Strictly Business

THE ESPERTI PETERSON INSTITUTE CONTRIBUTORY SERIES

Eileen Sacco, Managing Editor

Generations: Planning Your Legacy
Legacy: Plan, Protect, and Preserve Your Estate
Strictly Business: Planning Strategies for Privately Owned Businesses
21st Century Wealth: Essential Financial Planning Principles
Ways and Means: Maximize the Value of Your Retirement Savings
Wealth Enhancement and Preservation, 2d ed.

Strictly Business

PLANNING STRATEGIES FOR PRIVATELY OWNED BUSINESSES

*Practical Answers
from America's Foremost
Business Planning Authorities*

— A Special Edition —

David K. Cahoone   Larry W. Gibbs

Dennis C. Cook

Loren J. Richards

6010

ISBN 0-9674714-3-5
Library of Congress Control Number: 2001093939

Managing editor: Eileen Sacco
Senior technical editor: Richard Gumm
Project editor: Constance Hardesty
Project manager: Christy Allbee
Project assistants: Marcia Gresty and Jeremy Riggert
Marketing services: Lydia Monchak
Jacket design: Richard Adelson, china60@aol.com
Composition, design, & editing services: C+S Gottfried,
    www.lookoutnow.com/dtp
Printed and bound in Canada by Quebecor Printing

An Esperti Peterson Institute Book
by Quantum Press LLC
Quantum Alliance[3] Companies
621 17th Street, Suite 2250
Denver, CO 80293
303.893.2663

Contents

Foreword

Robert A. Esperti
Renno L. Peterson

Strictly Business is dedicated to those entrepreneurs who have already started their own businesses, those who are ready to do so, and those who may be inspired by our contributors to start their own small businesses.

The purpose of *Strictly Business* is to educate you about planning for your business, yourself, and your family. Our contributors define *business planning* to include starting and operating a business, choosing a business structure, expanding a business, and developing fringe benefits, retirement funds, and a succession strategy.

In our experience, business owners have different needs over time. Someone starting out needs help in selecting the right ownership structure and obtaining financing; owners of existing businesses need ideas for recruiting and keeping employees, expanding operations, and improving profitability; and long-time owners need guidance in estate planning, business succession, and exit strategies. Depending on your business situation—a start-up company, a flourishing operation, or a firm ready to see a transition in ownership and management—different parts of this book may be more relevant to you than others.

It is also our experience that all business owners have one constant need at all times: knowledgeable and motivated advisors. Business owners are entrepreneurs with ideas and spirit, but it is unlikely that they are also legal, financial, or tax experts or that they fully understand all the complexities and nuances of today's business world. While customers, competition, laws, and regulations change, sound business planning principles do not.

A major principle is to seek authoritative guidance when you are operating outside your area of expertise. Without proper guidance, a new business can get off poorly, an existing operation might wander off course, or a firm might falter during a crucial shift in ownership. A competent attorney, financial advisor, accountant, or other consultant can in many instances substantially contribute to the success of a business.

Never has this been more true than now, in the wake of the Economic Growth and Tax Relief Reconciliation Act of 2001. This act, with its broad-reaching and seemingly contradictory implications, is one of the most complex tax laws ever passed. While reducing taxes is not the sole or, often, the primary reason to plan, sound advice and cutting-edge strategies become increasingly important as shifting tax laws provide unexpected opportunities—and consequences.

Strictly Business was edited by our close friends and colleagues, David K. Cahoone and Larry W. Gibbs. They have done a masterful job of making the complex understandable. We are grateful for their efforts, and we commend them and our colleagues for undertaking the herculean task of assembling this resource for small-business owners.

As you read *Strictly Business,* look for new insights and ideas that will improve your business. Also, take note of the complex decisions you must make, and consider whose professional guidance you need most to implement new strategies that fit you best.

The contributors to *Strictly Business* stand ready to help you and your business attain the success you deserve. Seek them out, and see how far you can take your business.

Preface

Small businesses employ more than half of the private-sector work-force and provide about 75 percent of net new jobs. You and your business are critically important to the economic well-being of not only your family but also your employees, their families, and the entire country. It is important to many people that you succeed in your business enterprise.

Despite the owners' best efforts, and all that is riding on their success, many businesses fail. Studies indicate that 70 percent of all businesses fail in the first year, 10 percent in the second, and an additional 10 percent in the third. In *Strictly Business*, our contributors, many of whom are small-business owners, give you the benefit of their personal experience, along with the experiences of their thousands of business-owner clients, to help you plan correctly at the start of your business so that you can succeed in the first year and beyond.

Congress passed the Economic Growth and Tax Relief Recon-ciliation Act of 2001 in June of that year. Much has been made of this law's confusing and evolving approach to phasing out estate taxes—and the sunset provision that "magically" restores them. Commentators have called the 2001 tax act everything from the most complicated piece of tax legislation ever passed to the most hilarious estate tax law ever. Whomever or whatever you believe, it *is* the law. One point remains true: Flexibility in planning is the key. In *Strictly Business,* we explain the challenges and opportunities the 2001 tax act creates for business owners.

On the other hand, our contributors proffer that there are many other reasons to plan than simply to avoid taxes. Studies indicate that only half of all family-owned businesses last more than one generation and very few last more than two generations. Estate tax plays a role in this, but failing to plan for the succession of the business plays an equally important role. We and our contributors have collectively counseled thousands of business owners over the years, and these clients prove that point. For them, saving estate taxes is usually the aftereffect of planning for other goals: the successful start-up of a new business, the successful expansion of a business, a happy and comfortable retirement, and the succession of the business to co-owners, family, or key employees in the event of disability, disagreement, retirement, or death.

Strictly Business is the product of a national research project that involved the most talented estate, business, financial, retirement, and insurance planning attorneys, financial advisors, and accountants in the United States. It is not an annotated reference book intended to cover everything about business planning in the tiniest detail. All our contributing authors were challenged with a single goal: to provide readers with the best answers to the questions most frequently asked by their business-owner clients. Because of the book's question-and-answer format, even the newest entrepreneur will be able to make sense out of the many aspects of business planning.

Strictly Business offers insights into the issues that are important for planning. For many, just knowing which questions to ask a competent advisor will be a great help and will encourage participation in the planning process. Armed with the information in this book, you will be able to enter into business planning with more confidence.

The consistency of the questions provided by the contributors reinforced our belief that most business owners have similar concerns, regardless of differences in their cultures, economics, and geographic locations, as well as in the sizes or types of their businesses. This consistency has been the highlight of every Esperti Peterson Institute contributory book project.

The responses of our contributing authors reflect their differing professional views and feelings with regard to virtually every business planning issue. As editors, we have attempted to blend these differences into an overall perspective. At times, we included similar questions with different responses in order to present a variety of good approaches and allow readers to decide which one they are most comfortable with.

Experience tells us that few readers will read this book from cover to cover. As you skip around, reading specific sections, you will encounter much of the background information necessary to understand each topic. We encourage you to read the introduction at the beginning of each part to gain a broad view of the topic under discussion and a better understanding of the focus of each chapter in that part. We recommend that you read Chapter 1 for an overview of the effects of the 2001 tax act and read Chapter 2 to review business fundamentals before skipping to other chapters of the book.

Strictly Business is organized in six parts, covering what our contributors consider the most important aspects of business planning. Part One explains the 2001 tax act, business planning for new businesses, laws and regulations for operating businesses, and techniques for capitalization. Part Two discusses business structure: sole proprietorship, partnership, corporation, and limited liability company. Part Three offers techniques for providing fringe benefits, medical insurance, disability insurance, and retirement plans.

Part Four covers deferred-compensation plans, stock bonuses, stock options, and life insurance. In Part Five, our contributors discuss succession planning techniques, some of which are quite unique, for selling your company or giving it to family members or charity. Part Six focuses on passing your business to your family or others after your death. (It also discusses what may happen to the business after your death if you do not plan.)

We have included four appendixes. Appendix A lists resources for many of the topics covered in this book, the designations and accreditations of possible consultants, and the agencies that govern and regulate such professionals. Lists of referral organizations and professional organizations are also included.

The professionals who contributed to *Strictly Business* were chosen to participate in this project through a stringent application process that is fully described in Appendix B. Alphabetic and geographic lists of all the contributors are presented in Appendixes C and D.

Strictly Business contains the most current information on business, tax, estate, financial, and retirement planning. However, a few statistics relevant to these topics are indexed for inflation and are not yet available for 2002 and beyond. For this reason, our contributing authors used 2001 figures in a few explanations. In all cases, the theories and strategies behind the figures are completely up to date and incorporate the latest legislation affecting business, tax, estate, financial, and retirement planning.

As with all general reference works, readers should be careful not to treat the information in *Strictly Business* as a recommendation for any particular course of action in individual circumstances. No other concept came through to us more clearly than the diversity of successful strategies available to business owners, as well as the damage that can result from implementing the wrong strategy. This is especially true now in light of the 2001 tax act. The act may affect business owners in regard to retirement plans, buy-sell agreements, lifetime gifts to children, marital trusts, and other crucial planning strategies. *Strictly Business* addresses these impacts, but we specifically recommend that, in planning for your well-being and that of your family and business, you seek advice from competent professionals in each relevant discipline.

Strictly Business is the collaborative effort of many planning professionals. We are proud of the efforts our contributing authors made to bring you such practical information and strategies for effectively implementing business planning. We hope that the information in this book helps you, the reader, attain a better understanding of business planning.

We especially wish to thank Dennis C. Cook and Loren J. Richards for their contributions to *Strictly Business* and are honored to dedicate this special edition to them.

David K. Cahoone
Larry W. Gibbs
July 2001

Introduction

Dennis C. Cook
Loren J. Richards

The business of America is business.
—Calvin Coolidge (1872–1933)

Trade, commerce, and employment form the basis of any strong society, so we deeply appreciate the opportunity to join with our colleagues in the writing of *Strictly Business* to answer many of the questions that our clients ask us about business.

Although we have written articles, lectured, and conducted seminars on various aspects of estate and business planning over the years, we were drawn to this book project because of the opportunity it provided us to collaborate on a comprehensive work about business planning. Unlike books that present the opinions and experiences of only one or two authors, *Strictly Business* reflects hundreds of years of collective practical experience of some of the best estate and business planning lawyers, accountants, and financial planners in the country. We are honored to add our estate and business planning experiences to this marvelous collaborative effort.

Because most businesses in our country are small, closely held businesses, we believe there is truth in the principle "As businesses fare, so fares society." From local sole proprietorships to corporations with international markets, closely held businesses provide untold opportunities for personal, financial, and spiritual growth. We believe that the growth and improvement of our local community, our great State of Wyoming, and our nation is intimately dependent upon the creation, growth, continuation, and improvement of closely held businesses. We hope that *Strictly Business,* and our contribution to it, will help owners create, expand, continue, and improve their businesses.

Creating a business involves consideration of a myriad of issues: Which business-entity structure—partnership, corporation, or limited liability company—will be flexible enough to change and grow with the business? How do the different structures provide liability protection for owners and investors? How are they taxed? Which type offers the smoothest transfer of the owner's interest at his or her retirement or death?

Obviously, to make a profit, a business must be proficient in providing services or in manufacturing and marketing its products. It is sometimes less obvious that the choice of entity structure can have a major effect on the profitability of a business and the financial success of its owner.

Even beyond profitability, the choice of entity can involve many personal issues, ranging from how to pass the family business to children or key employees to teaching sons and daughters the meaning of personal achievement through operating a successful business. A proper choice of entity structure within a comprehensive business plan will not only protect or improve the bottom line but also complement the personal estate planning needs of the business owner. Concentrating efforts on one, to the exclusion of the other, wastes meaningful opportunities for both.

In our experience, nothing good comes from the failure to plan. Our objective is to help clients anticipate problems or issues, establish their goals, and then implement appropriate tools and techniques to meet their goals and avoid the problems. In achieving our objective, we have employed *values-based planning* for many years. That is, we design and create plans that represent the individual needs of our clients. The same planning tools and techniques are available for all clients, but not every tool is necessary or appropriate for each client or client family. Therefore, we base our planning effort on each client's unique goals and values, focusing on his or her issues and applying the most appropriate tools to address those issues. By matching and combining appropriate estate and business planning techniques with our clients' hopes, dreams, fears, and social values, we create unique solutions to meet our clients' estate and business planning goals.

In our experience, most business owners or "business owners to be" are familiar with the design process in which the skills of many specialists are combined to design a product or a building. Similarly, in our practice we recognize that as the complexity of an estate or business plan increases, the need for input from other professional experts increases proportionally. We experienced a great sense of relief when we finally recognized the simple truth that no one expects us to know everything to serve our clients' planning needs as long as we are willing to join with others whose knowledge supplements our own. In fact, we found that our clients were relieved to find that we do not profess to know everything but are willing to work with other professionals when necessary. We pride ourselves on our ability to collaborate with other professional advisors.

It is our goal in *Strictly Business,* and the goal of our colleagues, to educate owners of closely held businesses about the many planning opportunities available to them when they seek the assistance of competent estate and business planning professionals. We enjoyed the collaborative process of working on this book and we hope it brings some measure of enlightenment to those who read it.

Acknowledgments
Dennis dedicates this book to his wife, Margi, and their three children, Jennifer, Craig, and Scott. Loren dedicates this book to his wife, Christine, and their two children, Dustin and Brittany.

∞

Dennis Cook, J.D., was born and raised and now practices law in Laramie, Wyoming. He received a B.S. in mechanical engineering from the University of Wyoming, College of Engineering, in 1972, and his law degree from the University of Wyoming, College of Law, in 1982. Between 1972 and 1982 he served in the U.S. Air Force as a commissioned officer and pilot. Dennis is admitted to practice law before courts at all levels in Wyoming and Colorado and in numerous federal courts, including the U.S. Supreme Court. He founded the law firm of Cook & Associates, P.C., in Laramie, Wyoming, in 1993. Since then, his law practice has evolved into one that focuses primarily on estate and business planning. Dennis is a member of the National Network of Estate Planning Attorneys, the American Bar Association's Real Property and Probate Section, and the Southeast Wyoming Estate Planning Council. He is also a fellow of the Esperti Peterson Institute for Wealth Strategies Planning. Dennis and his wife, Margi, are the proud parents of three children, Jennifer, Craig and Scott.

Loren Joseph Richards, J.D., received a B.S. degree from the University of Wyoming, College of Agriculture, in 1973 and his law degree from the University of Wyoming, College of Law, in 1992. Loren has written for the *Land and Water Law Review* and served on its editorial staff as a comment editor. He is admitted to practice law before the state courts of Wyoming and Colorado, the Federal Court for the District of Wyoming, and the Tenth Circuit Court of Appeals. From 1992 through August 1997, Loren had a general practice as an associate attorney in a three-member law firm in Cheyenne, Wyoming, emphasizing the areas of contracts, real estate, corporations, wills, estates, and probate. Since August 1997, he has been an attorney with Cook & Associates, P.C., in Laramie, Wyoming, focusing his practice on business planning, tax planning, trusts and trust administration, probate, and real estate matters. He is a member of the National Network of Estate Planning Attorneys and a graduate of the Esperti Peterson Institute Advanced Studies for Estate and Wealth Planning. Loren is married to Christine, a schoolteacher. They have two children, Dustin and Brittany.

PART ONE

A Work
in Progress

So you have decided to leave the comfort of working for someone else and are ready to start or buy your own business. Congratulations. At some pont in their lives, many people have that goal, but few actually take the necessary steps to turn it into reality.

We appreciate that it is a little frightening to step out into the unknown and leave behind the perceived safety of being an employee with a steady paycheck and few management responsibilities. In our experience two things make the journey much easier: understanding the process of getting started and having a good road map of where you are going. It also helps to understand the larger context in which your business will operate.

The most outstanding and consistent element of today's business climate is change, so you should consider your business a work in progress. Thus Chapter 1 focuses on the need to be flexible, responsive, and ever-ready to harness the "winds of change." One key area that has seen much change in the past decade is federal tax law. Chapter 1 summarizes the main features of the Economic Growth and Tax Relief Reconciliation Act of 2001 (the "2001 tax act") as they relate to business owners. This summary is critical for all business owners, from those with well-established firms to those who are just starting out.

A logical way to begin the process of launching a new business is to prepare a business plan. In Chapter 2 our contributors discuss the main elements of a business plan and provide a detailed list of what you should consider and include in your plan. When you are starting a business, it is important that the plan address issues such as the legal structure of the business, the ownership of the business, and how the firm will be managed on a day-to-day basis. Chapter 2 also provides information on including an exit strategy in your business plan. You may be wondering why you should worry about an exit strategy before you even know if you have a successful business concept. One of the important habits in Stephen R. Covey's seminal work *The Seven Habits of Highly Effective People* is to "start with the end in mind." We and our contributors believe that at least considering an exit strategy is an essential element in starting off on the right track with a new business. It is much easier to reach your destination when you know, from the outset, where you want to go.

We are sure that it comes as no surprise that businesses in the United States are highly regulated. Your business will be governed by a regulatory body, be it federal, state, county, or municipality. Chapter 3 explains the many types of regulations that may apply to your business, and then it looks briefly at accounting methods. The final third of the chapter focuses on employment issues. After discussing when, how, and whom to hire, the chapter explains employment contracts, noncompete agreements, and confidentiality agreements.

Many businesses can start on a "shoestring," but if a business meets with initial success, it needs additional financing to take it to the next level, where real financial success can be achieved. Often the person or persons who started the business do not have the ability to provide significant new financing at this critical point in time. Chapter 4 focuses on ways to finance an existing business. While some of the techniques for raising capital are designed for a particular type of business, most of the concepts and many of the financing methods apply to all businesses.

chapter 1

Harnessing the Winds of Change

Gone are the days when a successful business owner could set a course for his or her business and stick to that course year after year. The twenty-first-century business world moves too fast for that. Today's successful business owners must react rapidly to changing customer demands, outside competition, and local, state, federal, and international regulations and tax laws within the context of sound business practices. Successful business owners view change as an opportunity not just to survive but to thrive.

As of this writing, President Bush has just signed into law the Economic Growth and Tax Relief Reconciliation Act of 2001 (the "2001 tax act"). This act significantly affects tax, estate, business, and retirement planning. It comes as no surprise. Congress enacted tax acts in 1976, 1981, 1986, and 1993 that each, in its own way, caused significant course changes for American taxpayers. This chapter focuses on the changes set in motion by the 2001 tax act that affect business owners and their families. It serves as an overview so that business owners can consider how best to chart a course not just to survive this "storm" and the ones we know are still coming but to thrive in spite of them.

When viewing the totality of the 2001 tax act, it is necessary to understand two very important facts:

1. Most of the tax relief provisions are phased in over the period 2002–2010. This 9-year lag provides future Congresses with many opportunities to slow down or even eliminate the scheduled tax cuts and repeals.

2. The act has a built-in self-destruct mechanism that will cause it to disappear on December 31, 2010. The last page of the 2001 tax act contains the following sentence, referred to as the "sunset" provision:

All provisions of, and amendments made by, this Act shall not apply (1) to taxable, plan, or limitation years beginning after December 31, 2010, or (2) in the case of title V, to estates of decedents dying, gifts made, or generation skipping transfers, after December 31, 2010.

The projected cost of the 2001 tax act is $1.3 trillion. If the act were to remain unchanged and in effect from 2011 to 2020, its projected cost would be an additional $4 trillion. This negative impact on the budget was so great that Congress considered it fiscally irresponsible to have the act continue beyond 2010 without affirmative congressional intervention, which the sunset provision requires.

After its repeal on December 31, 2010, the act will be deemed to have never existed at all and provisions of the Internal Revenue Code affected by the act will go back to what they were on June 7, 2001, before the act was signed. One commentator, Marc Hevrdejs, the executive editor of CCH Federal Tax Publications, has described the 2001 tax act as "arguably one of the most complicated pieces of legislation we've seen due to the wide range of unprecedented time-delayed tax law changes, with varying phase-ins and effective dates that span 10 years."

Of one thing there is no doubt: Flexibility in planning, now more than ever, is essential. It is critical that every business owner surround himself or herself with a group of professional advisors who work together for the owner's benefit.

Let's look at the 2001 tax act provisions that directly affect you, your family, and your business.

THE CHANGES

Income Tax Reductions

What are the new income tax rates?

Before the act the top individual income tax rate was 39.6 percent. If the tax cuts are fully phased in as scheduled, by 2006 the top individual income tax rate will be 35 percent, as shown in Table 1-1. In addition, a new 10 percent bracket, which went into effect retroactively in 2001, will lower many taxpayers' taxes. The income tax rates for corporations were not changed in the 2001 tax act, so the top corporation marginal rate is still 35 percent. Between 2002 and 2005 this rate will still be lower than the top individual rate, but beginning in 2006 the top individual and corporation rates will be the same.

How do the rate decreases affect business planning?

One of the reasons to consider operating your business as a corporation is to retain earnings inside the corporation so that they are taxed at the lower, corporation rates instead of distributing the profits to the shareholders, who will pay a "second" tax on the distributions at their higher individual rates. That may still be a major consideration between now and 2005; but beginning in 2006, when the

TABLE 1-1   Income Tax Cuts

Year	Income tax rate, %			
Before 2001 tax act	28	31	36	39.6
Taxable year beginning in				
2001	27.5	30.5	35.5	39.1
2002 & 2003	27	30	35	38.6
2004 & 2005	26	29	34	37.6
2006 & beyond	25	28	33	35

top individual and corporation tax rates are the same, you and your advisors may decide to establish—or to convert an existing C corporation to—a pass-through entity such as an S corporation, partnership, or limited liability company in which the distributions are taxed once and at a rate that is no more or less advantageous than the corporation rates.

On the other hand, if you believe that Congress will increase the individual tax rates again before 2006 or that it will decrease the corporate income tax rates, you may still want a C corporation for income tax planning purposes. But remember: Even if the 2001 tax act remains unchanged until 2010, the tax cuts will vaporize with the act on December 31 of that year. You and your advisors will want to examine these issues, along with any other relevant considerations discussed in this book, when you are selecting your business structure or considering a conversion to a different structure.

⅏ *Were any changes made to the alternative minimum tax?*

Although the tax act of 2001 did not overtly change the alternative minimum tax (AMT) rates, it is projected that over the next 10 years many more taxpayers will be subject to the AMT than ever before. The Joint Committee on Taxation estimates that in 2011 the number of individuals subject to the AMT will approach 16 million (compared to 140,000 in 1997). A disproportionate number of these individuals will be owners of small businesses. One of the reasons for this increase is the reduction in the income tax rates. Business owners and their tax advisors will need to focus on planning to avoid or at least minimize application of the AMT even more than in the past.

Retirement Plan Rules

⚐ Can you summarize the changes to the retirement plan rules and how they can help me in my business?

The 2001 tax act provides significant reform in employer-sponsored retirement plans by easing and simplifying rules and regulations and by increasing employer tax-deductible contribution limits and employee salary reduction deferrals. These beneficial changes phase in between 2002 and 2006 and sunset on December 31, 2010. The most important changes that affect business owners are outlined here:

EMPLOYER TAX-DEDUCTIBLE CONTRIBUTIONS: As a general rule, beginning in 2002 the tax-deductible amount that employers can contribute to profit-sharing, money purchase pension, 401(k), and SEP IRA plans is 25 percent of an employee's compensation, not to exceed $40,000, which will be indexed annually for inflation. Previously the contribution limits varied among the plans, and only the money purchase pension plan allowed up to a 25 percent tax-deductible contribution. In the past, employers had to combine a money purchase pension plan—with its mandatory annual contributions—with another plan in order to maximize the contributions for highly compensated employees. Now employers can achieve the same result with any one plan that has discretionary annual contributions.

EMPLOYEE BENEFITS: The amounts that an employee can defer to a 401(k) or SIMPLE IRA have been simplified into a schedule and increased (see Table 1-2). Employees 50 years of age and older may

TABLE 1-2   Retirement Plan Employee Contributions

	Plan	
Year	401(k)	SIMPLE IRA
2002	$11,000	$ 7,000
2003	12,000	8,000
2004	13,000	9,000
2005	14,000	10,000
2006	15,000	Indexed
2007 & beyond	Indexed	Indexed

make additional "catch-up" contributions to most contributory plans. In addition, before passage of the 2001 tax act, the employer contribution and employee salary deferral to contributory plans could not total more than 25 percent of the employee's compensation. Under the new law, the combined contributions can be 100 percent of the employee's compensation. For example, if an owner's compensation is $40,000, in 2002 he or she can defer $11,000 to a 401(k) and the company can contribute $10,000 (25 percent of $40,000) to a profit-sharing plan for a total contribution of $21,000. All these revisions allow employers to design plans that offer key employees, including the owners, better retirement accumulation than was possible under previous law.

TESTING REQUIREMENTS: New provisions may help employers meet top-heavy testing requirements. For example, the new law has simplified the definition of "key employee" and relaxed the criteria for meeting this requirement. Also, the 2001 tax act provides a new tax credit in 2002 through 2006 to encourage low- to middle-income individuals to contribute to a 401(k) plan. The credit is based on the amount of the contributions and is available to single taxpayers making $25,000 or less and married taxpayers filing joint returns who make $50,000 or less. To help meet top-heavy nondiscrimination requirements, business owners can promote this tax credit to employees who are not highly compensated and can thereby encourage more of them to contribute to 401(k) plans.

Part Five covers the latest information about each of the employer-sponsored plans under the 2001 tax act. The changes may allow you and your key employees to accumulate more in retirement accounts before the act sunsets in 2011. You should contact your advisors to discuss how you can take advantage of these changes now because you must incorporate some of them into your existing plan documents for the changes to become effective.

Gift, Estate, and Generation-Skipping Transfer Tax Provisions

⚖ *Do I still need an estate plan?*

Estate tax repeal—is it real? Because the most significant portions of the gift, estate, and generation-skipping tax changes are pushed so far into the future, there is considerable debate about whether they will ever become a reality. The 2001 tax act has three stages (outlined in Table 1-3):

1. Between 2002 and 2009, the old unified gift and estate tax structure essentially remains intact.
2. In 2010, the estate and generation-skipping transfer taxes are repealed, but as of this writing, the repeal is for only that year. Thus estate taxes are repealed only for individuals who die in the year 2010.
3. The act sunsets in 2011: the gift, estate, and generation-skipping transfer tax provisions are once again the same as they were in 2001 before passage of the act.

Because of these three stages of tax laws, additional, flexible planning is required for most Americans with estates in excess of $1 million, especially those who own businesses.

TABLE 1-3 Estate, Gift, and Generation-Skipping Taxes

Year	Gift tax TMR, %	Credit	Estate tax TMR, %	AEA	GST tax TMR, %	Exemption	State death tax credit
			Stage 1: Continuation of unified gift and estate tax system				
2001	55	$ 675,000	55	$ 675,000	55	$1,060,000	100%
2002	50	1,000,000	50	1,000,000	50	1,060,000*	75
2003	49	1,000,000	49	1,000,000	49	1,060,000*	50
2004	48	1,000,000	48	1,500,000	48	1,500,000	25
2005	47	1,000,000	47	1,500,000	47	1,500,000	−†
2006	46	1,000,000	46	2,000,000	46	2,000,000	
2007	45	1,000,000	45	2,000,000	45	2,000,000	
2008	45	1,000,000	45	2,000,000	45	2,000,000	
2009	45	1,000,000	45	3,500,000	45	3,500,000	
			Stage 2: Estate tax repeal				
2010	35	1,000,000‡	−§	−§	−§	−§	
			Stage 3: Return to pre-2001 tax act conditions				
2011¶	55	1,000,000	55	1,000,000	55	1,000,000	

TMR = top marginal rate; AEA = applicable exclusion amount.

*Indexed for inflation.

†Repealed. Beginning in 2005, there is a deduction for death taxes paid to any state with respect to property in the estate of a decedent.

‡Beginning in 2010, the amount is scheduled to be indexed for inflation.

§Repealed.

¶After the 2001 act terminates, all rates revert to what they were under the previous law. Since the exemption amount under prior law was scheduled to increase to $1 million in 2006, that is the amount in 2011.

◁ *How do I plan during stage 1?*

During stage 1 there is still a unified gift and estate tax system, but the 2001 tax act reduces the top estate and gift tax rates and increases the estate tax exemption amount over an 8-year period. Couples with standard marital and family trust (A-B trust) planning should meet with their advisors as soon as possible to discuss the effects of the exclusion amount increases on their existing plans and to examine options for revising their plans so that they continue to meet their personal goals.

While the act provides separate exemptions for estate and gift taxes, application of these exemptions is still "unified." For example, if you use your gift tax exemption to give $1 million of your business to your children during your lifetime, at your death your estate tax exemption amount is reduced by the $1 million you used during your lifetime.

Parents' primary motive for making lifetime gifts of business interests to their children was the same 50 years ago and will be the same 50 years from now: training the next generation to take over and successfully continue the family business while the older generation is still around to do the training. Reducing the tax impact of this transfer is usually the secondary motivation. It continues to make sense to shift ownership to younger generations by using lifetime gifts and, whenever possible, to use leveraging techniques to accomplish those gifts most efficiently.

During stage 1, the law remains the same with respect to a decedent's assets' being "stepped up" in tax basis to fair market value as of his or her date of death. Parents wishing to leave their businesses to children at death may have to plan differently for the stage 1 period, 2002 to 2009, and then for stage 2, 2010.

The good news is that many of the techniques planners have been recommending for years are just as effective, or even more so, after passage of the 2001 tax act as they were before it. Life insurance will continue to provide liquidity for estate taxes and a greater inheritance for loved ones.

⅍ *What do I do for stage 2?*

The magic year for estate planning is 2010. Persons "lucky" enough to die in that year will be able to pass their wealth to their heirs without any federal estate taxes. Unfortunately, estate tax repeal is as ephemeral as a mirage: the closer you get to it, the less likely that it's going to be there when you need it.

For now, however, repeal exists for 365 days during 2010. But it comes with a cost. A very significant *stealth* tax increase contained in the 2001 tax act calls for the elimination in 2010 of the step-up in basis for assets owned at a decedent's death. In 2010, under the 2001 tax act, the date-of-death step-up-in-basis system is replaced with a "carryover-basis" system which dictates that the beneficiary take the assets with the same basis as the decedent had before his or her death and thus be subject to potentially significant taxes on the gain in sale. The new law does provide partial relief by giving to each decedent's estate the ability to increase the basis to date-of-death fair market value for certain assets that are deemed to be owned by the decedent at his or her death—in effect, an exemption against the appreciation of the asset. In 2010, a decedent's administrator can increase by $1.3 million the basis of property owned by a decedent at his or her death. Also, property left to a surviving spouse that is considered "qualified spousal property" is entitled to an additional $3 million increase in basis.

One benefit of the current system is that the basis of inherited assets can be readily determined—the fair market value on the decedent's date of death. Under the new law, in 2010, when no step-up at death occurs, it will be necessary to keep records of the basis of all assets for generation after generation. In our experience it is difficult enough just keeping track of all the assets let alone the basis of each asset.

⚐ *Will these changes affect state death taxes?*

Many states impose an estate tax. Under prior law, estates were allowed a credit against the federal estate tax for a portion or all of the state death taxes paid. Most states peg the amount they collect in estate taxes to the maximum amount that is allowed as a credit for federal estate taxes. Under the 2001 tax act, the credit will be phased out over a 3-year period and turned into a deduction for state estate taxes actually paid. Many states will increase their state estate taxes to offset the revenue loss expected from the phase-out of the death tax credit, so individuals will need to plan for state estate taxes more than ever before.

⇗ *What happens when the act terminates in 2011?*

When the 2001 tax act ends, the gift, estate, and generation-skipping transfer tax provisions will be the same as they were in 2001 before passage of the act. As shown in Table 1-3, the gift, estate, and generation-skipping top marginal tax rate returns to 55 percent, the applicable exclusion amount for transfers of property during life or at death reverts to $1 million, and the generation-skipping transfer tax exemption reverts to $1 million.

Many tax planning professionals believe that the taxation trend is shifting away from the traditional estate tax system and toward the carryover-basis system. So even though the 2001 tax act vaporizes on December 31, 2010, the next law that Congress passes after that may still incorporate a form of the carryover capital gain taxation. Business owners and their advisors will have to consider this in planning for the transfer of a business to the next generation at the death of the owners.

⇗ *Is there any reason why I should change my current planning?*

Several commentators have indicated that there is no need to alter existing planning to address the carryover-basis scheme until we get much closer to 2010. However, in some scenarios inaction could prove devastating. First, business owners have buy-sell agreements in place which require that upon the death of an owner, the remaining owners must purchase the decedent's business interest from his or her family. If death triggers a buy-sell agreement in 2010 or thereafter and some form of the carryover-basis regime continues, the family of the selling owner may be faced with a huge capital gain tax.

Second, if an individual dies between now and December 31, 2009, leaving assets to his or her surviving spouse in a standard marital trust, that property will receive a date-of-death step-up in basis.

However, if the surviving spouse subsequently dies in 2010, none of that spouse's property remaining in the marital trust will be eligible for a basis increase because in stage 2 the law does not treat the marital trust property as "property owned by the surviving spouse." This is a radical departure from the law that applies before 2010, which does treat all marital trust property as being owned by the surviving spouse and includes it in the estate of the surviving spouse as it passes to his or her heirs. This critical change in the law may have drastic consequences for the unprepared.

TIME TO GO
TO WORK

How can I prepare for the effects of the 2001 tax act?

To ensure that your business and your wealth survive and thrive into the next decade, you must react quickly to the challenges and opportunities presented by the 2001 tax act. The key is to plan today for your goals and reevaluate your plan periodically as the act gradually changes from year to year and then sunsets in 2011.

The following chapters provide a wealth of ideas and opportunities that will help you plan during the years to come. We know the laws will continue to change. However, many of the time-tested concepts and strategies still work today, some will work better for you as your goals change, and some will evolve along with the legal changes we know are still coming.

We encourage you to embrace change because that is the only way you will be able to control it and plan for it. Successful entrepreneurs surround themselves with advisors who see every change as an opportunity to grasp greater success through collaboration.

chapter 2

Starting
a Business

After working many years in a large organization, I'm thinking of taking an early retirement to start my own business. Is that a good idea?

The answer depends on your expectations. Owning and running a business, especially in the early years, is anything but retirement—it's hard work and long hours. Operating a new business requires a completely different mind-set from working as an employee. You are independent and in control. You are accountable for the bottom line, but in some respects that is easier than being accountable for some vague departmental or governmental goals.

We read about new companies that are started on a shoestring and become amazingly successful on the Internet. Those are rarities. Starting a business that will eventually support you and your family involves hard work, research, and risk. Most new businesses fail in the first year. If you use your retirement funds to capitalize the business, you risk losing your retirement security as well.

17

However, the financial and personal rewards of going out on your own can be well worth the responsibility and risk. Many millionaires started out as small-business owners. You derive satisfaction from creating income and wealth through your efforts, talent, capital, and employees. As time goes by, if you have structured your business appropriately, you might even have more free time than you have now or, at least, have the freedom to structure your work schedule as you want.

If you have a good idea, the right temperament, appropriate skills, proper planning, and enough capital, starting your own business can be the beginning of an exciting and successful new career.

> *I'd like to turn my hobby into a business so that I can work and play at the same time. What's wrong with that?*

Sometimes the best way to ruin an enjoyable hobby is to turn it into a business! A hobby may cease to be fun when you are working at it day and night. It can become tedious, leaving no time for creativity. Running a business is much more than working at a hobby. As the owner, you must deal with many business issues that may take you away from the hobby you love. If you ignore the business issues, your business might fail or never reach its full potential.

> *Why do many businesses fail in their first year or two?*

Studies indicate that 70 percent of all businesses fail in the first year, 10 percent in the second, and an additional 10 percent in the third. There are many reasons why businesses fail.

Perhaps the owner did not carefully research the feasibility of the business. For example, who is the competition? What is the market for the product or service? What will it cost to produce the product or service?

Perhaps the business was not adequately capitalized. Many businesses are undercapitalized at the start. Let's face it: It takes a lot of money to start a business. You must subsidize the business in the early phase, until the cash flow covers your costs and returns a profit. Too much debt can be a major drain on the cash flow, drawing off money that could have been used for expansion. We've all heard stories of hugely successful companies that got their start in the founder's garage on a shoestring budget. Though some businesses may not require significant capital to commence operations, all businesses need large sums of capital to market their products or services to the masses. In our experience, adequate capitalization, either at the start or when products and services are ready to go to market, is critical for the long-term success of every business.

Perhaps the business was less fun and more work than the owner expected. Many new owners decide that the long hours and low pay are just not worth it. They may have thought that simply because they posted a sign on the door, put an ad in the paper, and got a site on the web, customers would beat a path to the door. Some owners may experience changes in their personal or family situations that force them to reorder their priorities.

Finally, perhaps the owner just does not have the temperament to own and run a business. Business owners face numerous issues involving personnel, government regulations, cash flow, accounting, competition, inventory, marketing, and, of course, the technical aspects of the business.

What basic components do I need to develop a successful business?

There are any number of answers to this question, but in very simple terms you need:

- A product or service that fits the needs of your customer base or is revolutionary enough to create a need if one does not exist
- A team of competent employees, advisors, and managers who can get the job done
- The ability to attract capital, whether it is debt, equity, or a combination of the two

If you have two of these things, you can usually attract the third. For example, if you have a great product and a good management team, you should be able to attract capital; if you already have the capital and the product, you can hire a strong management team.

PROFESSIONAL ADVICE

⋈ *Where can I get help with starting a business?*

The following are good sources of information and advice:

ADVISORS AND CONSULTANTS: Find consultants or advisors who are familiar with the type of business you want to start. For example, if you are starting a restaurant, you want advisors who know the restaurant business. If there is a restaurant owners' association in your city or state, contact it for the names of consultants or organizations that can assist you. If you are thinking of a franchise, the franchisor will help you.

Your attorney, accountant, or financial advisor may be able to help you develop a business plan or recommend an industry specialist who can help. Once you have decided to start your business, you will need an attorney, accountant, and financial advisor to assist you with long-range planning.

BANKER: Your banker may have informative booklets about developing a business plan and may be able to provide you with the names of consultants or industry contacts.

COMMUNITY AND SPECIALTY ORGANIZATIONS: Depending on the size of your community, there may be organizations that specialize in your industry or groups of retired individuals who specialize in helping small and start-up businesses. The American Association of Retired Persons may offer such help.

GOVERNMENT ORGANIZATIONS: One of the best resources is the Small Business Administration (SBA). It provides free copies of *The*

Resource Directory for Small Business Management, a catalog of publications and videotapes, which you can order from your local SBA office or from the Washington office. The SBA website includes detailed information on almost every aspect of starting a new business.

The U.S. Department of Commerce has "trade desks" that provide information on importing and exporting. Depending on the type of business you are starting, a local or state government agency may provide assistance. For example, many local governments promote economic development by providing assistance to entrepreneurs and certain types of businesses through the mayors' or governors' offices.

EDUCATIONAL INSTITUTIONS: Many educational institutions, such as your local college or business school, offer adult education courses on starting new businesses, and many of these are taught by consultants from various industries.

LIBRARY AND INTERNET: Both the library and the Internet offer rich resources for researching your type of business and finding consultants who can help you create your business plan.

Appendix A includes extensive lists of useful organizations and associations, along with addresses, phone numbers, and websites.

Whether or not you hire advisors to assist you in creating your business plan, we suggest you conduct your own research using the resources listed above and any others you can find. Educate yourself through books and courses. Learn all you can about the industry and the market you are entering, as well as management and finance in general. The more you learn, the more reliable the information in your business plan will be—and the more likely you will be to make the correct decision about the feasibility of your business idea.

≤∆ *Which advisors do I need to help me with my business, and what should I expect from each of them?*

Starting a business is easier when you work with a team of advisors who have the experience and qualifications to help you. Although there are many different types of advisors, the ones who typically help a small business succeed include:

- An *accountant,* who will help you plan for long-range financial, accounting, and tax issues
- An *attorney,* who will advise you on entity selection, long-term business planning, legal and contractual aspects of the business, and succession and estate planning strategies for you and your business
- A *banker,* who will help establish lines of credit and loans for start-up and expansion
- An *investment banker or another such consultant,* who will help raise equity
- An *insurance agent,* who will advise you on risk management
- A *financial advisor,* who will assist you with financing and cash-flow analysis
- A *consultant* who has experience in the type of business you are starting, knows its inner workings, and will advise you on business issues

You may need to hire other advisors from time to time.

The advisors who help with your long-range planning—your attorney, accountant, and financial advisor—should collaborate, because each advisor has his or her own specialty and perspective. It is not enough that you talk with each of them separately; they must work together to give you the best advice and to help you achieve the best results.

How do I choose the advisors who will help me plan?

You want advisors who have experience planning for a business like yours. As you might expect, all professionals do not have the same education and experience when it comes to business planning. Select advisors who are experienced or specifically educated in the area of owner-operated or closely held businesses. (The resources listed earlier in this section include several that can be used to find qualified advisors.) We suggest you interview the advisor to see whether he or she is right for you. Write down a list of questions and goals to take to the meeting. Ask the advisor for the names of several past clients whom he or she assisted in starting a new business. Interview them to determine how helpful this advisor is likely to be.

CREATING A
BUSINESS PLAN

⚜ *What planning should I do before I start or buy a business?*

At the very least, you should have a written business plan with verifiable statistical information, a 3- to 5-year budget, and reasonable cash-flow projections.

⚜ *Is it really necessary to write a business plan? What benefit could possibly come from all that work?*

We strongly recommend a business plan. Writing a business plan is a common assignment for students in undergraduate or master's business programs, and it is required in the real world to obtain commercial financing.

While the ultimate product, the written plan, is the obvious goal, the *process* of drafting it is just as, or even more, important. The process requires that you research every aspect of the potential business and think through the feasibility of the business from several angles. This involves, among other things, finding out if there are any customers who need or want the product or service and determining the price they are willing to pay for it, as well as preparing income and expense budgets for a 3- to 5-year period. Many new business ideas that "sound good" wind up in the wastebasket after rigid analysis reveals insurmountable cash-flow or other problems.

Often the process of developing the business plan convinces the entrepreneur to go forward with a new business that is slightly different from his or her original idea.

A business plan also serves as a management tool *after* you create the business. Periodically, you will compare the plan to how the business is actually developing. Deviations from the marketing plan and budget will alert you to unfounded assumptions and allow you to correct developing problems before they escalate. You can also use the business plan as a tool for communicating your goals to your employees and helping you recruit key personnel.

I want to try my hand at creating a business plan before I find a consultant. How do I start?

Ask your banker for an instruction booklet or sample outline if you have any intention of applying for financing. Or pick up one of the many business planning software programs that are available. The SBA provides information on creating a business plan, and you will find books on the topic at local and online bookstores.

Basic Elements

What goes into a business plan?

A business plan tells you where you want your business to be and how you plan to get it there. To start, envision your business as a success 3 to 5 years from now. What position will it hold in the industry, community, region, nation, or world? What need will it fill, or what benefit will it provide? In other words, what will the users of your product or service have then that they don't have now?

Your business plan should include everything you need to know or anticipate about your business. Table 2-1 summarizes the elements found in a typical business plan. However, if you will be using the plan to raise money, you may need additional information such as personal financial statements of the principals, pertinent contracts, and other legal documents. If you don't need financing from outside sources, your business plan can be less detailed—but it is no less important.

⚄ *Do I need to revise my business plan after I start the business?*

You must periodically review and update your plan. Because your business will continue to change, you should review all aspects of your plan at least once every year. Given the fast pace of business today, once a business plan is 1 year old, there is really no difference between a good plan and a bad one because by then they are both out of date.

⚄ *How do I find out about the legal requirements that govern my business?*

To get you started, we have outlined the most common legal requirements for all businesses in Chapter 3. Your advisors can assist you.

⚄ *What ownership questions need to be answered in the business plan?*

Several fundamental ownership issues must be addressed:

- How many owners will there be?
- Will there be more than one class of ownership?
- Will one owner have majority control?
- If not, what percentage of ownership will dictate control?
- Will the owners hire a manager?
- Will the owners have an absolute right to transfer all or part of their interest in the entity? Or will the owners have a restricted right to transfer all or part of their interest only to other owners or specific members of an owner's family?

TABLE 2-1   Elements of a Business Plan

	Marketing
Purpose	What will you do?
	For whom will you do it?
	What will your clients or customers get?
	Why won't they get it from your competitors—what makes your business unique?
Product	What product or service will you provide?
	Who will be your customers or clients?
Place	How will you deliver the product or service?
Promotion	How will you tell prospective customers or clients about your product or service?
	How will you sell it to them?
Pricing	What price strategies will you use?
Other	What opportunities and obstacles will you face?
	How do you plan to overcome them?

	Legal requirements
Business name	What will you call your business?
	Does the name of the business offend any person or group?
	Can the name of the business attract customers?
	Is the name being used by another business in your state?
Laws	What tax laws govern your business?
	Does your business idea infringe upon anyone else's patent, trademark, or copyright?
	What laws must you follow regarding hiring, firing, and ongoing employee relations?
Regulations	What safety regulations apply to your business or industry?
	Are there industry standards or regulations you must comply with?
	What other local, state, regional, or federal regulations apply?

	Operations
Location	Where will your business be located? Why?
	Does your location offer advantages or pose challenges to your business?
Facilities	What type of facility and equipment will you need?
	Will an inventory control system be needed? If so, what type?

TABLE 2-1 *Continued*

Ownership and capitalization	
Ownership	Who are the owners?
Legal structure	What legal entity will you use?
Capitalization	How will you finance start-up and operations?
	Where and how will you obtain additional capital?

Control and management	
Control	If there are multiple owners, who will make decisions and how will they do it?
Management	What is the business's management philosophy?
	If there are multiple owners, or you hire managers, who will manage day-to-day operations?
	Who are the key employees?
	How and when will you hire additional employees?
	What problems might you encounter in hiring employees from the local labor force?
	Will you require subcontract workers?
	How will you structure the organization chart?
	Will you compensate owners through distributions or salaries?
	How much will you pay employees?
	Will you offer employee benefits?
	What is the owner's exit strategy and management succession plan?

Financial data	
Projections and assumptions	What is the business's 3- to 5-year budget?
	Have you created 3- to 5-year projected income (profit-and-loss) statements, cash-flow projections, and balance sheets?
	Have you done a break-even analysis?
	What assumptions have you used to arrive at financial projections?
	What benchmarks will be used to track progress?

Other	
Advisors	Who are your legal, accounting, and financial advisors?

⇿ *What do I need to consider about capitalization and financing?*

How you capitalize the business and finance its ongoing operations will affect the ownership of the business. Consider the following:

- Where will you find the money to start your business and keep it going until it begins to make a profit?
- Can you capitalize it entirely on your own, or will you need loans?
- How much debt, if any, is appropriate?
- Will you raise funds for start-up or operations from the private sector by selling equity, thus giving up ownership interests?
- If there is a shortfall in operating funds, how and when will contributions from the owners be required? Can an owner lend money to the entity, and if so, what right to repayment does that owner have?
- What capital expenditures will be made? Should property be leased or purchased outright?

For information that will help you answer these questions and others you may have regarding capitalizing your business, see the section on financing in Chapter 4. The concepts for financing a start-up are the same as those for financing an expansion.

⇿ *What are the control and management issues?*

The most immediate concern of most business owners is control of the business. *Control* is the authority to make the day-to-day business decisions. Even if you are the sole owner, control is not necessarily certain, and it is much less certain when there are two or more owners. Some of the questions you will have to answer are:

- How will crucial operating decisions be made?
- How will expenses be approved? Who will have the authority to obligate the property of the business?
- What will need to be done about marketing, and who decides?

- How will fees or prices be determined? Will exceptions—"deals"—be made? If so, who will have the authority to determine whether or not an exception should be made?

- If another owner or partner comes into the business because you have to sell equity for capital, what potential control and conflict issues may arise?

My husband's parents are financially comfortable and generous, and they're willing to lend money to our new business so that we don't have to borrow from a bank. We want to protect them and treat them fairly. Do you think the loan is a good idea?

Prepare yourself for the possibility that when the risks are explained to your in-laws, they will either change their minds or insist that, as a condition of the loan, they become nonmanaging partners. When relatives or friends become partners, the arrangement can strain a relationship. Your in-laws' attorneys might urge that the business's promise to repay the loan be secured by a lien on your business interests. If repayment is delayed or neglected, your exclusive right to manage the business could be compromised by the lenders, creating tensions among the parties. This is a perfect example of why making decisions about ownership, management, and control is critical before you start the business.

What issues related to compensation and profits should my business plan address?

The plan should cover how you and other owners will be compensated. It should also address how and when profits will be distributed and what must be retained for operating purposes.

What questions should I consider regarding employees and benefits?

In developing your business plan, ask yourself questions such as these: Will I need to hire employees? If so, what types of skills will they need to have? Will family members work in the business? What will I pay employees, and what benefits will I provide?

Exit Strategy and Management Succession Plan

  What is an exit strategy?

An *exit strategy* is a long-range plan for the current owners to divest their ownership of the business upon certain events, including death, disability, or retirement. No one lives forever, and few people want to own and operate the same business forever. The only question is whether the transition of your ownership will occur before or after your death. Usually, the ability of key employees or second-generation family members is known early enough for you to decide whether one or more of these individuals can eventually take over the business—and you can plan for this. If your plan is to operate the business until you die, there will be no opportunity to test your successors' ability to operate it before they take over.

The exit strategy is often implemented through a business continuity or management succession plan.

  Why should I include an exit strategy in my business plan?

One of the most important things you will do after completing your business plan is choose an entity, or ownership structure, under which your business will operate. Including your exit strategy in your business plan ensures that the entity you choose will allow you to carry out your exit strategy.

A key to success in any venture is to "start with the end in mind." The same is true when you are developing your business plan. At some point you may want to transfer some or all of your business. Having the correct ownership structure in place will make that transfer much easier. For example, you may start out as the sole owner of the business but may want to sell a portion of the business to other parties in the future. Or you may want to take the business public someday. You may even consider transferring partial ownership to members of your family. Your exit strategy ensures that you get where you want to go. Throughout this book we will discuss which entity is best suited for your goals, including the eventual transfer of your business.

⚄ *What is a management succession plan, and why do I need to make it part of my business plan?*

A *management succession* or *business continuity plan* is the blueprint for implementing your exit strategy. It specifically directs who will operate, or perhaps own, the company in the event of your death, disability, or retirement.

When you look at your priorities, you will probably recognize that you want to avoid what could be catastrophic pitfalls. How concerned are you about your spouse's welfare? How much do you want to leave to your children, and when do you want them to have it? What do you want your employees to have? Your purpose and goals are the road map to the business transition.

⚄ *What do succession plans cover?*

Good succession plans cover, at minimum, the following scenarios:

Disability: What happens if you become disabled? Who will run the business? Will all the owners need to participate in the ongoing operation of the business? Will each owner need to devote his or her full time to the business? How will that be defined?

Death: What happens to the business if you die? When there are multiple owners, death raises several additional concerns. For example, will an owner be allowed to transfer his or her interest at death to someone other than the existing owners?

Transfer of ownership interests: Before death, will an owner be allowed to sell part or all of his or her ownership interest to a party who is outside the existing ownership? Will the plan allow transfers to revocable living trusts or other entities that have longevity without a "heartbeat"? What is appropriate in the beginning may be inappropriate years down the road.

OWNERSHIP INTERESTS AS BONUSES: Will the owners employ a manager? Will they give this person a percentage of ownership? Will there be incentive- or production-based compensation?

DIVORCE OR LAWSUITS: If one partner divorces or is sued, how will this affect the business? How will the owners protect themselves from business liabilities? And how will they protect the assets of the business from any personal liabilities the owners may incur?

BUSINESS VALUATION: How are businesses of this sort generally valued? How important will valuation be to future decisions?

SALE OF THE ENTIRE BUSINESS: Is it likely that you will sell the business as a going concern if you want to retire?

Financial Statements

What are the key financial statements that I'll need in my business plan and for the business once I start it?

You will need three basic financial statements in your business plan and after you start your business:

CASH-FLOW STATEMENT: Shows the sources, amount, timing, and uses of cash flowing into and out of the business for the same period of time as the income statement. A company should have enough cash to meet its needs at all times. Estimated receipts are added to the previous month's cash balance, and estimated expenses are deducted. If the resulting cash balance is insufficient, the amount must be made up through additional capital contributions or loans.

INCOME, OR PROFIT-AND-LOSS (P&L), STATEMENT: Shows the revenues and expenses for a specific period of time. It indicates whether the business achieved its primary objective—earning a profit.

Balance sheet: Lists the business assets (property or property rights) and liabilities (debts) as well as the equity (interest in the assets) of the owner or owners.

When you create these statements for your business plan, you use estimates based on your assumptions. After you start the business, you continue to use the estimates but also use actual historical data as they accumulate. All three financial statements are extremely important for investors, owners, and lenders.

You develop these financial statements on the basis of figures from your budget. This means that, for your business plan, you must prepare the budget first.

⊲ What is a budget?

A *budget* is simply your best guess of what will happen to the business on a financial basis. For a new business, it is your best estimate of monthly revenues and expenses and anticipated capital expenditures for the first 3 to 5 years. Once you start the business, the budget keeps you focused and helps you make decisions based on the long-term needs of the business.

Once the business is operating, it is extremely important to periodically compare the actual results of operations to the budget. This includes analyzing all significant variances and revising the budget, or rebudgeting, for the remainder of the year. The original budget should not be changed, but it should be amended to show the new expected results so that there will be no surprises at the end of the year.

From the budget you can estimate the cash-flow needs for start-up and operation. If the company is growing, it needs cash to buy more fixed assets or to fund its accounts receivable and inventory. Without careful cash-flow planning, the business, though profitable, might run out of cash for handling its growing needs.

⊲ What are the basic steps in preparing a budget?

The "master" budget consists of several budgets that collectively express the planned activities of the business. Typically a master budget has an operating budget and a capital expenses budget.

The *operating budget* includes the following:

SALES BUDGET: This includes an estimate of the products or services you will sell and the revenues you will collect as a result of the sales.

INVENTORY PURCHASE OR PRODUCTION BUDGET: If you have a merchandising business or any business that requires an inventory, you must prepare a budget for the purchase of the items. If you are manufacturing a product, you must prepare a production budget to show how many widgets you will produce each month. This budget includes the costs of raw materials, direct labor to produce the widgets, and overhead for the facilities.

SELLING EXPENSE BUDGET: Using the figures from your sales budget, you can estimate how much it will cost each month to sell your product or service.

GENERAL AND ADMINISTRATIVE (G&A) EXPENSE BUDGET: This usually includes administrative salaries, depreciation, interest expense, and the like. Some of these expenses may be based on sales volume, but most are probably based on other factors, such as management policies.

The *capital expenses budget* includes anticipated expenditures for facilities or equipment for the first 3 to 5 years of your new business. If your sales budget shows increases in sales over the first 5 years, your capital expenses will probably go up.

Using the information in these budgets, you should be able to prepare cash-flow statements, income statements, and balance sheets for the same 3- to 5-year period.

Once I start my business, how often should I update the budget?

We believe that budgets should be updated monthly. This is called *rebudgeting* or, sometimes, *reforecasting* the year. By doing this, you will always have a good idea of where your business is going. You should compare the original budget's estimated results throughout the year to each month's actual results. The rebudget will provide you with a revised estimate of how the year will turn out, based on the most current information available. Thus you can communicate with your lenders and investors about any significant changes in the estimated results for the year.

CHOOSING A
BUSINESS STRUCTURE

⅍ *If I determine that I have a viable business after I put the business plan together, what do I do next?*

You must choose the *entity*, or structure, under which you want to conduct business, and then you must legally form the entity. There are several entities to choose from: corporation, partnership, limited liability company, and so forth. In choosing an entity, consider the following topics:

- Ownership, capitalization, and financing
- Control and management
- Formation requirements
- Duration of the entity and how to terminate it
- Ownership of real estate
- Multistate operations
- Taxation
- Asset protection (avoiding unnecessary liability)
- Compensation
- Employee benefits
- Exit strategy and succession planning
- Estate planning

⚞ *Does my choice of entity affect my management decisions?*

The entity you select will determine how you operate the business, how you establish the rules determining who will have control of the business, and how you will resolve disputes. For example, if your business will have multiple owners and you think you want to conduct business as a general partnership, all of the general-partner owners will have an equal vote in decision making. On the other hand, if you choose a corporate form of business, the board of directors, elected by the owners, and/or the president will make most of the business decisions.

⚞ *Does my choice of entity affect my taxes?*

Yes. Each entity has its own set of tax rules. For example, Internal Revenue Code subchapter C corporations pay federal income tax on their income at rates up to 39 percent, in addition to any applicable state income tax. On the other hand, partnerships, limited liability companies, and subchapter S corporations are *pass-through* entities, and only the partners, members, or shareholders, respectively, pay tax.

⚞ *Does my choice of entity affect liability?*

Yes. Every business owner needs to be aware of the risks of doing business and the ways to limit liability. If business owners do not create limits on liability, they are putting their future at risk, because they are leaving the door open to debts or claims that may make their other assets (or their family's assets) liable.

In addition to protecting current earnings and assets, business owners must take steps to protect future earnings and assets acquired after the owner is no longer in business. Several types of entities can limit liability and cut off claims in the future.

Many business owners do not worry about creditor protection until it is too late. But without proper planning a business owner may easily be responsible for the obligations of the business. These obligations may include contractual liabilities to third parties, internal liabilities to other participants in the business, or lawsuits from people who claim to have been wronged by the business or its owner. By choosing the right entity, owners can shield themselves from many of these perils.

◁ Does my choice of entity affect compensation?

The entity you select can affect the true (after-tax) compensation and the value of benefits to you and your employees, as well as the costs to the business of providing those benefits. For example, if you are the owner of a pass-through entity, money you receive from the business includes compensation for your labor, which is subject to Social Security and Medicare taxes, and distributions that represent a return on your investment, which are not subject to Social Security and Medicare taxes. Proper entity selection may permit you to lawfully reduce the overall amount of taxes that you and your business pay.

◁ What does estate planning have to do with my choice of entity?

Enhancing and preserving the value of the business for yourself and your family should include consideration of the fact that the business will not be owned forever. The type of entity will affect what happens if you die or become disabled. For example, if one of the goals of starting your business is to leave something for your children to run after you are gone, you should choose an entity that can be easily transferred to them. This rules out a sole proprietorship. If you want to make your children, or trusts for the benefit of your children, owners of a portion of the business with you, you should choose an entity that provides for easy transfer but allows you to maintain control.

chapter 3

Operating a Business

GOVERNMENT REGULATIONS

⚐ *How do I find out about all the rules and regulations of doing business?*

A good way to begin is to meet with your business attorney and accountant. Your local chamber of commerce is also an excellent source of information on local, state, and federal regulations affecting businesses. If your business is operated under a franchise or a license, ask your franchisor or licensor for help. If you belong to a trade association, ask it for help. Table A-1 in Appendix A lists additional sources of information on rules and regulations.

⚐ *What are some of the compliance issues facing my business?*

Compliance issues common to most small businesses are:

- *Licenses and permits:* Obtaining a business license; controlling disposal of wastes or hazardous substances; working within the rules and restrictions on land use and building construction

- *Taxes:* Withholding and paying income, Social Security, and Medicare taxes; paying sales taxes, if applicable

- *Employee relations:* Complying with laws against sexual harassment and discrimination in employment; obeying laws with respect to minimum wages, maximum hours, and overtime pay; complying with workers' compensation requirements

- *Credit and collection practices:* Collecting debts in accordance with federal and state rules

- *Advertising and sales practices:* Advertising with appropriate disclosures

Depending on the nature of your business, it may face additional compliance issues, such as those regarding consumer protection; patents, trademarks, and copyrights; importing and exporting; and multistate operations.

Taxes

◄ *What are FICA taxes?*

FICA stands for *Federal Insurance Contributions Act.* FICA taxes are more commonly called Social Security and Medicare taxes. FICA taxes are based on the employee's salary and wages. The employer pays a portion, and the employee pays a portion through withholdings from pay. FICA taxes are divided into two parts:

- *Social Security* (Old-Age, Survivors, and Disability Insurance, or OASDI): This portion is 6.2 percent of an employee's wages, up to $80,400 in 2001. It is indexed annually for inflation.

- *Medicare:* This portion is 1.45 percent of all wages, with no ceiling.

The combined employee withholding tax rate is 7.65 percent. The employer is required to pay a matching amount to the federal government for each employee.

For example, Cecil Jones earned an annual salary of $60,000 from Acme Corporation in 2001. Cecil's gross wages per semimonthly pay period were $2500. Acme Corporation withheld $191.25 ($2500 × 7.65%) from Cecil's paycheck. Acme matched that amount and paid a total of $382.50 on Cecil's behalf to the federal government. Cecil's semimonthly take-home pay after FICA taxes was $2308.75, before further reduction by any income tax withholding.

⅄ What is the self-employment tax?

A self-employed person is an independent contractor or anyone who works in a business where there is no distinct employer-employee relationship, such as a sole proprietor, partner of a partnership, member of a limited liability company, or shareholder of an S corporation. A self-employed individual must pay both the employer's *and* the employee's portion of the FICA taxes. The 15.3 percent total amount (the employer's 7.65 percent plus the employee's 7.65 percent) is called the *self-employment tax.*

Self-employed individuals must estimate their taxes for the year and make quarterly deposits. Individuals must take care not to underestimate. If the amount of the tax deposits is insufficient to cover the tax liability, the IRS may impose penalties.

⅄ What is FUTA?

The *Federal Unemployment Tax Act (FUTA)* complements state unemployment systems for providing unemployment compensation to workers who have lost their jobs. Most employers pay both federal and state unemployment tax. In general, the wages employers pay to employees are subject to FUTA unless the wages are less than a specified amount in any calendar quarter ($1500 in 2001). In 2001, the FUTA tax rate was 6.2 percent on wages up to the feder-

al wage base of $7000. Employers must follow a formula for calcu-
lating and depositing FUTA taxes quarterly.

☙ *What are the federal income tax withholding requirements?*

The goal of the income tax withholding rules is to have each taxpayer pay most of his or her annual income tax liability periodically throughout the year. To accomplish this, the employer withholds
each employee's taxes from his or her paycheck and deposits those
taxes on a regular basis with the federal government.

The employer must obtain from each employee a completed W-
4 form. On this form, the employee computes the amount of money
the employer should withhold from his or her paycheck and pay to
the federal government as the employee's federal income tax. The
employer may rely on the W-4 submitted by an employee until the
employee submits a new form.

The purpose of the W-4 is to help the employee estimate his or
her total income tax liability for the year so that the employer can
withhold a pro-rata portion of that amount from each paycheck.
The computations necessary to determine the suggested amount of
withholding are based on tables provided by the IRS in a publication titled *Circular E*. The tables in *Circular E* take into account
whether the taxpayer is single or married and the number of
"allowances" claimed by the employee. Allowances are based primarily on the number of the employee's dependents. Employees need
to be careful of underwithholding, or they may be subject to IRS
penalties.

For example, Cecil Jones is married and has two children. Cecil
is allowed to claim four allowances: himself, his wife, and the two
children. The tables in *Circular E* for a married person with four
allowances who was paid $2500 semimonthly in 2001 indicate a
withholding amount of $264 per check. If Cecil chooses, he can
claim fewer allowances on his W-4 and have more taxes withheld.
Two reasons for extra withholding are to make up for other income
he earns or to create a tax refund (a forced savings plan). Cecil may
also claim more than four allowances to reduce his tax withholding

to adjust for other factors that will reduce his annual tax liability, for example, home mortgage interest payments.

⁂ *Are there ways to avoid an underpayment penalty other than by increasing the amount of withholding?*

Yes, you may make estimated payments of federal income tax to supplement the amounts withheld from wages. Such payments are most prevalent for sole proprietors and business owners who receive distributions rather than, or in addition to, wages.

Estimated tax payments are generally made on a quarterly basis. For example, for a calendar-year taxpayer, the quarterly income tax payments are due on April 15, June 15, and September 15 of the current year and on January 15 of the following year.

⁂ *When cash flow is tight, I sometimes don't make the required estimated tax deposit for my employees because the business needs the money to pay bills. Is this a good policy?*

No! In our experience the biggest mistake business owners make is failing to pay all withholding taxes when they are due. Often we are told that the limited cash is needed to pay suppliers, the landlord, utilities, and so on, in order to keep the business open. However, the IRS treats failure to deposit withholding taxes as theft by the employer. This can result in the owner's personal liability for the full amount of the tax, and the business can be shut down and all its assets sold. It is *never* okay to delay payment of withholding taxes, no matter how good the reason appears to be at the time.

Employee Relations

⁂ *What basics should I know about employer-employee relations?*

The main points you should know are that the relationship is highly regulated and the conduct required by the parties to comply with the laws is not always obvious. In fact, whole treatises have been devoted to this subject. Because of the number and complexity of the rules and regulations, guidance from an attorney with expertise in employer-employee relations is highly recommended as you begin to hire employees.

All employers should be aware of certain issues:

1. Every employer must carry workers' compensation insurance, even if there is only one employee. In certain states, exceptions may apply to employees who are also owners.

2. Federal and state occupational safety and health agencies publish guidelines related to worker safety. Failure to follow the guidelines can carry substantial penalties.

3. Federal and state wage and hour guidelines govern such things as when overtime must be paid, who is entitled to overtime compensation, how it must be calculated, and the circumstances under which "comp time" can be used in lieu of overtime compensation.

4. Minimum-wage laws affect how much an employer must pay to entry-level employees. An employer also must be aware of payroll systems and required withholdings and deductions. (Use of a good payroll service may be helpful.)

5. Federal and state antidiscrimination laws and the regulations of the administrative bodies that enforce them place substantial restrictions on employers with respect to hiring, firing, and other employment decisions.

6. Federal and state laws designed to prevent harassment based on sex, race, religion, and other protected categories, and to prevent wrongful termination, also affect employers' decisions and actions.

7. Several laws and regulations require that employers post certain notices in a conspicuous location at the workplace.

These are but a few of the legal issues confronting an employer, and this is by no means a comprehensive list.

⚜ *Do I have to pay a minimum wage to my employees?*

Most likely you do, since almost all jobs are covered by minimum-wage requirements. There are both federal and state laws governing employee wages. Consult your state's Department of Labor to see what specific requirements apply to your employees.

⚜ *If an employee is paid a salary, not an hourly rate, do I have to pay overtime?*

Under federal law, every employee, whether paid by the hour, on a salary basis, or otherwise, must receive overtime pay unless a recognized exemption to the overtime laws applies to his or her job. None of the exemptions are based solely on whether the employee is salaried. All of them depend on the employee's job responsibility and functions. Therefore, you should not assume that you can avoid paying overtime simply by paying someone on a salary basis, even if the amount of salary takes into consideration the excess hours you expect the employee will have to work.

The federal wage and hour laws and the classification of employees as exempt or nonexempt are quite complex. Many states also have their own wage and hour rules and regulations. Consequently, you should consult an attorney with expertise in this area before implementing any policy or taking any action if you are uncertain about its legality.

⚜ *Is there any requirement that men and women be paid the same amount?*

The Equal Pay Act of 1993 was adopted as an amendment to the Fair Labor Standards Act. It prohibits sex-based discrimination in matters of wages. Therefore, equal work on jobs that require equal skills, effort, and responsibility, performed under the same conditions, must be paid equally, regardless of the employee's sex.

⚜ *Can we employ our children in our business?*

The answer depends on your children's ages and the type of work involved. Basically, the Fair Labor Standards Act protects children under age 17 from being hired for dangerous occupations and industries. Between ages 14 and 15, children can be employed in some specifically approved jobs, such as those in retail stores, restaurants, and service stations. Under age 14, a child can be employed only in certain occupations, such as agricultural employment.

⊰ What rules protect older workers?

Congress adopted the Age Discrimination in Employment Act (ADEA) in 1967 to prevent employers from replacing older workers with younger workers at lower wages and at lower cost for medical benefits. Generally, the ADEA applies to persons 40 or older and to employers who have twenty or more employees. The ADEA prohibits discrimination in hiring, firing, promotions, compensation, privileges, or any other terms or conditions of employment.

⊰ What rules must I follow with regard to employees with disabilities?

Congress ensured civil rights protection to people with disabilities when it passed the Americans with Disabilities Act (ADA) in 1990. Employers with fifteen or more employees may not discriminate against a qualified applicant who has a disability. This national mandate defines a *disabled person* as someone who (1) has a physical or mental impairment that substantially limits one or more of the person's major life activities, (2) has a record of such an impairment, or (3) is regarded as having such an impairment.

This law applies to individuals with acquired immune deficiency syndrome (AIDS) and those with positive human immunodeficiency virus (HIV) test results. A person who has recovered from a previous disability is also protected by the same statute.

Employers must facilitate disabled persons' employment by making "reasonable accommodations." These include accommodating work schedules, making facilities accessible, restructuring jobs, and providing training policies and materials to qualified applicants.

If an employer suffers significant difficulty or expense in making reasonable accommodations and is able to show undue hardship, the employer may be exempted. This exemption necessarily includes a review of the employer's financial resources.

⚜ *What if a disabled applicant is simply not able to do the job?*

If the job involves a task that is a bona fide occupational qualification and a reasonable accommodation does not enable the applicant to do it, the employer is not required to hire the person. For example, if bending over and lifting 50 pounds on a regular basis is a job requirement, an employer would not be required to hire someone with a bad back.

⚜ *What do I need to know about hiring men or women for particular jobs?*

Although a job may have been traditionally held by a man or a woman, such preferences are deemed discriminatory unless actually required by the nature of the work. For example, it is not discriminatory to interview only women for a job modeling women's clothing. Clearly, in this example, gender is a bona fide occupational qualification. However, the courts have interpreted this qualification narrowly. Customer preference for a male or female employee does not qualify as a bona fide occupational qualification.

⚜ *Do we have to make accommodations for employees who are members of the military reserve or National Guard?*

The Military Selective Service Act protects the employment of men and women who serve in the military or the National Guard. For example, employees who attend 2 weeks of active duty in the summer or who are called up for active duty during a national or international crisis (such as the operations in Bosnia, Somalia, and Haiti) are protected from losing their jobs.

An employer cannot discriminate in hiring a person because he or she serves in one of the military branches. If an employee is called for active duty, the employer must reemploy that person upon his or her return without loss of seniority and must restore all benefits. The employee is entitled to all cost-of-living pay increases but not to merit pay increases. Further, the returning employee cannot be discharged without cause for 6 months after returning to work.

◢ Is there a federal law governing safety of workers?

Yes, the Occupational Safety and Health Act of 1970 regulates worker safety. It is enforced by the Occupational Safety and Health Administration (OSHA). Under its worker safety and health standards, OSHA requires that employers keep detailed records of workers' injuries and illnesses. The agency conducts workplace inspections and investigates workplace injuries and illnesses.

OSHA inspections are typically initiated as a result of an employee's written complaint. The employee's identity is kept confidential, and he or she is protected from discrimination for exercising his or her rights under the statute.

◢ Am I required to have a retirement plan for my employees?

No. If you choose to have one, however, and you decide that it will be a qualified plan, the terms of the plan must comply with the Employee Retirement Income Security Act (ERISA) of 1974. One of the primary ERISA requirements is that the plan not discriminate among employees. (See Part Three for more information on qualified plans.)

◢ If we suffer a theft in our business, can we require that our employees take a lie detector test?

Because the test, known as a *polygraph test*, must be subjectively interpreted by the test operator, Congress came to believe that many innocent persons were denied employment on the basis of inaccurate test interpretations. To correct this failing, the Employee Polygraph Protection Act of 1988 makes polygraph use unlawful in most instances. Permitted uses include national defense; ongoing investigations; drug security, theft, or diversion investigations; and armored-car and security issues.

To be protected under the ongoing-investigations exception, an employer must meet three requirements: (1) Polygraph tests must be administered in connection with an ongoing investigation involving economic loss or injury to the employer's business; (2) the employee must have had access to the property that is the subject of the investigation; and (3) the employer must have a reasonable suspicion that the employee was involved in the incident under investigation. All questions must relate to the incident, and the employee has the right to stop the test at any time. Employees cannot be fired solely for refusing to take a polygraph.

This is a very sensitive area. You should obtain legal advice before entering into polygraph testing or substance-abuse testing.

⚖ *Can I give a bad reference for a former employee?*

Employees are entitled to certain protection regarding information in their personnel files. Two legal theories apply: defamation and invasion of the right to privacy. *Defamation* can occur, for example, if you give a negative reference based on personnel-file information that is unfounded. An *invasion of the right to privacy* can occur if the termination reasons communicated to the prospective employer reveal ethical or other problems of the employee. Even if the reasons are beyond dispute, the communication may be considered an invasion of the employee's right to privacy. To be cautious, you may want to provide a prospective employer with only your former employee's ending salary, job title, and dates of employment.

Consumer Issues

⚖ *I want to sell goods and services to my customers on credit. Are there any laws I should be concerned about?*

Both state and federal laws govern the extension of credit to consumers. The primary federal law is known as the Consumer Credit Protection Act of 1968. This federal law has been amended several times with statutes that have been given popular names: Consumer Credit Cost Disclosure Act, commonly known as the Truth in Lending Act (TILA); Fair Credit Billing Act; Fair Credit Reporting Act; Equal Credit Opportunity Act; and Fair Debt Collection Practices Act. In addition to these federal laws, many states have their own laws that are known by such titles as Unfair Trade Practices Act, Installment Sales Act, Home Improvement Loans Act, and the like.

I've heard that the Truth in Lending Act gives consumers 3 days to reconsider and get out of a contract. Is this true?

Generally, consumers do not have 3 days to rescind. The exceptions relate to TILA's provisions governing contracts secured by a consumer's residence. Apparently, Congress was concerned that businesses might have an advantage over consumers in situations where consumers might put their houses in jeopardy. In these cases consumers have until midnight of the third business day after signing to rescind the contract. The consumer must be given notice of the right to rescind in addition to the other required TILA disclosures. The right to rescind does not apply to a creditor that lends money for the consumer to purchase a residence, as opposed to improving one. It also does not apply when an immediate home repair is necessitated by some emergency circumstance.

Are there special rules if we sell our products door-to-door?

Yes. Under Federal Trade Commission (FTC) regulations, buyers have the right to cancel within 3 business days any contract arising from door-to-door product sales, even if no credit is extended. The buyer must be provided with a written form that can be filled in and mailed to the seller to exercise the right to cancel the contract. If these rules are not followed, the consumer can cancel within 1 year.

What do I have to know to comply with the Truth in Lending Act?

In order to eliminate confusion, the Federal Reserve Board has issued both administrative rules that implement the Truth in Lending Act, known as "Regulation Z," and model forms for businesses to use when selling goods on credit. The rules described in Regulation Z apply to all businesses that, in the ordinary course of their transactions, lend money, sell on credit, or arrange for the extension of credit to consumers. The rules do not apply to sales between consumers or between businesses. Basically, the seller must describe the cash price; the down payment or trade-in allowance, if any; the unpaid cash price (the cash price minus the down payment) that is to be financed; the finance charge (the total amount of interest and other charges); and the annual percentage rate. Penalties for failure to comply include the actual damages plus twice the amount of the finance charge, as well as attorneys' fees.

What if I get into a dispute with a customer over the billing?

The Fair Credit Billing Act requires that creditors promptly correct errors in billing without damaging a person's credit rating. When a dispute arises, the consumer must notify the creditor in writing to explain the mistake. The customer must pay any *undisputed* amount while waiting for the creditor's reply. The creditor has 30 days to acknowledge the inquiry and 90 days to either correct the mistake or provide an explanation as to why the creditor believes there is no mistake. During this time, the creditor may not give an unfavorable credit report or attempt to collect the amount in dispute.

What discrimination rules do I need to be aware of in granting credit?

The Equal Credit Opportunity Act, passed in 1974, prohibits certain forms of discrimination. In short, if a person can pay the debt, he or she cannot be denied credit on the basis of race, color, religion, national origin, sex, marital status, age, or amount of income derived from public assistance.

⚜ *If people don't pay me on time, can I turn them over to a collection agency?*

Certainly. Just make sure you deal with a reputable collection agency that follows all the requirements for collecting debts and for reporting delinquent customers to credit report agencies.

⚜ *If we back up our products with a warranty, are there any special concerns?*

Both state and federal rules regulate product warranties. The Magnuson-Moss Warranty Act of 1975 established standards for consumer warranties. No seller is required to give a written warranty for consumer goods. But if the seller decides to give an express written warranty on a consumer product valued at more than $10, the warranty must be labeled "full" or "limited." A *full warranty* covers free repair or replacement of any defective part. A *limited warranty* indicates something less than a full warranty. For example, tires often come with a limited warranty under which the purchaser receives a pro-rated refund based on tread wear at the time the tire goes flat.

Consult the Uniform Commercial Code, which has been adopted in every state. This statute has specific provisions for express and implied warranties dealing with the sale of consumer goods.

⚜ *My business manufactures products for sale to the public. Are there any safety guidelines I need to follow?*

To help protect consumers from unreasonable risk of injury from hazardous products, Congress in 1972 adopted the Consumer Product Safety Act. Among its comprehensive provisions is the requirement that product manufacturers inform the Consumer Product Safety Commission about events involving their products that cause injury or death. Contact the Consumer Product Safety Commission for information on regulations that may apply to the products your business sells to the public.

⊌ *I want to start a business that prepares food for sale. What issues should concern me?*

The Food and Drug Administration (FDA) is charged with ensuring that food, drugs, therapeutic items, and cosmetics are safe and labeled correctly. Each state (and some cities) regulates and licenses businesses that prepare and sell food. For more information, check with your state authorities.

Advertising and Sales Practices

⊌ *We do a lot of advertising in our business. What laws apply to advertising?*

Since 1938, the FTC has had the authority to monitor deceptive advertising practices affecting consumers. Generally, any practice that would tend to mislead consumers is deemed to be unfair or deceptive. Most states (and many cities) have their own consumer protection laws and ordinances governing unfair trade practices, including advertising.

There are four major areas in which advertisements are challenged:

UNSUPPORTED CLAIMS: There must be reasonable, scientific evidence to substantiate advertising claims. Thus, if you claim that your product is faster than similar products, there must be sufficient testing to back up your claim.

FAILURE TO DISCLOSE IMPORTANT FACTS: While every negative fact need not be revealed in the advertisement, important ones must be. For example, it would be deceptive to advertise that anyone will qualify for credit without disclosing that, in fact, each consumer has to deposit several hundred dollars into an account to cover the extension of credit.

Statements that are less than the whole truth: In this instance, instead of omitting a material fact, the advertiser uses true statements out of context. For example, the FTC restrained the Parker Pen Company from making "guaranteed-for-life" statements when "life" meant the life of the pen rather than the life of the consumer.

False statements or claims: Misrepresentations about the quality, composition, origin, character, or availability of products are prohibited.

   Are there any special issues if we use the U.S. Postal Service to advertise or deliver our products?

The postmaster general has the power to return all mail either addressed to or mailed by a promoter who has made false representations. Postal regulations require that unordered merchandise contain a clear and conspicuous statement indicating that the merchandise is a free sample. The promoter can take no action to persuade a consumer to pay for unordered merchandise. For more serious violations, postal fraud statutes provide for criminal penalties. The FTC shares with the postmaster general the enforcement of regulations as they relate to mail-order houses. For example, if a business is unable to ship its goods within 30 days, it must notify the buyer of his or her option either to allow the delay or to cancel the order and receive a refund.

   I want to hire people to sell my product by telephone. What are the rules?

The FTC specifies the hours during which telemarketers can make unsolicited phone calls. Solicitors must inform subjects that the call's purpose is to sell goods and services. Certain states have laws that allow consumers to register with the state in order not to receive telephone solicitations. Penalties apply to telemarketers who call consumers who are on the no-solicitation list.

Other Regulatory Issues

✍ *I have a great idea that can make me a lot of money. How can I protect it?*

New and unique ideas can be very valuable. To encourage creative thinking, the United States has a system of patent, trademark, and copyright laws.

New inventions and processes can be protected by a patent obtained from the U.S. Patent and Trademark Office. The patent holder has the exclusive right to make, use, and market an invention during a 17-year nonrenewable period.

Authors and composers can protect their original works by obtaining a copyright. Others who use their works must pay compensation, usually called *royalties*. Generally, a copyright is valid for the author's or composer's life plus 50 years.

✍ *Our professional services firm has developed a few unique processes that differentiate us from competitors. Should we trademark these systems?*

In the twenty-first century, with its technological advances and the tremendous explosion of new information, it is very important to protect your "intellectual property." Going through the simple process of trademarking or copyrighting your unique systems is extremely beneficial for several reasons:

- The act of "branding" (or naming) the things you do gives you a sense of pride, ownership, and authorship.
- It enables you to prevent competitors from using the same techniques.
- The sooner you trademark your processes, the easier it is to

prove they are owned by you rather than by other companies that may have come up with similar systems at the same time.

- The legal work involved is somewhat inexpensive.

- Branding allows you to adopt a unique, proprietary "look and feel" that increases client awareness of and identification with your firm's services.

- It is easier to sell your business in the future if you own your systems and have a legal right to pass them on to the buyer of your practice.

⚞ *Where do we go to get information on importing and exporting?*

There are a number of agencies concerned with international business, including:

- *International Trade Administration (ITA):* Promotes export trading companies and grants exemptions from liability under certain antitrust laws

- *U.S. Customs Service:* Assesses and collects customs duties, excise taxes, fees, and penalties on imported merchandise

- *Small Business Administration:* Guarantees loans for certain types of import/export businesses and provides information

- *U.S. Department of Commerce:* Provides assistance through its "trade desks" for each country

- *State and local governments:* Often have commissions that help individuals set up import/export companies

- *Export-Import Bank (Eximbank):* Provides financing assistance to exporting and importing firms, typically by guaranteeing a transaction to a commercial bank, thereby allowing the commercial bank to make direct loans to a firm

The United States has entered into multiple trade agreements, such as the North American Free Trade Agreement (NAFTA), which is designed to promote free trade in the western hemisphere and to eliminate trade barriers between Mexico, Canada, and the United States. Websites devoted to these agreements may help you conduct business within the countries that are party to the agreements.

⚐ Are there limits on importing and exporting?

There are limits on what you can export or import, as well as restrictions on which countries you can do business with. The organizations listed in the previous answer can give you the specifics.

⚐ What legal requirements must I meet in order to do business in a state other than the one in which I formed my comapany?

Generally, whenever a company is "doing business" in a state other than the one in which it was established, it must file for authority to carry on its business in that state. Consult with your business lawyer to determine whether the nature and location of the activities conducted by your company require filing or registration in another state.

ACCOUNTING METHODS

⚐ Do I have a choice of accounting methods?

Businesses typically use the cash, accrual, or, less frequently, percentage-of-completion accounting method. The method you can use is dictated by generally accepted accounting principles (GAAP) and perhaps the IRS, depending on the type of business you own.

⚐ What is the cash method?

Under *cash-basis accounting*, the business records and recognizes revenue when it collects it and records and deducts expenses when it pays them. Usually, the business records depreciation using the tax method of depreciation; if the assets are minor, they are deducted when the company pays for them.

Sole proprietors may generally report income on a cash basis. As a general rule, the cash method of accounting is available to corporations only if they are S corporations, corporations engaged in the trade or business of farming and timber, or corporations with average annual gross receipts of $5 million or less. Partnerships and LLCs are subject to certain restrictions on the use of the cash method. They are prohibited from using the cash method of accounting if they are classified as a "tax shelter" or if they have a C corporation as a partner.

ᴴ᷃ What is the accrual method?

Under the *accrual method of accounting,* the business records and recognizes revenue when it makes a sale regardless of when the customer pays. The business records expenses when it incurs them regardless of when it actually pays the bills. The accrual method is the most accurate means of accounting because it matches the revenue with the expense regardless of the cash situation. If a business has a large amount of accounts receivable, inventory, accounts payable, accrued expense, and fixed assets, its financial statements will not be accurate unless it uses the accrual method of accounting, which GAAP requires in such circumstances.

Both individuals and corporations that maintain inventory for sale to customers are required to use the accrual method for determining the cost of goods sold unless gross sales are less than $1 million per year.

ᴴ᷃ When would I have to use the percentage-of-completion method?

GAAP requires the *percentage-of-completion method* for companies whose business is based on projects that span multiple tax years. Contractors, architects, and engineers may be required to use this accounting method in order to more accurately reflect their income and expenses as they relate to each project.

⋟ How should my accounting system be set up?

A company's accounting system must be easy to use and must provide management with current information on a timely basis. Most accounting systems have the following subsystems (not all systems are relevant to every business):

- A *human resource system* to incorporate all payroll and employee-related costs
- An *inventory system* to track cost and quantity of inventory
- A *sales/accounts receivable system* to record sales and payments
- A *vendor/accounts payable system* to record vendor expenses and payments
- A *property and equipment system* to keep track of capitalized assets and purchases and to record depreciation for both book and tax purposes (Depending on the number of assets, the system should keep track of their location.)
- A *reporting system* to produce monthly and year-to-date profit-and-loss (P&L) statements, balance sheets, and other financial statements
- For service companies, a *time and billing system* to record time and match it to client billing to measure profitability of both clients and personnel

HIRING CONSIDERATIONS

⋟ I'm so incredibly busy "doing" the business that I don't have time to manage the business. What can I do?

This is a common problem. New owners of start-up companies do everything, and owners and managers of fast-growing businesses keep taking on more and more work as the business grows. Dan Sullivan of Strategic Coach in Toronto, Canada, refers to this as hitting the "ceiling of complexity." If you spend all your time and energy working, you will lack the creative energy needed to see things in perspective. When you are tired, the first things to go are communication and proper delegation. You won't be able to recognize strategic opportunities. And you won't be having much fun.

Taking days off or extended vacations away from the business (without pagers and daily check-ins) can give you the necessary perspective, rejuvenation, and enthusiasm. You may find that the business actually gets along fine without you. You may also discover that with this free time, retirement is not such a big priority. At a minimum, you should take at least 1 full day each quarter to assess your goals, your progress, your opportunities, and your strategies. If you have employees, solicit input from the key employees and periodically involve them in the process.

Hitting the ceiling of complexity is typically a key indicator that it is time to hire more employees.

   ⚑ *My business isn't large enough to support more personnel. How do I go about building a team, especially on a budget?*

Dan Sullivan has created several tools to assist businesspeople in hiring the right employees for themselves, the jobs, and their businesses. According to Sullivan, we all do our day-to-day tasks at one of the following levels:

> Some things we do . . . we are incompetent.
> Some things we do . . . we are competent.
> Some things we do . . . we are excellent.
> Other things we do . . . we are in our *unique genius and ability*.

The most important thing for businesspeople to do, if they want to expand their businesses, is to accurately assess the tasks they do on a regular basis. Entrepreneurs can *do* a lot of things, but they usually can't do them all at the same level of commitment, energy, and ability. When people do things that are monotonous and boring or that they're not good at, they get fatigued and lose creativity. Business owners should ask themselves, "What do I do best? What can only I do? What unique talents do I bring to the table?"

The smart entrepreneur determines what his or her *unique ability* is, concentrates on tasks that require it, and delegates all other tasks to people who have unique abilities in those areas. This "smart synergy" allows an organization to be empowered with "endless energy."

A good exercise is to list all the things you do in your business. Then cross off all the "stuff" and identify just three things that you absolutely must do to provide the highest payoff for your business. Think about your unique talents. What gives you energy? What do people say you are really great at? Ideally, your unique abilities should come close to the three critical tasks you identified. Next, identify areas of excellence. You are very good at these, but not unique. Then identify areas of competence. You can do them, but you do not excel at them. Finally, identify your areas of incompetence. These are things that cause you stress.

Do this exercise with existing team members or potential new employees. (Your team can be as small as two people, or it can be a virtual team, with some tasks out-sourced to other providers.) You should delegate tasks to those whose skills complement—rather than duplicate—your abilities. Reorganize so that each person operates in the areas of his or her unique talents. You and your team members will all be happier and much more effective. You will find that your organization has excess capacity to tackle more opportunities, and you will have more time for strategic planning—and rejuvenating days off.

Selecting the Right People

❧ *To expand my business, I need to hire more people. Are there any hiring tips that will help me choose the right people?*

Employment agencies are a good source of help in screening and selecting applicants. There are also many types of personality and psychological tests that can help identify the right employees, and it is worth finding the one that best fits your needs. Many of the contributors to *Strictly Business* use a method developed by the Kolbe Corporation (www.kolbe.com) to assess current and prospective employees.

The Kolbe Conative Index identifies and measures a person's unique faculties or abilities on the basis of four major categories: "fact finder" (red); "follow through" (blue); "quick start" (green); "implementor" (yellow). Everyone has some measure of each of these "colors" but is highest in the color that correlates with his or her unique ability. Most entrepreneurs are by nature green: quick starters, risk takers, visionaries. They may not have enough red or blue to properly pay attention to the details of their businesses. This is where assessing existing staff and potential future staff becomes extremely important.

According to Kolbe, if a business has too many employees of the same color, major problems may occur. The Kolbe Team Assessment Index can determine whether a business's team is properly balanced. If imbalances are found, it is important to fill the gaps with new hires who complement the existing team.

Job descriptions tend to be best suited for specific colors, or unique abilities. For example, the CFO of an organization should have high red and blue profiles. As part of the screening process for prospective employees, Kolbe can profile the job description and then assess each applicant's ability to perform the job.

Family members

🔾 *Aside from legal measures, what can we do to increase the odds that our business stays in the family for generations?*

If you are successful in business, a part of your family's identity will be intertwined with the business enterprise. You will want to develop an interrelated family and corporate culture that reflects your values as a family. This culture should become so obvious and consistent as to be almost tangible to both insiders and outsiders.

⚜ *How can I be objective about hiring and promoting family members?*

Scott E. Friedman, in his article "A New, More Effective Planning Strategy for Family Businesses" (*Estate Planning*, June 1999), listed the following protocols:

- Create a system of fairness for dealing with family members in and out of the business.
- Seek consensus for decisions that directly affect either family members or the structure, direction, and future of the company.
- Create written hiring objectives, job descriptions, and qualifications, and apply them fairly and consistently to both family members and persons outside the family.
- Create objective tests based on demonstrated performance that can be used to evaluate and promote all employees, especially family members.
- When promoting someone, particularly a family member, discuss the objective criteria and performance with the family. If possible, gain consensus before making a decision.
- Hire or keep only those family members who are capable and who desire to increase the family's success.
- Have a system for treating nonparticipating family members fairly to reduce conflicts.

⚜ *That all sounds fine, but I'm a bottom-line person. I've succeeded without bureaucracy in the past, so why should I create so much structure now?*

If you are going to keep the business healthy for another generation or more, you need to begin creating a family business structure as soon as you start hiring family members. Many companies are founded by unique individuals who are capable of many things. It is unlikely that all the same capabilities are going to be found in a single successor.

If the company is large enough and profitable enough to support several family members, you probably need to specialize your management structure anyway. Give family members the opportunity to show their stuff, but use objective measures of success to judge the quality of those you promote to leadership roles.

Without objective measures of achievement, employees who are not family members may not strive to excel; they may conclude that only family members can get into top management. In addition, without an objective means of placing and advancing family members, family rivalries and friction may spring up as family members try to compete without a game board or rules.

⋙ *What should I be concerned about if I want to hire my spouse?*

Employing a spouse has its rewards and challenges. If you and your spouse work well as a team, the arrangement is highly satisfying and it keeps in the family the money that you would have paid to an outside employee. However, it can make it difficult to separate business from personal life, and it may lead to marital and business tensions. It can also create tension and confusion among employees.

Couples who succeed have learned to draw some boundaries between work and home. They can "turn it off" when they go home, forgetting about the roles they play at work. Likewise, they can turn off their roles as spouses when they are at work. They have also learned to carve out distinct territories of work responsibilities to minimize disagreements about tasks and how to do them.

⋙ *Does it make sense to employ my children, who are under age 18, in my business?*

There are reasons why you may or may not want to employ your children. Initially, you may want to consider whether they will be good employees, without any reference to the family relationship. Also, consider your personal relationship with your children to determine whether the employer-employee relationship might damage your parent-child relationship. If such considerations do not dissuade you, there are good tax reasons for employing your under-age-18 children.

Your business can pay them reasonable wages for the work they perform, and the wage payments result in income and self-employment tax deductions for your business. Additionally, your children's wages can be sheltered from personal income taxes up to each child's applicable standard deduction. Let's assume, for example, that single taxpayers receive a standard deduction of $4500 (as in 2001). If your business pays one of your children $4500 in annual wages, the business can deduct the $4500; that child reports the $4500 as income from wages and then deducts it as his or her standard deduction. Your children may also be able to shelter additional wages by contributing to an IRA.

⊀ *My son wants to work for my business, and I'd like to give him an entry-level position, but he wants to be a VP. How do I handle this?*

It's great that your son wants to work with you. But is your business the best place for him to start? Perhaps he should go to work for a competitor, where he can acquire valuable experience and industry knowledge to bring to the table when he is ready for a senior position. Alternatively, you could give him an entry-level position as a "gopher" for one of your department heads. After learning the ins and outs of the company, he might be ready for a more challenging position, and you could give him the opportunity to work his way up the ladder of jobs until you and he feel he has found his niche in the business.

Independent contractors

⊀ *Can't I avoid all the employment rules and withholding taxes by hiring an independent contractor instead of an employee?*

This is a very dangerous approach. As a rule of thumb, any person who works in your workplace and is not provided by an employment service is most likely an employee no matter what you call him or her. Your failure to withhold taxes from a paycheck and to follow other employment rules is an unnecessary risk and a threat to the success of your business. The rules for independent-contractor status have been tightened considerably in the past few years; if you contemplate this approach, it is essential that you obtain from the IRS and your state taxing agency the regulations governing the use of independent contractors.

There are other detriments: Independent contractors may not share the goals, camaraderie, and commitment that exist among employees. They may be more like "lone rangers" and may disrupt business morale.

⩜ *How does an independent contractor differ from an employee?*

Independent contractors need not be covered by workers' compensation insurance, are not covered by federal antidiscrimination laws, are not subject to tax withholding and contribution requirements, and cannot bring wrongful termination claims against you.

Merely labeling someone an "independent contractor" and paying him or her outside the payroll does not ensure that the person is not an employee under the law. Courts and enforcement agencies apply their own standards in determining whether an individual is an independent contractor or an employee.

The general test involves the extent to which the person or business for which the services are performed has the right to control and direct the individual who performs the services—not only the result to be accomplished but also the detail and means by which the result is achieved. In other words, an *employee* is someone subject to the will and control of the employer, not only for what will be done but also for how it will be done. It is not necessary that the employer actually direct or control how the services are performed; it is sufficient that the employer has the right to do so. In contrast, an *independent contractor* is expected to achieve a particular result but is left free to decide how it will be accomplished.

⅍ What risks are associated with misclassifying an employee as an independent contractor?

Incorrectly classifying someone as an independent contractor can have many unintended results. First, if the worker is injured and not covered by workers' compensation insurance, the company could be liable for damages and/or face statutory penalties for not having provided coverage. The business is also liable for having failed to make the required tax withholdings and employer contributions for Social Security and unemployment insurance. This liability usually entails payment of the uncontributed amounts along with penalties and interest, and the owners and persons responsible for withholding can be personally liable for these amounts. Finally, the worker may be able to assert claims against the company that are based on the existence of an employer-employee relationship, such as discrimination, harassment, or wrongful termination. The worker could also assert claims for benefits that extend to all other employees but not to him or her.

Using Written Agreements

⅍ When I hire employees, should I have written employment contracts with them?

Many employers find it helpful to use written contracts, either in the form of an "offer letter" or a more formal instrument. Certainly, strong consideration should be given to creating a written contract for all management-level employees, executives, and key employees. Written contracts have the benefit of expressly defining the relationship, clarifying the expectations of the parties, and minimizing disputes about what was agreed on. Contracts and letters are particularly useful in dealing with bonuses or nontraditional forms of compensation, vacation time, standard hours, and the like, as they commit to writing what the agreement is. Written agreements also can be helpful in minimizing the potential for wrongful-termination suits and avoiding jury trials through the use of mediation and/or arbitration provisions.

You should have employment contracts prepared or reviewed by an attorney who has expertise in this area of the law.

⋈ *If an employee leaves my company or is fired, can I keep him or her from setting up a competing business?*

Generally, former employees are free to compete against you as long as the competition is conducted fairly in the eyes of the law and does not infringe on your intellectual property rights. Some states allow employers to restrict postemployment competition through a contract entered into with the employee before the termination. Such *covenants not to compete* provide that the employee will not work for a competitor of the company or set up a competing business for some specified period of time after the end of his or her employment. Not all states recognize the enforceability of these contracts, and even in states where they are valid, they are often strictly scrutinized for reasonableness with respect to the duration of the noncompete period, the geographic scope, and what is considered a competitive activity. Seek the advice of a business lawyer who has experience in drafting such covenants to ensure that your document will achieve the desired results.

⋈ *Can I prevent a departing employee from soliciting business from my customers or trying to hire my employees?*

Your customers and employees are not considered your property under the law. However, certain information they have might be considered *trade secrets,* which a departing employee cannot use in competition against you. For example, the identities, contact information, and buying preferences of your customers might be considered trade secrets if the customers are known to want a specialized product or service.

Because your ability to protect your business against customer or employee "raids" will vary from case to case, depending on the particular facts and circumstances presented, you should contact an attorney with expertise in this area if you suspect you might be at risk.

⊿ What should I do to protect my proprietary business information?

To qualify as a trade secret, information must be subject to reasonable efforts to maintain its secrecy. Therefore, you should take all reasonable steps to maintain the confidentiality of your business information. You should have each of your employees sign a confidentiality agreement, acknowledging the confidential nature of your proprietary information and agreeing not to use or disclose it, except as necessary to perform his or her job functions. Access to sensitive information should be restricted to persons who have a need to know.

⊿ What should I include in a confidentiality agreement?

Because confidentiality agreements are an important part of protecting your proprietary business information, you should have them prepared or at least reviewed by an attorney with expertise in this area. At a minimum, the agreement should identify the types of information considered confidential and proprietary; provide an acknowledgment by the employee that the designated information is confidential and proprietary; and state the employee's agreement not to use or disclose the information during or after the term of employment, except as necessary for the performance of the job function. You might also want to specify that the employee will not use the proprietary information of a former employer during the course of employment with you; require an assignment to you of any inventions, ideas, concepts, designs, discoveries, and the like, developed by the employee during the course of employment with you; and, if permitted in your state, include a covenant not to compete for some reasonable period of time after the termination of employment.

chapter 4

Expanding
the Business

⚞ My business is fairly successful now. When should I consider expanding it?

Some business advisors will tell you "immediately" because "if you're not growing, you're going." Today, planning for the growth and expansion of your business is more important than ever because of the rapidly changing markets and technical environment of the early-twenty-first century. Businesses have to expand to move, to stay ahead of the competition; sometimes, if the margins in their industry are being squeezed, they need to increase sales volume just to remain at the same level of earnings. One of the most important and fundamental reasons for expanding your business is to increase its relative sales value so that it is in a better position should you decide to sell it.

⊉ *How can I expand my business?*

The most common ways to expand a business are:

- Increasing sales to existing customers
- Increasing hours of operation or the size of existing outlets or branches
- Penetrating new markets with existing products and/or services
- Adding new, related products and/or services
- Expanding geographically with new outlets or branches
- Acquiring another company or its assets
- Merging with another company
- Adding investment capital for growth or going public

With some of these approaches, owners may want or need to form an additional, new business for the expansion. There are many reasons for doing this, including to provide some protection for the existing business in case the expansion does not succeed.

The first five points are outside the scope of *Strictly Business;* we will leave those topics to the marketing and business development experts.

⊉ *Should I tell my employees about my expansion plans for the company?*

Yes, at the appropriate time. Employees can be an excellent "sounding board" for your ideas and a source of additional ideas on ways to expand. However, many employees may become nervous at the thought of change, so make sure you present this opportunity for growth in the most positive and exciting light possible: You're not expanding because business is bad; you're expanding because business is great and can be even greater, thereby providing more potential for income and benefits for everyone.

Consider using select "focus groups" of employees, existing customers, and suppliers to generate ideas on new and creative ways to expand. By asking for suggestions from people involved with your company, you are effectively communicating to them that you highly value their opinions. You are likely to be nicely surprised at their innovative and insightful ideas.

☙ *I want to attract new forms of capital. Do I need to convert to a new business structure, or can I use the existing one?*

This depends largely on the present structure of your business. For example, if it is a sole proprietorship, you must change the legal structure because a sole proprietorship has only one owner. If, however, the business is a corporation, a limited liability company, or a partnership, the existing structure may work for the expansion if you are willing to give up some of the ownership. We return to this topic at the end of the chapter.

FINANCING AN EXPANSION

☙ *How do I finance an expansion?*

One of the first things you should do is examine your existing operations to determine whether you can reorganize the business or make the operations more efficient and thus reduce sales expenses, production costs, and overhead. After this, you can finance the expansion of your business in one or more of the following ways:

- Tap internal sources of funding from retained earnings
- Improve profit margins by reorganizing existing management or operations
- Sell an ownership interest (equity) in the business
- Borrow working capital or secure long-term-debt financing
- Sell assets or a portion of the business

- Merge with a company that has the funds to expand your business
- Make an initial public offering (IPO)

How do I decide which of these methods is best for my business?

You decide which method (or combination of methods) is best for you with a great deal of help from your advisors. Choosing the optimum method of funding an expansion is a financially complex exercise. Each of the methods has advantages and disadvantages that will create long-range consequences for your company. Without assistance and advice from your accountant, attorney, financial advisor, and perhaps a business consultant, you could end up paying more than necessary for the financing or even place your entire business in jeopardy.

Why is choosing a financing method such a complex process?

You have to be certain that you can earn at least as much as it costs you to acquire the funds. Thus it is critical for the long-term success of the company that you find the least expensive financing method (or combination of methods).

For example, you must find a balance between debt financing and equity financing; this relationship is referred to as the *debt-to-equity ratio*. Debt is good up to a point, but beyond that point the risk of being unable to repay the debt increases, and this could be highly detrimental. Selling ownership interests up to a point can be good, but beyond that point the owner dilutes his or her equity position to such an extent that he or she no longer controls the company. Yet selling a portion of a more valuable company may be worth the trade-off.

The most successful approach to financing an expansion often entails a combination of methods. In this chapter, we discuss retained-earnings, debt, and equity financing. You will need to seek professional advice to determine the degree of each method that is the most beneficial for you and your business.

Financing with Retained Earnings

≱ What do I need to know about financing an expansion with retained earnings?

For many companies, the most important source of capital is retained earnings. By law, retained earnings belong to the current owners and can either be paid out to them as distributions or dividends or be reinvested in the business. As current profits are accumulated over the years, they become the most likely source of capital for growth.

A company's cost of using retained earnings must be determined in order to compare it to the cost of debt or equity financing. There is a cost associated with using retained earnings that may not be obvious but must be considered: the *opportunity cost* to the owners. If retained earnings are reinvested in the business, the owners lose the personal use of the dividends they would otherwise receive. Thus if the business generates a lower return on the reinvested earnings than the return the owners could earn from investing dividends elsewhere, the difference between the returns—the income forgone—is the owners' opportunity cost.

If you are the sole owner, this may be an easy decision for you to make. But if you share ownership with others, especially owners who do not work in the business, you will need to have solid projections of the likely investment return to convince them to leave earnings in the company to finance expansion.

Financing with Debt

≱ What types of debt are used for starting a business or financing expansion?

Lenders categorize loans as being either short-term or long-term. *Short-term loans* typically require repayment in 1 year or less and are secured by the assets of the company and/or by an owner's personal guarantee. Examples are working-capital loans, accounts receivable loans, and lines of credit. *Long-term loans* span from 1 to 7 years but can extend to 25 years for real estate and equipment. Generally made for capital expenditures, they are secured by the purchased asset.

A *line of credit* is a short-term loan usually for immediate cash-flow needs. It is likely to be a revolving loan: the company can borrow and pay down and then borrow again. The line of credit has a maximum limit, is usually for a 1-year term, and is renewable assuming the company is creditworthy the next year. A line of credit is often secured by accounts receivable, inventory, other company assets, and/or the owner's personal guarantee. Depending on the situation, a company should be able to finance up to 80 percent of its eligible accounts receivable and between 25 and 60 percent of its inventory.

Subordinated debt usually is provided by a shareholder, a venture capitalist, or an institutional investor and is used to supplement the normal borrowings of a company. Sometimes this debt is a "bridge arrangement," in which the company either will repay the debt when it raises equity or will convert the debt to equity when more equity is raised or certain benchmarks are achieved.

⚐ *Where can I borrow the money for start-up or expansion?*

If you are starting a new business, your options for capital will be limited to personal savings, friends and relatives, banks, and credit unions.

Whether you need financing to start a new company or expand an existing one, a good place to begin is the Small Business Administration (SBA). (The SBA defines a *small business* as being "independently owned and operated and not dominant in its field of operation.") Most, but not all, businesses are eligible for financial assistance from the SBA. Note, however, that the SBA does not directly lend money. Rather, it guarantees loans made through private-sector lenders; that is, you arrange for the loan through a bank or other lender that then submits the loan to the SBA for guarantee. In addition, the SBA's Prequalification Pilot Loan Program assists borrowers with creating their loan application packages and securing loans. Depending on the circumstances, there may or may not be a fee for this service.

As of March 2001, the SBA had fifteen different loan guarantee programs for small businesses within its 7(A) Loan Guarantee Program. These programs are designed with different loan limits, for different uses of the loans, and for different types of businesses. The programs guarantee loans ranging from $10,000 for short-term cyclical and seasonal cash-flow needs to $3.5 million for capital expenditures or a change in ownership. There are specific programs to help export businesses; businesses in low- and moderate-income areas and in markets that the SBA considers "new"; businesses in communities that suffer job losses because of trade competition with Mexico and Canada or because of defense budget cutbacks; and businesses owned by veterans, minorities, and women. You might find it helpful to investigate these programs before speaking to a banker or some other lender.

The SBA is also a major source of information on other topics and maintains an extensive website (www.sba.gov). Its catalog, *The Resource Directory for Small Business Management,* lists all the publications the SBA sells and is available free from any SBA office or via the website.

⩺ *What are the advantages of debt financing?*

The advantages of debt financing are:

- Assuming a fixed rate of interest, the company knows the amount of debt and its cost and can accurately forecast the debt service.

- The interest the company pays on the debt is tax-deductible. Therefore, if the business is profitable, the loan's effective rate of interest is reduced through tax savings.

- The owner can use debt as financial leverage to increase his or her return on equity.

- Because it is a loan and not a sale of equity, the debt does not reduce the owner's interest in the company.

⊰ *What are some of the disadvantages of debt financing?*

Some disadvantages of debt are:

- Interest is a fixed cost that increases the company's expense burden. If the company has a downturn in business, the interest may be difficult to pay.

- Repayment of the debt affects the cash flow of the company. Also, if the company is using a line of credit, the arrangement must be renewed on an annual basis and this allows the lender to raise the interest costs or change the terms and conditions of borrowing.

- The lender may require a personal guarantee from the owner.

- The debt may contain restrictive covenants that affect the company's mode of operation.

- Debt is not permanent capital, so as the company repays the loan, the balance sheet changes.

⊰ *What is a personal guarantee? How and why is it used?*

When a lender lends money to a business, the lender expects to be repaid from the cash flow generated by the business. In simple terms, the business is expected to generate a profit that will at least cover the repayment obligation (debt service). However, on all loans, the lender looks at other business assets for a secondary source of repayment. If the business doesn't have another identifiable source of repayment (for example, the assets might be intangible or previously pledged on other financing), the lender often looks to the owner's personal assets and guarantee as the secondary source of repayment. Vendors, suppliers, credit card companies, and landlords may also require a personal guarantee before setting up accounts for or leasing to a new business.

In most instances when the business is small, a lender or some other vendor requires that the owner or owners personally guarantee the debt in case the business cannot make the payments. The lender believes that the owners have such a large influence over the success of their business that it wants them to have a real interest in repaying the loan. The prevailing logic seems to be that if the owners personally guarantee the debt, they have a much greater incentive to make sure it is repaid.

When owners sign a personal guarantee, they put their personal assets at risk. If the business cannot repay the debt, the owners must do so by selling personal assets unless they have another source for the cash required.

What do you mean by "financial leverage," and how does it increase returns?

Financial leverage is the process of using a lender's money to increase earnings and thus the return on the owner's equity. Let's consider an example: the use of financial leverage by the Roadrunner Trucking Company.

As Table 4-1 shows, Roadrunner's return on equity was 40 percent in year 1. The company wants to purchase a truck so that it can open a new delivery route and thus expand its business. The truck will cost $200,000, but Roadrunner expects that in year 2 the new route will increase sales by $200,000 and earnings by $44,000, as shown in the table.

Roadrunner obtains a $200,000 loan at 10 percent. This means an additional $20,000 in interest expense, but 40 percent ($8000) is tax-deductible, leaving an interest cost of $12,000. The year-2 data in Table 4-1 present the result of this simple scenario. Roadrunner Trucking has used financial leverage to increase the return on equity from 40 to 52.8 percent. In addition, the company has expanded its business and increased its competitive edge.

Note: Although using debt as financial leverage usually generates better earnings as operating income goes up, beyond a certain point the risk of loan repayment becomes more difficult and can jeopardize a company's cash flow.

TABLE 4-1   Financial Leverage: Roadrunner Trucking

	Year 1	Year 2
Sales	$1,000,000	$1,200,000
Earnings before interest	–	$144,000*
Interest after deduction	–	– 12,000
Earnings	$100,000[†]	$132,000[‡]
Equity	$250,000	$250,000
Return on equity[§]	40%	52.8%

*12% of sales.   [†]10% of sales.   [‡]11% of sales.   [§]Earnings ÷ equity.

⚏ *What are the true costs associated with a line of credit or a term loan?*

There are many costs associated with a loan, some of which are very obvious to the borrower and many of which are "hidden." It is important that the borrower know the true cost of borrowing funds. The significant costs are as follows:

INTEREST: This is the amount of money the lender charges the borrower for borrowing the money; it is calculated on the average outstanding balance. Interest rates can be *fixed* for the life of the loan or can be *variable,* starting at a lower rate and increasing over the life of the loan on the basis of certain factors, usually the income level of the business. Typically, interest rates are based on the prime interest rate plus a percentage. For most customers the "plus" ranges from 1 to 3 percent, depending on the situation.

LOAN OR ORIGINATION FEE: The bank charges this fee for reserving the money for the borrower. Although there are no standard fees, charges are often between 0.5 and 1 percent of the loan commitment.

OTHER FEES: The lender may charge fixed processing, application, or brokerage fees and/or percentage "points" of the total loan as part of its loan processing. It might charge the borrower any costs it incurred for appraisals, outside counsel, and so on.

COMPENSATING BALANCES: If the lender is a bank, it may require that the borrower maintain a certain balance in its bank accounts. Thus, if the borrower has a loan of $1 million and the bank requires a compensating balance of $50,000, the borrower's interest rate has just increased by 5 percent.

FINANCIAL STATEMENTS: The lender might require that financial statements be prepared, audited, or reviewed on an annual or semi-annual basis by a certified public accountant. Without this requirement, the business might not normally incur the expense of CPA-prepared statements. The cost of preparing these statements, therefore, can be viewed as an additional loan cost.

≼ *What documents do I provide to a lender to obtain a loan?*

Obtaining a loan depends a great deal on how well you present yourself, your business, and your financial needs to the prospective lender. According to the SBA, the best way to do this is to prepare a written loan proposal, which should contain your business plan (as described in Chapter 2), updated to include the following:

- Business name and address, and names and Social Security numbers of the owners
- The exact amount of the loan you are seeking
- Why you need the loan and exactly what you will use the proceeds for
- The specific assets you are willing to pledge as security for the loan
- The history and the age of the business
- The number of employees
- The business's assets
- A management profile, including each owner's and key manager's background, education, experience, skills, and accomplishments
- A profile of your customers
- Balance sheets and income statements for the last 3 years; for a

start-up company, projected balance sheets and income statements

- Each owner's personal financial statements and tax returns

In addition, you may want to invite the lender's representative to tour your operations and meet the key personnel. This will give him or her a real sense of what your business is all about.

Financing through Sale of Equity

What are the advantages of financing my business expansion through equity investors?

The advantages of equity financing are:

- It does not increase the company's existing expense structure.
- As long as the equity investment is not preferred stock, it typically does not have to be repaid, so there is no effect on cash flow.
- It is not a liability on the balance sheet.
- Using equity financing will generate higher reported earnings if there is no interest cost on the equity investment.

What are the disadvantages of funding my business through equity investors?

The disadvantages of equity financing are:

- You may be required to hire an appraiser to value the company in order to put a price on the ownership interests you are selling.
- You may be diluting the existing ownership to the point of losing control of the business.

- The new equity holders may exercise some control or conflicting influence over the business through voting rights.

- Majority owners have a fiduciary responsibility to minority shareholders.

- If you operate as a regular C corporation, issue stock, and pay dividends, equity financing will affect cash flow and dividends are not tax-deductible to the corporation.

I am trying to obtain capital to expand my business. Whom should I consider as possible investors?

If there is no particular person you want to bring into the business, you might consider a venture-capital firm. Venture capitalists help companies expand in exchange for equity. Your advisors, business consultant, or banker may be able to refer you to a venture capitalist. The SBA created the Angel Capital Electronic Network (ACE-NET) to help small companies find investors and investors find opportunities. Contact the SBA for information on ACE-NET.

Another alternative is the possibility of current employees as investors. They have a vested interest in the continued success of the company and may surprise you with their interest in your proposal. You might offer them the ability to invest through cash or salary reductions or in exchange for pay raises. Provide a written overview of your expansion needs and outline the proposed return on investment. At the least, your employees will be grateful that you considered them.

You might consider speaking with your advisors about using an employee stock option plan if it meets some of your other goals (as discussed in Parts Four and Five).

I'd like to raise money by selling ownership interests. Are there any issues I should know about?

Although your "offering" of an ownership interest may be exempt, this is a highly regulated area of the law, at both state and federal levels, that may affect your situation. For example, there are complex registration requirements relative to the sale of securities—stock, member interests, limited partnership interests, bonds, and notes.

The regulations are concerned with protecting people who purchase securities. The law distinguishes between "accredited" and "unaccredited" investors. It defines *accredited investors* as those who do not need protection. They have incomes over $200,000 or net worths over $1 million. Institutional investors and the selling company's directors and officers are generally considered to be accredited investors. The law defines *unaccredited investors* as those who need protection, and it requires that they receive complete disclosure.

Often, state and federal laws allow exemptions for small issuances of securities. If there is any doubt or if a business proposes to offer an equity interest to more than five people, the owners should consult with an experienced securities lawyer.

⊰ What types of business equity can I sell?

The types of equity interests used to raise capital for a business depend on the legal structure of the business. For example, C corporations can sell common stock, preferred stock, and debt instruments that can be converted into common or preferred stock. In contrast, S corporations can sell voting common stock, nonvoting common stock, and debt instruments that can be converted into voting or nonvoting common stock. With limited partnerships and limited liability companies, there are limited partnership interests and member interests, respectively, and debt instruments that can be converted into limited partnership interests or member interests.

⊰ What is the difference between preferred stock and common stock?

There are many differences between the two. Here we discuss the major ones.

With *common stock,* the stockholder's percentage ownership of the company depends on how many shares he or she owns. For example, if 100,000 shares are issued and outstanding and you own 40,000 of them, you own 40 percent of the company. Usually only the common stockholders have voting rights, although this is not a requirement. Many companies have only common stock, and therefore the equity structure is very simple and easy to understand.

Preferred stock is an additional class of stock that some companies issue to their investors. Preferred stock typically has dividend rights which require that the company pay a specific dividend amount to the preferred stockholders and that it do so before paying any dividends to common stockholders. Preferred-stock dividends can be cumulative or noncumulative. Cumulative dividends accrue even if they are not paid; noncumulative dividends do not accrue if they are not paid. If the company is forced to liquidate, the preferred stockholders get paid before common stockholders do. Investors who are interested in a conservative investment with a more certain return tend to invest in preferred stock rather than common stock and prefer cumulative preferred over noncumulative.

If you are thinking about selling stock to raise capital for start-up or expansion, you need to consider the pros and cons of both classes of stock and determine which rights to give each class in order to make your company attractive to investors.

⅍ *What is a convertible-debt instrument?*

Convertible debt is a loan that can be converted into equity of the borrowing company. Many companies want to finance an expansion with debt, but investors often want equity. The convertible-debt concept lets both sides meet somewhere in the middle. In some cases, the debt can be paid back at the option of the company before being converted to equity. Since the interest is deductible, this is better for the company, assuming it can pay back the debt. For the investor, convertible debt provides an annual return—the interest—and places the investor in the role of creditor, which is superior to common- and preferred-equity holders in the event of the liquidation of the company.

⊰⧉ *I want to raise capital by selling 30 percent of my company's stock to my friend. What rights do I have to give her as a shareholder?*

Generally, state law dictates exactly what rights must be given to a shareholder. These rights usually include the right to attend shareholder meetings; the right to vote on issues brought before the shareholders, including the right to elect directors; and the right to receive annual financial reports of the company. While these rights may sound significant, you must look closer to determine their practical application. The right to attend shareholder meetings does not include the right to present agenda items. The right to vote one's shares must be assessed against the total voting shares of the corporation. Thus, if your friend holds a 30 percent interest, there is a 70 percent interest that might vote against her.

The shareholders of a closely held corporation are allowed to enter into shareholder agreements or buy-sell agreements, which set forth the rights of the shareholders, even regarding the reacquisition of stock should specified events occur. Either at the formation of the corporation, at a subsequent sale of stock, or at the time an employee is rewarded with stock, the parties can execute a contract that provides for reacquisition of the stock by the corporation or by the remaining shareholders. The agreement can and should set out either the price at which the stock will be acquired or a formula for determining what the price will be. (Buy-sell agreements are discussed in detail in Chapter 21.)

Debt versus Equity

⊰⧉ *Can you give an example that compares how using financial leverage and selling equity affect earnings?*

Yes. Let's expand the example of Roadrunner Trucking, using our previous assumptions: Roadrunner's current equity is $250,000, and the company needs $200,000. Its owners want to compare the results of using only financial leverage, only equity financing, and a combination of both:

A. *Borrow* the full amount: The interest rate is 10 percent, and the interest cost is tax-deductible.

B. *Sell equity* to raise the full amount: Sell 20,000 shares.

C. *Combine debt and equity:* Borrow $50,000 and sell 15,000 shares at $10 per share.

Table 4-2 shows the earnings per share that result from each option in three different scenarios: (1) if the company earns exactly what it did before the financing ($100,000), (2) if it meets the goal of $144,000 in earnings after the financing, and (3) if it exceeds projections and earns $250,000 after the financing. (For ease of computation, we have not taken the company's total taxes into account, including the fact that it could carry losses forward to future years, and we have not included a cost of capital to sell equity.)

Financial and Operating Ratios

⚄ *What data do lenders or investors look at when deciding whether to lend or invest?*

Lenders, investors, creditors, and business appraisers use financial ratios to analyze a business's finances and operations. A *ratio* is a mathematical comparison of entries on the company's balance sheet and income statement. Financial and operating ratios provide valuable information regarding the company's financial condition and performance.

Ratios are important to you, as the owner of a business, as they enable you to monitor your business's progress and condition. By itself, a ratio does not have much significance; but when you compare ratios from one period to the next, you can monitor progress and spot unfavorable trends over time. Another way to monitor your business's performance and condition is to compare its ratios to those of similar companies in your industry. You can obtain this information in publications such as *Annual Statement Studies* (Risk Management Association), *Almanac of Business and Industrial Financial Ra-*

TABLE 4-2　Effect of Debt and Equity on Earnings: Roadrunner Trucking

	A Debt only	B Equity only	C Debt + equity
Debt (10% interest)	$200,000	0	$50,000
Equity	$250,000	$450,000	$400,000
Common stock ($10/share)	25,000	45,000	40,000
(1) EBIT*	$100,000	$100,000	$100,000
Less: Interest	20,000	0	5,000
Earnings before taxes	$ 80,000	$100,000	$ 95,000
Less: Taxes	12,000	0	3,000
Earnings after taxes	$ 68,000	$100,000	$ 92,000
Shares	25,000	45,000	40,000
Earnings per share†	2.72	2.22	2.3
(2) EBIT	$144,000	$144,000	$144,000
Less: Interest	20,000	0	5,000
Earnings before taxes	$124,000	$144,000	$139,000
Less: Taxes	12,000	0	3,000
Earnings after taxes	$112,000	$144,000	$136,000
Shares	25,000	45,000	40,000
Earnings per share	4.48	3.2	3.4
(3) EBIT	$250,000	$250,000	$250,000
Less: Interest	20,000	0	5,000
Earnings before taxes	$230,000	$250,000	$245,000
Less: Taxes	12,000	0	3,000
Earnings after taxes	$218,000	$250,000	$242,000
Shares	25,000	45,000	40,000
Earnings per share	8.72	5.55	6.05

*Earnings before interest and taxes.
†Return on equity.

tios (Prentice-Hall), and *Key Business Ratios* (Dun & Bradstreet), which are all published annually. Trade associations often provide financial- and operating-ratio benchmarks for their industries.

In addition, you can use ratios for budgeting. Since accounts on the income statement and the balance sheet will maintain a given percentage relationship to sales, you can use a percent-of-sales ratio for each category on these statements to project future needs. Suppose, for example, that a company maintains inventory equal to 12.5 percent of sales and that sales are currently $100,000, requiring inventory of $12,500. If the owner projects that sales will increase to $150,000, the company needs to increase inventory to $18,750.

The questions and answers in this section cover the five most common types of financial and operating ratios. Not all the ratios are equally important to everyone. Some of them are more important to investors, some are more important to short-term creditors, and so on. Valuation experts and lenders use them to compare one company to other companies in the same profession or industry. (In Part Five, we explain how valuation experts and sales specialists "normalize" and "recast" financial statements to fine-tune these ratios.)

We discuss these ratios for your general knowledge. Entire master's degree programs are built around analyzing financial ratios because the analysis is different for each industry. For example, a 180-day inventory turnover might be quite good for a publisher but very bad for a restaurant. Industry benchmarks or your accountant, valuation expert, and business consultant can help you analyze your company's ratios and put them in context when you need or want more detail.

⚐ What are profitability ratios?

Profitability ratios measure a company's ability to earn an adequate return—how well it is using all its resources. These ratios are also a measure of a company's operating performance and will usually be of crucial interest to an investor. In general, owners would want these ratios to increase from period to period. There are four main profitability ratios.

Profit margin shows the percentage return on sales:

$$\text{Profit margin} = \frac{\text{net income}}{\text{total sales}}$$

Regardless of how the assets were financed (debt, equity, etc.), *return on assets* calculates the percentage return of all assets:

$$\text{Return on assets} = \frac{\text{net income} + [\text{interest expense} \times (1 - \text{tax rate})]}{\text{average total assets}}$$

Return on equity measures the percentage return on the owner's invested capital:

$$\text{Return on equity} = \frac{\text{net income} - \text{preferred dividends}}{\text{common stockholder's or owners' equity}}$$

When the return on equity is higher than the return on assets, the company is said to be "trading on the equity" because it is using more creditors' funds than equity to finance the business.

Investors are most interested in a company's reported ratio of *earnings per share:*

$$\text{Earnings per share} = \frac{\text{net income} - \text{preferred dividends}}{\text{common shares outstanding}}$$

What are growth ratios?

A company's positive or negative growth rates in sales and in earnings from one period to the next are measured by *growth ratios*. Owners would want to see these ratios increase from one period to the next. The percentage increase or decrease in sales from the previous period to the current period is expressed by the *sales growth* ratio:

$$\text{Sales growth} = \frac{\text{current-period sales} - \text{previous-period sales}}{\text{previous-period sales}}$$

The percentage increase or decrease in earnings from the previous period to the current one is covered by the *earnings growth* ratio:

$$\frac{\text{Earnings}}{\text{growth}} = \frac{\text{current-period earnings} - \text{previous-period earnings}}{\text{previous-period earnings}}$$

⚐ What are asset utilization ratios?

Asset utilization ratios measure the speed at which accounts turn over. The higher the number is, the better (except for the average collection period). These ratios are of special interest to short-term creditors.

The *accounts receivable turnover* ratio measures the number of times the company turned accounts receivable into cash during the year:

$$\frac{\text{Accounts}}{\text{receivable turnover}} = \frac{\text{sales on account}}{\text{average accounts receivable balance}}$$

The number of days it takes to collect the receivables is given by the *average collection period* ratio (ideally, this should be close to the number of days for credit terms):

$$\text{Average collection period} = \frac{365 \text{ days}}{\text{accounts receivable turnover}}$$

The number of times in a year that the company sold inventory is shown by the *inventory turnover* ratio:

$$\text{Inventory turnover} = \frac{\text{cost of goods sold}}{\text{average inventory balance}}$$

The *fixed-asset turnover* ratio measures the number of times in a year that the company paid for its fixed assets (and thus indicates how productive fixed assets are in generating sales):

$$\text{Fixed asset turnover} = \frac{\text{sales}}{\text{fixed assets}}$$

The *total-asset turnover* ratio shows the number of times in a year that the company paid for its total assets (and thus indicates how productive all assets are in generating sales):

$$\text{Total-asset turnover} = \frac{\text{sales}}{\text{total assets}}$$

What are liquidity ratios?

Of most interest to short-term creditors, *liquidity ratios* measure a company's liquidity: its ability to pay off short-term obligations without having to liquidate or depend too heavily on inventory, especially when sales might be down because of economic or other conditions. Generally, the higher the liquidity ratio, the healthier the company.

Does the company have sufficient current assets to pay current liabilities? One uses the *quick*, or *"acid test,"* ratio to find out:

$$\text{Quick (acid test)} = \frac{\text{cash + current receivables}}{\text{current liabilities}}$$

A ratio of 1:1 is viewed as minimally acceptable, but 2:1 is generally safer.

The *working-capital* ratio is more a measure of cash flow than it is a ratio:

$$\text{Working capital} = \text{current assets} - \text{current liabilities}$$

The greater the working-capital amount, the greater the assurance that short-term debts can be paid when due.

⚔ What are debt utilization ratios?

Debt utilization ratios measure a company's overall debt position in light of its asset base and earning power. They are likely to be of primary importance to long-term creditors and of secondary importance to investors.

The *debt-to-assets* ratio is the percentage of debt used to capitalize a company:

$$\text{Debt to assets} = \frac{\text{total liabilities}}{\text{total assets}}$$

A high ratio may indicate a riskier company to invest in because of higher levels of debt.

The *debt-to-equity* ratio shows the percentage of capital contributed by creditors versus that contributed by owners:

$$\text{Debt to equity} = \frac{\text{total liabilities}}{\text{total equity}}$$

The higher the ratio, the greater the risk assumed by long-term creditors.

The number of times the company's income (before interest and taxes) covers the interest obligation is shown by the *times-interest-earned* ratio:

$$\text{Times interest earned} = \frac{\text{income before interest expense and income taxes}}{\text{interest expense}}$$

The higher the ratio, the stronger the firm's ability to meet its interest payments.

The *fixed-charge coverage* ratio is the number of times the company's income can cover all fixed obligations:

$$\text{Fixed-charge coverage} = \frac{\text{income before fixed charges and taxes}}{\text{fixed charges}}$$

Note that failure to meet any financial obligation will jeopardize the position of the company.

What are operating ratios?

Operating, or *cost control,* ratios measure management performance. They are indications of the company's operating environment and operating efficiency. Increasing ratios may indicate that competition is forcing the company to cut profit margins or that costs are out of control and/or that the company should pass on its increasing costs to the customer.

The *cost-of-sales* ratio shows how much it costs the company to make its sales:

$$\text{Cost-of-sales ratio} = \frac{\text{cost of sales}}{\text{sales}}$$

The *operating expense* ratio indicates management's ability to control its operating expenses:

$$\text{Operating expense ratio} = \frac{\text{operating expenses}}{\text{sales}}$$

The *gross margin* ratio measures the efficiency of producing what is sold:

$$\text{Gross margin ratio} = \frac{\text{gross margin}}{\text{sales}}$$

PURCHASING ANOTHER
BUSINESS OR ASSETS

How can I purchase a sole proprietorship?

To purchase a sole proprietorship, you need to purchase each of the assets individually. The business itself is often so closely tied to the sole proprietor that it is difficult to identify or evaluate assets, such as goodwill, other than the tangible assets used in the business. You want to purchase the assets free of any claims or liability, so you should comply with "bulk-sale" procedures and obtain clearances of any encumbrances.

What is the difference between buying the assets of a corporation and buying the stock of a corporation?

When you buy the assets of a corporation, you are acquiring the specific assets you want. Often in an asset purchase, the buyer acquires equipment, furniture and fixtures, goodwill, work in progress, customer lists, and so on. When you buy the shares of a corporation, you are acquiring ownership rights in the company itself, everything it owns, and its liabilities and obligations. For example, if you bought the assets of ABC, Inc., and those assets consist of two forklifts, you own just two forklifts. However, if you purchased the stock of ABC, Inc., you own ABC, Inc., as an ongoing business, with its existing clients, accounts receivable, inventory, contracts, and obligations, in addition to the two forklifts.

Why would I want to purchase the assets of a corporation rather than its stock?

If the ongoing business is not earning an adequate return and you don't think you can change that situation but you could use the firm's equipment to expand your own production or sales capacity, you want to buy the assets instead of the stock of the business. Also, when you purchase assets, you receive a step-up in basis on those assets, which may provide income tax benefits if you depreciate the assets.

When I buy a business, why can't I just pay cash and avoid the lawyers who insist on preparing a pile of documents for everybody to sign?

In a perfect world one might avoid the pile of documents, but we live in a world of people who make mistakes. To lessen the risk of mistakes when you purchase a business, your business lawyer and other business advisors will use documents to encourage everyone involved in the transaction to pay attention to the following questions:

- Does the seller have unencumbered title to all the offered real estate?
- Does the seller have unencumbered title to the equipment and other tangible assets?
- Are there hazardous materials or subsurface defects?
- Does the Internal Revenue Service have a lien on the seller's property?
- Do the seller's business records accurately reflect the business's operations so that you, as purchaser, have a reliable basis for predicting the success of the business?
- If you are buying accounts receivable, what guarantees are there that the accounts can be collected?

Skilled professionals representing your interests will see that promises, called *warranties,* are made in the documents. Requiring a seller to make written promises in answer to the above questions improves your chances of success in operating the purchased business. The professionals will also assist you in what is called *due diligence*—investigating the business and assets of the seller. Sometimes a seller of business assets tries to collect the sale price without paying the business's creditors. You won't want to pay lawyers to resist a lawsuit in which you try to prove that you didn't know the seller was trying to cheat the business's creditors. Your resistance to a pile of documents may well be overcome by your appreciation of the protection they provide for your personal wealth as well as your investment in the new business.

GOING PUBLIC

⅏ *What does "going public" actually mean?*

Going public is the process whereby the equity of a company—usually consisting of common stock, preferred stock, and, possibly, bonds—is offered for sale to the general public for the first time, in what is called an *initial public offering (IPO)*. If the securities are actually purchased by the public, the offering is successful and the company is public from that point on.

⅏ *What are some of the advantages of going public?*

The key advantages of going public are:

- Going public can generate a huge infusion of cash for funding expansion plans.
- In the process of going public, owners usually sell some of their holdings and thus acquire cash that they can invest elsewhere. This provides owners with critical diversification that they didn't have before.
- The company can attract key employees by offering stock options.

⅏ *What are some of the disadvantages of going public?*

Some disadvantages of going public are:

- The initial cost of taking the company public is very expensive and extremely time-consuming.

- Even though the general public can buy and sell a company's stock, the officers, directors, and principal stockholders of the company may have restrictions on selling their stock.

- After a company goes public, it must publish its financial activity on a quarterly basis, and this entails additional fees to accountants and attorneys. Also, to meet ongoing requirements for SEC reporting, the company must either have experienced staff on hand or hire another company's services.

- Since most of the shares are owned by the public, management will lose voting control.

- Compensation for all significant officers and directors must be disclosed in annual reports.

- There is no longer anything "private" about the company: SEC and shareholder reporting requires disclosure about most facets of the company's operations and financial condition.

CREATING A NEW COMPANY OR STRUCTURE

Why would I want to create a new company to expand?

Creating a new, additional company keeps the new venture separate from the existing business. This arrangement is desirable in many situations. Some of the most common are:

- There is risk associated with the new venture, so by creating a new company the old business is protected from liabilities incurred by the new business.

- There are individuals who want to, or can only, invest in the new business. For example, if your current company is an S corporation and your new investor is a nonresident alien, you either have to give up the S election or create a new company. There are many other reasons why this might be the case.

- The new business is in a different state or country or some other location away from the existing business. To keep ownership, control, and taxes separate, the owners may create a new company.

- The new business needs to be a "partnership" with other businesses. In this case, multiple partnerships, joint ventures, limited liability companies, corporations, or any combination of these may form a new company for the new business venture.

⋈ Can you give an example of expanding a business by creating a new company but not changing the existing ownership?

John is the sole owner of a restaurant that is about 5 years old and has done quite well. All of his customers have suggested that John open a new restaurant in another part of the city. After finding professional advisors who will help him set up the new venture, he decides to purchase and remodel an existing restaurant that has not done well but is in an excellent location.

John's advisors recommend that he form a limited liability company (LLC) to own each restaurant: JJ's Purloined Sirloins 1, LLC, for his existing restaurant and JJ's Purloined Sirloins 2, LLC, for the new restaurant. John has his attorney create the two LLCs, of which he owns 100 percent. John and his attorney transfer the assets of the existing restaurant to JJ's 1 in exchange for the membership certificates. John's accountant sets up the accounting system so that each of the restaurants is a separate unit for financial reporting. Through JJ's 2, John arranges a loan from his bank for the down payment on the purchase and remodeling of the new restaurant. The seller agrees to take back some debt that JJ's 2 will repay over 5 years.

In this case, John formed a new company to own the new restaurant, obtained financing for the expansion (a term loan from the bank and a purchase loan from the seller), kept 100 percent of the ownership, and segregated his successful restaurant from the new venture for asset protection purposes. This was not John's only option, however. He could have formed a single corporation with a subsidiary for each restaurant. As with the LLCs, this would reduce the risk of the new venture's affecting the financial condition of his existing restaurant, and John could still retain 100 percent of the ownership.

⊀ *Can you give an example of expanding a business by using new equity investors?*

We can use the same situation as above except this time John decides that investors should put up most of the money to purchase and remodel the new restaurant. John transfers the existing restaurant to the new JJ's Purloined Sirloins 1, LLC, of which he owns 100 percent. For JJ's 2, he invests $100,000 and raises $900,000 from other investors.

John will be the managing member of the new restaurant, so he enters into a management contract with JJ's 2 and in return receives a salary. The LLC agreement for JJ's 2 states that the profits are allocated 90 percent to the investors and 10 percent to John (the same percentages as their investments) until the outside investors have been repaid their original investment. Afterward, the profits are allocated 50 percent to the investors and 50 percent to John.

In this case, the outside investors put up most of the money for the new venture, but John now has a group of investors that could back him in purchasing additional restaurants. If this new restaurant is not successful, they can shut it down, but John will still have 100 percent ownership and control of his first restaurant.

PART TWO

Entity Primer

Many years ago the task of choosing the right entity, or ownership structure, for a business was easy because the only options were general partnerships or regular corporations. Today there are general partnerships, limited partnerships, corporations, limited liability partnerships, limited liability companies, S corporations, professional corporations, and on and on. This smorgasbord of opportunities makes finding the right entity for your new business venture an important task.

101

The last 20 years have seen hundreds of thousands of Americans leave the perceived security of large corporations to start their own businesses. One of the challenges facing the budding entrepreneur and his or her advisors is accurately assessing the needs of the new business venture and determining the ownership structure that will best allow the business to fulfill its mission. To provide entrepreneurs and their advisors with criteria that can guide the selection process, our contributing authors have compiled an overview of the most commonly used business structures.

Chapters 5 through 8 discuss each of these entities. The chapters are organized in a similar fashion so that you can easily compare the various business structures on the basis of significant factors. Reviewing the specific criteria for each entity will help you identify the features that are most important to you and thus the type of business you will conduct.

The most elemental type of business is the sole proprietorship. Chapter 5 discusses the essence of individual ownership, including its limitations. Once a business has any employees, income of any significance, or possible liability issues or creditor issues, other types of entities are preferable.

Partnerships come in two basic types: general and limited. Chapter 6 discusses both types in great detail. The limited partnership structure is widely used because it offers opportunities to minimize business income tax, limit liability, and have a number of owners. In recent years, the limited partnership has become very popular among families as a means of achieving business, financial, and estate planning goals.

The corporate structure is versatile and often works as well for a private, one-owner business as for a public business owned by tens of thousands of individuals. Chapter 7 explores various types of corporations. The regular C corporation is the most common type among businesses with a large number of owners, but it can be beneficial for those with few owners, or even one owner, as well. The S corporation is a special type with many characteristics that are similar to those of limited partnerships. The chapter also discusses several more specialized types: the personal service corporation, profes-sional corporation, and close corporation.

Chapter 8 discusses the limited liability company. Although this is one of the newest ownership structures, it is quickly becoming one of the most preferred. Combining the most favorable features of limited partnerships and corporations, it offers an incredibly flexible way of doing business.

In Chapter 9, our contributing authors briefly evaluate the enti-ties in terms of business goals and choices. Their answers explain how particular ownership structures will affect specific situations in the life of a business and its owners.

After reading Part Two, you will have a good understanding of the various types of businesses and the advantages and disadvantages of each.

chapter 5

Sole Proprietorship

What is a sole proprietorship?

A *sole proprietorship* is a business in which an individual (which, for IRS purposes, can be a husband and wife) owns all the business assets. Usually the owner is the only person who operates the business. No formal business structure, or entity, separates the business assets and operation from the individual. For all practical purposes, the business and the person are the same. While the business may operate under a distinct business name, it is more formally recognized and referred to as being operated in the name of the individual, such as "John Doe, doing business as (dba) Widgets." The owner may be the only employee, or the business may employ any number of employees, although typically the number of employees is few. The sole proprietorship is the simplest and least expensive way to form a business.

OWNERSHIP

⚖ *What is the ownership structure of a sole proprietorship?*

A sole proprietorship is owned by an individual. In community property states (Arizona, California, Idaho, Louisiana, Nevada, New Mexico, Texas, Washington, Wisconsin, and Alaska, by election), the nonparticipating spouse may legally own up to one-half of the business, even if the owner had the business before the marriage.

⚖ *How do I finance a sole proprietorship?*

Since a sole proprietorship by definition has only a single owner, all the assets and financing come from the owner and, possibly, from loans from third parties.

⚖ *How do I take money out of the business or pay myself a salary?*

This is one of the advantages of a sole proprietorship. You don't have to worry about how much to pay yourself in salary, as you might with other business structures. You simply write a check from your business account to yourself whenever you want for whatever amount you want.

FORMATION

⚖ *How do I form a sole proprietorship and commence business?*

The sole proprietorship is the easiest type of business to commence. You simply start engaging in the activities of the business. No formal documentation is required. If the business involves activities that are subject to government regulations, such as paying wages to employees or collecting and paying sales taxes, compliance with the regulatory provisions is a necessary part of the formation process.

It is a very good idea to open a business bank account that is separate from your personal bank account. Although a business account is not required with a sole proprietorship, having one will help you keep track of business income and expenses.

⚞ What name can I use for my business?

You may conduct your sole proprietorship under your own name, without registering the name, as long as it does not infringe on the trade name of another business. Alternatively, you may use a name other than your own, but in this case a certificate must be filed and some jurisdictions require that it be published in a general-circulation newspaper. (The certificate is known as a *doing-business-as certificate, assumed-name certificate,* or *fictitious-name statement.*) However, even if you file a fictitious-name statement, you do not have the right to use a trade name or logo that is already owned or used by a competitor. If you intend to invest substantially in a trade name or logo, you should first conduct a search to ensure that it is not being used by any other business.

MANAGEMENT

⚞ How is a sole proprietorship managed?

A sole proprietorship is generally managed by its owner. Nevertheless, since it is fairly common for a sole proprietorship to have a few employees, the owner could delegate management of the company to an employee. For example, Bob Smith could delegate day-to-day management of Bob's Pool Service to a manager. However, the ultimate responsibility for operations and, therefore, liability rests with the owner.

⚞ What formalities are required to maintain a sole proprietorship?

A sole proprietorship does not have to maintain any documents showing how management decisions are made.

As a sole proprietor, however, you do need to keep books and accounting records for the business operations, listing income, expenses, costs of assets, and inventory acquired. These records will help you track the progress of your business, prepare your individual income tax returns, and prepare the depreciation schedule for assets used in the business.

◄ *How do I track and report business income and expenditures?*

Many sole proprietors set up categories of expenditures. At the minimum, these categories should match those listed on Schedule C of Form 1040. However, many Schedule C categories are very broad, so it is a good idea to delineate expense categories in more detail. Many accountants will tell you that how an expense is categorized often determines whether or not it is fully deductible as a legitimate business expense. Therefore, you should have your accountant help you establish categories that are appropriate for your business.

If you have different income sources, you should set up different categories for them as well. In addition to reducing tax preparation costs, a good accounting system can be an excellent management tool for analyzing income and expenses over different time periods.

DURATION

◄ *How long does the business last?*

A sole proprietorship continues until the owner stops doing business, sells it, liquidates it, or converts it to a different entity, or ownership structure.

◄ *What happens on the death of a sole proprietor?*

The death of the owner ends a sole proprietorship. This is one of the major disadvantages of a sole proprietorship. Although a sole proprietor may leave the business *assets* at death by way of a trust or will, he or she cannot leave the ongoing business itself. Each asset of the business becomes part of the owner's estate, and business debts and liabilities are debts and liabilities of the estate. It may be necessary to have the business wound up by the personal representative of the estate. Because of this, sole proprietorships provide few succession planning opportunities.

⚜ How do I stop doing business as a sole proprietorship?

There are two ways to end a sole proprietorship.

You can *sell the business*. This means selling both the tangible and the intangible assets of the business. You may want to follow *bulk-sale* procedures and obtain clearances of any encumbrances so that the buyer can purchase the assets free of any claims or liabilities. Many states have bulk-sale laws addressing the sale of business assets. However, each state has its own rules on how to give notice and what steps to follow. If you are married and reside in a community property state, your spouse may have rights (including the right of notice to the sale), so the proper steps should be followed. You should retain the services of a knowledgeable attorney and establish an escrow for the transfer of the payment and assets.

You can *close the business*. If you close the doors and stop doing business, your liability for business obligations continues until satisfied. You should notify customers and creditors (so that accounts can be settled), as well as the appropriate local authorities, if required. The services of a knowledgeable attorney are essential to make sure no item is overlooked and to bring all liabilities to an end.

TAXATION

⚜ How is the income of a sole proprietorship taxed and at what income tax rate?

Each year, the sole proprietor reports all income of the business on his or her personal income tax return. This is true whether the money from the business is kept in a business account or in the owner's individual bank account. The income from a sole proprietorship is taxed at the owner's individual income tax rate. Thus, at the federal level, the tax rate on such income can range from as low as 15 percent to as high as 39.6 percent. The owner includes the business income on Schedule C of his or her 1040 federal income tax return.

⚖ *How does the sole proprietor file tax returns?*

Business income is taxed directly to the sole proprietor. The owner simply completes a separate Schedule C for each sole proprietorship he or she operates (or Schedule F, for farming operations) and reports the income or loss from the business or businesses on his or her regular IRS Form 1040. The owner also files Schedule SE to report any self-employment tax that is due.

⚖ *As a sole proprietor, when do I pay income taxes on my business income?*

Since you include your sole proprietorship income on your personal tax return, you pay your taxes on that income when you file your personal tax return—April 15, unless you file for an extension. Depending on the amount of income you have, you may need to pay your income tax liability in quarterly installments to avoid tax penalties. In summary, keep track of your income and deductions throughout the year, and consult a professional advisor to determine when and how much you should pay.

⚖ *Can a sole proprietorship have a tax year that is different from the owner's personal tax year?*

A sole proprietorship is 100 percent owned and controlled by the sole owner, so the business must maintain a tax year that is exactly the same as the owner's individual tax year. In most cases, this is the calendar year.

⋈ *Does the self-employment tax apply to a sole proprietorship?*

Yes. This is one disadvantage of operating a business as a sole proprietorship. In 2001, a 15.3 percent self-employment tax applied to the first $80,400 of income; income above that level was subject to a 2.9 percent Medicare tax. At those rates, $100,000 of income from a sole proprietorship will result in over $12,000 of federal self-employment tax alone. The sole proprietor uses Schedule SE (self-employment), along with his or her regular Form 1040, to determine the self-employment tax.

⋈ *Do I need a separate tax identification number for a sole proprietorship?*

If you have no employees, the answer is no. You report income and expenses on your individual income tax return. However, if you have employees, you must file IRS Form SS-4 to obtain an employer identification number (EIN) for paying FICA and employee income taxes that you withhold.

LIABILITY

⋈ *As a sole proprietor, what protection do I have from contract liabilities of the business?*

None. If your business breaches a contract, such as failing to pay a supplier, you can be sued for breach of contract. You are personally liable for payment of the judgment, even if the business has no money. The sole proprietorship structure provides no protection from contract liabilities of the business. When your sole proprietorship enters into a contract, it is entering into the contract through you as an individual. Any claims against your business are against you individually; therefore, your personal assets are continually at risk.

⚘ *As a sole proprietor, how can I protect my assets from the contractual liabilities of the business?*

The best way to protect yourself from contract liabilities is to carefully review contracts before signing them. Attempt to limit your exposure within the terms of the contract by including a limitation-of-liabilities or liquidated-damages clause or by specifically defining the limits of your obligations (e.g., "Seller shall not be responsible for delivering more than 500 widgets within any 30-day period"). To limit your risk of liability, it is very important that you have your business lawyer review any contract before you sign it.

The way you title your nonbusiness assets may protect them from exposure if the means of ownership is in place before the debt or liability occurs. For example, if state law provides for tenancy-by-the-entireties ownership and you and your spouse own property as tenants by the entireties, that property is generally exempt from the sole proprietorship's creditors.

⚘ *What protection does a sole proprietorship offer its owner from tort liabilities of the company?*

None. If during the course of carrying out his or her duties on behalf of the sole proprietorship an employee, agent, or representative of the business commits a *tort,* which is an injury to another person or a wrong done to another person, such as the personal injury or death of another, then the owner can be sued for such conduct. The owner is personally liable for payment of the judgment, even if the business has no money.

⚘ *How can I protect my business assets from my personal liabilities?*

Unfortunately, not much legal protection can be given to a sole proprietor's business assets. Thus, if you are at fault for a traffic accident (even if it occurs when you are not engaged in business activities), the victim of your negligence can recover from your business assets as well as your personal assets. The same is true if you default on your home mortgage or on any other installment purchase. The best protection in these circumstances is insurance, although usually you cannot insure against contractual liabilities.

RECOMMENDATIONS

In what situations is a sole proprietorship appropriate?

Small businesses with no employees and no need for large amounts of equipment tend to be sole proprietorships. In these limited cases, a proprietor may not need the liability protection and other benefits of a more formal business structure. The following types of businesses are sometimes sole proprietorships: small consulting or service businesses, small retail establishments, businesses that operate out of the proprietor's principal residence, and start-up businesses in cases where the owner is not sure whether the "idea" of the business will work and therefore seeks to lower the cost of establishing the business.

However, it is rarely advisable to conduct any business activity as a sole proprietorship. This is especially true when the business requires more than one owner; the ownership needs to be separate from the management; there are employees; complex financing may be needed; the owner requires limited liability; businesses in its industry customarily have a different structure; or continuity of the business is important.

I'm starting a construction company. Should I begin as a sole proprietorship?

No, you should not. One of the biggest disadvantages of a sole proprietorship is the unlimited liability of the owner. Operating your construction business as a sole proprietorship would create significant legal exposure for you. For example, if your company was sued by a customer, your personal assets would be exposed and subject to the customer's claim if he or she won. Talk with your advisors to determine the best ownership structure to use before establishing your construction company.

ADVANTAGES
AND DISADVANTAGES

Can you summarize the advantages and disadvantages of a sole proprietorship?

Advantages

- A sole proprietorship is simple to establish and operate; little ongoing documentation is needed.
- The sole proprietor is the only owner of the business, so he or she has complete control.
- The sole proprietor can take any amount of compensation or withdrawals, and there are no adverse tax consequences from such distributions.
- Since the sole proprietor does business in his or her own name or under an assumed name, no real difference exists between the individual and the business.
- From a legal standpoint, the business is not a separate entity and thus does not require a separate federal income tax return.

Disadvantages

- The sole proprietor generally has unlimited personal liability for all business activities, debts, obligations, and other liabilities. Most of the owner's personal and business assets may be taken by a creditor to satisfy a court judgment against the business.
- If there are employees or others working under the sole proprietor's direction, he or she can be held legally responsible for their acts.

- Assets used in the business are not protected from the sole proprietor's personal creditors, other than through insurance.

- Insurance is limited to individual coverage unless there are employees.

- All income is subject to self-employment tax up to the annual limitation amounts.

- Retirement plans are limited to SIMPLE and SEP plans.

- As the sole owner, the proprietor can obtain capital for the business only from his or her own money or through personal loans.

- Sole proprietorships are often perceived as amateurish and lacking credibility.

- A sole proprietorship terminates at the death of the owner; there are no options for continuing the business.

- Transferring a sole proprietorship from one person to another is cumbersome. Because the owner holds title individually to each business asset, he or she must transfer each asset separately.

chapter 6

Partnership

COMMON FEATURES
OF ALL PARTNERSHIPS

⚖ *What is a partnership?*

A *partnership* is a unique, personal, and voluntary relationship between two or more persons who have reciprocal rights and duties. A partnership has five distinct elements: (1) an association (2) of two or more persons (3) who carry on a business (4) as co-owners (5) for a profit. The relationship can be written (formal) or oral (informal). There are three types of partnerships: general partnership, limited liability partnership, and limited partnership. Joint ventures have some similarities to partnerships.

Partnerships have a long history, with a distinct body of law attached to their development in the United States. Each state has statutory law governing partnerships. The laws are primarily based on uniform acts pertaining to either general or limited partnerships.

For *general partnerships,* the two most common forms of legislation adopted by the states are the Uniform Partnership Act (UPA) and the Revised Uniform Partnership Act (RUPA). These statutes dictate the legal relationships among the partners as well as the conduct of the business from creation to termination. They generally apply to a partnership only if the partners have not entered into a written agreement governing their relationship or if the written agreement does not address a matter that is covered by the state's partnership act.

For *limited partnerships,* the two most common forms of legislation are the Uniform Limited Partnership Act (ULPA) and the Revised Uniform Limited Partnership Act (RULPA). To establish a limited partnership, the partners must enter into a written agreement. State limited partnership laws apply to situations that the limited partnership agreement does not address.

Thus, according to the state statutes, "unless the partnership agreement provides otherwise," the partnership act dictates how a matter is treated. Furthermore, most partnership agreements specify that if the agreement is silent on an issue, governing state law will apply. This dual approach acts as a fail-safe mechanism to cover as many matters subject to interpretation as possible.

What is the most important factor in a successful partnership?

The relationship among the partners is probably the most important factor in a successful partnership. A partnership is both a legal relationship and a human relationship. It is important that the duties and responsibilities of the partners be clearly defined and understood by each partner. In many ways, a partnership is like a marriage.

Who can be partners in a partnership?

The partnership acts provide that any individual or entity may be a partner in a general or limited partnership. Thus, all of the following can be partners: a natural person, another general partnership, another limited partnership, a limited liability company, a trust, an estate, an association, or a corporation. However, some statutory limits may prevent licensed professionals from sharing profits and losses with nonprofessionals.

Capitalization

⚜ *How is a partnership capitalized?*

Typically, on the formation of a general or limited partnership, each of the partners contributes money or other property to the partnership in exchange for his or her general or limited partnership interest. In some instances, a partner may contribute services instead of money or property to obtain his or her partnership interest. If additional capital is needed, the partnership may obtain outside loans from lending institutions or other third parties.

⚜ *Do the tangible assets used in a general partnership need to be formally transferred to the partnership?*

When the partners contribute assets other than cash to the partnership, a formal transfer is generally required. If there is no transfer instrument that indicates the existence of the partnership or an individual's capacity as a partner, the property may be deemed *not* to be partnership property, even if it is used for partnership purposes. Some state statutes allow a general partner to hold partnership property in his or her own name and still have the property treated as if it belongs to the partnership. This nominee ownership on behalf of the partnership should be used only after consultation with an attorney to weigh its advantages and disadvantages.

Partnership Interests

⚜ *Do all the partners have equal interests in the partnership?*

There are two forms of interests in a partnership. The first is an interest in a share of the distributions of profits and losses from the partnership business. This *distributive share* is based on the ratio of a partner's partnership contribution to the total contributions of all partners. Therefore, a partner's interest in distributions may or may not be equal to the other partners' interests. The second interest is a *management interest.* The management and control of the partnership depends on the type of partnership, regardless of the partners' percentage interests in the profits and losses.

⚐ *What does a partner actually own?*

A partner owns a percentage of the partnership. The partnership owns the partnership assets.

A partner does not own partnership assets and cannot individually transfer the assets. If the partnership owns a parcel of real estate, partners cannot sell the real estate or any part of it individually, even though they may be equal partners. Any sale has to be from the partnership itself. On the death of a partner, the interest that passes to the deceased partner's heirs is the interest in the partnership, as opposed to an interest in the assets of the partnership.

⚐ *How do partners share in the profits of a partnership?*

Typically, the general partners of a general or limited partnership decide whether to distribute profits, and when, or to retain profits for the needs of the business. In some circumstances a partnership agreement provides for a special allocation of distributions in favor of one or more of the partners. Consult with your tax advisor to determine if a special allocation is appropriate in your circumstances.

Documentation

⚐ *What should a written partnership agreement contain?*

There are no formal requirements for a written partnership agreement. It can include whatever provisions the partners agree on, but it should cover every facet of their relationship. The agreement should address such issues as who the partners are; the formation of the partnership; the partners' initial contributions; the partners' percentage of ownership interests; and the partners' ownership rights, including allocations of income, expenses, and preferences on dissolution. The agreement should also address how voting, management, profit distribution, and other partnership affairs are controlled. It should specify any restrictions or rights regarding a partner's transfer of his or her share of profits and losses. If the agreement does not address these issues, statutory default will probably apply.

Individuals entering into a partnership should always consult their state's partnership statutes to ensure that their written agreement covers each area of concern or that the application of statutory provisions will give the desired results. A written partnership agreement should expressly provide that any area not specifically covered by the partners' written agreement will be determined in accordance with the applicable state statute. The state partnership statutes should be referenced to identify any partnership rights and obligations that cannot be altered, even by mutual agreement.

⚄ *Do we need to document operations in a partnership?*

Often, other than the initial partnership formation documents that may be required by the partnership acts and local jurisdiction, no other formal ongoing documentation is required. The partnership agreement often dictates, expressly or by implication, any additional operational documentation that is required, such as minutes of partners' and committee meetings and the financial books and records needed for maintaining control of the partnership's affairs.

All transactions of the partnership should be documented. In addition, most advisors recommend that the partners have annual meetings at which they discuss the management and operation of the partnership and that they keep minutes of the meetings. The partnership is a business, and anything the partners can do to clearly reflect this fact is beneficial.

Taxation

⚔ *How is a partnership taxed?*

A partnership is recognized as an entity separate from its partners and thus is required to file an income tax return (IRS Form 1065). However, the partnership itself does not pay income taxes. Partnerships are "flow-through" or *pass-through* entities, meaning that the profits and losses pass through to the individual partners in accordance with their ownership interests or as provided in the partnership agreement. The partnership provides each partner with a K-1 form that states the partner's share of all partnership pass-through items—income, losses, deductions, and credits. The partner uses this form when preparing his or her personal income tax return.

The partnership does not withhold monies for income tax, FICA, or FUTA from distributions it makes to the partners.

⚔ *How are my cash distributions from the partnership taxed?*

Each partner is responsible for paying the income taxes resulting from his or her pro-rata interest in the pass-through items of the partnership. Distributions are generally income tax–free to the extent that the partner has *basis* in his or her partnership interest. Any distribution exceeding the partner's basis is generally treated as income.

General partners' distributions and guaranteed payments are subject to self-employment tax. Distributions to limited partners are not subject to self-employment tax, but any guaranteed payments, such as salary or professional fees, are.

⚔ *What is a partner's basis in his or her partnership interest?*

Initially, a partner's *basis* in his or her partnership interest is equal to the basis of the property he or she contributes to the partnership. For cash contributed to the partnership on formation, the basis is equal to the amount of cash. For contributions of property other than cash, a partner's basis is the property's initial cost—which may be increased by capital improvements and decreased by depreciation. A partner's basis in the partnership is increased by his or her basis in the encumbered property, increased by the partner's pro-rata share of the liability encumbering the property, and decreased by the amount of the liability allocated to the other partners.

For example, John Smith is one of two equal partners in a partnership. John contributes property with a basis of $70,000; a fair market value of $150,000; and a mortgage of $40,000, which the partnership assumes. John's basis in his partnership interest is $70,000 + $20,000 (half of the debt, representing John's 50 percent interest in the partnership) = $90,000.

A partner's basis in his or her partnership interest increases or decreases annually as a result of partnership income and gains allocated to the partner, the allocation of losses, and actual distributions made to the partner.

◁ What happens when the partnership business experiences losses?

When a partnership is unprofitable, its losses pass through to the individual partners. Such losses may be used to offset a partner's income from other sources, depending on whether the losses are characterized as active or passive. As a general rule, passive losses may be used only to offset passive income; however, there are exceptions to this rule. Consult your tax attorney or accountant for detailed information about partnership losses.

◁ What is phantom income?

As it applies to a partnership, *phantom income* is income earned by a partnership but not distributed to the partners. Often, a provision in the partnership agreement gives the general partner the right to retain income for the reasonable future needs of the partnership. Even if the general partner decides to do so and the partners do not receive distributions in a particular year, the federal government requires that the partners pay tax on their pro-rata share of the income.

⚜ *What choice of taxable year do I have with my partnership?*

Generally, a partnership must conform its tax year to the tax year of its partners, that is, the tax year used by the majority-interest partner (the tax year of one or more partners that own in total more than a 50 percent interest in the partnership profits and capital). However, the partnership can have a different tax year if it can establish a business purpose for doing so. For example, if all the partners are individuals, the partnership would normally use a calendar tax year.

⚜ *Are there any tax consequences when partners contribute to a partnership?*

Generally, no gain or loss is recognized by the partners or the partnership on the contribution of cash or other property in exchange for an interest in the partnership. The contribution is treated as a tax-free exchange. The partnership's basis in the contributed property is the same as the transferor's basis in it before the transfer, and the partner's basis in the partnership interest is the same as his or her basis was in the cash or other property transferred. An exception to tax-free formation occurs if the property transferred to the partnership is encumbered by debt in excess of its basis. Another exception occurs when marketable securities are transferred to the partnership to accomplish diversification and the securities account for more than 80 percent of the partnership assets.

Taxable diversification occurs when the partners contribute different marketable securities that are not diversified. For example, if partner A contributes IBM stock and partner B contributes Dell stock, both of them would have gain recognition on formation equal to the appreciation in the contributed stock. However, if A contributed a mutual fund portfolio and B contributed a different mutual fund portfolio, there would be no gain recognition, since both A and B had diversified investments before funding the partnership.

To avoid any income tax surprises, always consult with a tax advisor before contributing marketable securities and debt-encumbered property to a partnership.

GENERAL
PARTNERSHIP

What is a general partnership?

A *general partnership* is an association of two or more persons who carry on, as co-owners, a business for profit. Issues such as management rights and responsibilities, sharing of profits and losses, and other matters affecting partner relationships and partnership operations should be set out in a written agreement for the reasons discussed earlier in this chapter.

If I start operating a business with my friend on a handshake, how will our relationship be treated?

For legal purposes, a general partnership is often the "default choice" of ownership structure. If two or more persons agree to operate a business together with the intent of making a profit but they do not form a corporation, a limited liability company, or some other entity recognized by statute, state law usually deems that they have formed a general partnership.

In the absence of a written agreement, as in your case, the legal relationship between you and your partner, as well as the conduct of your business, will be governed by state partnership laws (UPA or RUPA).

If I hold property jointly with another person, is this a general partnership?

No. Titling assets in joint tenancy, tenancy in common, tenancy by the entireties, or part ownership does not, of itself, create a partnership. However, if a share of profits is received from an asset titled in one of these ways, that is a strong indication that a partnership exists. For example, if you and your brother own a piece of farmland in joint tenancy and rent it to someone, the law may deem that you and your brother have a general partnership.

Ownership

☙ Do general partners own the partnership equally or in proportion to the amounts they contribute to the partnership?

As explained earlier, partners own both distributive and management interests in a partnership. Without a specific written agreement to the contrary, by law the general partners in a general partnership own equal distributive interests in the partnership and have equal management rights in the business. In a community property state, a partner's spouse may also have an ownership interest in the partnership.

If there is a written partnership agreement, the partners can own the partnership equally or unequally, as set out in the agreement. If the partners have made unequal contributions to the partnership, it is of paramount importance that the partnership agreement reflect the different values of the contributions and the ownership interests of each partner. The agreement should direct how profits and losses are allocated among the partners, since the allocation need not correspond to the partners' respective capital contributions.

Management

☙ Who is responsible for the management of a general partnership?

In the absence of a written agreement to the contrary, the law states that a general partnership is managed and controlled equally by its partners. Each partner has the authority to obligate the partnership for matters in the normal course of the business, including signing agreements, such as contracts and leases, in the name of the partnership. A partner cannot obligate the partnership for matters outside the normal course of the partnership's business, such as disposing of the goodwill of the business or confessing a judgment.

If the partners want to override state law, they must spell out their desires in a written partnership agreement. For instance, if they want their percentages of ownership to determine the strength of their control and management authority, want to designate one specific partner to have day-to-day management authority, or want to employ third parties for management of the business, this must be specified in their agreement.

✑ *Who has control of the partnership if the partners cannot agree?*

Deciding in advance on the management and control of a partnership is one of the reasons that it is so important to have a written partnership agreement. Partners should have a mechanism for resolving disputes in place before they arise. If there is no agreement among the partners, the law assumes that all partners have equal control of the business. Often, resolving a dispute without a written agreement requires litigation in which, ultimately, a court may order the dissolution of the partnership. Alternatively, the partners may simply agree to dissolve the partnership.

✑ *What are a general partner's legal obligations to the partnership?*

Partners must be loyal to the partnership in their business dealings. The law creates a *fiduciary* relationship among partners and between the partners and the partnership. Any assets or profits acquired by a partner through the business belong to the partnership. A partner holds these items on behalf of the partnership and cannot take them individually. Also, a partner cannot compete with the partnership during its existence.

Compensation

✑ *Can general partners be compensated for working in the partnership business?*

As previously discussed, general partners typically receive distributions of income in accordance with the written or oral partnership agreement or on a pro-rata basis. General partners are not employees of the partnership and so cannot receive salaries. Instead, they may receive guaranteed payments, or "draws," for the work they do in the partnership business. Sometimes, partners begin working without understanding how they will be compensated. Without a written agreement to the contrary, many states' partnership laws provide that no partner is entitled to compensation, so there is no compensation adjustment when one partner spends more time than another working for the business. The partners can share the profits of the business only through distributions.

⅏ *Are these distributions subject to the self-employment tax?*

Distributions to general partners, whether characterized as distributions or guaranteed payments, are considered ordinary income and thus are subject to the self-employment tax. However, they are not subject to any withholding tax by the partnership.

Transfer rights

⅏ *Can we restrict a general partner from selling or transferring his or her partnership interest?*

You can and you should. Most general partnership agreements prohibit the transfer of a general partner's interest without the consent of all the other partners. One reason for this is obvious: A general partnership is established by people who want to conduct business together. Also, all general partners are liable for the actions of any one general partner if that partner is acting within the scope of his or her authority. Therefore, you want to make sure that you will not be forced to accept a partner who is not of your choosing.

Formation and Duration

⅏ *How do we form a general partnership?*

You form a general partnership by entering into an agreement to conduct a general partnership. Your agreement may be written, oral, or implied by law.

Typically, no formal documents need to be filed with a government agency to establish a general partnership. However, in some cases, various types of documentation are required. For example, a few state and local governments require registration of a partnership to identify the business and its partners, primarily to protect consumers and to prevent duplication of business names. Many state and/or local laws require that a business obtain a vendor's or sales tax license. If a business adopts a name other than the names of the partners, it may be necessary to file a fictitious-name registration. In addition, if a partnership has employees, it must obtain a tax identification number from the IRS for payment of withholding taxes, and it must also register with the state's workers' compensation and unemployment compensation programs. We strongly suggest that partners work with an experienced attorney when creating their partnership.

If a written agreement isn't necessary, and my partner and I understand how we want to do things, why should we bother drafting a partnership agreement?

The best reason for creating a written agreement is to prevent confusion, misunderstandings, and even disputes. While a partnership may begin in perfect harmony, with a mutual oral agreement on how the business will operate, over time that harmonious relationship may become tenuous due to the many issues that inevitably arise among the individual partners. Often, memories regarding the initial oral agreement become clouded, and matters that are outside the scope of the original agreement arise. Difficulties and misunderstandings may lead to premature termination of an otherwise viable and valuable partnership. A written partnership agreement is critical and should be as unambiguous as possible to avoid disputes over interpretation. We advise that parties to general partnerships have an experienced attorney draft a written agreement.

≫ *How long does a general partnership last?*

A general partnership can last for an unspecified period of time, for a specified period of time, or long enough to complete a project. Normally, a partnership terminates at the end of a stated period of time or at the completion of a project. However, if the partners continue to do business, the partnership also continues.

For example, two partners operate a fish and tackle store. One of the partnership assets is the building in which the store is located. The partners decide to close the fish and tackle store but rent the building to another business. Even though the initial purpose of the partnership has ended, the partnership itself continues by renting the property.

≫ *Is the duration of a general partnership limited?*

A general partnership does not have perpetual existence. Under both the UPA and the RUPA, a partnership may be dissolved when certain acts or events occur. Under the UPA, in the absence of provisions to the contrary in the partnership agreement, a partnership is generally subject to dissolution if any of several events occur, including the following:

- The conclusion of the stated term of years or specific objective of the partnership
- A partner's express will for dissolution, if the partnership is without a definite term or particular undertaking
- A partner's violation of certain provisions of the partnership agreement
- The resignation or death of a partner
- The partnership's bankruptcy
- The order of a court with appropriate jurisdiction

RUPA contains similar provisions but also permits a partner to disassociate himself or herself, or be disassociated from, the partnership without necessarily impairing the partnership's continuity.

Many partnership agreements contain provisions that attempt to reduce the ability of a single partner or a minority number of partners to cause the partnership's dissolution.

Liability

Actions of the business

⤨ *What liability do I face from my general partnership?*

Each partner in a general partnership is responsible for all the acts of the partnership, as long as the acts are committed in the ordinary course of business. The partners are equally responsible for business contracts and all injuries or losses to others. For instance, a partner is responsible for the lease of office space even if the lease was signed by a different partner. Similarly, if an employee is involved in an auto accident while on company business, each partner is responsible for the damages.

⤨ *What protection from contract liabilities of my partnership can I expect?*

Under the UPA, the partners of a general partnership are "jointly" liable to third parties for the partnership's contract debts. *Joint liability* means all partners are liable for a pro-rata share of the amount at issue. Under the RUPA, partners have *joint and several liability,* which means that each partner is responsible for the whole amount. For instance, if there is a judgment of $100,000 against a partnership with five partners, the creditor may collect the entire judgment from any one of the five partners. However, a creditor who is owed money by a general partnership must first attempt to recover the debt from the partnership before attempting to recover from the individual partners. Some UPA states have changed their contract liability to match RUPA's unlimited joint and several liability.

If a partner satisfies an obligation of the partnership by paying more than the pro-rata amount of his or her capital contribution, that partner may be entitled to seek reimbursement from the other partners for any amounts they should have paid.

≱ *What protection from tort liabilities of my partnership can I expect?*

The rules regarding liability for tort claims against the partnership are similar to the rules regarding liability for contractual claims. Under both the UPA and the RUPA, partners are subject to unlimited joint and several liability for tort claims against the partnership, regardless of whether the tort (such as the personal injury or death of another) is committed by a partner, an employee, or some other representative while acting on behalf of the business. A partner who pays more than his or her pro-rata share to satisfy a claim or judgment may be entitled to seek reimbursement from the other partners. Under the RUPA, a creditor must proceed against the partnership first; only if the partnership's assets are insufficient to satisfy the judgment may the creditor proceed against one or more individual partners.

≱ *If I become a member of the partnership after a contract liability is incurred, am I still liable? What if I resign from the partnership after a liability is incurred?*

A person who becomes a partner after a claim is made under a contract generally is not personally liable to third parties for the claim.

On the other hand, if a partner resigns after the partnership incurs an obligation, he or she remains liable for the obligation even after resigning. To minimize your liability after you resign, you should notify the public that you are no longer a member of the partnership. You can do this by publishing a notice in a general-circulation newspaper in each county in which the partnership does business. In addition, you should make your resignation known to third parties that transact business with the partnership so that in the future they will not rely on your participation in the partnership.

⚮ *How can I protect my personal assets from liabilities incurred by the general partnership?*

The best way to protect personal assets from negligence claims against the partnership is to ensure that the partnership has a good liability insurance policy. It is also a good idea to know your partners well. Be very cautious about being in partnership with someone who is habitually careless or unconcerned about the rights or well-being of others.

The best way to protect yourself from contract liabilities is to limit your exposure within the terms of the contract by including a limitation-of-liabilities or liquidated-damages clause or by specifically defining the limits of your obligations (e.g., "Partnership shall not be responsible for delivering more than 1000 widgets within any 30-day period"). It is very important to have your business attorney review and, if necessary, revise contracts before you sign them to limit your risk of liability.

The way you title your nonbusiness assets may protect them from exposure if the means of ownership is in place before the debt or liability occurs. For example, assuming state law provides for tenancy-by-the-entireties ownership, if you and your spouse own property as tenants by the entireties and your spouse is not a partner with you, the property is generally exempt from the partnership's creditors.

Additional methods of providing protection are discussed later in this chapter.

Actions of the general partners

⚮ *Are the assets of my general partnership protected from my personal creditors?*

Property owned by a general partnership is not usually available to the personal creditors of a general partner. Thus, someone who has obtained a personal judgment against you generally cannot seize a piece of equipment that is owned by your general partnership.

However, your ownership interest in the general partnership is available to your personal creditors through a charging order. A *charging order* is simply a court order that constitutes a lien on the debtor's transferable interest in the partnership.

⌁ *My partner was just sued on a $25,000 loan he had cosigned with his ex-wife. If he loses the lawsuit, will I, or our partnership, have to pay for it?*

If a judgment is entered against your partner, the creditor will certainly look around for assets your partner owns that can be attached in order to ultimately satisfy the judgment. One asset your partner owns is his interest in the partnership. While state laws vary somewhat, the general rule is that the creditor is entitled only to a charging order against the debtor partner's partnership interest. The court generally may *not* order partnership assets or the assets of the other partners to be attached or sold in satisfaction of the debt unless it has the written consent of the partners or the partnership. Whenever a distribution is made by the partnership, the creditor will receive the amount allocated to the general partner's interest that is subject to the charging order. The creditor is not in a position to force a distribution and usually must just wait it out. As a result, this may be a good opportunity for your partner to negotiate a different arrangement for paying or settling the debt.

LIMITED LIABILITY PARTNERSHIP

⌁ *What is a limited liability partnership?*

A *limited liability partnership (LLP)* is a relatively new business structure. Several states have modified their general partnership statutes to allow the creation of LLPs. An LLP is a general partnership in all respects except the following: who can be partners, how the partnership is formed, how it is managed and controlled, and the partners' liability.

⚜ Who owns the LLP?

The ownership structure of an LLP is the same as that of a general partnership except that the partnership interests must be owned by two or more individuals in the same profession.

⚜ Who is in charge of an LLP?

Unless otherwise agreed to in the partnership agreement (if there is one), LLP statutes require that the partners make decisions by majority vote on the basis of their percentage of ownership of the partnership.

⚜ How is a limited liability partnership formed?

The name of the business must include the words "limited liability partnership" or the abbreviation "LLP," and the partners must file a certificate of limited liability partnership with the secretary of state. The contents of the certificate are governed by state statute but typically include the name of the partnership; the business, profession, or activity in which the partnership engages; the term of the LLP; the name and address of the LLP's registered agent and registered office; and the name and address of any partner who is responsible for the management of the business.

⚜ What happens if an LLP does not properly file with the secretary of state?

The partnership is legally deemed to be a general partnership instead of an LLP, and the partners lose their limited liability benefit.

⅍ *What protection does an LLP offer its partners from the contract liabilities of the company?*

An LLP offers great protection to the partners for contractual debts or obligations of the company. If the business fails to repay a bank loan and a lawsuit arises, the LLP can be held liable for the bank loan but, generally, the individual partners cannot be held liable. Obvious exceptions exist—for example, in situations where the limited liability partnership is used to perpetrate a fraud.

⅍ *What protection does an LLP offer its partners from the tort liabilities of the company?*

An LLP offers good protection to the partners for torts committed by the company's employees, agents, and representatives. If the LLP's partners, employees, agents, or representatives commit a tort (such as the personal injury or death of another) while acting on behalf of the business, the LLP and the person who caused the harm can be held liable for such conduct but partners who did not cause the harm cannot be held liable.

LIMITED PARTNERSHIP

⅍ *What is a limited partnership?*

A *limited partnership (LP)* is a specialized type of partnership created under state law. It has two classes or categories of partners—one or more general partners and one or more limited partners—that, together, hold 100 percent of the business interests.

Almost every state has adopted some form of the Uniform Limited Partnership Act (ULPA) or Revised Uniform Limited Partnership Act (RULPA) to control the conduct and operation of the partnership and the relationships among the partners, but many of the state rules can be modified by a written partnership agreement.

⚖ *What's the difference between a general partner and a limited partner?*

The rights, duties, obligations, and liabilities of the two types of partners vary considerably. The *general partner* (or partners) controls the operations of the partnership and has full personal liability for its debts and obligations. The *limited partners* are passive investors; generally they own the lion's share of the partnership interests and their liability is limited to their individual capital investments in the partnership.

⚖ *How are the general partner's and limited partners' interests decided?*

The general partner contributes property to the partnership in exchange for the general partnership interest. It is common for the general partner to have a very small interest in the limited partnership, often only 1 or 2 percent. If the general partner wants a greater interest in the LP, he or she typically contributes cash or property to the partnership in exchange for the larger interest. Limited partners own the percentage of the LP that is not owned by the general partner. Typically, the limited partners provide most of the capital and receive most of the interests in the limited partnership.

Management

⚖ *How is the management of a limited partnership structured?*

The general partner is vested with complete management of and responsibility for the limited partnership and its business.

⚖ *Who controls my limited partnership?*

Since the general partner has the sole right to manage the partnership's business, he or she has the right to control its business and therefore to control how the partnership assets are used and invested. By law, a limited partner cannot participate in the management and control of the limited partnership. This restriction justifies placing full liability for the partnership's actions on the general partner.

> *If a dispute arises among the general partners, can a limited partner decide to control partnership affairs after the LP is formed?*

A limited partner who participates in the management of the partnership's affairs runs the very real risk of being deemed a general partner for liability purposes, regardless of the provisions of the limited partnership agreement. Typically, such agreements do not allow management by a limited partner. It is a bad idea, in any event.

Compensation

> *How are partners in a limited partnership paid?*

The general partner typically receives a guaranteed payment for managing the day-to-day activities of the LP's business. In addition, the general partner receives a pro-rata share of all partnership distributions, based on his or her ownership percentage in the partnership.

Limited partners, who are typically only passive investors in the LP, receive distributions from the partnership on a pro-rata basis if and when the general partner deems it appropriate to make distributions. If a limited partner is also an employee of the partnership, he or she receives a salary for the services performed.

> *Do partners need to pay self-employment tax on distributions from the partnership?*

Usually, only the general partner's guaranteed payments and distributions are subject to self-employment tax; limited partners' distributions are not. However, if limited partners participate as employees, their compensation is subject to self-employment tax.

Transfer rights

⊰ *Can a partner transfer or sell his or her LP interest to someone else?*

Most limited partnership agreements place rigid transfer restrictions on the partnership interests so that they cannot be transferred without the consent of all partners. By giving the partners the right to approve any proposed transfer, these restrictions prevent the transfer of interests to unknown or undesirable parties.

By law, a transferee, or the recipient of a transferred limited partnership interest, typically receives only an *assignee interest* and is not entitled to become a limited partner. A transferee who is merely an assignee receives the distributions of income that the transferor would have received but has no other rights. State partnership statutes allow a new partner to become a full general partner or a limited partner if all the remaining partners agree to this or as the partnership agreement may provide.

⊰ *Can you give an example of a typical transfer restriction?*

The limited partnership agreement can require that a partner first offer his or her interest to the remaining partners before transferring or assigning the interest to someone outside the existing ownership. Typically, a written notice and valid offer from a third party are required to trigger the right to exercise the right of first refusal.

⊰ *What happens if it's difficult for the remaining owners to quickly raise the cash needed to purchase the interest?*

It is not unusual for the partnership agreement to provide that the existing owners can have an extended period of time to pay for the interest and that the limited partnership operations can finance the purchase so that there is no need for outside financing. A predetermined interest rate and term of years may be specified in the agreement.

Formation and Duration

⋈ *How do we create a limited partnership?*

To create a limited partnership, the partners must file a certificate of limited partnership with the secretary of state and pay a filing fee. Filing requirements and fees vary from state to state. The ULPA or the RULPA determines what information must be included in the certificate of limited partnership.

The partners must also enter into a written partnership agreement. Everything pertaining to the formation of the limited partnership should be documented. An accurate list of all assets contributed to the partnership and their value is critical. In addition, it is recommended that partnership certificates similar to stock certificates, reflecting ownership by the general partner and the limited partners, be issued.

⋈ *What's in the certificate of limited partnership?*

Typically, the certificate must include the name of the limited partnership and the address of its principal office, the name and address of a registered agent for service of legal papers, the name and address of every general partner, and the duration of the partnership. In some cases, a description of the assets contributed and their agreed-upon value must also be included.

⋈ *How long can a limited partnership last?*

Depending on state statutes, a limited partnership can last for a stated period of time or indefinitely.

⋈ *What happens to a limited partnership on the death of a general partner?*

The answer depends on the terms of the partnership agreement or state law. Generally, under state statutes, the death of the last remaining general partner terminates the limited partnership unless the remaining limited partners agree to continue the partnership and select a new general partner.

⚖ *What happens to a limited partnership on the death or withdrawal of a limited partner?*

Typically, any withdrawal due to the death, disability, or voluntary departure of a limited partner does not cause the partnership to dissolve unless there is no remaining limited partner. A limited partner may withdraw at a time specified in the partnership agreement or on the occurrence of an event specified in the agreement (such as disability). Under some state statutes, if the agreement does not specify such times or events or provide a definite time for the partnership to be dissolved, a limited partner may withdraw 6 months after giving written notice to each general partner.

Liability

Actions of the business

⚖ *What protection do general partners have from contract liabilities of their limited partnership?*

A limited partnership offers no liability protection for the general partners. Each general partner is responsible for the contractual debts and obligations of the partnership. For example, if the limited partnership fails to repay a bank loan and a lawsuit arises, the partnership itself and its general partners can be held liable for the loan.

⚖ *What protection do general partners have from tort liabilities of their limited partnership?*

A general partner of a limited partnership has unlimited liability for the partnership's tort liabilities, such as the personal injury or death of another, to the same extent as the liability with a general partnership. (For details, see the earlier question on tort liability, under "General Partnership.") A general partner has the right to be reimbursed by other general partners if they did not contribute their prorata shares to the amount he or she paid and by the limited partners up to the amount of their investment.

⧫ How can I, as a general partner, protect myself from personal liability for the partnership's debts and obligations?

Since the general partner is fully responsible for the management and control of the limited partnership and bears the economic risk of its debts, obligations, and liabilities, the best liability protection is to have a general partner that has limited liability features. It is possible, and even preferable in most cases, to create a separate entity to be the general partner so that you can avoid exposure to personal liability.

The entity you choose to be the general partner should insulate its members or interest holders from personal liability for its debts and activities. This is usually best accomplished by using a corporation or limited liability company as the general partner. For example, you can own a corporation that becomes the general partner of the partnership. As long as control and management are exercised through this general partner, your personal liabilities are limited to your investment in the corporation.

Each type of business that can be used as a general partner has advantages and disadvantages that you must review to determine which type would produce the greatest overall benefit.

⧫ What entity is the best choice as general partner?

Any entity that can provide control through centralized management, continuity of life, limited liability, salaries to officers (or members) and employees, and fringe benefits is a good choice as the general partner. The most popular choices are C corporations, S corporations, and limited liability companies. The LLC, in particular, is very popular due to its excellent protection, ease of formation, and flexibility.

Chapters 7 and 8 discuss entities that protect owners from the activities of the entity's business. If you are doing business as a partnership, it is often prudent to own the partnership interest inside one of these other business structures.

⚐ Can you give me an example of how two entities would work together?

Assume you form a limited partnership to operate a family business and you want to control the management decisions. To protect yourself from the partnership's liabilities, you form an LLC to be the general partner of the limited partnership. You are the sole owner of the LLC that owns the general-partner interest. The LLC protects you personally from the liabilities of the partnership, and your 100 percent ownership of the LLC allows you to control the limited partnership.

⚐ Is avoiding personal liability the only reason I would use a company as the general partner?

No. Another reason for using a company as a general partner is to avoid involuntary or inadvertent termination of the partnership as the result of your becoming incompetent or dying. Most state limited partnership laws call for the automatic dissolution of a limited partnership if the general partner dies or becomes incompetent, insolvent, or bankrupt. While a successor general partner may be appointed by the remaining partners, there are strict deadlines for doing so. In addition, federal tax regulations provide that if 50 percent or more of a partnership's interest is sold or exchanged during any 12-month period, the partnership is terminated for federal income tax purposes. Therefore, the disability or death of an individual acting as the general partner could result in the premature termination of an otherwise valuable business. Using a corporation or limited liability company as a general partner, and providing for transition to individuals to control and manage the company in the event of your disability or death, prevents these problems.

In addition, remember that the general partner is entitled to fair compensation from the partnership for services rendered. Using a company as general partner may yield beneficial business and income tax planning opportunities, such as allocating income through the general-partner company to individuals or providing fringe benefits and income tax deductions that are not available to individuals.

⍦ *Are there any other ways to help reduce the general partner's liability?*

You could form multiple limited partnerships. As a general rule, you should not mix "safe" assets, "vulnerable" assets, and "dangerous" assets in the same partnership. *Safe assets*—mutual funds, stocks, or bank accounts—ordinarily do not subject the owner to liability. For example, a share of General Motors stock is safe because the stockholder is not personally liable for injuries caused by a faulty General Motors vehicle. *Dangerous assets* could subject the owner to personal liability merely because he or she is the owner. Examples of dangerous assets include vacant land with hazardous waste on it, dangerous equipment, or a business producing a product that could injure people. *Vulnerable assets* are neither safe nor dangerous. Most assets are vulnerable assets.

If the partnership itself owns dangerous assets and a lawsuit results in a judgment against the partnership, all the partnership's assets—safe, dangerous, or vulnerable—can be used to satisfy the judgment.

Just as you should not mix safe assets and dangerous assets in the same partnership, you may want to separate vulnerable assets into different partnerships. If you own six apartment houses, you may want to create a separate limited partnership for each one. In this way, you will avoid exposing all your apartment houses to the liabilities that might arise with respect to any one property.

⅍ *What business liability exists for the limited partners in a limited partnership?*

Limited partners are not liable for the partnership's debts and other liabilities beyond the amount of their investments in the partnership. State law limits the liability of limited partners because they have little or no right to participate in management decisions of the partnership.

⅍ *What if a limited partner does get involved in the management of the partnership?*

A limited partner can work in, with, or for the partnership as an employee. However, if a limited partner becomes involved in the management and control of the partnership, he or she loses the limited-partner protection and is liable for the partnership's debts to the same extent as a general partner is.

Also, if a limited partnership fails to observe the formalities of the home state's partnership law or if a limited partner holds himself or herself out to third parties as a general partner, the limited partner may lose limited liability protection.

Actions of the partners

⅍ *Are the assets of my limited partnership protected from my personal liabilities?*

Generally, property owned by a limited partnership is not available to the personal creditors of a general or limited partner. Thus, someone who has obtained a judgment against you personally cannot repossess a piece of equipment that is owned by your limited partnership.

Personal creditors have no right to any property owned by the limited partnership. A limited partner's creditors cannot obtain any power over the partner's interest and may not interfere with the partnership's affairs. If a creditor obtains a monetary judgment against a limited partner, the court may issue a charging order. This order gives the creditor only the right to receive distributions that would otherwise be paid to the debtor partner. The limited rights that charging orders grant to creditors are a very important asset protection benefit of a limited partnership over a corporation.

FAMILY LIMITED PARTNERSHIP

I've heard people talk about a family limited partnership. What is that?

A *family limited partnership (FLP)* is a limited partnership in which all the partners are family members. The Internal Revenue Code (IRC) addresses several issues that pertain to FLPs. For example, the IRC provides that individuals who are given an interest in a limited partnership are treated for all purposes as limited partners as long as the partnership assets are "a material income-producing factor." This requirement is intended to prevent a parent from transferring his or her personal services to a partnership in order to allocate the income from those services, for income tax purposes, to his or her children at their lower income tax rates.

Why would I want to form a limited partnership with only family members?

People form FLPs mainly for estate planning. The FLP may be used to own family assets, manage them, protect them from creditors, spread income among family members, or provide an efficient, tax-effective way to pass assets from one generation to the next.

In *Strictly Business,* we also discuss using a limited partnership in cases where a business owner wants to transfer his or her business to younger family members without giving up control of the business while the younger generation is learning to manage it. The owner can create a limited partnership for a new business or convert an existing business to a limited partnership.

ৰ্থ *Who owns the family limited partnership?*

The general partner and the limited partners own the FLP. The general partner has full control of the FLP, even if he or she owns only a small percentage of it. The limited partners, as passive investors, have few rights in, and no control of, the partnership.

Usually, when parents or grandparents create a limited partnership, they initially own 100 percent of it as the general partners, because they owned 100 percent of the assets they transferred to the FLP. Then, depending on their estate and business planning goals, the senior-generation general partners, either immediately or over time, transfer 99 percent of their ownership interest to other family members, thereby making them limited partners.

ৰ্থ *Is it important to document the operations of a family limited partnership?*

Yes. Documenting all transactions and operations is even more critical for an FLP than it is for a standard limited partnership. Although not required by partnership law, we recommend that the partnership have annual meetings to discuss the management and operation of the partnership and that it keep minutes of the meetings. The FLP is a business; everything you can do to clearly reflect that fact is beneficial.

ৰ্থ *My husband and I established a limited partnership several years ago to operate our dairy farm. Can we change the ownership structure to involve our children in the business?*

It is common for parents to bring their children into their business when the children show interest and are old enough to participate. You and your husband can give or sell limited partnership interests to your children. You should work with your accountant, attorney, and financial advisors to create the best plan for your situation.

JOINT VENTURE

⚖ *I have a friend who is involved in a joint venture. What is that?*

Legally, a *joint venture* is like a general partnership that is formed for a short time, usually to complete a particular project. It is not uncommon to see corporations or other entities engage in a joint venture for a particular activity.

⚖ *Why would unrelated businesses agree to form a joint venture?*

A joint venture enables businesses to exploit a particular business opportunity without getting tied into a long-term association. Usually, each company in the venture looks to the other company to provide a resource needed to do one project. For example, small oil companies frequently form joint ventures to perform drilling projects: one company owns the drilling rights but does not have the financial resources to explore the site, while the other company has the finances and likes the prospects of that particular site. A real estate developer may form a joint venture with a construction company to build an office complex: the developer owns the land and the construction company has the financial resources to build the complex. Airbus airplanes were developed through a joint venture involving multinational corporations.

In a joint venture, both businesses are stakeholders and have a direct interest in the project.

⚖ *How do I form a joint venture?*

You can form a joint venture through an oral or a written agreement. We generally recommend that the parties enter into a written joint venture agreement, which is similar to a partnership agreement. It should cover such topics as capital contributions, control of daily operations, distribution of profits and losses, management decisions, and duration of the project. Generally, without a written agreement, the profits, losses, and control are apportioned equally among the parties.

More than likely you will use a fictitious name for your joint venture project, so you must file a certificate with the secretary of state specifying the name under which you are doing business. Usually, all the employees working in the joint venture are employed directly by one of the joint venturers. However, if the joint venture itself hires employees, it must follow federal and state rules and regulations related to withholding and paying taxes, workers' compensation coverage, and the like.

What protection do joint venturers have from contract and tort liabilities of the business?

In most respects, the joint venture is similar to a general partnership in terms of liability. Typically, all joint venturers are responsible for the joint venture's contracts, as well as for any joint venture activities of the individual venturers. Because of this, joint ventures tend to be particularly risky when one of the parties has limited financial resources. If one party cannot meet its joint venture obligations, it is likely that the other joint venturers will be called on to complete those obligations, regardless of the financial arrangement between the venturers.

However, if the joint venturers are limited partnerships, corporations, or limited liability companies, their individual partners, shareholders, or members are not personally liable for actions of the joint venture.

Are joint venture assets protected from the liabilities of the joint venture partners?

For liability purposes, the joint venture is treated as a general partnership. For a detailed explanation, see the liability questions under "General Partnership," earlier in this chapter.

RECOMMENDATIONS

When would a general partnership be an appropriate entity for doing business?

Because of liability issues, a general partnership is best suited for companies that already provide protection from personal liability but desire flexibility in jointly operating and controlling a business. Always consider the general partnership form of business when two or more corporations or LLCs want to start a business.

Should I form a family limited partnership?

A family limited partnership is simply a limited partnership that has two or more members of the same family as partners. FLPs are sophisticated management, gift, estate, and asset protection planning tools, and they require attention to detail in their operation. If you want to establish an FLP, you should do a complete FLP plan with experienced advisors.

When is it appropriate to form a joint venture?

When two businesses want to combine their resources to complete a specific project without merging into a single entity for the long term, they frequently use the joint venture form of business. For example, two competitors might form a joint venture to manufacture a specific product that requires different patents owned by each or different skills possessed by each. Two companies might create a joint venture to have the resources needed to compete with a larger company in regard to a specific product or service without losing their separate identities. Alternatively, a joint venture might enable a company to operate in a location where only the other venturer is authorized to conduct business.

ADVANTAGES
AND DISADVANTAGES

⚑ *What are the advantages and disadvantages of a general partnership?*

Advantages

- A general partnership is simple to form; most states do not require a written partnership agreement (but we recommend it).
- No ongoing formalities are required (but regular meetings are advisable).
- Relations between partners are largely left to their own agreement, subject to the principle that each partner must refrain from actions detrimental to the other partners.
- The partners can specify how they will share and distribute profits and losses and what events will trigger a termination or dissolution of the enterprise.
- The partnership is not subject to income taxation; all income, deductions, and losses pass through to the partners.
- Partnership assets are usually protected from the personal liabilities of the general partners.

Disadvantages

- Each partner is liable for the debts and obligations of the partnership and for liabilities incurred by other partners while engaged in partnership activities.
- In community property states, the community property of both

spouses may be at risk even if the nonowner spouse takes no part in the business.

■ Unless a written partnership agreement states otherwise, there is no centralized management.

■ Each general partner has equal authority to manage the business and thus can bind the partnership and partners to any transaction related to the business.

■ Any distributions to general partners are treated as ordinary income and subject to self-employment tax.

■ General partners must report partnership profits as income on their individual income tax returns even if they do not take the profits as distributions.

■ There is limited opportunity to expand the business since financing primarily depends on contributions from general partners and loans obtained through the partnership.

■ Transfer of a general partnership interest is subject to the approval of all the other partners, unless otherwise specified in a partnership agreement.

■ The partnership will terminate on the death, disability, or bankruptcy of a general partner unless the remaining partners agree to continue the partnership.

≤⅃ *What are the advantages and disadvantages of a limited liability partnership?*

Advantages

The advantages of an LLP are the same as those listed above for a general partnership, with one important exception:

■ All partners have limited liability protection from the debts, obligations, and judgments of the LLP.

Disadvantages

An LLP has the same disadvantages as a general partnership (other than unlimited liability), plus:

- The rules and laws governing LLPs are relatively untested, so there is uncertainty regarding how they will be enforced.
- Not all jurisdictions allow LLPs; in those that do not, an LLP may be treated as a general partnership.
- An LLP limits the opportunities for business continuity and estate planning.

Can you summarize the advantages and disadvantages of a limited partnership?

Advantages

- A limited partnership is easy to form; states require only a certificate of limited partnership (but we recommend a written partnership agreement).
- There are no requirements for ongoing documentation of operations.
- Only general partners can manage the partnership.
- Limited partners may be employees of the business.
- General partners can take a salary for day-to-day management of the business.
- Both general and limited partners can receive distributions.
- General partners have the authority to make distributions or to retain profits in the business.
- The partnership is not subject to federal taxation; all income, deductions, and losses pass through to the partners.
- General partners may restrict transfers of partnership rights under the terms of the partnership agreement.
- The limited partners' assets are protected from the liabilities of the partnership.
- Partnership assets are usually protected from the personal liabilities of the general and limited partners.
- Limited partners can invest in the partnership without being involved in management and with limited exposure to the partnership's liabilities; this facilitates expansion.

- The partnership can continue after the death, disability, or retirement of a general partner if the written partnership agreement provides for the selection of a new general partner.
- The partnership can continue after the death, disability, or retirement of a limited partner.

Disadvantages

- The general partner has unlimited liability for the debts and activities of the partnership (unless the general partner is a company with limited liability protection).
- Limited partners may consider any restriction on their right to transfer their ownership interests to be a disadvantage.
- There is limited opportunity to expand the business since financing primarily depends on contributions from partners and loans obtained through the partnership.
- Any distributions or guaranteed payments to general partners are treated as ordinary income and subject to self-employment tax.

Can you list the advantages and disadvantages of a joint venture?

They are the same as those listed for a general partnership. See the first question in this section.

chapter 7

Corporation

What exactly is a corporation?

A *corporation* is a type of entity, or business ownership structure. Corporations are created by state law. Every state provides rules for the formation of corporations. While the rules are not exactly the same from state to state, every state recognizes a corporation as an entity that is separate from its owners, provided certain formalities are followed. A corporation conducts business, enters into contracts, incurs liability, and acquires assets in its own name, not in the name of its owners, who are called *shareholders* or *stockholders*.

While the shareholders can vote on issues that control the corporation, they do not conduct the day-to-day affairs of the business. In exchange for this limited managerial authority, shareholders are insulated from personal liability for the debts and claims of the corporation. The day-to-day management of a corporation is often left

155

to corporate officers, who are responsible to the directors, who in turn are responsible to the shareholders. In many small corporations the shareholders, officers, and directors are the same individuals.

People refer to several types of corporations. Each type is simply a variation of the same basic structure—the corporation—that is formed under general state statutes. The primary differences among the types of corporations relate to who the owners can be (e.g., professional corporations), how the corporations choose to be taxed (as C versus S corporations), or how they sell their stock (public or closely held). In addition to the general rules that apply to all corporations, special rules apply to each type of corporation.

◢ What are some characteristics of a corporation?

The most important characteristics of a corporation are limited liability, continuity of life, and centralized management.

◢ What is meant by "continuity of life"?

A business is deemed to have *continuity of life* if it can continue even after the death, insanity, bankruptcy, retirement, departure, or removal of an owner. A corporation has *perpetual life:* when its owner (the shareholder) dies, it goes on "living" until someone takes action to legally dissolve it or fails to take action needed to keep it in existence. After the death of the original owner, the shares can be transferred many times to new owners, any of whom can die without affecting the viability of the corporation.

◢ What is centralized management?

With *centralized management,* the management decisions are made by the corporation's elected directors and appointed officers, rather than by all the owners. The shareholders, in their capacity as shareholders, are not involved in the day-to-day decision making.

⚅ *What is a public corporation?*

A *public,* or *publicly traded, corporation* sells its stock, on a stock exchange, to individuals or companies. A public corporation may have hundreds of thousands of shareholders all over the world; the shareholders "vote their shares" to elect a board of directors that sets company policy and to appoint or hire officers who run the company. Only C corporations can sell stock to the public on a stock exchange. The Securities and Exchange Commission and other authorities impose many controls upon such corporations.

⚅ *What is a closely held corporation?*

A *closely held corporation,* like a public corporation, is formed as a regular corporation under state statutes. However, a closely held corporation's shares are not publicly traded on a stock exchange; they are owned by a small number of shareholders or even one shareholder. Closely held corporations differ from public corporations in several other ways:

- Closely held corporations can choose to be taxed as C or S corporations.
- Because there are few shareholders, the owners also function as directors and officers. Thus, they have active control of the corporation.
- Because the shares of a closely held corporation are not publicly traded, they are difficult to value. Thus, there is a limited market for the shares.
- Because the shareholders of a closely held corporation know each other and have chosen to do business together, they usually impose restrictions that limit the transfer or sale of shares to "outside" parties.

Some states have formalized this structure as a distinct type of corporation called a *close corporation.* Close corporations are created by state law to provide the benefits of corporate status to corporations owned by an individual or by a small group of shareholders.

TYPES OF
CORPORATIONS

⚖ *What is a C corporation?*

A *C corporation* is a corporation that is taxed under Subchapter C of the Internal Revenue Code (IRC). Under Subchapter C, income or losses are determined and income taxes are assessed at the entity level.

⚖ *What is an S corporation?*

An *S corporation* is initially formed under state law as a C corporation. After formation, the business elects to be treated as an S corporation for federal income tax purposes.

As an S corporation, the business is *not* taxed as a separate taxable entity. Instead, all the S corporation's income or losses "pass through" to the shareholders on a pro-rata basis in accordance with their percentage ownership of the company. The shareholders then report the income on their own income tax returns. Although an S corporation must file its own income tax returns, generally no income taxes are assessed against the corporation.

⚖ *What is a personal service corporation?*

The IRS defines a *personal service corporation (PSC)* as one that meets the following criteria: It is set up as a C corporation; its principal activity is providing personal services; the personal services are substantially performed by the employee-owners; and the employee-owners own, on any day, more than 10 percent of the PSC's outstanding stock. Most personal service corporations are in the fields of health, law, engineering, architecture, accounting, actuarial science, performing arts, or consulting.

The major drawback to PSCs is that their income is taxed at a flat rate of 35 percent rather than at graduated tax rates of the standard C corporation. A corporation can avoid being classified as a PSC by choosing to be taxed as an S corporation.

⚓ What is a professional corporation?

Although several states allow professionals, such as architects, lawyers, and doctors, to incorporate as either a regular corporation or a professional corporation, most states require that they incorporate as a *professional corporation (PC)*. Professional corporation statutes include special rules regarding who can be shareholders, officers, and directors. We discuss these rules in detail later in the chapter.

⚓ Is a close corporation the same as a closely held corporation?

No. A close corporation is a type of corporation, authorized by the statutes of some states, in which the shareholders regulate the corporation's internal affairs among themselves.

General corporation statutes mandate specific formalities regarding the formation and operation of corporations. Yet there are fundamental differences between closely held corporations, which have only a few shareholders, who actively work in the business, and publicly traded corporations, which have many passive shareholders. Recognizing these differences, some states have enacted close-corporation statutes that dispense with many of the formalities required of regular corporations, such as bylaws, directors, and annual meetings. In addition, the statutes allow flexibility in the control of the corporation and restrict the number of shareholders.

To maintain liability protection, owners of close corporations must comply with their state's close-corporation statute. Owners should work with their attorneys to create and maintain this type of corporation.

⚔ *Can a close corporation be an S corporation?*

Yes. A close corporation can choose to be taxed as an S corporation.

OWNERSHIP

Structure

⚔ *Who are the owners of a corporation?*

The owners of a corporation are the shareholders or stockholders. Generally, shareholders invest in the corporation by contributing money or other property in exchange for all or a portion of the corporation's stock. This is called "buying stock." *Stock* is simply a paper certificate that shows the portion of the corporation, or the number of *shares,* that a shareholder owns.

⚔ *I'm going to be the only shareholder of my corporation. Why doesn't my attorney issue all the available shares to me?*

To answer this question, let's discuss some important terms: *authorized shares* and *issued and outstanding* shares. State statutes and the articles of incorporation govern how many shares of stock corporations are authorized to issue, or sell. When you file your articles of incorporation and your state accepts them, your company is authorized to issue a specified number of shares of stock.

Let's use Ohio as an example. If you want to pay only the minimum incorporation fee ($85 in 2001), the state will authorize your corporation to issue 850 shares of stock. If you purchase all 850 shares, you own all the stock your corporation is authorized to sell. You will never be able to sell additional shares to take in a co-owner, reward an employee, and so on, without amending your articles and paying additional professional fees and state filing costs. Why close off your options? If you issue and purchase just 50 shares, those are the only shares issued and outstanding; you are still the sole shareholder and 100 percent owner, but you have 800 authorized shares for future use.

C corporation

⋈ *Who can have ownership in a C corporation?*

The C corporation is the most flexible type in terms of ownership. Any number of individuals or businesses can own shares of stock in a C corporation.

⋈ *How is the ownership of a C corporation structured?*

If its articles of incorporation so authorize, a C corporation may issue different classes of stock. The two most common classes of stock are *preferred stock* and *common stock*.

⋈ *What are the differences between preferred stock and common stock?*

Preferred stock is said to be "preferred" over common stock for two reasons: liquidation and dividends. Upon *liquidation* of the corporation, creditors are first in line to be paid from any assets, bondholders are second, and preferred stockholders are third. Last in line are the common stockholders.

Dividends are payments, to shareholders, of a portion of the corporation's profits. Holders of common stock receive dividends based on their percentage ownership of the corporation. Preferred stock, on the other hand, is issued with a fixed rate of return on the stockholder's investment. For example, the owner of 7 percent preferred stock receives dividends based on a fixed rate of return of 7 percent of his or her initial investment—to the extent that the corporation has earnings and profits to pay dividends. The preferred dividend can be structured in many ways, and there can be various types of preferred shareholders with various investment returns.

Preferred shareholders receive their dividends before common shareholders do. In other words, the corporation must pay all preferred dividends in full before it pays any common-stock dividends for any given year. Moreover, preferred dividends are typically cumulative: if the corporation does not pay all or any portion of the preferred dividends in any year, the dividends accumulate and the corporation must pay them in future years before it can declare and pay any common-stock dividends. After the corporation pays its creditors and its preferred stockholders, it can use the remaining earnings to pay the common stockholders—but it doesn't have to. The corporation can either pay the residual earnings to the common stockholders as dividends or keep them in the company as capital for future growth. Keeping the earnings for future growth should benefit the common stockholder: as the company grows, the price of the common stock should increase accordingly.

⋙ Who has the voting rights: common or preferred stockholders?

It is not unusual for the common stock to have all the voting rights and the preferred stock to have no voting rights. However, there is no restriction on giving different voting rights to each class as long as the corporate articles and bylaws address the nature of the voting rights given to each class of stock.

⋙ Why would a company want to issue two classes of stock or stock with different voting rights?

Corporations create different classes of stock for many reasons and to accomplish many goals. For example, a corporation might create a class of preferred shares in order to raise capital for initial formation or business expansion. Investors may be more inclined to invest in the corporation if they know that they will profit from their investment on a preferred basis over those who own common shares. Alternatively, some owners may want to realize a return on their investment before others. Finally, owners may issue voting and non-voting shares of stock in order to share the business with family members or valued employees without giving up the control that goes with the right to vote.

S corporation

✍ Are there any special ownership requirements for electing S corporation status?

To qualify, the corporation must be organized under the laws of any state or U.S. territory as a domestic corporation, and all shareholders must consent to the election. S corporations have the following ownership requirements:

- The shareholders must be individuals, estates, or certain types of trusts. They cannot be partnerships or corporations.
- The shareholders must be U.S. citizens or residents.
- The corporation can have only one class of stock.
- There can be no more than seventy-five shareholders. (Note that a husband and wife are counted as one shareholder.)
- The corporation cannot be a member of an affiliated group, a financial institution, an insurance company, a Section 936 election corporation, or a current or former domestic international-sales corporation.

✍ How many classes of stock can be issued by an S corporation?

An S corporation can issue only one class of stock, and the outstanding shares must confer identical rights to distributions and proceeds of liquidation. An S corporation may issue voting stock and nonvoting stock, which are not deemed to be two classes of stock.

Professional corporation

✍ Who can own a professional corporation?

Generally, only professionals licensed in the same occupation can be shareholders of a professional corporation.

Each state has its own list of qualifying professions; in general, however, if the professionals involved can be sued for malpractice, they can establish a professional corporation. Examples of qualifying professionals include accountants, architects, chiropractors, dentists, engineers, harbor pilots, attorneys, pharmacists, psychiatrists, psychologists, physicians, nurses, optometrists, osteopaths, podiatrists, surgeons, surveyors, and veterinarians. Examples of professionals who do not qualify include insurance salespeople, nurse anesthetists, and real estate brokers.

⚘ Can the members of a professional corporation practice in more than one specialized profession?

No. Professional corporations are limited to one profession. An exception is made for professionals in the overlapping areas of architecture, engineering, and surveying but only to the extent allowed by the ethical rules of each profession.

Capitalization

⚘ What are the legally recognized forms of consideration that can be exchanged for stock?

Consideration can be in the form of money paid, labor performed, services actually rendered to or for the benefit of the corporation during its formation or reorganization, debts or securities canceled, or tangible or intangible property actually received either by the issuing corporation or by a wholly owned subsidiary. Promissory notes (unless adequately secured by collateral other than the shares acquired or unless permitted by law under an employee stock purchase plan) and future services are not permissible.

On the basis of these guidelines, the board of directors—or the shareholders, if the articles of incorporation give them the authority—determines which forms of consideration can be exchanged for the company's stock.

⊌ *My state's corporation statute says I must have $1000 of "paid-in" capital before I start business. What happens if I don't have $1000 in the bank?*

The answer depends on the state corporation statute. Under most states' laws, if a corporation begins business with less than the required $1000 paid-in capital, the directors of the corporation are personally liable for the unpaid balance, that is, the difference between $1000 and the amount of capital the corporation had when it started business. Note that all corporation statutes limit the liability to the unpaid balance.

⊌ *How much capitalization is enough?*

In general, a corporation should have enough available capital to meet its obligations. If the amount of capital is illusory or trifling compared with the business activity and the risks of loss, sufficient grounds might exist for denying the existence of the corporate entity. Courts frequently refer to "inadequate" capitalization as a basis for "piercing the corporate veil"—that is, finding individual shareholders personally liable. However, little discussion has been devoted to what degree of undercapitalization is sufficient to pierce the corporate veil. Clearly, at the time of formation, stock should be issued only in exchange for consideration that is recognized as sufficient under the law, and the amount of cash and other liquid assets on hand should be sufficient to meet the start-up costs and short-term obligations of the corporation. During operations, adequate capitalization should be looked at in terms of a combination of equity capital, loans, anticipated receipts from operations, insurance, and other sources of available funds.

Transfer Rights

⊌ *Can we restrict the transfer of shares of our closely held corporation?*

Yes. Depending on your point of view, restrictions on the transferability of shares are either one of the major benefits or one of the major detriments of closely held corporations.

⚜ How can the restrictions be a benefit or a detriment?

Because closely held corporations are usually both owned and operated by a close-knit group of individuals, it is essential that the owners be able to work together. Restricting the transfer of stock helps ensure that the shareholders can decide with whom they will work in managing the affairs of their closely held corporation.

On the other hand, share transfer restrictions can significantly affect the shares' value because they limit the market for the shares. For that reason, if statutes or agreements create transfer restrictions, owners should establish a specific market for, and price of, the shares of departing or deceased shareholders. Owners usually do this through buy-sell agreements that both restrict and define the market for closely held shares.

Buy-sell agreements can take several forms. *Stock redemption agreements* provide that the corporation will purchase the shares of a departing shareholder. *Cross-purchase agreements* provide for the purchase of shares by the remaining shareholders. Many buy-sell agreements are combination agreements that allow for either redemption of the stock by the corporation or a cross-purchase of the stock by the remaining shareholders. (These are called *wait-and-see agreements.*) In addition to establishing the market for the shares, a major purpose of a buy-sell agreement is to establish the value of the shares. (We discuss buy-sell agreements in detail in Part Five.)

⚜ As one of three shareholders, what can I do to prevent a shareholder from selling his or her shares to a stranger, thereby forcing me to own a business with someone not of my choosing?

If you want to restrict the ability of a shareholder to sell or otherwise transfer shares, you must do so specifically in the articles of incorporation, corporate bylaws, or separate shareholder agreements. For example, the provision can specify that a shareholder is allowed to transfer stock only to the corporation or other shareholders.

You must state your restrictions in the corporate documents because standard corporation laws were created primarily for publicly held corporations, for which restrictions are the exception rather than the rule.

I have close-corporation stock. How do I know whether transfer restrictions apply?

Many state statutes require that transfer restrictions be noted on close-corporation share certificates. For example, Wyoming's statutes provide that the following statement must appear conspicuously on each share certificate issued by a statutory close corporation:

> The rights of shareholders in a statutory close corporation may differ materially from the rights of shareholders in other corporations. Copies of the articles of incorporation and bylaws, shareholders' agreements, and other documents, any of which may restrict transfers and affect voting and other rights, may be obtained by a shareholder on written request to the corporation.

FORMATION

How do I form a corporation?

You form a corporation by filing articles of incorporation with the secretary of state in the state in which you want to incorporate. The state of incorporation is often, but not always, the state in which the corporation will conduct its business activities. If you incorporate in a different state, you must qualify the corporation to do business in the state in which it will conduct its principal activities.

Forming a corporation can be very complex. We recommend that you work with your business attorney, accountant, and financial advisor to determine whether the corporate structure is the best for your situation and to form it correctly.

☙ Why would I incorporate in one state and conduct business in another?

A prime reason is to take advantage of the laws of a particular state. For approximately 80 years it has been common for businesses to incorporate in Delaware because the state has a reputation for handling shareholder or control disputes quickly and efficiently. Unfortunately, Delaware also has a franchise tax on businesses incorporated there. Other states that are popular for incorporating large businesses include New York, Ohio, Illinois, Texas, and California.

For smaller corporations, the laws are not substantively different among the states. Still, some states may be better for incorporation than others. Delaware's franchise tax is a deterrent to small corporations, but states such as Nevada, Indiana, Florida, Minnesota, Wisconsin, and Washington may be of interest because they traditionally do not tax businesses simply for incorporating. However, unless there is a key advantage to incorporating in a different state, most businesses are advised to stay in their local jurisdictions.

☙ How do I form an S corporation?

To form an S corporation, first create a C corporation. After the formation of the C corporation, you can elect S corporation status for federal income tax purposes.

☙ How do I form a professional corporation?

You form a professional corporation the same way you form any other type of corporation—by filing articles of incorporation. In addition, most professional corporations must register with the agency that regulates the profession, for instance, the state bar association for attorneys.

⊰ *How do I form a close corporation?*

The procedure is the same as that for forming a regular corporation, but there may be additional requirements. For instance, forming a close corporation may require (1) a statement signed by all the shareholders in which they agree to be a close corporation and specifically acknowledge applicability of the close-corporation statute and (2) a conspicuous notice on every stock certificate stating that the agreement exists and applies to the shares.

Corporate Name

⊰ *Can I pick any name I want for my corporation?*

Yes—within certain limits, of course. You cannot incorporate under a name that is already in use, that is very similar to another name in use, or that might mislead the public. Also, there may be special restrictions on names for certain types of businesses, such as banks and savings and loan institutions. State requirements vary. For example, many states require that a corporate name include "Inc.," "Incorporated," "Co.," "Company," "Corp.," or "Corporation"—as notice to customers or creditors that they are doing business with a corporation. Your attorney will explain what your state law requires.

Common sense, marketing philosophies, and other legal restrictions should also prevail. For instance, you would not want to use a name that infringes on a trademark or trade name; that is libelous, offensive, or unrelated to your primary product or service; or that is hard to spell, difficult to remember or pronounce, or extremely long. Some states set a maximum length for corporate names. Name length is a practical issue as well: being known as "The Corporation Formerly Known as Prince" might make your commercials too long for radio spots!

⊰ *How do I name my professional corporation?*

You must include the words "associated," "professional association," or "professional corporation," or an abbreviation of any of those terms, in the name. It is not uncommon for the corporation to carry the name of one or more of the licensed professionals. However, this is not required, and many states allow the business to operate under a trade name or fictitious name. All other naming requirements are generally the same as those for any other type of corporation.

⚔ *What is a fictitious business name, and what do I have to do to obtain one?*

A *fictitious business name,* also known as a *doing-business-as (dba) name,* is a name that is different from the name of the legal entity. For example, you might form the XYZ Corporation but operate the business as Pets Galore. "Pets Galore" is a fictitious business name, and XYZ Corporation must file a fictitious-business-name or trade-name statement with the required authorities, generally the secretary of state and perhaps offices of the counties in which Pets Galore operates.

Articles of Incorporation

⚔ *What do I have to include in the articles of incorporation?*

Each state's corporation statutes specify exactly what must be contained in articles of incorporation. Generally, articles of incorporation describe the purpose and structure of the company; some or all of the following information is included:

- Name of the corporation
- Duration of the corporation, which may be perpetual
- Purpose or purposes for which the corporation is organized (This may be stated as "any or all lawful business for which corporations may be incorporated.")
- Name of each director, with a minimum of one director
- Capital stock structure, including class, quantity, and rights of stock (e.g., "two classes of common stock, 50,000 shares each,

one voting and the other nonvoting"); par value, if any, of the stock; and statement as to whether there are preemptive rights in the stock and, if so, the terms (With *preemptive rights,* if there is a new issuance of stock for cash, current stockholders have the right of first refusal to purchase new shares, thereby preventing a dilution of their percentage of ownership.)

- Name and address of the statutory or registered agent
- Name and address of each incorporator
- If incorporated in carrying out a merger or plan of conversion, a statement to this effect

These are the typical, minimum requirements. The articles of incorporation may also include items not required. Frequently, attorneys add clauses about stated capital, voting requirements of shareholders, and protective provisions for directors and officers.

◢ᐤ *What is a statutory or registered agent?*

Imagine that you want to bring a lawsuit against a corporation. On whom would you serve the court papers? A shareholder? A director? An officer? An employee? And how would you know the identity and whereabouts of that person?

To facilitate the procedure, state laws require that a *statutory agent* or *registered agent* be appointed when a corporation is formed. This person resides in the state of incorporation and is the individual designated to accept service of process on behalf of the corporation. His or her name and address is a public record on file with, typically, the secretary of state, and anyone can obtain that information by phone.

A corporation must have a registered agent in each state in which it is registered to do business.

◢ᐤ *What is an incorporator?*

The *incorporator* is the person who signs the articles of incorporation. There can be one or more incorporators. The incorporator does not have to be a natural person; it could be another business, but a natural person must sign on the business's behalf.

If you are starting a corporation, you or your attorney will typically act as the incorporator. If your local newspaper regularly publishes a list of new corporations (obtained from state records), it most likely includes the name of the incorporator after the name of the corporation. Thus, the principal of the new business is implied. If you want to publicly announce your new enterprise in this fashion, ask your attorney to list you as the incorporator. If you want to retain your privacy for a while (e.g., you don't want your current employer to know you are forming a business), ask your attorney to sign the articles for you. Also discuss with your attorney whether it is typical in your region for the incorporator to receive a flood of direct-marketing mail, and discuss your preference regarding who should receive this mail.

Other Requirements

⋈ *What are corporation bylaws?*

Bylaws, also called *codes of regulations* in some states, are a written statement of day-to-day management procedures that govern the business actions of the corporation. Procedures that might be covered include how meetings of the shareholders are called and conducted, what constitutes a quorum, and how many votes are needed to pass a resolution; directors' minimum qualifications, terms, election, compensation, and liability and how their meetings are called and conducted; description of the officers' functions, powers, and duties; choice of fiscal year and other items related to corporate finances; provisions regarding share certificates and transfer restrictions; adoption of a close-corporation agreement, if applicable; and provisions for amending the bylaws or codes.

⋈ *What should we include in a close-corporation agreement?*

Ask your attorney to check your state's statute. Typical close-corporation agreements include provisions that:

- Eliminate the board of directors
- Designate in advance who will be the officers and directors (thus eliminating the need for annual elections)
- Create special voting requirements, such as unanimous approval or the binding of the shareholders in advance on how they will vote
- Give the power to dissolve the corporation at will to certain shareholders
- Determine who will be employed by the corporation, how long they will be employed, and how much they will be paid
- State how to distribute profits
- Require arbitration to resolve any deadlock

❧ *What else is required to form a corporation?*

You commence the business of the corporation, which is called *perfecting* the corporation. Perfecting a corporation includes, among other things, the following:

- The incorporator appoints a board of directors.
- The board of directors adopts the bylaws.
- The board issues, or directs the issuance of, corporate stock in exchange for the shareholders' capital contributions.
- The board may also appoint corporate officers to run the day-to-day affairs of the corporation.

❧ *Are there any other steps I should take at or near the time of incorporation?*

The corporation should apply for a federal employee tax identification number; obtain workers' compensation and unemployment insurance, as required by state law; select an accounting system (cash or accrual basis); select a bank or financial institution as a depository for corporate funds and, if necessary, have an adoption of a bank resolution; secure any necessary liability insurance and special licenses; and determine what, if any, sales taxes must be charged and paid to the proper authorities.

<hr style="width:30%">

MANAGEMENT

≼ *How do I determine the management structure of my corporation?*

A corporation has three distinct groups: shareholders, directors, and officers.

The *shareholders* own the corporation. Usually, they meet annually to elect the members of the board of directors. Shareholders generally vote to decide major items of business, such as mergers, acquisitions, and sale of the entire business or a major part of it. The types of decisions that require a shareholder vote are usually spelled out in each state's laws or in the articles of incorporation and bylaws of the corporation.

The *directors* have the general duty of managing the corporation. They do not manage the corporation on a day-to-day basis but, rather, establish corporate policy, goals, and objectives, which are implemented by the officers. Normally, the board of directors meets at least once each year, at which time the board elects the officers and conducts its other business. Some states' rules allow a small corporation to operate without a formal board of directors.

Officers carry out the directors' agenda and handle the day-to-day operations of the corporation. Generally, a corporation must have at least one officer who is authorized to record the minutes and maintain the records of the corporation. The bylaws can create as many officers as necessary to operate the corporation. Many corporations have, at minimum, a president, vice president, treasurer, and secretary. Generally, the president supervises the other officers and has the authority to execute all contracts in the corporation's name. The president's additional duties and responsibilities are stated in the bylaws. "Vice president" is the title given to any other officer who has the authority to administer departments, projects, or other responsibilities in the president's stead. The treasurer is responsible for supervising the financial books. The secretary is responsible for maintaining all the corporate records.

Can a person hold more than one office or be both an officer and a director?

Yes. In many closely held corporations, the board of directors consists of the persons who hold the majority of the stock, and the same persons fill all the officer positions. In corporations with only a single shareholder, it is not unusual for him or her to be the sole member of the board of directors and to serve as all the officers.

In corporations with few shareholders who also act as the directors and officers, the shareholders sometimes enter into a shareholders' agreement that allows the corporation to dispense with formal meetings by the board of directors. Management is vested exclusively with the shareholders, and all their decisions are binding on the corporation without the necessity of a formal meeting or board resolution.

How does the board of directors make decisions?

The board of directors generally acts by passing resolutions at a meeting of the board. The board cannot transact business unless a quorum—usually a majority—of directors is present at the meeting. Decisions are made by a majority vote.

In regard to small, closely held corporations, where the directors are also the shareholders, there is a common misconception that the "weight" of a director's vote, or the number of votes he or she can cast, is related to the number of shares he or she owns. For example, if there are two directors on a board, one of whom owns 51 percent of the outstanding stock and the other of whom owns 49 percent, many people erroneously believe that the director with 51 percent can carry the day on any vote because he or she owns more than half the corporation. This belief is based on confusion about the distinction between shareholders and directors and their respective powers. For the limited matters that are subject to a vote of the shareholders, the voting power of a shareholder is directly related to the number of shares he or she holds. For the far greater number of decisions that fall within the scope of the directors' authority, however, each director has a single vote, regardless of how many shares of stock he or she owns or whether the director is even a shareholder at all.

Written minutes of board meetings must be kept. Any resolutions passed should be reflected in the minutes, with the vote of each director properly noted.

While this might seem like a cumbersome decision-making process, it should be remembered that decisions on day-to-day operations are made by officers and the managerial employees working for them. In addition, if there is no dissent among the directors, they can pass resolutions without meeting by having all the directors sign a form commonly known as a "written action by the board of directors through unanimous consent." Such written actions must be kept with the minutes of the corporation.

I'm starting a company by myself. My attorney says I shouldn't be the only named officer. Why?

While it is perfectly acceptable for you to be the sole shareholder, sole director, and president, treasurer, and secretary, it may be necessary or prudent to have at least one other person as an officer. Some states require that corporate share certificates be signed by both the president and the secretary and that one person cannot sign in both capacities. In this case, you might want to name a spouse or another family member as assistant secretary (assuming the statute allows an assistant to sign) or as secretary (with you as assistant secretary).

Your attorney might also be thinking of practical considerations, such as the possibility that you might be absent due to illness or vacation. It might be a good idea to have someone else empowered to act for the corporation in an emergency. The role of vice president, assistant secretary, or assistant treasurer is commonly used for this purpose.

⊰ Who runs the professional corporation?

A professional corporation operates in much the same way as a regular corporation does. It is run by its officers, employees, and agents. Generally, in all decisions that relate to the practice of the licensed profession, only officers, employees, and agents who are properly licensed can participate. However, state statutes vary somewhat on the specifics of when an officer or director must be a licensed professional. Consult with your business advisor if you have any questions.

DOCUMENTATION

⊰ What are corporate formalities?

Corporate formalities are the steps a corporation must regularly take to ensure that its legal existence will be recognized as separate from that of its shareholders: A corporation must keep careful records of the stock it issues. A corporation must conduct at least one annual meeting of its shareholders and at least one annual meeting of its board of directors. Minutes of each meeting should be kept and must be made available for shareholders to inspect. A corporation must regularly report to the secretary of state the names of its officers and directors. And it must file annual tax returns with the IRS and, generally, state taxing authorities.

⊰ Why is there so much emphasis on these formalities?

One of the major reasons for doing business as a corporation is to protect shareholders and officers from personal liability for the actions of the business. If you fail to follow the corporate formalities, creditors may later claim that the corporation's separate existence should be disregarded and that the corporation's liabilities should pass through to its shareholders. This is particularly true when the shareholders have more money than the corporation. The corporation's creditors want to look beyond the assets of the corporation to those of its shareholders; that is, they would like to "pierce the corporate veil." If creditors can establish that the corporate formalities were not maintained, a court may allow the creditors to collect judgments from the personal assets of the shareholders, directors, or officers.

Documents showing that corporate formalities were observed are crucial to establish the fact that the corporation is a separate "person" from the shareholders.

COMPENSATION

≱ *How can I compensate myself as the owner, director, and officer of my corporation?*

You can compensate yourself in the following ways: corporate dividends, salary for your duties as an officer, a fee as a member of the board of directors, a fee for any corporate loan that you personally guarantee, and an auto allowance, as well as fringe benefits, retirement plans, health insurance, life and disability insurance, financial tax planning assistance, and the like. There are many ways for an owner to be "reasonably" compensated. Proper planning will help you determine the best forms of self-compensation.

≱ *Do I need to follow any formalities to set an executive salary?*

Yes. The board of directors should set the dollar amount of the salary at the beginning of the year; explain how it determined the salary; and keep a written record of the decision in the corporate minutes or the employment contract.

⚜ *You mentioned reasonable compensation. Why is this important?*

For income tax purposes, the corporation may deduct only "reasonable compensation." If the IRS determines that an employee's salary is excessive and the employee is a shareholder of the company, the IRS treats the excess compensation as a taxable dividend and the company may not deduct the excess amount. As long as compensation is reasonable, a shareholder's entire distribution from the company could be characterized as compensation, for which the company would receive an income tax deduction.

For some publicly traded corporations, the IRS limits reasonable compensation to $1 million for certain employees.

⚜ *How do I determine what's reasonable for my closely held corporation?*

Some of the factors to consider in determining reasonable salary are:

- What is the executive's job description?
- What are the executive's job qualifications?
- Is the salary comparable to other executives' salaries in similar positions at other companies?
- How large and complex is the company?
- How does the salary compare to the income of the company (e.g., is it 10 percent or 70 percent of the income)?
- What are the current economic conditions of the industry or profession and the community?

⚜ *As president of our S corporation, I put in many more hours than the other shareholders, so we've discussed increasing my salary. Can the IRS challenge the deductibility of my salary if it deems the amount to be unreasonable compensation.*

No. From the IRS perspective, S corporation status eliminates unreasonable-compensation problems for executive officers who are shareholders in the corporation.

⚞ *What does the IRS look for in determining whether payments are dividends or salary?*

Factors that alert the IRS that payments are dividends rather than salary include:

■ The corporation paid the employee-shareholder a bonus close to the end of the company's tax year.

■ The company paid only a small dividend or no dividend at all in recent years.

■ The salary or bonus was out of proportion to the employee-shareholder's stockholdings.

⚞ *Why are earnings usually paid out as salary in a personal service corporation?*

Personal service C corporations are taxed at a flat rate of 35 percent of taxable income; they can never be taxed at a rate lower than 35 percent. Therefore, unless the individual taxpayer's effective tax rate is more than 35 percent, it makes sense to pay all earnings out as salary.

DURATION

⚞ *How long does a corporation last?*

A corporation typically has perpetual existence. It will remain in existence forever unless:

■ The directors or a majority of the shareholders dissolve it.

- An inaction, such as failure to meet the state's filing requirements, causes its termination by default.
- It merges with another corporation.

Perpetual life is one of the benefits of the corporate structure and a major reason that many closely held businesses choose the corporate form of organization. The corporation does not terminate on the death of a shareholder, even if the shareholder is the sole shareholder. As a result, ownership of the corporation can be passed from generation to generation fairly easily, assuming that the shareholder has done proper succession planning.

⚖ *What happens if the shareholder of a professional corporation dies?*

Most states require that the shares be sold back to the corporation or be sold to another licensed professional. The sale must occur within a certain time limit; otherwise, the corporation may lose its status as a professional corporation. It is good planning to make arrangements ahead of time for the sale of stock on the death of a shareholder. Some states' PC statutes even require that the shareholders enter into a buy-sell agreement.

⚖ *Does a professional corporation immediately lose its PC status when a member dies and leaves his or her stock to a spouse who is not a licensed professional?*

State laws vary on this issue. Generally, the laws provide for a grace period so that professional corporation status is not immediately terminated when PC stock is left to a beneficiary who is not a licensed professional. The grace period is usually no longer than 6 months. During this period, the nonprofessional beneficiary may not participate in management of the business as it relates to rendering professional services. If the beneficiary does not transfer the shares to a qualified owner by the end of the grace period, the professional corporation will lose its status.

TAXATION

Tax-Free Formation

⋑ *I'm going to transfer some appreciated property to my company in return for stock. Do I have to recognize gain?*

Generally, no gain or loss is recognized by a person who contributes cash or other property to a C or S corporation solely in exchange for stock in the corporation, provided that the person is in control of the corporation immediately after the contribution. "In control" means that the person owns at least 80 percent of the total combined voting power of all classes of stock entitled to vote and at least 80 percent of the total number of shares of all other classes of stock. The corporation's basis in the property received is the same as the basis when the property was in the hands of the shareholder.

⋑ *I contributed assets to my corporation on its formation. What is my basis in the stock I received in exchange for the contribution?*

The basis of your stock is equal to the basis of the assets you contributed to your corporation for the stock. If any gain is recognized on the contribution of property to the corporation, your stock basis is increased by the amount of that gain.

⋑ *If one shareholder receives stock solely for the performance of services, what are the income tax consequences to other shareholders?*

The tax-free incorporation rules apply only to persons who transfer *property* to a new corporation. As the IRS rules state, "Stock or securities issued for services rendered or to be rendered to or for the benefit of the issuing corporation will not be treated as having been issued in return for property." Shares received by a person solely for services rendered are not counted in determining whether the transferors are in control of the corporation. As a result, if stock being transferred for services causes the rest of the shareholders who transfer property to own less than 80 percent of all classes of stock immediately after the exchange, the exchange will fail the tax-free incorporation rules and all transferors will be subject to tax on any resulting gain or loss.

≥ *Can we do anything to include the stock received for services in determining the required 80 percent control?*

If, in addition to rendering services, a person also transfers property in exchange for stock, the stock received is counted in determining control if the value of the stock received for property is not relatively small compared to the value of the stock received for services. The IRS has stated that if the fair market value of the property transferred is at least equal to 10 percent of the value of the stock received for services, the stock received for the property will not be considered as having a relatively small value.

≥ *When we set up our corporation, we were issued IRC Section 1244 stock. What is that, and are there any special rules I need to know about it?*

Internal Revenue Code *Section 1244 stock* is small-business corporation stock that was originally issued to an individual or partnership in exchange for money or property, and on the exchange the shareholders owned at least 80 percent of the authorized stock. Code Section 1244 defines a *small-business corporation* as one whose total capital and paid-in surplus do not exceed $1 million.

Special rules apply to Section 1244 stock. A loss on a subsequent sale or exchange or some other disposition of the stock is an ordinary loss to the selling shareholder rather than a capital loss. Ordinary losses are much more useful because they offset ordinary income, whereas capital losses can offset only capital gains and up to $3000 of ordinary income each year. The Section 1244 loss is limited to $50,000 for an unmarried individual or $100,000 for a married couple filing a joint return, and in either case it cannot exceed gross income.

If you transfer Section 1244 stock to a trust or sell or exchange it at a gain, it loses its Section 1244 status. However, if you leave it on death to your heirs, it retains its status.

⊴ *Is there an income tax advantage to having a C corporation treated as a qualified small business?*

The owners of qualified-small-business stock receive special income tax benefits on its sale if certain requirements are met. If the owner sells the stock after owning it for more than 5 years, he or she is entitled to exclude 50 percent of the gain recognized on the sale.

Qualified-small-business stock is any C corporation stock originally issued after August 10, 1993, in a qualified small business. A *qualified small business* is any active qualified trade or business whose assets never exceed $50 million. A qualified business is any business *not* involved in the following:

- The performance of services in health, law, engineering, architecture, accounting, actuarial science, performing arts, consulting, athletics, financial services, or brokerage services
- Banking, insurance, financing, leasing, investing, or similar business activity
- Any farming business
- The production or extraction of oil, gas, or other natural deposits
- The operation of a hotel, motel, or restaurant

Satisfying all the requirements to obtain the gain exclusion on sale is best accomplished by working closely with your tax advisor.

Taxes and Deductions

⫸ How are cash distributions to shareholders treated by the corporation?

A distribution of cash is generally treated as a dividend and does not result in any gain or loss to an S corporation or a regular C corporation. However, if the distribution is appreciated property, the gain is recognized at the corporate level. For this reason, be cautious when distributing corporate assets to shareholders. The distribution may force the corporation to pay income tax on the difference between the corporate cost basis in the asset and its fair market value.

⫸ If services are rendered to the corporation in exchange for stock, is the corporation entitled to an income tax deduction?

In general, a person who receives stock for services must treat the stock as compensation income at the time the right to receive the stock becomes unconditional. The amount of the income equals the stock's fair market value as of the date received. For the corporation, the income tax treatment is determined by whether the services were for an ordinary business expense or were related to the acquisition or creation of an asset. For example, if the stock is issued to an attorney in exchange for organizing the corporation, the stock's value is capitalized by the corporation as organization costs and thus is subject to amortization.

C corporation

⫸ How is a C corporation taxed?

A C corporation is subject to federal income tax on its income. The tax on the corporation may result in what is called *double taxation*. Double taxation means that the profits accumulated after the payment of corporate-level tax, if any, are subject to further federal income tax at the shareholders' level when those profits are distributed to them.

☙ What are the federal corporate income tax rates?

A C corporation's income is taxed at the C corporation's marginal income tax rates, as shown in Table 7-1.

☙ Can you give me an example of double taxation?

Let's assume ABC Corporation's adjusted gross income is $150,000 and the company pays dividends totaling $50,000 to its three shareholders, all of whom are in the 31 percent marginal tax bracket. On its gross income, ABC pays corporate taxes of $41,750 (see Table 7-1: $22,250 + [39% × $50,000]). In addition, on their dividends, the shareholders pay income taxes totaling $15,500 (31% × $50,000). Thus, the dividends are taxed twice: as part of gross income and as dividends.

☙ What is the corporate accumulated earnings tax?

Because of the double taxation of dividends, some corporations avoid dividend distributions to minimize taxes. Instead, they let the corporation's earnings accumulate. The *corporate accumulated-earnings tax* is a penalty tax imposed on corporations that accumulate too much in earnings rather than distributing the earnings to shareholders. The accumulated-earnings tax is equal to the highest individual tax rate imposed on single-return filers.

A corporation has a minimum credit of $250,000 ($150,000 for certain personal service corporations) against accumulated earnings and profits and a maximum credit equal to the amount of money necessary to meet the reasonable future needs of the business. Consequently, once a corporation's accumulated earnings and profits exceed $250,000, the corporation may be subject to the accumulated-earnings tax penalty if it cannot establish that it retained the excess amount for reasonable business needs.

TABLE 7-1   Federal Corporate Income Tax Rates

If taxable income is		The tax is	Of amount over
Over	But not over		
$ 0	$ 50,000	15%	$ 0
50,000	75,000	$7,500 + 25%	50,000
75,000	100,000	$13,750 + 34%	75,000
100,000	335,000	$22,250 + 39%	100,000
335,000	10,000,000	$113,900 + 34%	335,000
10,000,000	15,000,000	$3,400,000 + 35%	10,000,000
15,000,000	18,333,333	$5,150,000 + 38%	15,000,000
18,333,333	–	35%	

S corporation

⚑ How is an S corporation taxed?

An S corporation is a special type of corporation for federal income tax purposes. Ordinarily, the corporation does not bear any federal income tax at the corporate level. All corporate-level income or loss is treated as being distributed, or passed through, directly to the shareholders. The shareholders are taxed on their distributive share of income or loss.

⚑ Are there any cases in which S corporations, not the shareholders, are subject to federal income tax?

Yes. There are a few situations that could generate corporate taxation. For example, an S corporation could be subject to capital gain tax and built-in gains on corporate assets, which may be triggered when the corporation distributes appreciated property to its shareholders. Also, if an S corporation is deemed to have too much passive income, it could be taxed on any excess net passive income. Check with your tax advisor for details.

Tax Filing Requirements

C corporation

⅍ *What are the tax-return filing requirements for a C corporation?*

Taxable income is computed for a period of time called a *tax year,* which is usually a calendar year or a fiscal year. C corporations enjoy flexibility in selecting their tax years and usually can choose tax years that are different from the tax years used by shareholders. In addition, newly formed corporations usually may choose any approved accounting period they want to use, without obtaining the consent of the IRS.

C corporations using a fiscal year must file annual tax returns 2½ months after the end of the fiscal year. C corporations using the calendar year must report business income or loss on Form 1120 on or before March 15 of each year. Like many individuals, C corporations using the calendar year must pay their federal income taxes at least quarterly. Quarterly payments are due on March 15, June 15, September 15, and December 15.

Federal taxes are deposited in local banks. If the state requires quarterly deposits, the payments must be sent directly to the state. The amounts and frequency of tax deposits depend on several factors, including the amount of taxes paid in the previous year, the amount of profits earned during the current year, and whether the corporation is considered a "large corporation" for federal income tax purposes.

⅍ *My C corporation does business in several states. Does it have to file a tax return in each of these states?*

As a general rule, yes. If your corporation is registered in a state and does business in that state (even if it does not have an office there), it must file a tax return for that state and pay state taxes. The allocation of taxable income is proportionate, generally based on the revenue earned in the state or a percentage of total revenue.

Because each state is unique, proper state tax planning is critical to minimize overall state taxes. Find an advisor with a good working knowledge of the tax laws of the states in which your firm operates.

S corporation

⚔ *How do I make the election for S corporation status?*

All the shareholders must sign IRS Form 2553. If even one shareholder objects, the corporation cannot be an S corporation. Form 2553 must be filed with the IRS before the fifteenth day of the third month after the earliest of the following: (a) the date the company first had shareholders; (b) the date the company first had assets; (c) the date the company began operations; or (d) the beginning of the company's taxable year. If you make the S election later, the company is treated as a C corporation for its first year. The S election automatically becomes valid for the next taxable year without any further action on the part of the company or the shareholders.

⚔ *Is it possible to elect S status and later change it?*

Yes. You can terminate an S election by written request or by matter of law, such as obtaining a nonqualifying shareholder, which automatically terminates the election. To terminate by written request, submit the request within the first 75 days of the company's taxable year.

Timing the termination of your corporation's S status can be critical, because you must wait 5 years before you can reelect S status. Because of the difference in tax rates for corporations and individuals, properly timed S election and S termination can be excellent tax-planning tools. Use them wisely!

⚔ *What choice of tax year do I have with an S corporation?*

Generally, an S corporation must use the calendar year, unless it can establish a business purpose for having a different tax year.

≥∆ *What are the tax-return filing requirements for an S corporation?*

An S corporation using the calendar year must report business income or loss on Form 1120S on or before March 15 of every year.

Taxation of Dividends

≥∆ *Are noncash distributions to shareholders subject to income taxes?*

Corporations generally may not distribute cash or property to shareholders in a tax-free manner. Distributions of property result in income just as if the property had been sold by the corporation for its fair market value. If the corporation is an S corporation, the gain, if any, is recognized by the shareholder, rather than the corporation.

C corporation

≥∆ *How are cash distributions from a C corporation treated by the shareholders for tax purposes?*

Distributions of a C corporation's earnings and profits (E&P) generate dividend income for shareholders up to the amount of the E&P. After all the E&P has been distributed, any excess distributions are treated as a tax-free return of capital, that is, a reduction of the shareholder's stock basis. When the stock basis is reduced to zero, any further distributions are taxed as capital gain.

TABLE 7-2   S Corporation Pass-Through: Owners' Taxes

Owner	Distribution		Marginal tax bracket, %		Tax due
Bob	$25,000	×	.15	=	$3750
Carol	25,000	×	.28	=	7000
Ted	25,000	×	.31	=	7750
Alice	25,000	×	.36	=	9000

⊿ *How are distributions of earnings and profits to shareholders of a C corporation taxed to the shareholders?*

Dividends paid from a C corporation are taxed at the ordinary-income tax rates of the individual shareholder receiving the dividends.

S corporation

⊿ *How does the pass-through of profits and losses of S corporations work?*

As a practical matter, since there is no income tax at the corporation level, no benefit is achieved by artificially inflating salary rather than distributing dividends. Amounts distributed to individual shareholders are dividends (to the extent that there are accumulated or current earnings and profits). The dividends are subject to ordinary-income treatment by the shareholders.

For example, let's assume we have an S corporation with four shareholders, each of whom has 25 percent ownership. Let's also assume that all the owners are in different individual marginal income tax brackets. The corporation earned $100,000 during the last taxable year. Each owner is deemed to have received $25,000 in S corporation income, whether it was distributed or not. The income tax consequences to each owner differ as this income is applied to each individual's personal income and tax situation. Each owner's income tax consequence is shown in Table 7-2.

⊿ *How are cash distributions from an S corporation treated by the shareholders for tax purposes?*

When an S corporation has no accumulated earnings and profits, the taxation of a distribution totally depends on the shareholder's basis in his or her stock. The distribution is nontaxable up to the value of the stock basis. Distributions received after the stock basis has been exhausted are treated as capital gain.

If an S corporation has earnings and profits, tax-free distributions generally can be made up to the corporation's *accumulated adjusted account (AAA)*. After all the AAA has been distributed, any excess distributions are treated as a return of capital and a reduction of stock basis. When the stock basis is reduced to zero, any further distribution is taxed as capital gain.

⊿ *What is the tax result when distributions from an S corporation are more than the corporation's earnings in that year?*

Distributions from an S corporation that are greater than current-year earnings are considered a return of principal and lower the tax cost basis of the subchapter S stock position. Let's assume the cost basis of shares is $10,000. If the corporation's earnings are $5000 and distributions are $6000, the excess $1000 distribution reduces the shareholder's cost basis of the stock to $9000. (See Table 7-3.)

If the cost basis of the stock is reduced to zero, any additional distributions that exceed the cost basis are taxed. Let's assume this time that S earnings are $5000 and distributions are $16,000. The consequences are shown in the right-hand column of Table 7-3. The cost basis of the shares is now zero for all future distributions. The result, this year, is a $1000 taxable distribution.

LIABILITY

Actions of the Business

⊿ *What protection do I have from the contract liabilities of my corporation?*

As a general rule, a corporation's shareholders are not liable for the corporation's contract liabilities to third parties beyond the amount

TABLE 7-3   S Distributions in Excess of Earnings: Tax Result

| | Distributions greater than | |
	Earnings	Stock cost basis
S earnings	$ 5,000	$ 5,000
S distribution	6,000	16,000
Distribution in excess of earnings	1,000	11,000
Shareholder's cost basis of shares	10,000	10,000
Shareholder's reduced cost basis	9,000	
Taxable distributions	–	1,000

of the shareholder's investment. There are, however, a few exceptions:

1. Some states subject shareholders to liability for wages due to corporate employees.

2. A shareholder is liable for the contract debts of the corporation when he or she guarantees those liabilities. The guarantee can be express, as in the case of a written guarantee, or it can be implied, as is the case when a shareholder fails to make clear that he or she is acting for the corporation when entering into a contract.

3. A shareholder can be liable for the corporation's contract debts when a court determines that corporate formalities have not been met and the corporate veil should be pierced.

What do you mean when you say that corporate formalities haven't been met and creditors can pierce the corporate veil?

An advantage of doing business as a corporation is that it is a legal entity separate from its owners and, as such, is responsible for its own actions. A legal doctrine known as *alter ego* provides the exception to this rule. Basically, alter ego means that there are defects in the formation and maintenance of the corporation—the shareholders have failed to treat the corporation as a separate legal entity and instead have treated it as their own "alter ego." This is a matter of serious concern to the owners of closely held corporations.

In almost any lawsuit involving a corporation, the first thing the creditor's attorney will do is check with the secretary of state or department of state to determine whether the corporation has filed all the required documents and is in good standing with the state. In addition, the creditor's attorney will obtain a court order to examine corporate records to see whether they meet required corporate formalities.

The courts have considered many factors in applying the alter-ego doctrine. Some of the more prevalent circumstances giving rise to personal liability include:

- Failing to adequately capitalize a corporation or maintaining it with a near-total absence of corporate assets
- Commingling the funds or other assets of the corporation with those of the shareholders or improperly diverting corporate funds or assets to personal use
- Failing to issue stock or issuing stock for insufficient consideration
- Failing to hold annual shareholders' and board of directors' meetings, to maintain minutes, and to otherwise comply with required formalities
- Using the corporation as a mere shell or conduit for the personal activities of the shareholders
- Shareholders' failing to maintain an arm's-length relationship in their personal transactions with the corporation

If the court determines that the corporation did not follow the required formalities, it may decide that the alter-ego doctrine applies. In such cases. the court may allow a creditor to "pierce the corporate veil," meaning that the creditor can proceed directly against the shareholders to satisfy its claim. You do not want to find yourself in this position.

⚐ *How do I minimize potential alter-ego liability?*

First and foremost, make sure you comply with all the requirements for forming, perfecting, and maintaining your corporation. In addition:

- Hold annual meetings of the shareholders and board of directors, and maintain minutes and proper corporate resolutions.

- Issue stock certificates in exchange for the consideration that is recognized as legally sufficient under the law.

- Correctly classify shareholders who perform services for the corporation as employees, and pay them through a payroll system with proper deductions and withholdings. These shareholders should not take draws from the corporate account.

- Be reasonable in relating compensation for services to the actual services rendered, and maintain some retained earnings.

- Make distributions to shareholders as dividends. Make distributions only when allowable under the recognized accounting tests.

- Keep personal transactions between the shareholders and the corporation on terms and conditions within the range one would expect to see between two unrelated individuals or entities, and properly document all such transactions.

For example, a loan to a shareholder from the corporation or to the corporation from a shareholder should be supported by an authorizing resolution from the board of directors and should reflect reasonable business terms.

⚜ *How do I minimize potential alter-ego liability when I have two corporations?*

In addition to following all the procedures described in the previous answer, you should:

- Maintain separate books of account. Ensure that any consolidated financial statements are prepared according to generally accepted accounting principals.
- Maintain separate bank accounts.
- If the two corporations share office space, have separate leases for each corporation, or have one corporation sublease from the other. Separate suite numbers are helpful, as are separate telephone lines and numbers.
- If the corporations share employees, make sure both corporations pay for their services, either by using direct payroll or by having one corporation reimburse the other.

⚜ *My spouse and I own all the stock of our corporation. If our business goes bankrupt, will we lose our house?*

If you have treated your corporation as a separate legal entity and respected the formalities that go with a corporation, your personal assets will be at risk only if you personally guaranteed the corporation's debts. Tenacious creditors will sometimes attempt to reach your personal assets by arguing, for instance, that the corporation was undercapitalized or that it was your alter ego.

In general, according to court rulings, if you adequately capitalize the corporation, document all transactions between you and the corporation, keep good records, title the corporation's property in the name of the corporation, don't commingle your funds or property with the corporation's funds and property, and generally treat the corporation as a separate legal entity, you should enjoy the limited liability protection that corporations offer. However, the reverse is also true: people have been held personally liable for the debts of a corporation because they did not respect the corporation as a separate legal entity.

⅍ *As a shareholder in a professional corporation, am I protected individually from being sued by the creditors of the business and from liability for any professional negligence by my business partners?*

No business entity insulates licensed professionals from liability if their actions amount to malpractice. However, for liabilities that are not related to the rendering of professional services (e.g., paying rent under a lease arrangement), a professional corporation or some other limited liability entity shields shareholders from the liabilities of the business. In addition, a professional corporation shields each professional within it from liability for malpractice by the other member professionals.

⅍ *As an officer of the corporation, can I incur liability?*

Generally, no officer of a corporation can be held liable simply on the basis of acting within the scope of his or her authority. However, all officers have an obligation to perform their duties in good faith and with the degree of care that a reasonably prudent person in a similar position would use under similar circumstances. Officers are liable for any breach of this obligation. In addition, officers have been held to be fiduciaries of the corporation, which imposes on them a high standard of conduct in the best interests of the corporation and strictly forbids any self-dealing or fraud. Any breach of this fiduciary duty would result in personal liability.

Officers of a corporation also can be liable for payroll withholding taxes and for any Social Security and Medicare taxes or union dues withheld from employees' paychecks. Each state may impose additional duties and responsibilities, so check with an attorney in the state of incorporation.

⅍ *What protection do officers, directors, and shareholders have from their corporation's tort liabilities?*

A corporation offers great protection from tort liabilities. If a corporation, while acting through its employees, agents, or representatives, commits a tort, such as personal injury or wrongful death, the corporation and the person who caused the harm can be sued for the conduct. However, the officers, directors, and shareholders cannot be sued unless they actually caused the harm. This is particularly relevant in the service industry, where a shareholder-employee might be personally liable for his or her own acts in providing services to a customer of the corporation. For example, a real estate agent handling the purchase of a house could be held liable for fraud or negligence in connection with the transaction even though the real estate business is operated as a corporation.

Actions of the Shareholders

*Are the assets of my corporation protected from its shareholders'
personal creditors?*

A corporation is ordinarily not responsible for the debts and liabilities of its shareholders. There are several exceptions to this rule, however.

The corporation may be liable for the debts of one or more of its shareholders if those employee-shareholders reasonably caused parties with whom they contracted to believe that they were acting on the corporation's behalf and not on their own behalf.

A second exception is sometimes referred to as a *reverse piercing* of the corporate veil. In a reverse piercing, the assets of the corporation are deemed to be indistinguishable from the assets of one or more of the corporation's shareholders. Courts that follow the reverse-piercing doctrine are more likely to apply it in situations similar to those under which the courts might pierce a corporate veil. As discussed earlier, such situations involve failure to observe corporate formalities, fraudulent or illegal conduct by a shareholder, or other conduct that is inequitable or contrary to public policy. Courts may be less likely to impose a reverse piercing when there are innocent shareholders, because those shareholders' interests in the corporation will be applied to satisfy the debt at issue.

REAL ESTATE OWNERSHIP

✒ *Should my C corporation own the real estate on which the business is conducted?*

As a general rule, it is not a good idea for a C corporation to own real estate. This is primarily a tax issue. Since C corporations are separate taxable entities and most distributions of their assets are taxable to the recipient, the result is double taxation. Thus, when a corporation is ready to conclude its operations and dissolve its business, the sale of its assets could be a taxable event (capital gain taxes). Later, when it distributes the proceeds of the sale to the shareholders, the shareholders will pay tax on those proceeds. The same result occurs if the corporation distributes its assets "in kind" to the shareholders and then the shareholders sell the assets.

A better arrangement is for you to own the real estate individually, or create a limited liability company or limited partnership to own it, and then lease the real estate to your C corporation. The benefit of this is that there will be no entity-level tax when the real estate is sold or distributed to you.

✒ *Are there any other benefits of my corporation's not owning the land and office building?*

Yes. If you, your LLC, or your limited partnership own the office building and land, there are several benefits in addition to avoiding corporate taxation on a future sale of the property. You receive additional remuneration in the form of rent, and you recognize appreciation on the property. You can plan more easily for income and estate taxes. After you retire, you will have a stream of income in the form of rent, without having to reduce Social Security benefits.

✒ *If I plan on owning real estate, should I still consider making an S election?*

When an S corporation distributes appreciated property to its shareholders, the distribution is treated as if the corporation sold the property for its fair market value. If the property has a value in excess of its basis, the corporation must recognize the gain at the corporate level. The taxable gain is the amount by which the distributed property's fair market value exceeds its adjusted basis on the date of distribution to the shareholders.

Thus, if you don't expect to distribute the real estate or other appreciated property to the shareholders, but expect to keep it in the corporation or sell it while the corporation owns it, an S election may be appropriate. However, if at some future time you might want to distribute the property to the shareholders, an S election may not be appropriate. You may want to consider a limited liability company instead, because the limitation does not apply with LLCs.

There is a caution: If the property is depreciated, the same rules apply to the extent of the difference between the depreciated cost of the property and the fair market value when distributed to the shareholder.

CONDUCTING BUSINESS
IN OTHER STATES

How can my corporation do business in more than one state?

State laws vary. Generally, the corporation must file a document with the secretary of state to register as a "foreign" corporation. The filing qualifies the corporation to do business in that state. Check the state laws for other requirements, such as annual renewal of the foreign corporation registration.

Can a professional corporation conduct business in states other than the one in which the corporation was formed?

A professional corporation can conduct business in another state as long as at least one shareholder is a licensed professional in that state. For example, a law firm corporation that operates in both California and Nevada must have at least one shareholder who is licensed to practice law in both states.

RECOMMENDATIONS

◢ Does a C corporation work well for start-ups?

For many start-ups, no. Start-ups require large investments of money during the first years of operation, when greater losses tend to occur. Shareholders generally want to obtain tax deductions for the losses they incur, but losses in a C corporation do not pass through to the shareholders; they must be retained in the corporation to offset any future net income. However, if the business expects to go public quickly, the organization must be a C corporation when the time to go public arrives.

◢ Should we use a corporate structure for our family business?

One of the greatest concerns, especially for small family-owned businesses, is that the required corporate formalities can be difficult to maintain. It is not uncommon to find family-owned corporations that have never issued shares of stock, never conducted meetings as required by law, and never complied with other important corporate formalities. In such cases a creditor may be able to pierce the corporate veil; that is, a court may determine that the business is a partnership instead of a corporation, that the corporation is simply the alter ego of the owners, and therefore that all the owners are jointly and severally liable for the debts and other liabilities of the business.

Generally, taxation is one of the most important issues to consider when you are selecting an ownership structure. The double taxation of C corporations can be avoided with an S corporation. Other taxes to consider are Social Security and Medicare taxes. Usually, distributions of income to shareholders of C or S corporations are not subject to Social Security and Medicare taxes.

ADVANTAGES AND DISADVANTAGES

Can you summarize the advantages and disadvantages of corporations?

Advantages

- A corporation provides centralized management.
- Corporate shareholders have limited liability protection from the corporation's actions.
- The corporation's assets are protected from shareholders' creditors.
- Shareholders may be restricted by a shareholders' agreement from freely transferring ownership interests to outside parties.
- The corporate structure is excellent for complex financing or raising capital.
- Corporations commonly obtain both equity and debt financing.
- The issuance of stock, either to existing or new shareholders, is an easy means of raising capital for expanding the business.
- A corporation can have perpetual life; that is, the business can continue after the death, disability, or retirement of the original shareholders.

Disadvantages

- Forming a corporation involves filing articles of incorporation, issuing stock certificates, and, generally, having the shareholders enter into an agreement governing the operation of the corporation.

- To receive limited liability protection, owners must treat the corporation as a separate entity: corporate formalities must be followed, the corporation must have its own bank account, and the corporation's funds cannot be commingled with shareholders' funds.

- Persons performing services for the corporation, including shareholders, must generally be considered employees and paid through payroll, with state and federal withholdings and deductions made.

- Shareholders generally are not allowed to "draw" from the corporate funds.

- Scrutiny by the IRS and state taxing authorities might affect the amount of compensation a shareholder or employee can receive in the form of salary, bonuses, and the like, as opposed to just taking dividends from after-tax profits.

- Corporations have a very defined and rigid management structure. Generally, shareholders have to elect a board of directors, who in turn appoint officers to run day-to-day operations. This might be cumbersome and confusing if there are only a few shareholders.

- In some states, a corporation must pay a minimum tax every year even if it shows a loss on paper.

Are there any advantages and disadvantages that pertain only to C corporations?

Yes. In addition to the items listed above, the following apply to C corporations:

Advantages

- A C corporation can be owned by an unlimited number of any type of "persons" (corporations, partnerships, trusts, estates).
- A C corporation may issue different classes of stock with various

rights, so it is the best ownership structure if shareholders want to go public.

■ Fringe benefits for owners who are employees are usually fully deductible against the corporation's income.

■ If the C corporation is a qualified small business, the owner may exclude 50 percent of the gain on the sale of his or her stock if certain requirements are met.

Disadvantages

■ Typically, there is double taxation: a C corporation pays corporate income tax on its earnings and the shareholders pay income tax on the dividends they receive from the corporation.

■ C corporations cannot pass losses through to their shareholders. Only when the shareholders sell their stock at a loss do they have the opportunity to generate a loss for tax purposes that may offset income from other sources.

⚮ *What are the specific advantages and disadvantages of an S corporation?*

An S corporation has the same advantages and disadvantages as corporations in general (see the first question in this section), as well as the following:

Advantages

■ There is no taxation on income at the corporate level.

■ Income and losses pass through to the shareholders.

Disadvantages

■ An S corporation is limited to seventy-five shareholders, all of whom must be certain individuals, certain types of trusts, and certain types of estates.

- An S corporation can have only one class of stock, although it can be issued with voting and nonvoting rights.
- The S election can be terminated unwittingly by not adhering to the IRS requirements.
- All corporate-level income is treated for tax purposes as if it had been distributed to the shareholders, whether it was actually distributed or not.

Are there any particular advantages and disadvantages of a professional corporation?

Advantages

Professional corporations offer all the advantages of either a C corporation or an S corporation, depending on which corporate form the professionals select.

Disadvantages

In addition to having the same disadvantages as other corporations, PCs have two other drawbacks:

- Generally, stock can be sold only to persons licensed in the specific profession or back to the corporation.
- The professionals cannot use the corporate shield for actions taken as part of rendering their professional services.

What are the advantages and disadvantages of a close corporation?

Close corporations have the same advantages and disadvantages as other corporations, as well as the following:

Advantages

- Statutes allow more flexibility in structuring close corporations (e.g., permitting management by shareholders rather than boards of directors, reducing corporate formalities, and recognizing the needs of minority shareholders).

Disadvantages

- The number of shareholders is limited.
- There are restrictions on the transfer of shares.
- Not every state has adopted the statutory close corporation.

chapter 8

Limited
Liability
Company

⚶ *What is a limited liability company?*

The *limited liability company (LLC)* is a fairly recent entity. Its creation and operation are governed by state law. The owners are generally referred to as *members.* An LLC is a hybrid business form that combines the best characteristics of the limited partnership and the corporation. The LLC provides flexibility in structure and organization that few other entities can match:

FORMALITIES: An LLC requires fewer formalities than a corporation to create and maintain, but it provides shareholders with the same level of liability protection as a corporation does.

TAXATION: An LLC can be taxed as a partnership, a corporation, or even a sole proprietorship (in the case of a single-member LLC). The vast majority of multiple-member LLCs choose to be taxed as a partnership to receive most of the tax benefits of the partners in a limited partnership. Virtually all single-member LLCs choose to be taxed as a sole proprietorship.

LIMITED LIABILITY: Members of an LLC enjoy limited liability without strict formality constraints. There is no requirement that *any* member have unlimited liability, as is the case with the general partners of a general or limited partnership.

MANAGEMENT: An LLC offers flexibility in the management of the business. The LLC can be managed by members or managers without the necessity of electing a board of directors and appointing officers, as is required for a corporation. The management function can be completely severed from ownership, so members of an LLC can be actively involved in management without losing their limited liability. This is unlike the case in a limited partnership, in which a limited partner may not work in the business without the risk of losing the limited liability protection.

⅍ *What is a professional LLC?*

A *professional LLC* is an entity that is formed by certain licensed professionals under special state statutes. Many states have special rules for professionals, such as accountants, lawyers, or insurance agents, who want to form an LLC. Some states treat professional LLCs as regular LLCs; others refer to them as *professional limited liability companies (PLLCs)*.

OWNERSHIP

⅍ *Who owns an LLC?*

An LLC is owned by its members. It may issue certificates (similar to stock certificates for corporations) to its members as evidence of their membership interests. A membership interest in an LLC is personal property; this means that a member has no interest in the specific property of the LLC but only a percentage interest in the LLC.

⚐ *Who may be a member of an LLC?*

Any person or entity that can legally enter into a contract may be a member of an LLC. This includes any domestic or foreign corporation, partnership, limited partnership, trust, estate, and natural person, as well as another LLC.

⚐ *How does a person become a member of an LLC?*

Generally, a person becomes a member of an LLC in accordance with the terms and procedures set forth in the *operating agreement,* which is the controlling document of an LLC. Normally, doing so requires a contribution of capital (typically cash or property) to the LLC when it is initially created.

After the formation of the LLC, a person may be admitted as a member by acquiring a membership interest directly from the LLC or from an existing member who, under the operating agreement, has the right to transfer his or her interest. Unless the operating agreement provides otherwise, some states require the vote of two-thirds of voting members for admission of new members, while other states require only a simple majority vote.

⚐ *Can members have different ownership rights?*

An LLC's articles of organization and operating agreement may provide for different classes or groups of members with different rights, powers, preferences, and limitations. For example, the operating agreement may allow, or withhold from, one or more classes of members the right to vote on any matters, on the basis of their respective capital contributions.

⚐ *What happens if our agreement does not specify each member's rights?*

If the operating agreement and the articles of organization do not state otherwise, under state statutes members are entitled to (1) participate in managing the LLC; (2) vote in person or by proxy on a wide variety of issues, including admission of new members, approval of additional liabilities for the LLC, changes in the articles of organization or operating agreement, dissolution or continuation of the LLC, approval of a merger or consolidation with another LLC, and transfer of assets; (3) share the profits (and losses) and distributions; and (4) assign membership interests to outside parties.

⚥ How do we capitalize an LLC?

To capitalize an LLC, the initial members make contributions to the LLC in exchange for membership interests. Capital contributions may be in any form, including cash, property, promissory notes, services rendered, or any combination of these.

Transfer Rights

⚥ Can a member transfer his or her ownership interest?

Under typical state statutes, members of an LLC have "free-transfer" ability. This means they can transfer their ownership interests in the LLC to people who are not members without obtaining the consent of the other LLC members. However, the statutes usually provide that the transferee receives only an assignee interest and has no right to participate in the management and affairs of the LLC, unless otherwise specified in the operating agreement, until all the members approve the transfer and the transferee has complied with any procedure set forth in the articles of organization or the operating agreement.

⚥ Can we restrict the transferability of interests within our LLC?

Certainly. Many people create LLCs with restrictions on transfers so that members of the LLC have some control over whom they are in business with. These restrictions are set forth in the operating agreement.

Compensation

How are profits distributed to the members?

The operating agreement stipulates how gains, profits, losses, assets, and deductions are to be allocated among the members. For the most part, distributions are made on a pro-rata basis according to members' ownership interests in the LLC.

If a member works in the business, he or she typically receives compensation for the services provided, in addition to the pro-rata share of the distributions made to all members.

What are the income tax consequences of distributions to members?

A member generally has no taxable gain on distributions of cash or property as long as the distributions do not exceed the member's basis in his or her LLC interest. A member's basis is decreased by cash and other property distributed from the LLC to the member.

What is a member's basis in his or her LLC interest?

As a general rule, the basis of the member's interest is equal to the amount of cash and the basis of the assets the member transfers to the LLC in exchange for his or her interest.

FORMATION

Are the statutes governing LLCs similar from state to state?

Yes, but "similar" is the operative word. All the statutes provide for the basic formation and features of LLCs. However, many aspects differ, such as the number of members, duration, and regulations for doing business in other states. Therefore, you should meet with an attorney who is familiar with the specific requirements for the state in which you will create your LLC.

⚞ *How do I create an LLC?*

Generally, the rules for establishing LLCs are provided in state statutes. The process is commenced by filing articles of organization with the secretary of state and paying the filing fee.

The relationship among the members is governed by an operating agreement, which is analogous to a corporation's bylaws or a partnership agreement. Members of an LLC generally prescribe in the operating agreement the structure of their organization and the rules by which they will conduct business. If there is no operating agreement or the agreement does not address an item that is covered in the state LLC statute, the state statute governs.

⚞ *What must I include in the articles of organization for my LLC?*

The specific requirements of what must be included in the articles of organization are set forth in the LLC statutes of each state. Common requirements include:

■ The name of the limited liability company (including "LLC" or "PLLC," whatever your state requires)

■ The address of the LLC's business office

■ The name and address of the registered agent (the person on whom legal process can be served)

■ The purpose of the LLC (which may be stated as "any or all lawful business for which limited liability companies may be formed")

■ The initial contribution to be made to the LLC by each member

■ Whether the LLC will be managed by members or managers

■ The number of years that the LLC will exist

⚞ *Is it important for us to have an operating agreement?*

Like a corporation's bylaws and a partnership's partnership agreement, the operating agreement is the heart of an LLC's operating structure. We believe it is essential to have an operating agreement, even though your state's law may not require one. You should have a written operating agreement in place from the beginning to avoid future problems among members and to reinforce the fact that the LLC is a separate legal entity from the individual members.

≱ What should an operating agreement contain?

A well-drafted operating agreement should contain all of the most important aspects of the arrangement between the members. At a minimum, the agreement should address the following:

- The initial capital contributions from the members
- The rights of the members to receive distributions
- Members' voting rights
- Whether members will have equal management authority or whether they will elect or hire managers to conduct the affairs of the LLC
- The authority of and limits on the members or managers in managing the business
- Restrictions on the transfer of a member's interest
- The circumstances under which members can enter or leave the LLC
- The circumstances that would give rise to a member's right to a formal accounting, personal liability, or expulsion

This list is not comprehensive. If you are considering an LLC, it is important that you seek the advice of an attorney who can help you properly draft an operating agreement.

≱ What kinds of transfer restrictions can I put in our operating agreement?

You can include many types of transfer restrictions in the operating agreement. For example, the agreement can provide that (1) members can sell, transfer, or assign their interests only to other members; (2) existing members have the right of first refusal before a membership interest may be sold to an outside party; or (3) members can sell, transfer, or assign their interests to anyone, but the person receiving the interest obtains only the benefit of distributions (and the right to an accounting) but cannot participate in management. The operating agreement can also provide that a transfer that is in violation of any transfer restrictions will cause dissolution of the LLC.

⚖ Should we require the consent of a majority of the member interests or a unanimous agreement to perform certain actions?

It is not uncommon to require a "super majority" or a unanimous decision to accomplish any of the following:

- Dissolve the company or substantially sell all the property in liquidation or dissolution of the business
- Allow a sale or transfer of an interest to an outside party or add a new member
- Amend the articles of organization or the operating agreement
- Engage in any act that would subject any member to liability
- Change or reorganize the company into another legal form
- Make a non-pro-rata distribution or return of capital to any member
- Purchase, sell, or otherwise dispose of company property outside the ordinary course of business
- Add or substitute a manager of the company

⚖ Do I need an operating agreement to form a single-member LLC?

State statutes do not typically require an operating agreement for single-member LLCs. This is altogether sensible, since it is difficult for one person to make an "agreement" with himself or herself.

However, you might want to consider creating a simplified operating agreement to help establish the fact that the LLC is a separate legal entity. Such an agreement may also be of great practical value in obtaining bank accounts and other documents which require that you provide some evidence of organizational authority.

MANAGEMENT

⚔ How is an LLC managed?

There are two basic types of LLCs: member-managed LLCs and manager-managed LLCs. A *member-managed LLC* is operated much like a general partnership: the members have an equal say in the management of the business and an equal right to obligate the business by executing contracts on its behalf. A *manager-managed LLC* is operated like a corporation: the LLC appoints or hires one or more individuals or an entity, which may or may not be members, to manage the LLC. The choice of management structure must be stated in the articles of organization and in the operating agreement.

⚔ If members manage my LLC, can each member enter into agreements on behalf of the company?

If your LLC is member-managed, each member has the power to bind the LLC. Of course, this power can be modified in the operating agreement or the articles of organization. It can be stated, for example, that a majority vote of the managers is required before entering into any agreements that obligate the LLC.

⚔ If we have a manager-managed LLC, do the managers owe a fiduciary duty to members?

The managers of an LLC owe a fiduciary duty to its members. That is, they must act in good faith in business concerning the LLC, not take personal advantage of LLC opportunities, and act with reasonable care.

DOCUMENTATION

⚐ *What formalities must be observed in an LLC?*

Generally, by statute, very few formalities are required. However, it is important to run the LLC as a separate legal entity and to follow the formalities that help preserve the separateness of the company and the individual. It makes good business sense to have periodic meetings and to have members or managers keep notes of the meetings.

⚐ *Is an LLC required to maintain any records?*

Many LLC statutes require that a domestic LLC (one that is formed in the state where it has its principal offices) must maintain certain records, such as a current list of the names and addresses of members, along with their respective contributions and shares of profits and losses; a current list of the names and addresses of managers, if the LLC is manager-managed; a copy of the articles of organization and any amendments; a copy of the operating agreement and any amendments; and a copy of the LLC's federal, state, and local tax returns for the 3 most recent fiscal years. These records may be maintained in paper or electronic format.

⚐ *Do alter-ego issues or the formalities of maintaining a separate legal entity affect the limited liability of LLC members?*

LLC statutes do not require the meetings and minutes that corporate statutes typically do. However, members of an LLC are subject to the same arguments and issues surrounding alter ego and piercing the corporate veil that apply to corporations. These may apply if the LLC is undercapitalized or if a member treats the LLC as a personal checking account. (See Chapter 7 for details on alter ego and piercing the corporate veil.) To be cautious and to bolster members' limited liability protection, it makes sense to document all meetings and all actions taken on behalf of the LLC.

DURATION

⅍ *What is the duration of an LLC?*

State laws vary. In some states, an LLC may not exist indefinitely; it must state a specific length of time that it will be in existence. In these states, an LLC is usually terminated on the earliest of the following events: the agreement of the members to dissolve it; the bankruptcy of the LLC; the retirement, resignation, dissolution, bankruptcy, or death of a member; or the expiration of the term of the LLC selected by the members.

Other states allow an LLC to specify its duration as "perpetual." Since 1997 many states, including New York and California, have amended their statutes to grant perpetual existence to LLCs. Under these laws, an LLC is presumed to continue forever, even on the termination of a member's membership. LLCs formed in these states under the old laws (which presumed dissolution on the termination of any member's membership) may amend their operating agreements and articles of organization to acquire continuity of life.

Most often, the duration of the LLC must be stated in the articles of organization. It is important to verify this requirement with the state agency before filing the articles.

⅍ *My partner and I each own 50 percent of our business. What happens to our LLC if my partner dies or becomes mentally incompetent?*

Generally, despite the occurrence of one of these termination events, an LLC may continue if all the remaining members agree to have it do so. Most LLC operating agreements specify how member interests are treated on the death or disability of a member. Since single-member LLCs are now valid in all 50 states, you may be able to continue the business on your own after acquiring the deceased or incompetent member's interest.

⚖ *What happens to a member's interest in the LLC at his or her death?*

Typically, members can transfer their interests to their heirs through a will or trust, as they would any other personal property. Generally, the executor or administrator can exercise all the rights formerly available to the member, including the right to sell the interest in the LLC.

TAXATION

Taxes and Deductions

⚖ *What are the tax options for LLCs?*

For federal income tax purposes, a multiple-member LLC can be treated as a partnership or as a corporation, whichever the members choose. A single-member LLC can be taxed as a sole proprietorship or a corporation. If treated as a sole proprietorship or a partnership, the LLC passes income, expenses, gains, and losses to the member or members for inclusion on their individual tax returns.

⚖ *What happens when an LLC is taxed as a partnership?*

If the LLC chooses to be treated as a partnership, the profits and losses of the partnership typically pass through to the members in the manner dictated by the operating agreement. In this way the

LLC does not pay income taxes on its profits. (See Chapter 6 for details on partnership taxation).

◢ If my LLC elects to be taxed as a corporation, is it subject to double taxation?

An LLC treated as a corporation may be subject to the double taxation applicable to C corporations. In such cases, the LLC must recognize income and pay tax at the entity level; and when it makes distributions to members, the individual members must recognize income and pay tax on their distributions at their individual tax rates.

Often, this undesirable result can be avoided by having the LLC make an S election. However, to qualify to be taxed as an S corporation, an LLC must meet requirements concerning the number of owners and type of ownership (discussed in Chapter 7).

◢ How is my single-member LLC taxed?

If you wholly own the LLC, it is often advantageous to choose to be taxed as a sole proprietor. In this case, you file Schedule C, on which you report the business's profits and losses, as part of your IRS Form 1040. For many single-member LLCs, this is a simple and attractive option. A single-member LLC may also choose to pay taxes as an S or a C corporation. It cannot be taxed as a partnership since a partnership must consist of two or more persons.

◢ How are distributions treated by the LLC?

If the LLC is treated as a partnership or sole proprietorship, a distribution of cash or appreciated property generally does not result in any immediate tax gain or loss to the LLC. Such distributions are not subject to FICA or FUTA withholding. The LLC is a pass-through entity: the tax consequences of a distribution, if any, are borne by the member receiving the distribution.

⚔ *Is my LLC exempt from state taxation?*

In most states, no. Although some states have no income tax and do not tax businesses, most states follow the federal tax treatment election that the LLC makes. Thus, they tax LLCs treated as corporations but not those treated as partnerships or sole proprietorships. Texas imposes a franchise tax on LLCs.

Tax Identification Numbers

⚔ *Is a federal tax identification number required for an LLC?*

Yes, an LLC must have a federal tax identification number. In almost all cases, LLCs are required to file federal tax returns. The exception is a single-member LLC that chooses to be taxed as a sole proprietorship; however, if such an LLC has employees, it needs a federal tax identification number for reporting payroll taxes.

⚔ *What choice of tax year do I have with an LLC?*

The answer depends on how the LLC is taxed. A partnership generally must conform its tax year to the tax year of its members unless the LLC can establish a business purpose for having a different tax year. An LLC must use the same tax year as that used by the member with the majority interest (that is, the tax year of one or more members who own in total more than a 50 percent interest in the LLC profits and capital).

A C corporation, other than a personal service corporation, can adopt a fiscal year different from the calendar year. An S corporation must generally use the calendar year unless it has a business purpose for using a different year.

Member Income Tax Issues

⚔ *Our LLC is treated as a partnership. What are the tax effects of member contributions?*

No gain or loss is recognized by the LLC or the individual when cash or unencumbered property is contributed in exchange for a member interest on formation of the LLC. Contributions of property encumbered by debt generally result in no recognition of gain to the member if his or her basis in the property exceeds the amount of the debt. For example, John Smith is one of two equal members in an LLC. John contributes property with a basis of $70,000; a fair market value of $150,000; and a mortgage of $40,000, which the partnership assumes. John's basis in his LLC interest is $90,000: $70,000 + $20,000 (half the debt, representing John's half-interest in the LLC).

A member's basis in his or her LLC interest increases or decreases annually as a result of the allocation of LLC income and gains, the allocation of losses, and actual distributions to the member. If a member renders services to an LLC for an interest in profits only (not for a capital interest), he or she can receive the member interest without a recognition of income. In this case, when the member receives a distribution of the profits, the distribution is considered compensation for the service and is taxed. If an individual contributes his or her expertise for a full member interest in the LLC, the member must recognize income equal to the value of the services rendered.

☙ Do I avoid self-employment tax with an LLC?

In a limited partnership, usually only the general partner is subject to self-employment tax on distributions and guaranteed payments, whereas limited partners who do not participate as employees do not pay self-employment tax on their distributions.

In the context of an LLC, it is less certain that the members are not subject to self-employment tax on distributions. A member who has an active management role incurs self-employment tax, but on what income? The IRS proposed regulations in 1997 that would have required all LLC members to pay self-employment tax on distributions from the LLC except for distributions derived from passive investments generating rents, dividends, and interest. The Taxpayer Relief Act of 1997 prohibited the IRS from enacting these regulations before July 1, 1998. Although the 1998 deadline has long passed, the IRS is reluctant to take further steps without a directive from Congress. Consult your accountant for assistance in determining how much, if any, self-employment tax to pay on distributions from your LLC.

LIABILITY

⩗ *What protection do members have from the contract liabilities of the LLC?*

An LLC offers members great protection from contractual debts or obligations of the LLC. For example, if the LLC fails to repay a bank loan and a lawsuit arises, the LLC can be held liable for the bank loan but, generally, the members cannot be held personally liable. Exceptions to this rule exist for situations in which the LLC is used to perpetrate a fraud or the members failed to treat the LLC as a separate entity (e.g., not holding meetings and documenting decisions made on behalf of the LLC).

⩗ *What protection from tort liabilities of the business do LLC members have?*

Generally, members of an LLC are not personally liable for tort liabilities committed by other members of the LLC or by its employees.

⩗ *What protection does an LLC have from my personal creditors?*

Property owned by an LLC is generally not available to someone who has a claim against you personally. Thus, someone who has obtained a judgment against you cannot seize a motor vehicle that is titled in the name of the LLC. However, your ownership interest in the LLC is subject to the claims of your personal creditors.

CONDUCTING BUSINESS
IN OTHER STATES

⚐ *Can my LLC do business in states other than the one in which it was formed?*

Yes, but like corporations and partnerships, your LLC is required to register in each "foreign" state in which it does business. Each state's LLC statute explains the registration procedure that out-of-state LLCs must follow to conduct business in that state.

RECOMMENDATIONS

⚐ *The LLC seems like the perfect ownership structure. Is it?*

No one business structure can be perfect for all situations, but the LLC may come close. However, even the LLC has drawbacks in certain circumstances. For instance, some regulated trades and businesses require a corporate charter or are subject to strict regulatory prerequisites that an LLC cannot meet.

Because the LLC form is relatively new, there are few reported court decisions interpreting applicable statutory provisions; therefore, no consistent body of law exists to predict how courts will deal with LLC statutes. Also, an area of much concern is the lack of uniformity among the states in regard to the formation, management and operation, and conversion and merger of LLCs. Many issues need to be settled by statute or litigation, including whether "thinly" capitalized LLCs protect their members from personal liability for actions of the business; whether LLCs are subject to actions comparable to piercing the corporate veil (Colorado has statutorily provided for piercing the LLC); whether the failure to follow certain formalities affects members' personal liability; and how LLCs formed under various state statutes will be treated in the international business world.

Over time these issues will be addressed, and it is likely the LLC will enjoy a larger role in the business world, nationally and internationally. Even so, it is not likely that the LLC will ever be the one perfect business form for all situations.

⚐ *What businesses run best as LLCs?*

Start-up enterprises often work very well as LLCs. When the members need the most outside investment, the investors can be taxed like partners and claim the business's losses on their personal tax returns. As the business grows and the initial investors want to take the business public, they can convert the LLC into a C corporation.

⚐ *How can I convert my sole proprietorship to an LLC?*

To establish a single-member LLC, transfer each asset you use in your sole proprietorship to the LLC and file an election with the IRS to have the LLC taxed as a sole proprietorship. This conversion to an LLC provides a significant advantage for owners who want to continue their sole proprietor status for income tax purposes but also want to have some liability protection.

ADVANTAGES AND DISADVANTAGES

⚐ *Can you summarize the advantages and disadvantages of an LLC?*

Advantages

■ Forming an LLC requires only articles of organization (we recommend an operating agreement as well, although not required).

- No ongoing formalities are required (we recommend regular, documented meetings).

- Members can decide whether to have centralized management or not.

- Members can choose to equally manage the LLC, can elect a specific member or members to run the business, or can hire managers to do so.

- The managing member or operating manager can take a salary for day-to-day management of the business.

- Nonmanaging members may receive distributions from the LLC.

- In general, without an agreement to the contrary, members can transfer only an assignee interest in the LLC, not a full ownership interest.

- By agreement, members can be restricted from transferring any of their ownership interests without the consent of the other members.

- All members have limited liability protection from the debts, obligations, and judgments of the LLC.

- LLC assets cannot be taken to satisfy personal debts, obligations, and judgments of members.

- An LLC can have an unlimited number of members, who may be individuals or businesses.

- Funds for the business can come from capitalization from the members or from outside financing.

- An LLC does not terminate on the death or incapacity of a member; thus, LLC interests can be transferred to the member's family.

- Single-member LLCs can be taxed as a sole proprietorship or a corporation.

- Multiple-member LLCs can be taxed as a partnership or a corporation.

- Under taxation as a sole proprietorship, a partnership, or an S corporation, the LLC is not taxed since all income and losses pass through to the members.

- Distributions to managing members may be treated as ordinary income and subject to self-employment tax.
- Distributions to nonmanaging members are usually not treated as compensation subject to self-employment tax.

Disadvantages

- An LLC cannot go public; doing so requires conversion to a C corporation.
- If an LLC reorganizes or is acquired by another organization, there may be problems in obtaining a tax-free exchange of LLC interests for stock of the acquiring organization.
- As yet, no consistent body of law exists to predict how courts will deal with LLC statutes.

chapter 9

Evaluating
the Entities

BUSINESS GOALS

⅏ *I'm going to start a new business. Which ownership structure should I use?*

Your goals will help you decide which entity is appropriate:

OWNERSHIP: A one-person business may be operated as a sole proprietorship, a corporation, or an LLC. However, the formalities required to create and maintain a corporation may be burdensome for a single owner. In addition, a C corporation may entail double taxation on business profits if the corporation's expenses, including your salary and fringe benefits, do not offset the corporation's taxable income. If you perceive that double taxation may occur, you could avoid it by making a timely S corporation election. You should also find out whether your state's LLC statutes allow single-member LLCs.

If there are multiple owners, you can consider forming a partnership, corporation, or LLC.

LIABILITY PROTECTION: If you need personal protection from the liabilities of the business, you can consider a corporation, LLP, limited partnership, or LLC.

CAPITALIZATION: Investors will want to be insulated from the liabilities of the business and may want preferred distributions of profits. If you need to bring in additional capital from outside investors, you might consider a corporation, LLC, or limited partnership.

MANAGEMENT: If there are multiple owners, your choice of entity depends on whether the owners will be equal partners in all respects. In a general partnership, all partners could be equal in ownership, management and control, and exposure to liabilities. In a limited partnership, the general partner has full rights and responsibilities in regard to managing the business and binding the partnership, while the limited partners have no rights. The limited partnership structure offers centralized management, while the general partnership does not.

Corporations and LLCs generally offer more flexibility and benefits for businesses with multiple owners.

SALE OF THE BUSINESS: If you want to sell your business, a corporation or LLC may help facilitate the transfer and distinguish business assets from other assets (e.g., the land on which you operate your business, which you may want to retain after selling the business). If you want to achieve certain tax advantages, investigate which entities qualify for them (e.g., tax-free mergers are available only to corporations). In any case, a limited partnership, LLC, or corporation may be the best choice if this is your priority.

In order to go public, your business must be a C corporation. If you have an LLC, you must convert it to a C corporation. If you have an S corporation, you must terminate the S election to become a C corporation.

Estate planning: To facilitate estate planning, you may need a business entity that allows multiple owners. You may consider forming a limited partnership or a corporation so that you can maintain control over the business even after you transfer a majority of the equity to your family. With careful planning and implementation, this is also possible with an LLC.

Taxation: The taxation of business profits varies among entities (e.g., in some, they are treated as dividends or distributions; in others, as wages or self-employment earnings subject to FICA or self-employment taxes). Consider the effects of the double taxation of C corporations in comparison with the pass-through taxation of partnerships, S corporations, and LLCs.

Owner and employee benefits: Any entity other than a sole proprietorship allows you to take advantage of fringe-benefit planning opportunities, including deduction of such benefits. Generally, a C corporation is best for taking maximum advantage of owner and employee benefits.

LIABILITY COMPARISONS

⨳ *We are a group of doctors who will have offices in two states. Should we form a professional LLP or an LLC?*

In a professional LLP, a professional partner usually is liable for his or her own acts or omissions and for those of someone he or she supervises but is not liable for the acts or omissions of anyone else employed by the partnership. However, not all states provide for LLPs, and the laws of those that do vary in regard to what must be done to obtain the benefits of an LLP. On the other hand, all states recognize LLCs. Bottom line: Seek the advice of your business advisor, who will look at the states involved and help you choose the best entity for your situation.

⋆ *I'm an attorney. How do I limit my liability to creditors?*

Like any other businessperson, you can limit your personal liability to creditors by forming a separate business in which to practice rather than practicing as a sole proprietor. You could form an LLC, LLP, or corporation. Each of these provides a separate identity for the business and thus reduces individual creditor liability. No matter which one you establish, you will be protected from personal liability for the malpractice of any attorneys who are partners or employees. Remember, however, that as an attorney you are always liable for malpractice claims against you.

⋆ *I have a great idea for a business but need money. My friend Luke owns a successful company and is willing to invest in my business for a share of future profits, but he wants to be a "silent partner" and doesn't want any liability for the actions of the business. What's the best way to accomplish this?*

Depending on your goals, one option for you and Luke is to create a new corporation. By forming a C corporation, you can be a stockholder and Luke's business can be a stockholder. You and Luke can determine what percentage of the corporation each will own and how the company will be operated. You can be the president of the corporation *and* run the day-to-day operations, and Luke can be as "silent" as he wants to be. In addition, Luke can be on the board of directors, thereby providing advice to the corporation as needed.

⋆ *I know that a general partner has unlimited liability for the obligations of a limited partnership and that having a corporation as general partner will protect shareholders from personal liability for the obligations of the corporation and of the partnership. I'd like to form a corporation so that I can be the general partner of my limited partnership. What should I know about this?*

Consult your tax advisor about partnership income, gains, losses, or deductions that might be allocated to a corporation as a general partner under federal income tax laws. Your corporation must meet state requirements to give you the desired personal protection from the liabilities of the corporation (including liabilities of the limited partnership). State law might require that, for you to be protected, the corporation must have enough initial assets to have a reasonable chance of business success. Your tax advisor will inform you of income tax issues that might result from getting money or property out of the corporation and into your hands. In addition, the laws of most states, in limited circumstances, allow a creditor of a limited partnership to pierce the corporate veil of the corporate general partner and hold a corporate shareholder liable for the obligations of the limited partnership. However, you are not likely to encounter this situation if your use of the corporation is characterized by good faith, fair dealing, and commercial reasonableness.

TAXATION COMPARISONS

⊰ *With each type of entity, what limitations exist on loss recognition?*

At-risk rules apply to the owners of partnerships, LLCs, and S corporations. These rules limit an owner's ability to use losses to offset his or her taxable income. This is accomplished by limiting loss deductions to the amount of the owner's investment in the business, borrowed amounts for which the owner is personally liable, and pledged assets not used in the activity as security for the borrowed amounts.

There are also complex *passive-activity loss rules* that apply to owners of limited partnerships, LLCs, S corporations, and personal service and closely held corporations. Generally, losses from passive activities may be deducted only against passive income, not against other regular income. Any disallowed loss is suspended and carried forward as a deduction from passive activities in the next succeeding tax year.

⚑ *Are there any special considerations regarding the alternative minimum tax with each entity?*

All types of businesses are directly or indirectly subject to the alternative minimum tax (AMT). For sole proprietorships, the AMT is calculated on the sole proprietor's tax form. For partnerships, S corporations, and LLCs, the tax preferences and adjustments are passed through from the business to the partners, shareholders, and members, and the AMT is calculated together with the owners' other preferences and adjustments. For C corporations, the AMT is calculated on the tax form with the corporation's taxable income. The corporate AMT rate of 20 percent is less than the individual AMT rates of 26 and 28 percent, but on later distribution of corporate assets, another tax will be exacted at the shareholder level.

⚑ *We are setting up a new corporation and expect losses during our first few years. Should we elect S corporation status?*

Yes. New businesses that expect losses in their early years generally should choose a pass-through business structure, such as an S corporation, so that the losses are passed on to the shareholders. Just make sure you can meet the S corporation requirements.

PART THREE

Benefits for All Employees

Business owners offer fringe benefits to attract and keep good employees. Part Three provides both practical and technical discussion of traditional fringe-benefit planning, which, if offered, must be offered to all employees. A typical benefit package might include health insurance, life insurance, long-term disability insurance, and an employer-sponsored retirement plan.

Five key questions govern the selection of a fringe-benefit plan for all employees:

1. Does the plan help recruit and retain good employees?
2. Is the fringe benefit deductible by the employer for federal and state income tax purposes?
3. Will the fringe benefit be taxed to the employee?
4. Does the employee realize the significance of the benefit?
5. Is the plan contributory (employee contributions allowed) or noncontributory?

Part Three aims to help small-business owners answer these questions and understand the advantages and disadvantages of each plan in the context of a privately owned business.

Most employers provide, at the very least, medical insurance coverage to employees as a fringe benefit. Federal law governs many aspects of a medical expense/health care plan. Statutory and federal regulations include nondiscrimination requirements, the Family Medical Leave Act, and COBRA. As a general rule, the expenses of group medical, disability, and life coverage are deductible by the employer for tax purposes, and premium costs are not taxed as income to covered employees. Chapter 10 examines the options available to employers for providing medical benefits and presents innovative and creative methods that employers can use to provide fringe benefits to employees.

Qualified and simplified employer-sponsored retirement plans must comply with requirements specified in the Internal Revenue Code and/or the Employee Retirement Income Security Act. Congress intended that the 2001 tax act would simplify the rules governing these plans and increase the amounts that individuals could contribute to the plans. However, in the rush to pass the act, the wording of the revisions has left much to be desired. The revisions amend several sets of previous revisions to a law that was already very complex. As we go to press with *Strictly Business,* plan administrators, professionals who specialize in retirement planning, and the IRS are still analyzing the changes in the 2001 tax act and how they apply to defined-contribution retirement plans. Many of these experts claim that there are discrepancies and conflicts in the law. If that is the case, Congress will pass a technical corrections act. Business owners should keep in mind that the exact figures and percentages will always change over time, whether necessitated by a technical correction to the law or just indexed for inflation. More important, however, is understanding the overall benefits, concepts, and rules of qualified and simple retirement plans, which our contributors explain in the next five chapters.

Chapter 11 presents an overview of qualified retirement plans and the features common to all of them. These features include limitations on contributions and benefits for highly compensated and key employees, vesting rules, fiduciary standards, and typical distribution requirements.

A defined-benefit plan specifies the *benefit* to be paid to participating employees. The defined benefit can optimize the employer's tax-deductible contributions for older employees. Chapter 12 explains this type of plan and its advantages and disadvantages.

A defined-contribution plan specifies the *contribution* that an employer is required to make to a qualified plan. Various defined-contribution plans are discussed in Chapter 13: profit-sharing plans, money purchase pension plans, employee stock ownership plans, and the very popular 401(k) plans, including the safe-harbor 401(k).

Chapter 14 covers the simplified plans, including the savings incentive match plan for employees (SIMPLE) and the simplified employee pension (SEP) plan. As their names imply, these are the least complex, and least expensive, plans for employers to sponsor.

Which retirement plan is best for your business depends on your objectives. Chapter 15 evaluates the plans in terms of costs and complexity. Sophisticated concepts for maximizing contributions for highly compensated employees are also presented. You are not limited to one plan. You can, for example, combine a 401(k) plan with a profit-sharing plan to maximize contributions for owners and other key employees.

chapter 10

Fringe Benefits

MEDICAL INSURANCE

⚑ *Do I have to provide medical coverage for my employees?*

A prospective employee will probably need and expect medical insurance as a fringe benefit. In the absence of a national health care plan, Congress shifts the burden of providing health insurance to employers. For almost every medical or health insurance plan, the employer receives an income tax deduction. The benefit is not taxed to the employee.

⚑ *What options do I have for providing health care coverage to my employees?*

Your basic choices include group health care insurance, health flexible-spending accounts, and self-insurance programs.

Group Health Care Insurance

⚜ *What are the general characteristics of a group health care plan?*

Group health care plans are usually underwritten by an insurance policy. A *basic plan,* or policy, provides health care services connected with medical diagnosis, treatment, and hospitalization. Dental and pregnancy benefits may be optional additions to a basic plan. A basic plan can provide services through a health maintenance organization (HMO) or a preferred provider organization (PPO), or it can allow employees to choose between the two. A basic plan almost always has limits on coverage and includes a deductible.

A basic plan may be supplemented with a *major medical policy* that covers some or all of the excess expenses that can be incurred in medical treatment. A *comprehensive plan,* or policy, combines the coverage provided by basic and major medical plans in one single plan.

In addition to these types of insurance coverage, employers may sponsor a *medical expense reimbursement plan* as an employee fringe benefit. Such plans are "made to order" and may be used to pay a deductible or to cover specified care not included in a basic or comprehensive medical insurance policy. A customized plan may include a health flexible-spending account to permit employees to pay for additional medical expenses, such as vision or dental expenses, with pretax dollars.

⚜ *Who must be covered under a medical expense reimbursement plan?*

These plans cannot favor the owner or other highly compensated employees. They must cover all employees except for those who have fewer than 3 years of service, are under 25 years of age, are part-time employees, are nonresident aliens, or are members of a union.

⚜ *What is an HMO?*

A *health maintenance organization (HMO)* is an independent organization designed to deliver health care services. The HMO receives a prepaid premium from employers. Physicians may be employed directly by the HMO or may be subcontracted. There are two basic types of HMOs: prepaid group practices (PGPs) and individual practice associations (IPAs).

In PGPs, practitioners are usually located together and may be organized under a staff model or group model. Under the staff model, physicians are hired by the plan and paid a salary. Under the group model, physicians are contacted by the plan and paid on a fee-for-service basis.

ᴁ What is a PPO?

In a *preferred provider organization (PPO),* the insurance company contracts with health care professionals who agree to deliver cost-effective care under negotiated fee schedules. In the most rigid form of PPO, the *exclusive provider organization,* subscribers must use affiliated health care providers. Under the newer *point-of-service plans,* subscribers may select a primary care physician, who then refers them to specialists from a list of affiliated providers.

Typically, the insured subscriber pays a single copayment at the time services are rendered. If service is provided outside the network, deductibles and coinsurance come into play. Often, insured subscribers who go outside the network pay a higher deductible and copayment.

ᴁ What are the income tax consequences of a health plan?

C corporations can deduct premiums and nondiscriminatory employee reimbursements for noninsured health care expenses. These payments are fringe benefits for which employees are not taxed.

A self-employed person is not classified as an employee for income tax purposes. In regard to fringe-benefit qualification, self-employed persons include partners in a partnership, members of an LLC that is taxed as a partnership, and shareholders who own more than 2 percent of an S corporation's stock. As a general rule, fringe benefits paid to a self-employed person are deductible by the business but are included in the gross income of the self-employed person for income tax purposes. Special rules apply for health insurance. A self-employed person may deduct a percentage of the health insurance cost paid by the business (70 percent in 2002 and 100 percent in 2003).

⅍ *Must I provide health care insurance for new employees with pre-existing conditions?*

Congress adopted the Health Insurance Portability and Accountability Act in 1996 to protect employees who change jobs voluntarily. When an employee changes jobs, he or she must be accepted by the new employer's group health insurance. There may be an exclusion period for preexisting medical problems, but preexisting conditions cannot be grounds for denial of coverage.

⅍ *Can I pay a higher percentage of health insurance costs for some employees and a lower percentage for others?*

Generally, no. A health care plan must comply with nondiscrimination rules. (Restricting eligibility to employees with a specified term of service is not considered discriminatory.) However, an employer may provide greater health care coverage to management-level employees if the excess benefit is reported as taxable compensation to the employee who receives the benefit.

⅍ *Rather than paying the higher premiums for insurance with a low deductible, I'd like to pay my employees a bonus that they could use to cover a higher deductible. Is this a good idea?*

Employees pay tax on the bonus, even though they use it to pay health care costs. However, an employer may benefit from the bonus arrangement in several ways: (1) Bonus compensation is fully deductible. (2) Bonus compensation is not subject to antidiscrimination rules, so highly compensated employees may receive larger bonus payments. (3) Employees are less likely to "abuse" the insurance if they must pay the deductible; careful and limited use of the coverage may result in lower premiums.

⚑ *Am I legally required to continue to provide health insurance for terminated employees?*

The Consolidated Omnibus Budget Reconciliation Act (COBRA) requires that coverage be continued for the following periods of time:

- Eighteen months for employees and their spouses and dependents if the employee loses coverage because of reduction in work hours or termination of service for any reason except gross misconduct
- Thirty-six months for spouses and dependents if (1) the employee dies, legally separates, or divorces or (2) the spouse and dependents lose benefits because the employee becomes eligible for Medicare

Employers must notify employees who are entitled to COBRA benefits of their right to continue as members of the plan. Employees must accept coverage within 60 days of the triggering event; otherwise, they lose all rights to continue their medical coverage. The former employee pays the entire insurance premium due under the group plan, plus a 2 percent surcharge.

While COBRA does not require that a business offer medical insurance, if an employer covered by the act discontinues a health plan, it must give employees the option to purchase individual coverage, regardless of their health status.

⚑ *Are there any special insurance rules regarding the Family Medical Leave Act?*

Employers must offer health care benefits to an employee who is on a Family Medical Leave Act (FMLA) leave of absence. If the employee chooses to continue coverage and pay his or her share of the premiums, the employer must also continue to pay its share of the premiums.

Regardless of whether an employee continues coverage during his or her absence, the employer must allow the employee to resume coverage when he or she returns to work. This has tax implications: the employee can choose whether or not to pay the premiums with after-tax dollars during an FMLA leave of absence; however, when the employee returns to work, he or she must be allowed to resume making such payments with pretax dollars.

Health Flexible-Spending Accounts

⇘   *What is a health flexible-spending account?*

A *health flexible-spending account,* or *health FSA,* is a benefit program funded through salary reductions or employer contributions that uses pretax dollars to reimburse employees for specified medical expenses. A health FSA can be offered under a cafeteria plan or in addition to one of the other health care plans.

⇘   *How does a health FSA plan work?*

The plan is easiest to understand through an example: Susan works for an employer that provides a health FSA plan. Each pay period, through a paycheck deduction, she contributes $12.50 to her health FSA (for an annual total of $300). She pays no income tax on this $300 income, and her employer takes the full amount as a deduction. Susan's contribution is not subject to FICA.

Susan needs new prescription glasses, which are not covered by her employer's group health care plan. The cost of her new glasses is $300. She uses her contribution to her health FSA to pay for the glasses. By paying with pretax dollars, Susan saves about $120 on the purchase of the glasses: 28 percent federal income tax, 5 percent state income tax, and 7 percent Social Security and Medicare. So the net cost of Susan's new glasses is $180 ($300 actual cost minus $120 in tax savings).

Alternatively, Susan could use the $300 to pay for medical expenses that are subject to the deductible limits of her employer's health insurance plan. For example, if her employer's health plan covers glasses but requires a $200 deductible, Susan could use the health FSA funds to pay the deductible on her glasses—and have $100 left in her health FSA for other deductibles or expenses she might have during the year.

Employees may use the funds in their health FSAs for medical and dental benefits that are not covered under their employer's group plan if the expense is otherwise deductible as a qualified medical expense for income tax purposes.

⍦ *What if it is March 1 and Susan has contributed only $50 to her FSA account. Does the employer have to reimburse her for the full $300 for her glasses?*

Yes. Beginning on the first day of the plan year, the employer must make available to the employee the entire amount of the contributions that the employee will make to the account during that year. For example, even though Susan's employer has withheld only $50 from her pay for her health FSA so far, it must reimburse her the entire $300 when she buys her glasses.

⍦ *What if Susan uses her year's worth of contributions and then quits before the end of the year? Does she have to reimburse her employer?*

No. The employer bears the risk that employees will use up their accounts and leave before the plan year has ended. This same type of risk applies to employees under the "use it or lose it" principle: If they don't use up the contributions they made during the plan year, they forfeit the use of those funds.

Self-Insurance Programs

◄ *What is a self-insured health plan?*

A *self-insured health plan* separates the various costs of health insurance. The primary costs are administration; "specific" insurance protection for large individual claims; "aggregate" insurance protection limiting the annual claims exposure for the employer; hospital, physician, and drug network access fees, which secure discounts for the employer; large case-management fees; and claims costs. Employers may choose to include or exclude other costs and expenses.

The largest single variable is claims costs. Under self-insured plans, the employer agrees to be liable for the claims costs up to the limits prescribed by the plan. Many self-insured plans are actually partially insured plans. The employer contracts with an insurance company to cover the amount of a claim in excess of a large deductible limit. The company is self-insured to the deductible amount.

Self-insurance health plans can be very attractive if claims are low, but they are expensive if claims are high.

◄ *How many employees should an employer have before considering a self-funded health insurance plan?*

An employer should have a minimum of 100 employees before considering self-insurance. Companies with fewer than 100 employees can experience very unpredictable swings in claims costs. Insurance is based on statistics; with a large number of covered individuals, statisticians can predict costs with relative accuracy. Statistics show that employers with fewer employees have more risk.

◄ *What are the advantages of a self-insured health plan for an employer?*

As opposed to fully insured plans, self-insured health plans offer employers several advantages:

- *Flexibility:* The employer can decide what benefits to include and how much coverage to provide.
- *Reports:* Detailed reports disclose the types of claims that are most prevalent among the employees. This can help the employer reduce claims by taking steps to improve working conditions and the overall health and well-being of employees.
- *Planning:* Reports indicate which providers employees use most frequently, so the employer may be able to secure volume discounts from some providers.

Cost savings alone should not govern the use of a self-insured program, since they are too unpredictable. Because the savings can vary from year to year, a self-insured program requires a long-term commitment and long-term planning.

DISABILITY INSURANCE

Why is disability income coverage important?

Most financial experts agree that disability coverage is not only important but essential. Typically, an individual's ability to create income is his or her most valuable asset. Without this ability, a person could lose everything he or she worked to build.

During a person's working years, the odds of becoming disabled are significantly higher than the odds of dying prematurely. Statistics show that a 35-year-old male has more than a 50 percent chance of being disabled for at least 90 days before age 65. Some individuals will be disabled for years—or for life—yet most people are ill-prepared to financially survive a disability as brief as 6 months.

What is the maximum benefit amount most insurers will issue for disability coverage?

Most insurers will insure up to 60 percent of an employee's income.

They set this limit so that the insured person will have an incentive to go back to work if possible.

⚐ What are the eligibility requirements?

Usually, an employee is eligible for benefits if the disability restricts his or her ability to work or prevents the employee from performing the substantial and material duties of his or her regular occupation. Some plans provide coverage if the employee suffers at least 20 percent loss of income due to a disability and is under the care of a physician.

⚐ How long must an employee wait before disability benefits begin? How long do they continue?

Income replacement benefits vary from plan to plan. Many plans for business owners and professionals provide for 30-, 60-, 90-, 180-, or 365-day waiting periods. The benefits may continue for 2 years, for 5 years, to age 65, or for the lifetime of the disabled employee.

⚐ Are premiums for disability coverage tax-deductible?

C corporations can deduct the premiums paid for employees, as they are qualified fringe benefits. The premiums are not considered compensation income to the employees.

Disability insurance premiums paid by a self-employed person, a partner, or a shareholder who owns more than 2 percent of an S corporation's stock are deductible as business expense but are included in the income of the self-employed person, partner, or shareholder. Members of an LLC are considered partners if the business is taxed as a partnership for federal income tax purposes.

⚐ Are disability benefits paid by an insurer included in the taxable income of the employee?

The general rule is that an employee must recognize disability payments as ordinary income if the employer pays and deducts the policy premiums. Disability-benefit payments are excluded from taxable income if the employee pays the premiums. The insured person is treated as having paid the premiums if he or she includes the premium amount as taxable income for the year. This also applies to self-employed persons, partners, and those who own more than 2 percent of the stock in an S corporation who are required, as a matter of tax law, to recognize compensation income for the disability insurance policy premiums. In each of these instances, the employer's tax deduction for premiums paid is actually a compensation deduction, not a qualified fringe-benefit deduction.

Must an employer offer disability insurance coverage to all employees, or can the employer be selective?

A plan satisfies the nondiscriminatory requirement only if two conditions are met: (1) Each benefit, right, and feature provided must be available to a *group of employees* that satisfies the minimum coverage requirements of Code Section 410(b), without regard to the average benefit percentage test, and (2) the group of employees must *not* substantially consist of highly compensated employees. A disability insurance plan that covers only management-level employees may be discriminatory if it favors highly compensated employees, especially highly compensated employees who are also owners.

Assume that a company offers disability insurance coverage to a prospective chief operating officer, a benefit not available to other employees of the company. The company can do so, but the new executive will be taxed on the discriminatory fringe benefit as additional compensation. No rule of law prohibits a company from providing special perks to executives. These perks may include a company-owned residence, a luxury automobile, and personal use of the company's aircraft. The executive must report the value of his or her personal use of the residence, automobile, and transportation as compensation income. The company realizes a business income tax deduction for compensation paid to the extent that the total compensation package is fair and reasonable.

⚰ *What's the difference between individual disability coverage and group coverage?*

Group coverage is usually less expensive. Individual coverage sometimes costs 50 percent more, or higher, than does group insurance. As with medical insurance, a difficult-to-insure employee may qualify for coverage under a group plan even though he or she might be uninsurable under an individual contract.

On the other hand, individual disability insurance contracts have the following advantages:

- Individual contracts generally provide better coverage.
- They have options not available in group programs.
- Individual coverage can move with the employee, with no change in coverage, if he or she changes jobs.
- For an individual policy the amount of coverage an employer can purchase for the employee is reduced by the amount of any other individual or group disability coverage the employee has. (Group coverage generally does not reduce benefits on the basis of other contracts.)
- Future premiums for some individual coverage may never increase or may increase only if entire blocks of business increase.
- Some group contracts reduce disability payments if Social Security disability benefits are paid to the employee. This is called *integration.* Individual contracts usually do not permit reduction of disability income payments through integration.

CAFETERIA PLANS

⚰ *What is a cafeteria plan?*

A *cafeteria plan* (sometimes called a *flexible benefit plan*) is an employer-sponsored benefit plan that allows employees to choose from a "menu" of cash and nontaxable (qualified) benefits according to their needs. It provides tax advantages to both employees and employers. The employer deducts the costs of the plan, and the employee does not pay payroll taxes on employer contributions to the plan.

With a cafeteria plan, the employer allocates a predetermined amount of money for each employee, and the employee may either take the benefits or take the allocated amount as cash in lieu of benefits. (The employer must allow the employee to make this choice.) For example, the employer may allocate $200 per month for each employee. If an employee does not need any of the benefits in the plan, perhaps because he or she is covered under a spouse's company plan, that employee may choose to take the $200 in cash each month. A cash distribution is treated as ordinary compensation. If the employee chooses to take the benefits, he or she has the right to apply the dollar amount to any one or more of the benefits that the plan provides.

◢ Can employees contribute to the plan to purchase more benefits?

Cafeteria plans are often funded through salary reduction agreements. Under a *salary reduction agreement*, the employee agrees to contribute a portion of his or her salary on a pretax basis to pay for some or all of the benefits. The reduction of the employee's salary and subsequent contribution of that amount is actually considered a contribution by the employer. The employer can still make its own separate contribution.

◢ What is a qualified benefit?

With a few exceptions, a benefit is *qualified* if it is excluded from an employee's gross income when offered outside a cafeteria plan and if the benefit does not defer the receipt of compensation, other than contributions to 401(k) plans.

◢ What benefits can we include in a cafeteria plan?

A cafeteria plan must offer participating employees a choice of two or more classes of benefits consisting of cash and qualified benefits. A cafeteria plan may offer:

- Accident, health, or dental insurance
- Group term life insurance up to $50,000 of coverage
- Disability insurance
- Medical and dental expense reimbursement accounts or flexible-spending accounts
- Coverage under a dependent care assistance program
- Group legal services plans (Contributions cannot be made on a pretax basis.)
- Contributions to a 401(k) plan
- An adoption assistance program

A cafeteria plan may also offer participants the opportunity to "buy" benefits with their own after-tax contributions. Benefits may include those listed above plus elective, paid vacation days and after-tax employee contributions to a 401(k) plan.

⚵ What benefits aren't qualified?

The Internal Revenue Code specifically excludes certain employer-provided benefits, such as employee merchandise discounts, scholarships or fellowships, educational assistance programs, moving expense reimbursements, and long-term-care insurance.

Meals and lodging furnished for the convenience of the employer are also not permissible options under a cafeteria plan because they are not elected in lieu of other benefits or compensation.

⚵ Who can participate in a cafeteria plan?

A cafeteria plan must comply with the nondiscrimination rules that generally apply to all employee benefits. (For details on nondiscrimination rules, see Chapter 11).

All participants in a cafeteria plan must be employees or former

employees. Former employees may participate if the plan group consists predominantly of active employees. Self-employed individuals,
that is, partners in business partnerships, shareholders in an S corporation who own more than 2 percent of the corporation's stock,
and members of an LLC, may *not* participate in a cafeteria plan even
if they are employees.

⌬ *When must employees choose the benefits they want?*

Each employee must make an affirmative choice between the cash
and qualified benefits (and, if the latter, specify which qualified benefits) before the first plan year (period of coverage) in which he or
she will receive the benefits. Failure to choose could jeopardize the
status of the cafeteria plan.

⌬ *Can employees change their selections?*

Generally, employees can make changes only during an "enrollment
period," which must occur before the start of each plan year. Choices are irrevocable after the plan year begins. An election is considered not to have been made if it can be revoked after the plan year
begins.

In certain limited circumstances, employees can change their
choices during the plan year. These circumstances involve a change
of status, such as losing coverage under another plan or changes in
family or job status. For example, if an employee had medical insurance under another plan and lost it, he or she can elect to take the
health care benefit under the cafeteria plan. Changes in family status include marriage, divorce, death, or a change in dependents.
Changes in job status include a change in the number of hours
worked or termination of employment.

chapter 11

Qualified Retirement Plans

⚜ *What is a qualified plan?*

A *qualified plan* is an employer-sponsored retirement plan that complies with the requirements specified in the Internal Revenue Code (IRC) and the Employee Retirement Income Security Act (ERISA). One requirement is that the plan cover a broad group of employees, not just key employees or owners.

To encourage employers to establish retirement plans, the government provides income tax incentives to both employers and employees for contributing to or participating in retirement plans. The employer realizes a current income tax deduction for contributions it makes to a qualified plan. The employer's contributions are not included in the employee's compensation and therefore are not subject to FICA and FUTA taxes. If employee contributions are permitted, they may be made on a tax-deferred basis, allowing the employee to save more for retirement. (*Tax-deferred* means that qualified participants do not pay income taxes on their contributions until they receive distributions on retirement, disability, or some other termination of service.) Although employee contributions are tax-deferred, they may be subject to FICA and FUTA taxes.

There is another very important attribute of qualified retirement plans: Income and capital gains accumulate tax-free within the plan. Compounding of untaxed income and gain can produce significant growth in value over time.

ᴁ *What types of qualified plans are available?*

There are two major categories of qualified plans: defined-benefit plans and defined-contribution plans. In a *defined-benefit plan,* the benefit the employee will receive at retirement is defined (a fixed dollar amount or fixed percentage of compensation) when the plan is established. The amount of the employer contribution is not fixed by law.

In a *defined-contribution plan,* the employer makes regular contributions of specific amounts for each employee, but the value of the future benefit is not guaranteed. Defined-contribution plans include the traditional profit-sharing plan, the money purchase pension plan, and the 401(k) plan. These plans have become more popular in recent years.

Other retirement plans employers may use include the simplified employee pension (SEP) plan and the savings incentive match plan for employees (SIMPLE). Technically, these are not qualified retirement plans because they are not governed by ERISA. Special IRC rules govern the creation of these plans. (See Chapter 14.)

ᴁ *What is a contributory plan?*

Employer-sponsored retirement plans, whether qualified or unqualified, are sometimes categorized as contributory or noncontributory. A *contributory plan* permits employee contributions (called *salary deferrals*). The most common contributory plan is the 401(k) plan.

A *noncontributory plan* does not allow employee contributions. Noncontributory plans include the defined-benefit plan, profit-sharing plan, and money purchase pension plan. Profit-sharing and money purchase pension plans can be paired with a 401(k) plan that does allow employee contributions. Pairing contributory and non-contributory plans is a sophisticated technique for maximizing contributions for key employees (see Chapter 15).

BENEFITS

❧ *Why should my business invest in a qualified retirement plan?*

As a business owner, you should consider sponsoring and investing in a qualified retirement plan for these reasons:

■ Assets that grow tax-deferred compound faster. If you earn 8 percent on your retirement plan assets, their values will double in 9 years. If you earn 10 percent, their values will double in just over 7 years.

■ Contributions are 100 percent deductible (within limits) for your business in the current tax year.

■ A retirement plan is the most tax-efficient way to provide additional compensation for yourself and other employees. This is because participants pay no income taxes on employer contributions to a qualified retirement plan.

■ A retirement plan is an excellent means of diversifying your personal holdings. When you reach retirement age, the liquidity offered by the plan can provide income while you wait for the right time, price, and buyer for your business.

■ A retirement plan is second in importance only to health insurance for employees who want fringe benefits. A qualified retirement plan is an excellent way to attract and retain good employees, motivate them to be more productive, and offer them the opportunity to retire earlier and more comfortably.

⚐ Does my business get a tax break for the costs of setting up a qualified plan?

As part of the 2001 tax act, Congress created a special tax break for eligible employers to encourage them to establish qualified retirement plans. The new law provides a nonrefundable tax credit of 50 percent (up to $500) of the cost of establishing and administering a new qualified retirement plan. This credit is available for 3 years after the plan is established. For employers not eligible for the credit (or once the credit has been fully utilized), the costs connected with maintaining a qualified or simple retirement plan are deductible as a business expense.

Eligible employers include those that do not employ more than 100 employees who each earned $5000 or more in the preceding calendar year and those that do not maintain any other qualified, SIMPLE, or SEP retirement plan.

COMMON FEATURES

⚐ What law governs qualified retirement plans?

Two bodies of federal statutory law govern the establishment, administration, and eventual termination of qualified retirement plans: the IRC and ERISA. Table 11-1 summarizes some of the rules governing these plans. In addition, general state fiduciary and trust law requirements apply when they are not in conflict with the IRC and ERISA.

⚐ What general rules apply to the establishment of a qualified retirement plan?

The following general rules apply:

■   The plan must be in writing and must be permanent.

TABLE 11-1   Rules Governing Qualified Retirement Plans

IRC

Eligibility: Which employees must or may participate; when employees must be allowed to participate.

Nondiscrimination: The same eligibility requirements, contributions, and allocations for everyone; cannot discriminate in favor of highly compensated or key employees.

Vesting: When the plan funds must become nonforfeitable to participants.

Contributions and allocations: How often and in what manner contributions must be made; how much the deductible contributions can be; how much and in what manner contributions are allocated to employees.

Distributions: When and how the funds may be distributed.

ERISA

There must be written documents containing required provisions that must be followed.

Assets must be held in a trust.

Fiduciaries must be appointed to oversee the operation of the plan and must act in the best interest of the plan and participants (prudent-investor standard).

No self-dealing or unjust enrichment is allowed.

There can be no interference with participant rights.

Title IV provides pension guaranty insurance to defined-benefit plans through the Pension Benefit Guaranty Association.

- The plan cannot discriminate among employees in terms of overall coverage, contributions, or allocations of benefits.
- The plan must limit the amount of contributions made by an employer and the amount of benefits available to participants.
- The plan must have vesting requirements.
- The plan usually must have incidental death benefits. (A defined-contribution plan, e.g., must specify the beneficiary of an employee's account.)
- The plan must be communicated to employees in a meaningful manner.

⚘ *Do I have to provide for all my employees in a qualified plan?*

The general rule is that *all* full-time eligible employees must be permitted to participate in a qualified plan. Some exceptions apply.

⚘ *What are the participation and eligibility rules for qualified plans in general?*

A qualified plan must cover full-time employees who are 21 years of age or older and have worked in the business for at least 1 year. It may exclude employees who are not 21 years of age.

Part-time employees may be excluded from defined-benefit plans, money purchase plans, and profit-sharing plans but not from 401(k) plans. A *part-time employee* is a person who works less than 1000 hours per year.

Nondiscrimination Rules

⚘ *What nondiscrimination rules apply to qualified plans?*

The IRC spells out three basic compliance requirements:

1. Contributions or benefits must not discriminate in favor of highly compensated or key employees.
2. The benefits, rights, and features provided under the plan must be made available to employees in a nondiscriminatory manner.
3. The effect of plan amendments (including grants of past-service credit) and plan terminations must be nondiscriminatory.

⚘ *What constitutes a highly compensated employee?*

A *highly compensated employee* is either (1) a 5 percent owner at any time during the current plan year or a preceding plan year or (2) any employee who realizes compensation greater than $85,000 (in 2001), indexed annually for inflation.

⚜ *Who is a key employee?*

Effective 2002, the term *key employee* refers to any employee (or, in some cases, any former or deceased employee) who, at any time during the plan year, is either (1) an officer of the employer receiving compensation of more than $130,000, indexed annually for inflation; (2) an owner who owns 5 percent or more of the employer; or (3) an owner who owns 1 percent or more of the employer and receives annual compensation in excess of $150,000.

If more than 60 percent of the plan's benefits or contributions go to key employees, the IRS considers the plan to be "top-heavy" and assumes that key employees receive larger contributions than other employees. If the plan is top-heavy, current law mandates a 3 percent minimum contribution on behalf of all participants and a vesting schedule that is more generous than that required for a plan that is not top-heavy.

⚜ *How do the rules about highly compensated and key employees actually affect qualified plans?*

Generally speaking, the government is concerned that all qualified plans be designed and in fact operate so that all employees, not just highly compensated and key employees, benefit from the plans. To that end, the IRC imposes several restrictions and nondiscrimination tests that focus on the benefits received by highly compensated and key employees as compared to those received by other employees. Many of these tests must be met every year that the plan is in operation. For example, all qualified plans must generally pass one of the following tests with regard to employer contributions:

- The plan must benefit at least 70 percent of all non-highly compensated employees in the company.
- The percentage of non-highly compensated employees who are covered under the plan must be at least 70 percent of the highly compensated employees who are covered by the plan.
- The average dollar-amount benefit provided to non-highly

compensated employees must be at least 70 percent of the average dollar-amount benefit provided to highly compensated employees.

Additional nondiscrimination testing rules for 401(k) plans are discussed in Chapter 13. In some instances employers can incorporate "safe-harbor" rules that permit a 401(k)plan to qualify without meeting one of the preceding tests.

The 2001 tax act simplified the top-heavy testing rules, but its elimination of the limit on combined employer contributions and employee deferrals could present problems in passing nondiscrimination tests if every employee defers the maximum amount. Nondiscrimination testing rules are still complex, but they are not insurmountable. Employers should seek professional advice on establishing qualified plans and monitoring them so that they remain qualified.

Vesting Rules

⚐ *What are the vesting requirements you mentioned?*

If the plan allows employee contributions, the contributions and the benefits produced from them must be 100 percent vested at all times. A participant's rights to his or her accrued benefit resulting from the employer's contributions in a qualified plan must vest (become nonforfeitable) at certain rates during the years of his or her employment.

An employer is free to establish a more generous vesting schedule, but the IRC imposes the following minimum requirements for vesting:

- *401(k) plans:* A 2- to 6-year graded schedule requiring 20 percent vesting after 2 years of service and 20 percent–per-year vesting for each year of service thereafter, reaching 100 percent vested in year 6; or a 3-year "cliff" schedule that produces full vesting after 3 years of service.

■ *All other qualified plans:* A 3- to 7-year graded schedule requiring 20 percent vesting after 3 years of service and 20 percent–per-year vesting for each year of service thereafter, reaching 100 percent vested in year 7; or a 5-year "cliff" schedule that produces full vesting after 5 years of service.

In addition, employers' contributions must immediately vest 100 percent when an employee attains the normal retirement age prescribed by the IRC or an earlier retirement age if the plan so provides; the plan is terminated or partially terminated; or the employer stops contributing to the plan.

⋈ What are the vesting requirements if the plan is top-heavy?

If the plan is top-heavy, the IRS requires more liberal vesting options, as follows:

■ An employee who has completed at least 3 years of service with the employer must have a nonforfeitable right to 100 percent of his or her accrued benefit.

■ An employee who has completed at least 2 years of service must have a nonforfeitable right to at least the following percentages of his or her accrued benefit: 20 percent after 2 years of service, 20 percent more for each of the next 3 years of service, and 100 percent after 6 years of service.

⋈ What happens to the "unvested" portion when an employee's service terminates before full vesting?

Depending on the type of qualified plan, forfeited employer contributions must be either distributed to the remaining employees' accounts or used to offset the employer's required contribution for the year.

Fiduciary Standards

⫤ You said ERISA requires that plans appoint fiduciaries. What is a fiduciary?

In the context of qualified retirement plans, the term "fiduciary" is broadly defined to include the employer sponsoring the plan and any person who either:

- Exercises any discretionary authority or discretionary control respecting management of the plan
- Exercises any authority or control respecting management or disposition of the plan's assets
- Renders investment advice for a fee or other compensation, direct or indirect, with respect to the plan's assets or has any authority or responsibility to do so
- Has any discretionary authority or discretionary responsibility in the administration of the plan

ERISA stipulates the duties and responsibilities of a fiduciary. A *fiduciary* must conduct plan business under established standards of care and is prohibited from engaging in, or causing the plan to engage in, certain transactions. Fiduciaries who breach these requirements often are held personally liable for their actions with respect to the plan.

⫤ What are a fiduciary's basic duties with regard to a qualified plan?

A fiduciary must administer a qualified plan for the exclusive purpose of providing benefits to participants and their beneficiaries. A fiduciary must administer the plan with care, skill, prudence, and diligence under the circumstances then prevailing. The fiduciary's actions with regard to investments are governed by the prudent-investor rule. A fiduciary must diversify the investments of the plan to minimize the risk of large losses unless the circumstances then prevailing indicate that it is clearly prudent not to do so. A fiduciary must act solely in the interest of the plan and its beneficiaries, establish a written investment policy, invest prudently, diversify assets, monitor investment performance, control investment expenses, and avoid prohibited transactions.

✍ Which plans require that the employee maintain responsibility for managing investments?

The employer retains all management control over defined-benefit plan investments. Defined-contribution plans may permit or require the employer to create segregated accounts for each participating employee and may permit each employee to direct the investments of his or her account. An employer's liability profile for investment decisions may be substantially diminished if the employer uses a defined-contribution plan (instead of a defined-benefit plan) and the plan requires segregated accounts and employees' responsibility for investment decisions with regard to their individual accounts.

✍ Can a business owner, using a third-party corporate trustee, transfer liability as a fiduciary and avoid being sued in the event of a breach or a prohibited transaction?

No. Many business owners believe this, but it is not true. A plan sponsor (employer) cannot transfer its responsibility and liability as a fiduciary to a third party (corporate trustee, investment advisor, custodian). Typically, investment managers will, in return for fees, accept cofiduciary status to help make plan decisions in the best interests of plan participants and beneficiaries.

Investment consultants who provide cofiduciary status must purchase errors-and-omissions insurance for each retirement plan they administer.

✍ Why is it important that the company have a written investment policy?

All employee benefit plans should establish and maintain a written *investment policy statement (IPS).* This is the only way a fiduciary can meet obligations and legally defend future actions. The objectives and purposes of the plan provide the standards against which the fiduciary will be judged.

Items that should be included in the investment policy statement are benchmarks against which to compare investment performance, risk tolerance, asset allocation, liquidity requirements, allowable investments, methods for minimizing risk, procedures for selecting and dismissing investment managers, and so on. The IPS does not have to be overly complex, but the objectives must be specific enough to define the plan's needs and goals.

Most business owners and those having fiduciary responsibilities require professional assistance to meet many of ERISA's requirements. ERISA encourages fiduciaries to use financial professionals, on the assumption that most fiduciaries do not possess the skills required to adequately discharge their duties. Delegation alone will not protect a fiduciary, but a system of delegation and oversight should reduce exposure to risk.

⚶ What are prohibited transactions under ERISA and the IRC?

Under ERISA and the IRC, a fiduciary may not engage in, or cause the plan to engage in, a prohibited transaction. Prohibited transactions include:

- The following transactions between the plan and a party in interest or a disqualified person: the sale, exchange, or lease of any property; loans or any other extension of credit; and the furnishing of goods, services, or facilities

- The transfer of any plan assets to, or for the use or benefit of, a party in interest or a disqualified person

- The acquisition on behalf of the plan of any employer security or employer real property in violation of ERISA Section 407

- Self-dealing by a disqualified person (i.e., the person uses plan income or assets for his or her own interest)

- The receipt of any consideration by a fiduciary from anyone in connection with a transaction involving the income or assets of the plan

⅃ Who is a disqualified person or a party in interest?

Basically, a person, partnership, trust, estate, or controlled corporation falling into one of the following categories is a *party in interest* or a *disqualified person:*

- Any fiduciary, including but not limited to any administrator, officer, trustee, employee, or custodian of or counsel for the plan
- A person providing services to the plan
- Any employer whose employees are covered by the plan
- An employee organization whose members are covered by the plan
- A direct or indirect owner of 50 percent or more of either (1) the combined voting power of all classes of stock entitled to vote or the total value of shares of all classes of a corporation's stock; (2) the capital interest or the profit interest of a partnership; or (3) the beneficial interest of a trust or unincorporated enterprise that is an employer or an employee organization described above (The secretary of labor, after consultation with the secretary of the treasury, may by regulation prescribe a percentage lower than 50 percent.)
- A relative of any individual identified as a party in interest, including a spouse, ancestor, lineal descendant, or spouse of a lineal descendant

Contributions, Distributions, Loans

⅃ As an employer, how much money am I required to contribute to a qualified plan?

The amount depends on the specific plan you choose and the plan design. As a general rule (effective 2002), the employer's maximum tax-deductible contribution to a qualified plan is either 25 percent of the employee's compensation up to $200,000 (indexed annually for inflation) or $40,000 (indexed annually for inflation), whichever is less. Compensation includes regular pay, bonuses, and overtime pay. Most companies contribute no more than the deductible amount. (See the chapters on specific plans for more details.)

✻ *Once my business adopts a qualified plan, must it make annual contributions to the plan?*

Defined-benefit plans require annual contributions. Defined-contribution plans vary: money purchase pension plans require annual contributions; traditional profit-sharing plans and 401(k) plans do not require annual employer contributions, but contributions must be "recurring and substantial."

✻ *When does payment of benefits begin?*

Unless a participant elects otherwise, payment of retirement benefits begins when the employee reaches normal retirement age, as specified in the plan documents. It must begin either by the time the participant reaches age 65 or, if he or she was not a participant in the plan for at least 5 years before age 65, by the fifth anniversary of the employee's plan participation.

✻ *Can a participant borrow from a qualified plan?*

The general answer is yes, if the plan document permits loans. A loan must bear a fair rate of interest; require, at the least, quarterly payments of principal and interest; and be repaid within 5 years (but can be up to 30 years if the loan is for the purchase of a principal residence). If the participant does not make prompt payments, the outstanding loan balance can be considered a premature taxable distribution from the plan, which may be assessed a 10 percent penalty if the participant has not reached the age of 59½ years.

Loan provisions can provide incentive for young employees to participate in a qualified plan because they can use the plan as a source of emergency cash. In general, loans are not permitted if the employer is a sole proprietor.

≼ *Are the assets in a qualified plan safe from the claims of creditors?*

ERISA protects assets in a qualified retirement plan from the claims of both the employer's and the employee's creditors.

ADVANTAGES AND DISADVANTAGES

≼ *Would you list the advantages and disadvantages of qualified retirement plans?*

Advantages

- They are the most tax-efficient way to provide additional compensation to owners and other employees.
- A qualified plan is an excellent way for the owner to diversify personal holdings; at retirement, it offers liquidity while the owner waits for the right buyer and price before selling the business.
- Within prescribed limits, contributions are tax-deductible by the employer.
- Vesting schedules are permitted, and forfeited amounts can be used by the employer to offset required annual contributions.
- Qualified plans promote retention of employees.
- Contributions are not currently taxable to participants.
- Employer contributions are not subject to FICA or FUTA taxes.
- Income and capital gains increase tax-free inside the plan, allowing greater compounding.

Disadvantages

- Qualified plans are strictly regulated by ERISA and the IRS with regard to employee eligibility, vesting, fiduciary responsibilities, tax deductions, distributions, and reporting requirements.
- The plan cannot favor highly compensated or key employees—including the owner.
- Contribution limits are set by law.

chapter 12

Defined-Benefit Plans

⊰ What is a defined-benefit plan?

A *defined-benefit plan* is a qualified retirement plan in which the benefit is defined as a specific dollar amount or a percentage of the employee's income before retirement. For example, the plan may say that all employees at age 65 with 30 years of service will receive 80 percent of their salaries for the rest of their lives. Defined-benefit plans almost always specify a reduced benefit for early retirement, death, or disability.

The defined benefit is a contractual obligation of the employer. The amount of payment is not increased or decreased according to the investment performance of the retirement trust fund. Defined-benefit plans use actuarial assumptions (age and life expectancy of employees, employee turnover, interest rates, investment projections, probable increases in compensation levels) to calculate the amount

269

an employer must annually contribute to the plan to adequately fund it.

≫ Who controls the investments, and who bears the investment risk?

Employer contributions are aggregated in one account or trust fund for the benefit of all the participating employees. The employer controls the fund and the investments, although it is common for the employer to use the services of a professional investment manager and a professional administrator. The employer bears the investment risk.

≫ How is the benefit determined in a defined-benefit plan?

Various formulas are used to calculate an employee's retirement benefit. The most common formula is years of service *times* a percentage *times* salary level. Variations for determining benefits include averaging the last 5 years' salaries or averaging the highest 5 of the last 7 years' salaries.

If the plan has insufficient funds to pay the retirement benefit, the employer must make up the difference from current cash flow. Starting in 2002, the maximum benefit amount that can be paid to an employee is $160,000 (indexed annually for inflation).

≫ Are there minimum contribution requirements for a defined-benefit plan?

Defined-benefit plans are subject to a minimum funding formula. A company may be required to make very substantial annual contributions to the plan if it has an older workforce, because the company has a shorter period of time within which to build up the older employees' retirement benefits. This "negative" attribute may be positive if (1) the company owners are older and want to fund a larger amount of money into their plan or (2) the company wants to contribute a lot of money quickly to a pension plan in order to gain an income tax deduction to offset extraordinary levels of profit.

◢ Who can help me establish a defined-benefit plan?

Business owners who want to establish defined-benefit plans usually employ a pension plan consultant or an advisor who specializes in managing pension plan investments. The terms of a plan must be customized to fit the employer's particular needs. Thus, the administrative costs of a defined-benefit plan may be higher than those of a standard defined-contribution plan or a simplified plan. Often, however, the flexibility of setting the benefit calculation formula and, in many cases, the higher income tax deduction for contributions are worth the added expense.

◢ What are the advantages and disadvantages of defined-benefit plans?

Defined-benefit plans have the same advantages and disadvantages as all qualified retirement plans, as well as the following:

Advantages

- Employees know the amount of the benefit they will receive at retirement.
- An owner-employee who has no other retirement plan and is nearing retirement can maximize the amount of annual contributions.

Disadvantages

- Defined-benefit plans are complex and more costly than other plans to establish and maintain.
- Once the contribution amount has been set, it is fixed and the employer must make annual contributions regardless of profits.

- The employer is responsible for making contributions; employees are not allowed to do so.

- The employer bears full fiduciary responsibility for investment management.

- The plan can be difficult to explain to participants because of the actuarial computations and the various distribution options.

- Overfunding the plan will cause a 50 percent excise tax and may cause a reversion of plan assets to the employer.

chapter 13

Defined-Contribution Plans

⩕ *What is a defined-contribution plan?*

A *defined-contribution plan* is a qualified retirement plan that does *not* promise any particular monetary benefit to the participant other than payment of the ultimate value of the account. The contribution, not the benefit, is defined. The employer's annual contribution, up to a maximum amount set by law, is determined by a formula.

A defined-contribution plan can be employee-directed. Such plans are designed to segregate the account of each participating employee and to permit (or require) each employee to direct the investments in his or her account. A participant is entitled to the balance of his or her account, whatever that amount may be, on retirement or termination of service, subject to vesting requirements, if any.

Many companies are replacing defined-benefit plans and employer-directed defined-contribution plans with employee-directed defined-contribution plans. Employers no longer want the liability produced by an employee's claim that the retirement benefit is unsatisfactory because the employer-investor did not realize higher returns. An employee-directed plan shifts the responsibility for investment return to the employee.

Defined-contribution plans include profit-sharing plans, money purchase pension plans, employee stock ownership plans, and 401(k) plans.

PROFIT-SHARING PLANS

⚄ *What is a profit-sharing plan?*

A *profit-sharing plan* is a "discretionary" defined-contribution plan in which an employer shares company profits with employees by making contributions to a profit-sharing retirement plan. It is discretionary because the employer-sponsor of the plan decides how much the company will contribute to the plan each year and which years contributions will be made. The employer must make contributions to the plan in at least 3 out of 5 years.

⚄ *How much can the employer contribute to the profit-sharing plan?*

In any year that the employer makes a contribution, the maximum amount the employer can deduct for tax purposes is either 25 percent of the employee's compensation or $40,000 (indexed annually for inflation), whichever is less.

⚄ *How are contributions to the plan allocated among the participants?*

Contributions must be allocated among participating employees according to a predetermined formula, such as

$$\frac{\text{Participant's compensation} \times \text{total contribution}}{\text{Total compensation paid}}$$

Allocations are earmarked for each participant's specific account. Starting in 2002, the maximum amount will be $40,000 (indexed annually for inflation) or 100 percent of the employee's compensation, whichever is less.

≱ *Can employees contribute to their accounts in a profit-sharing plan?*

No. A profit-sharing plan is noncontributory, in the sense that all contributions must come from the employer. However, employee contributions can be accommodated by linking a 401(k) plan to the traditional profit-sharing plan. This combination provides the advantages of the profit-sharing plan while allowing employees to defer a portion of their salaries as well.

≱ *Who directs the investments for a profit-sharing plan?*

In a profit-sharing plan, the amount credited to an employee's account is a bookkeeping entry. The profit-sharing trust remains as a whole under the administration of the employer, and the employer is responsible for the investment of plan assets.

MONEY PURCHASE PENSION PLANS

≱ *What is a money purchase pension plan?*

A *money purchase pension plan* is an employer-sponsored defined-contribution retirement plan in which each participant's benefit is determined solely by the amount that the money in the account can "purchase" at retirement. The plan requires an annual employer contribution, the amount of which is fixed at the time the plan is created. The amount of the contribution is typically based on a percentage of the participants' salaries. Employers who fail to make a mandatory annual contribution face IRS penalties.

Before the 2001 tax act, employers with a steady cash flow sufficient to make the annual contributions and companies with younger owners and younger key employees used the money purchase plan because it had a higher tax-deductible contribution limit than did other defined-contribution plans (25 versus 15 percent). Also, employers who wanted to maximize their tax-deductible contributions would combine the money purchase pension plan with a profit-sharing plan. However, the 2001 tax act has made the tax-deductible limits the same for all defined-contribution plans, so we believe that the money purchase pension plan no longer offers any advantages over the other plans. If the 2001 act ends and the money purchase pension plan returns to a higher tax-deductible contribution limit, it would again be a useful means for employers to maximize their tax-deductible contributions.

How much can an employer contribute to a money purchase pension plan on a tax-deductible basis?

Effective in 2002, employer contributions to the money purchase pension plan will be deductible up to 25 percent of the employee's compensation or $40,000 (indexed annually for inflation), whichever is less.

How much can I, as a business owner, allocate to each participant?

Starting in 2002, the maximum amount will be $40,000 (indexed for inflation) or 100 percent of the employee's compensation, whichever is less.

⍆ *Who directs the investments in the money purchase pension plan?*

The employer can retain responsibility for the investment of plan assets or can allow employees to direct their own investments.

EMPLOYEE STOCK OWNERSHIP PLANS

⍆ *What is an employee stock ownership plan?*

An *employee stock ownership plan (ESOP)* is similar to a profit-sharing plan, the major difference being that an ESOP may own shares of the sponsoring corporation, which a profit-sharing plan cannot do.

In a typical ESOP, a corporation establishes an ESOP plan and an ESOP trust as the qualified retirement plan. The plan is filed with the IRS for approval. The majority shareholders (or shareholder) then sell their shares to the ESOP trust at fair market value. If the company is not publicly traded, the fair market value must be determined by an independent business appraiser for every year that the plan exists.

The company makes its annual profit-sharing contribution to the ESOP by "releasing" from an escrow account a number of shares on the basis of the fair market value of the company at the time set for the allocation, usually the last day of the plan year. The shares are allocated annually to each employee's account in the ESOP trust, according to a formula set forth in the ESOP plan (e.g., each employee receives 10 percent of the value of the shares being released).

When an employee leaves the company, he or she usually sells the shares in his or her account to the ESOP at an amount equal to the fair market value of the shares at the time of separation and as established by the appraisal at the beginning of the plan year in which separation of service occurs.

An ESOP is a sophisticated planning tool used by employers for both retirement and succession planning (see Chapter 22). We cannot overstate the need for qualified advisors in establishing an ESOP. Whether an ESOP is appropriate for a small-business owner depends on the owner's situation, the profitability of the business, and the goals and objectives of all shareholders.

◢ How does the ESOP get the funds to purchase the stock?

The plan permits the ESOP to borrow funds to purchase the stock. The employer usually guarantees the loan repayment. The Small Business Administration offers a special loan-guarantee program for ESOPs.

◢ Can an S corporation establish an ESOP?

An S corporation may sponsor an ESOP. An S corporation that becomes 100 percent owned by an ESOP can effectively become a tax-exempt entity, because earnings produced by pass-through distributions and allocations are allocated to the ESOP trust and indirectly to the ESOP participants. Because the ESOP is a tax-exempt organization, the dividends are tax-deferred.

Note, however, that the S corporation ESOP is controversial. There is no assurance that Congress will continue to permit this unique planning opportunity.

401(k) PLANS

◢ What is a 401(k) plan?

A *401(k) plan* is a profit-sharing plan that includes a *cash-or-deferred arrangement (CODA)* that allows employees to contribute to their own retirement accounts. Employee contributions may be made in either of two ways, both of which are free of withholding for income, FICA, and FUTA taxes:

1. In a *salary reduction* (or *savings*) *plan,* each employee elects to reduce his or her pay by a certain amount, expressed either as a dollar amount (e.g., $200 per pay period) or as a percentage (e.g., 5 percent of salary). The employer withholds that amount from each paycheck and contributes it to the employee's 401(k) account.

2. In the *bonus* or *cash option plan,* the employer offers employees a bonus, typically at year's end. Each employee decides whether to defer all or a portion of the bonus to his or her 401(k) account instead of receiving it in cash.

Employers can combine these options and offer a bonus to workers in addition to ongoing salary deferrals. If you customarily pay year-end bonuses anyway, setting up this type of plan does not create a new expense for your business.

With either option employers must give employees the choice of receiving the cash at present or deferring receipt of the cash and its taxation until a later time. The employee contributions are known as *elective contributions.*

The employer may be a partnership, a corporation, or a limited liability company. A 401(k) plan is available to sole proprietorships only when they have employees.

⤳ *What are the eligibility requirements for 401(k) plans?*

A 401(k) plan must cover full-time employees who are 21 years of age or older and who have worked in the business for at least 1 year, and it must cover part-time employees (those who work less than 1000 hours per year). It may exclude employees who are not yet 21 years old.

In contrast, defined-benefit plans, traditional profit-sharing plans, and money purchase pension plans may exclude part-time employees.

⚅ *Must all employees participate to make a 401(k) plan work?*

No. However, regulations prohibit discrimination in favor of highly compensated employees, that is, those who earn $85,000 or more (in 2001), indexed annually for inflation.

Nondiscrimination Rules

⚅ *What are the nondiscrimination rules for 401(k) plans?*

In addition to meeting the nondiscrimination rules for qualified plans (see Chapter 11), a 401(k) plan must pass one of two special nondiscrimination tests. Because under a cash-or-deferred arrangement lower-paid workers are more likely than others to take the cash instead of deferral, it is possible that a 401(k) plan would provide a greater benefit to highly compensated employees. To prevent this situation, the rules require that non-highly compensated employees must defer salary at a certain percentage rate compared to that of highly compensated employees in order to allow highly compensated employees to contribute their maximum amount to the plan. The plan must satisfy at least one of the following tests:

1. The actual deferral percentage (ADP) of the eligible highly compensated employees does not exceed 125 percent of the ADP of all other eligible employees.
2. The ADP of the eligible highly compensated employees is not more than twice the ADP of all other eligible employees, and if the ADP for highly compensated employees is higher than the ADP for all other eligible employees, it is not more than 2 percentage points higher.

For example, for 2002, the five highly compensated employees of Mc-Dowell Engineering made elective contributions to their 401(k) accounts as shown in Table 13-1. The other eligible McDowell employees, on average, deferred 3 percent of their compensation in 2002.

The plan fails the first test because the average ADP of the highly compensated employees (4.6 percent) exceeds 125 percent of the ADP of all other eligible employees (125% × 3% = 3.75%). The plan passes the second test, however, because 4.6 percent is less than twice the other employees' ADP (2 × 3% = 6%) *and* the difference between 4.6 percent and 3 percent is less than 2.

Though the IRS imposes additional nondiscrimination tests on the 401(k) plan, it also provides alternate, simplified methods of satisfying the tests. They are called "safe-harbor" requirements, and we discuss them later in the chapter.

⊿ *How can I encourage my employees to participate in the 401(k) plan so that I can avoid having a top-heavy plan?*

Obviously, the most important thing you can do for employees is match their contributions. The 2001 tax act has helped employers in this effort. For years 2002 through 2006, it provides new, additional tax incentives to low- and moderate-income employees to encourage them to contribute more to 401(k) plans. Illustrate these new incentives to your employees.

TABLE 13-1   401(k) Contributions: McDowell Engineering

Highly compensated employee	Compensation	Deferred to 401(k)	Percentage of compensation
Bob	$100,000	$ 5,000	5
Carol	86,000	6,020	7
Ted	89,000	0	0
Alice	130,000	9,100	7
Harry	90,000	3,600	4
Total	$495,000	$23,720	23
Average	$99,000	$4,744	4.6

Also explain the added benefit of having contributions increase on a tax-deferred basis. For example, take a situation in which the employee contributes $100 and the employer matches it. If the employee is in the 15 percent income tax bracket, then his or her contribution to the plan really costs only $85 (the IRS was going to get the other $15 anyway), but the amount in the plan, growing on behalf of the employee, is $200.

You can offer the services of a financial advisor to help employees choose their investments or to teach classes on the subject.

If none of this works, you might consider incorporating a safe-harbor option (discussed later in the chapter).

Contributions

What are the employee's tax-deductible contribution limits?

In 2002, the tax-deductible limit on employee deferrals is $11,000. Then the limit increases $1000 each year, reaching $15,000 in 2006. Thereafter, it is $15,000 indexed annually for inflation. Also starting in 2002, workers over 50 may contribute an additional $1000 per year to the plan until 2006, when they reach the limit of $5000.

Are employer contributions required under 401(k) plans? If I, as an employer, want to contribute, how can I do so?

If you set up a CODA (cash-or-deferral arrangement) salary reduction option, you generally are not obligated to make contributions to the plan unless you cannot meet the nondiscrimination rules. To encourage non-highly compensated employees to participate, employers often "sweeten the pot" by matching employees' elective deferrals at a specified ratio. For example, for each dollar contributed by an employee, the employer may contribute a matching dollar, 50 cents, or some other set amount. You can also set up a CODA bonus plan option. This allows you to offer bonus contributions in addition to matching contributions for the salary reduction plan.

Because a 401(k) plan is also a profit-sharing plan, you can make additional discretionary contributions to the plan without giving employees the option of receiving cash instead.

⩕ *What are the employer's deductible contribution limits for a 401(k) plan?*

Effective in 2002, the maximum amount the employer can deduct for tax purposes is 25 percent of the employee's compensation or $40,000 (indexed annually for inflation), whichever is less.

⩕ *Are there any requirements for creating the formula I use to match employee contributions?*

No. The employer can establish any type of formula for matching contributions, as long as it is the same formula for all participants. Many employers use generous formulas to encourage non-highly compensated employees to contribute. For example, some employers provide a 50 percent match on all contributions or a 100 percent match on the first 5 or 6 percent and a reduced match on the balance.

⩕ *Are there any limits on the combined amount of the employer contribution and the employee deferral?*

Before passage of the 2001 tax act, the employer contribution and employee salary deferral could not, together, be more than 25 percent of the employee's total compensation. Under the new law, the combined contribution cannot exceed 100 percent of the employee's compensation.

⩕ *Can there be a vesting schedule for the employer's contributions?*

Employees' elective contributions must be 100 percent vested immediately, but employer contributions can be subject to a vesting schedule, as described in Chapter 11.

⅍ Who manages the investments in the 401(k) plan?

The plan may be invested by the plan fiduciary, or it may allow employees to direct the investments for their own accounts. If the employer wants to shift the fiduciary liability for investing to the employees, the employer must comply with several ERISA requirements, including (1) give the participants at least three investment options, (2) let the participants make their own choices among the options, and (3) let them change the investments at least every 3 months.

Safe-Harbor 401(k)

⅍ What exactly is a safe-harbor 401(k) plan?

Safe-harbor options are alternate, simplified methods of satisfying the nondiscrimination tests. Plans that adopt one of these methods are referred to as *safe-harbor 401(k) plans.* Safe-harbor options can also be used with SIMPLE 401(k) plans.

The 401(k) plan with safe-harbor language requires that the employer elect between two *mandatory* contribution options:

MATCHING CONTRIBUTION: For all non-highly compensated employees, the employer makes matching contributions equal to 100 percent of the employee's elective deferral of up to 3 percent of his or her compensation *and* 50 percent of the employee's elective deferral of between 3 and 5 percent of compensation. Other matching formulas may be used under certain circumstances.

NONELECTIVE CONTRIBUTION: The employer makes a nonelective contribution of at least 3 percent of compensation for each non-highly compensated employee, regardless of whether the employee makes an elective deferral.

With the nonelective safe-harbor option, the 3 percent contribution also ensures that the top-heavy minimum-contribution rule is satisfied. This allows the business owner and other highly compensated employees to defer up to their maximum-contribution dollar limit per year and to receive additional matching or profit-sharing contributions from the employer.

The safe-harbor contributions must be fully vested and are non-forfeitable, even if there are other employer contributions to the plan that may be subject to a vesting schedule. Full vesting is simply the "toll charge" that owners pay for the relaxed testing that allows them to provide significant benefits for highly compensated and key employees.

⋡ How do I determine which of these options is best?

The decision of which safe-harbor option to use depends on the company's facts, circumstances, and demographics. If employees are already deferring at a significant rate and the plan is not top-heavy, the matching incentive may be the appropriate one. For example, if the employer is currently making 50 percent contributions up to 6 percent of compensation and participation by non-highly compensated employees is very good, using the matching safe-harbor option increases the budget a bit but allows highly compensated employees to defer up to their annual limits.

If the plan is in danger of becoming top-heavy, the employer should make the 3 percent nonelective contribution. While this choice may be more expensive in terms of cash flow, it generally accomplishes three objectives: (1) It satisfies the top-heavy minimum required contribution of 3 percent to all participants. (2) There is no more ADP deferral testing. (3) The 3 percent counts as a base contribution toward meeting most other qualified plan nondiscrimination rules as well.

⋡ Are there any drawbacks to the 401(k) with safe-harbor options?

Potential drawbacks for an employer are:

- Employer contributions are mandatory.
- Safe-harbor contributions are 100 percent vested immediately, with no forfeitures available to offset employer contributions.
- There are more administrative expenses than is the case with other plans.
- The employer must provide a special annual notice to each participant.

≤┤ *When should an employer consider adopting a 401(k) with safe-harbor options?*

An employer should consider a safe-harbor 401(k) plan if the employer either:

- Has a large percentage of highly compensated employees
- Expects low participation by non-highly compensated employees
- Has trouble passing ADP/ACP tests with existing 401(k) plans
- Doesn't want the responsibilities and expense of nondiscrimination testing
- Wants the highest limits for employee contributions
- Wants to maximize employer contributions to highly compensated employees
- Has low employee turnover (since the safe-harbor contributions are nonforfeitable)

ADVANTAGES
AND DISADVANTAGES

≤┤ *What are the advantages and disadvantages of defined-contribution plans?*

Defined-contribution plans have the same advantages and disadvantages as all qualified retirement plans, as well as the following:

Advantages

- Most are easy to understand and explain to employees.
- Employers can integrate Social Security contributions into the contribution formulas to offset required contribution amounts and increase contributions for highly compensated employees.

Disadvantages

- Ultimate benefits depend on investment performance, so employees have no guarantee of the dollar values of their future retirement benefits.

≱ *Are there any advantages and disadvantages that pertain specifically to profit-sharing plans?*

Yes. In addition to the items listed above for all defined-contribution plans, the following apply to profit-sharing plans:

Advantages

- Employers can decide on the contribution amounts each year.
- Contributions are required in only 3 out of 5 years.
- The flexibility of contribution requirements permits employers with an erratic cash flow to make small contributions or skip years and employers with a highly profitable year to have a current deduction without committing to future annual contributions.
- Employers can incorporate allocation formulas into the plan to increase contributions and allocations for highly compensated and key employees.
- Employers can combine the profit-sharing plan with a 401(k) plan to maximize contributions for highly compensated and key employees.

Disadvantages

- Employers are responsible for making contributions; employees are not allowed to do so.
- Employers bear full fiduciary responsibility for investment management.
- Employees have no assurance that employers will make annual contributions to the plans.
- Without the use of allocation formulas or a 401(k) plan, a profit-sharing plan may not be the best means for older or highly compensated employees to accumulate retirement funds.

⚜ *What are the particular advantages and disadvantages of a money purchase pension plan?*

A money purchase pension plan has the same advantages and disadvantages as defined-contribution plans in general (see the first question in this section), as well as the following:

Advantages

- Employers can incorporate allocation formulas into the plan to maximize contributions for highly compensated and key employees.
- Employers can combine a money purchase plan with a 401(k) plan to maximize contributions for highly compensated and key employees.
- Employees can be given responsibility for investment management.

Disadvantages

- Employers are responsible for making contributions; employees are not allowed to do so.
- Annual contributions are mandatory, whether or not the company has profits.

- The contribution amount is fixed when the company establishes the plan.

- Without the use of allocation formulas or a 401(k) plan, a money purchase plan may not be the best means for older or highly compensated employees to accumulate retirement funds.

What are the advantages and disadvantages of an ESOP?

In addition to the items listed for defined-contribution plans in general (see the first question in this section), an ESOP has the following advantages and disadvantages:

Advantages

- The employer's contributions to the plan can be stock, so the employer's cash flow is not affected.

- An ESOP allows all employees to become owners.

- For majority stockholders, an ESOP can facilitate estate and financial planning objectives by providing (1) a liquid market if they want to sell their stock at retirement and (2) substantial tax benefits that allow them to defer (or avoid) taxable gain on a sale in the future when the company has appreciated in value.

Disadvantages

- ESOPs are costly to establish and maintain, with allocation and valuation services required each year.

- Employers are responsible for making contributions; employees are not allowed to do so.

- Majority stockholders must personally guarantee the loans to the ESOP for stock purchases.

Can you summarize the advantages and disadvantages of a 401(k) plan?

A 401(k) plan has the same advantages and disadvantages as

defined-contribution plans in general (see the first question in this section), as well as the following:

Advantages

- The employer does not have to make contributions unless the plan is top-heavy.
- It is easier for employees to participate because contributions are made in the form of payroll deductions.

If the employer contributes:

- This encourages more employees to participate, so costly top-heavy penalties can be avoided.
- Investment responsibility can be shifted to employees.
- The employer can decide on the contribution amount each year.
- The employer can choose between matching employee contributions and using a direct contribution formula.
- The flexibility of contribution requirements permits employers with an erratic cash flow to make small contributions or skip years and those with a highly profitable year to get a current deduction without committing to future annual contributions.
- The employer can establish a vesting schedule on its contributions.
- The employer can incorporate allocation formulas into the plan to maximize contributions and allocations for highly compensated employees.
- The employer can combine the 401(k) with a profit-sharing plan or money purchase pension plan to maximize contributions and allocations for highly compensated and key employees.

Disadvantages

- Employees have no assurance that the employer will make any contributions to the plan.

If the employer contributes:

- The employer may need to incorporate special provisions into the plan so that highly compensated employees can defer the maximum amount allowable each year.

- Without the use of allocation formulas or another plan, a 401(k) may not be the best means for older or highly compensated employees to accumulate retirement funds.

If only employees contribute:

- This may discourage many employees from participating, and the employer may have to make contributions to satisfy ERISA's top-heavy nondiscrimination requirements.

- The employees bear full responsibility for investment management and may have insufficient knowledge for prudently investing the funds in their accounts without the help of an investment manager or financial advisor.

- The employees cannot accumulate as much for retirement.

- Highly compensated and key employees may be unable to maximize their annual contributions if not enough other employees participate.

chapter 14

Simplified Retirement Plans

SAVINGS INCENTIVE MATCH PLANS FOR EMPLOYEES

≰ *What is a SIMPLE?*

A *savings incentive match plan for employees,* or *SIMPLE,* is a low-cost alternative for the employer that wants to offer a retirement program to employees but cannot sponsor a qualified plan. The Small Business Job Protection Act of 1996 created the SIMPLE. There are two types of SIMPLE plans: the IRA version and the 401(k) version.

≰ *What is a SIMPLE IRA?*

A *SIMPLE IRA* is an employer-sponsored individual retirement account. SIMPLE IRA plans allow an eligible participant to contribute money to his or her SIMPLE IRA or to fund an individual retirement annuity through payroll deductions. Employers can contribute by matching contributions or by making nonelective mandatory contributions. Within prescribed limits, employer contributions are tax-deductible to the employer. A SIMPLE IRA plan is not subject to the nondiscrimination and top-heavy rules that generally apply to qualified plans. In addition, reporting requirements are simplified. Within limits, employees do not pay tax on contributions to a SIMPLE IRA plan until they withdraw funds.

⅍ What is the difference between a SIMPLE IRA and a personal IRA?

A SIMPLE IRA is an employer-sponsored plan that permits larger annual contributions than a personal IRA allows.

⅍ What is a SIMPLE 401(k) plan?

A SIMPLE 401(k) plan is essentially a scaled-down version of a regular 401(k) plan, with the following exceptions:

- The plan need not comply with nondiscrimination or top-heavy rules.
- The maximum employee deferral in 2002 is $7000, and the maximum employer matching contribution in 2002 is $7000.
- Employer contributions *must* immediately vest 100 percent.
- The plan assets are maintained in a common fund, and the employer is the trustee and investment manager on behalf of the plan assets for all participants.
- An employer may *not* have any other retirement plan in place.

The SIMPLE 401(k) plan is more cost-effective and less complicated to administer than the standard 401(k) plan. In our experience, however, employers rarely use SIMPLE 401(k) plans. This is because these plans are subject to contribution limits, administration requirements, and a restriction against combining the SIMPLE 401(k) plan with another qualified plan to increase contributions. All things being equal, these restrictions and requirements make other plans more attractive to business owners.

We discuss only the SIMPLE IRA plan in this chapter. If you are interested in learning about a SIMPLE 401(k) plan for your company, please ask your financial advisor for more information.

⚜ Can any company establish a SIMPLE IRA plan?

Only small employers (including tax-exempt and government employers) qualify. Eligibility criteria include (1) the employer must not employ more than 100 employees who each earned $5000 or more in the preceding calendar year and (2) the employer may not maintain any other qualified, SIMPLE, or simplified employee pension (SEP) retirement plan. Sole proprietorships, partnerships, corporations, and LLCs that meet these criteria may establish SIMPLE IRA plans.

For these plans, compensation for self-employed individuals (sole proprietors, partners, and some LLC members) includes net earnings from self-employment, determined without subtracting any contributions made under the SIMPLE IRA plan on behalf of the self-employed individual.

⚜ What employees are eligible for a SIMPLE IRA?

Employees who *must* be permitted to participate in a SIMPLE IRA plan are employees who received $5000 or more in compensation from the employer during any 2 prior years (not necessarily consecutive) and who are reasonably expected to receive at least $5000 in compensation during the current year, part-time employees, and employees under 21 years of age.

⚜ Can an employer include employees who make less than $5000?

Yes. An employer may relax (or eliminate) the participation requirement for employees who earn less than $5000. An employer may make all eligibility requirements more open but not more restrictive.

Contributions

⋇ *How much can employees contribute to a SIMPLE IRA?*

After passage of the 2001 tax act, the limit for employee elective salary reduction contributions was $6500 in that year. The limit is $7000 in 2002, and then it increases $1000 each year, reaching $10,000 in 2005. Thereafter, it is $10,000 indexed for inflation.

Employee and employer contributions are not subject to income tax until the employee withdraws the funds. Employee contributions are subject to FICA, FUTA, and Railroad Retirement Act taxes, but employer contributions are not.

⋇ *How are employer contributions calculated?*

If the employer chooses to contribute to the SIMPLE IRA, it must use one of the following methods:

MATCHING CONTRIBUTION: The employer matches each employee's elective salary reduction, dollar for dollar, up to 3 percent of the employee's total compensation or the maximum allowable employee contribution limit for the year (e.g., $7000 in 2002), whichever is less. For any 2 out of 5 years, the employer can elect a lower match. However, the match cannot be less than 1 percent of the employee's compensation, and the percentage must be the same for all participants.

NONELECTIVE MANDATORY CONTRIBUTION: Each year the employer must contribute 2 percent of total compensation up to a base of $200,000 per employee (in 2002), whether or not the employee contributes to the plan. The maximum annual contribution to each employee is $4000 in 2002.

The employer makes contributions to the financial institution serving as the account's custodian and realizes an income tax deduction for its permitted contributions.

What are the vesting rules for a SIMPLE IRA?

All contributions made by the participant *and* the employer must be 100 percent vested at the time the contributions are made.

Who directs the investments in a SIMPLE IRA?

A SIMPLE IRA operates like a personal IRA. The investments are self-directed. Most custodians who manage IRAs can handle SIMPLE IRAs as well.

Withdrawals and Loans

Are there any special rules regarding withdrawals from SIMPLE IRAs?

Yes. Participants may withdraw funds from their SIMPLE IRAs before separation of service. If a participant withdraws funds within 2 years of the date he or she began participation, the IRS assesses a 25 percent penalty (instead of the 10 percent penalty for early withdrawal from qualified retirement plans and personal IRAs).

May employees borrow from their SIMPLE IRAs?

No. Participants may not borrow from their SIMPLE IRAs.

Creation and Administration

How does an employer establish a SIMPLE IRA plan?

The IRS publishes model forms an employer can use to establish a

SIMPLE IRA plan. Many financial institutions and mutual fund companies have IRS-approved plan documents ready for use.

An employer can establish a SIMPLE IRA plan with a single financial institution or can permit each employee to establish a SIMPLE IRA at the financial institution of his or her choice. If the employer selects the institution, the participant may transfer his or her account to another institution or another SIMPLE IRA without cost or penalty.

⩔ *What are the employer's compliance and reporting requirements for a SIMPLE IRA?*

The employer must notify each eligible employee (usually on or before November 2 of each year) of the employee's right to enter into a salary reduction agreement or to modify a previous agreement. The employer must provide each eligible employee with a copy of the summary plan description supplied to the employer by the trustee.

If the employer elects to reduce the matching contributions below 3 percent or to make nonelective contributions in lieu of the matching contributions, the employer must provide written notice of the election to the participants at least 60 days in advance so that they have time to revise their salary reduction agreements. The notification must also disclose the employee's ability to select a financial institution to serve as trustee for his or her account.

⩔ *When must an employer actually make the contributions to a SIMPLE IRA plan?*

The employer must transfer employee contributions to the plan custodian no later than the close of the 30-day period following the last day of the month for which the amounts would otherwise have been payable to the employees in cash. The employer must make its matching or nonelective contributions no later than the date for filing the employer's income tax return (including extensions) for the taxable year for which the contributions are made.

SIMPLIFIED EMPLOYEE
PENSION PLANS

⚐ *What is a simplified employee pension plan?*

A *simplified employee pension (SEP)* plan is an IRA or an individual retirement annuity established by an employer for employees. Under a SEP, the employer contributes funds to an IRA (called a *SEP-IRA*) established for each eligible employee. The employee owns and controls the account, and the employer makes contributions to the financial institution that serves as the account's custodian.

The SEP was designed to be less complicated than a money purchase pension plan or profit-sharing plan and to allow greater contributions than those for deductible IRAs. The SEP is very popular with sole proprietorships, partnerships, and LLCs with few employees.

⚐ *Who is eligible to participate in a SEP?*

In general, any employee who meets the following criteria is eligible and must be allowed to participate: an employee who is 21 years of age or older; earns at least $450 during the year (in 2001, indexed annually for inflation); and has performed services for the employer in at least 3 of the preceding 5 calendar years. The employer may make eligibility less restrictive but not more restrictive.

Contributions

⚐ *Can employees contribute to the SEP?*

No. Employee contributions are not allowed.

⚐ *How much can employers contribute to a SEP?*

Effective 2002, the maximum tax-deductible amount that employers can contribute is 25 percent of the employee's compensation or

$40,000 (indexed annually for inflation), whichever is less. The employer's contributions on behalf of employees are deductible to the company and are excluded from the employee's current gross income.

↩ *Is an employer required to contribute to a SEP each year?*

Employer contributions are discretionary. The employer may decide from year to year how much, if any, to contribute. When the company does make contributions, the percentage of compensation that "defines" the contribution must apply to all employees, including owner-employees. In other words, if you decide to contribute 7 percent of an employee's compensation to the plan, you must contribute that percentage for all employees.

↩ *Are SEPs subject to any nondiscrimination rules?*

Yes. SEPs are subject to top-heavy testing. If the test indicates that the plan favors key employees, current law mandates a 3 percent minimum contribution on behalf of each participant who is not a key employee.

↩ *When are the contributions vested?*

Contributions to SEP plans must vest immediately and must be nonforfeitable.

Loans

↩ *May an employee borrow money against his or her SEP or otherwise use the account as collateral for a loan?*

No. An employee may list the account in a financial statement submitted to a bank with a loan application. This information may help the employee qualify for a loan, but the account may not be pledged as security for the repayment of a loan.

Creation and Administration

⚐ Is a SEP expensive to establish and maintain?

A SEP costs almost nothing to establish, and reporting is minimal. The employer usually completes a simplified IRS Form 5305-SEP to start the plan. In most cases, there are no annual IRS or Department of Labor reports to complete.

ADVANTAGES
AND DISADVANTAGES

⚐ Can you summarize the advantages and disadvantages of this chapter's simplified retirement plans?

For the most part, SIMPLE IRA and SEP-IRA plans have the same advantages and disadvantages. The following items pertain to both:

Advantages

- They are tax-efficient ways to provide additional compensation to owners and other employees.
- Within prescribed limits, contributions are deductible by the employer.
- The plans promote retention of employees.
- They are simple for small businesses to establish and administer; they do not require Form 5500 filings with the IRS.
- The employer has no investment responsibility.
- The plans are not subject to ACP nondiscrimination testing rules
- Contributions are not currently taxable to participants.
- Employer contributions are not subject to FICA or FUTA taxes.
- Income and capital gains grow tax-free inside the plan, allowing greater compounding.

- Business owners who hire their children, even part-time, can provide them with the advantages of a retirement plan while shifting income to the children.
- The employer can use a vesting schedule to reward employees for longevity and has forfeited amounts to use.

Disadvantages

- Employees have no guarantee of future benefits.
- Older and highly compensated employees may not be able to accumulate sufficient funds for retirement and may bring pressure on the employer to provide additional retirement benefits.
- The investment risk rests with the participant.
- The investment choices available to a participant may be limited.
- Loans are not permitted.
- Funds may not be protected from attachment by creditors.

✒ *Are there any advantages and disadvantages that pertain only to SIMPLE IRAs?*

Yes. In addition to the items listed above, the following apply to SIMPLE IRA plans:

Advantages

- The employer can choose between a discretionary matching contribution or a mandatory annual contribution.
- The plan is not subject to ADP or top-heavy nondiscrimination testing rules.
- Employees may be allowed to contribute.

Disadvantages

- The employer may not sponsor a qualified retirement plan in addition to a SIMPLE IRA.
- Part-time employees may not be excluded.

■ Employer contributions are immediately vested, and participants have complete portability of their accounts, including cashing out the IRA while still employed by the company.

⚑ Are there any particular advantages and disadvantages of a SEP-IRA?

The SEP-IRA has all the advantages and disadvantages listed in the first question of this section, as well as the following:

Advantages

■ Part-time employees may be excluded.

■ The employer may sponsor a qualified retirement plan in addition to a SEP.

■ Annual employer contributions are discretionary from year to year.

■ The plan is not subject to ADP nondiscrimination testing rules.

Disadvantages

■ The plan is subject to top-heavy nondiscrimination testing rules.

■ Employee contributions are not permitted.

■ There is no guarantee that the employer will contribute annually and no guarantee of what the contribution amount will be.

chapter 15

Evaluating Retirement Plans

BUSINESS GOALS

How do I determine the best plan for my business and my employees?

First, you must have a clear vision of your business goals. Some of the most common goals of business owners are:

- To be competitive in attracting new employees and in retaining existing employees
- To help all the employees save for retirement
- To have a plan that is both cost-effective and simple to establish, administer, and explain to employees

- To have a plan that requires the least amount of reporting to government agencies
- To be able to modify or change the plan as the company and its goals change
- To contribute the maximum amount on a tax-deferred basis to the owner's retirement
- To reward a few key or highly compensated employees with contributions that are greater than those made for other employees

Your goals and priorities will, in large part, determine the best plan for your business.

❧ Do my retirement plan options depend on the ownership structure of my business?

While most plans are available to every type of entity, some benefits and features may differ among the various business structures. For example, since contributions to a qualified plan are based on an employee's "compensation," shareholders of an S corporation may have to pay themselves more compensation (and pay the payroll taxes) and take less profit in the form of dividends (which are not subject to payroll taxes) in order to contribute the maximum amount to a qualified retirement plan for themselves.

Otherwise, the amounts that can be contributed to any qualified retirement plan are relatively the same across the board, regardless of the entity.

❧ How can I evaluate the available plans?

To help you evaluate retirement plans, Table 15-1 compares the plans on the basis of their features and Table 15-2 suggests plan options for various goals and situations.

In establishing any retirement plan, work with your financial advisor, attorney, and accountant. These professionals will help you analyze your choice in terms of your overall planning goals and properly implement the plan you choose.

COST AND COMPLEXITY CONSIDERATIONS

⚛ *Should I use a prototype plan or hire an attorney to draft a custom plan?*

Every retirement plan must be submitted to the IRS for review and approval. *Prototype plans* are models that have already been submitted to and approved by the IRS, usually by financial services companies and other plan administrators and custodians. Prototype plans are less expensive to establish and to amend as the law changes.

A *custom plan* is more costly; however, you can structure it to fit your exact needs and requirements as the employer-sponsor. A custom plan usually provides your company with more control and benefits in terms of vesting requirements, payment of vested balances to terminated employees, and formulas for allocating plan contributions.

If you do not need special provisions in your retirement plan, using a prototype plan offered through a financial institution, financial firm, third-party administrator, or law firm is the least expensive option. If you require or want special options, you will need to employ the services of a financial advisor and an accountant to help you design the plan and of an attorney who specializes in retirement plans to draft the plan documents and submit the plan to the IRS for review and approval. It is also possible to start with a plan prototype and revise it as needed; IRS approval is still required, but starting with a prototype should reduce the cost of establishing the plan. Your current advisors can assist you in determining whether you need a custom plan and in finding an attorney to draft it.

TABLE 15-1 Retirement Plans: Comparison of Features*

Features	Qualified retirement plans					Simplified plans	
	Defined-benefit	Profit-sharing	Money purchase pension	ESOP	401(k)	SIMPLE IRA	SEP-IRA
Eligibility:							
Available to companies with any number of employees	Yes	Yes	Yes	Yes	Yes	100 max	Yes
Available to all entities	Yes	Yes	Yes	Corps only	Yes	Yes	Yes
Must allow part-time employees	No	No	No	No	Yes	Yes	No
Must allow employees under 21	No	No	No	No	No	Yes	No
Loans: May be allowed in plan documents	Yes	Yes	Yes	Yes	Yes	No	No
Investment responsibility: Employer must retain	Yes	Yes	No	Yes	No	No	No
Asset protection: ERISA creditor protection available	Yes	Yes	Yes	Yes	Yes	No	No
Reporting: Annual reporting requirements	Yes	Yes	Yes	Yes	Yes	No	Minimal
Employer contributions:							
Mandatory annual contributions	Yes	No	Yes	Yes	No	–†	No

Contributions vest 100% immediately	No	No	No	No	No	Yes	No
Maximum tax-deductible contribution per person	Actuarial calculation	$40,000	$40,000	$40,000	$40,000	–‡	$40,000
Maximum allocation per participant	NA	$40,000	$40,000	$40,000	$40,000	–‡	NA
Integration of formulas to maximize contributions for highly compensated employees	No	Yes	Yes	Yes	Yes	No	No
Employee contributions:							
Contributions allowed	No	No	No	No	Yes	Yes	No
Maximum contribution	NA	NA	NA	NA	$11,000	$7000	NA
Nondiscrimination testing:							
Top-heavy required	Yes	Yes	Yes	Yes	Yes	No	Yes
ACP required	Yes	Yes	Yes	Yes	Yes	No	No
ADP required	NA	NA	NA	NA	Yes	No	No

*All figures are based on 2002; NA = not applicable.
†May choose discretionary or mandatory.
‡Discretionary max: $7000; mandatory max: $4000.

TABLE 15-2   Plan Options Based on Goals and Situations

	Plan options
Goals	
No mandatory annual contributions	Profit sharing, 401(k), SEP-IRA
Flexibility in plan design to allow maximum contribution for key employees	Profit sharing, money purchase pension, 401(k), safe-harbor 401(k)*
Minimal complexity, administration costs, reporting	SIMPLE IRA, SEP-IRA
Limitation on employees' ability to withdraw from plan	Defined benefit, profit sharing, money purchase pension, 401(k) employer contributions
Situations	
More than 100 employees	Defined benefit, profit sharing, Money purchase pension, 401(k), SEP-IRA†
High employee turnover in first few years of service	Defined benefit, profit sharing, money purchase pension, 401(k)‡
Large number of part-time employees	Defined benefit, 401(k), SEP§
Older workforce (including owner-employees) deserving substantial retirement contributions	Defined benefit
Younger, stable workforce with many years to accumulate retirement funds	401(k) with no employer contributions, SIMPLE IRA, SEP-IRA

*With age-weighted, cross-tested, and Social Security integration formulas.

†All but the SEP-IRA are best suited for companies that require flexibility in plan design and can cost-justify higher expenses of administration.

‡Use vesting schedules; allocate forfeitures of departing employees to the accounts of loyal employees who continue with the company, or use them to offset required future employer contributions.

§Defined-benefit and 401(k) plans *must* exclude part-time employees who work less than 1000 hours in a year; SEP plans *may* exclude part-time employees on the basis of hours of service.

≱ *How do I calculate the costs of prototype plans?*

You should evaluate the plans and services for consulting and administration on the basis of a number of factors. Many firms bundle the costs of planning and formation with the annual cost of administration and record keeping. You should separate, to the extent possible, the cost of the services and determine the applicable fees for each level of service.

Department of Labor regulations require complete and full written disclosure of all fees and expenses associated with the operation and management of a qualified retirement plan. For more information on fees, visit the website for the Department of Labor's Pension and Welfare Benefits Administration (www.dol.gov/dol/pwba).

≱ *I am the only person in my business. What are my retirement plan options?*

As the sole owner-employee of your business, you have the advantage of not having to consider employee cost or benefit in your retirement plan decision. The goal is to maximize your own benefit at the lowest expense. Most one-person businesses like the ease, simplicity, and minimal cost of a SIMPLE IRA or a SEP-IRA plan. You can also consider some nonqualified retirement plan alternatives, such as a deferred-compensation plan.

≱ *What is the least expensive plan to establish and maintain?*

The SIMPLE IRA and SEP-IRA plans are the least expensive to establish and maintain.

MAXIMIZING CONTRIBUTIONS

≱ *How can I contribute more money for some employees without running into problems with nondiscrimination rules?*

Employers can incorporate additional options into profit-sharing, money purchase pension, and 401(k) plans so that they can contribute more for certain employees. For example, if Camelot Industries' profit-sharing plan provides for an employer contribution to employees of 4.8 percent of their salaries, this would amount to only $4800 for a key employee making $100,000 per year—even though the maximum amount Camelot could contribute to the plan (in 2002) for this employee is $25,000 (25% × $100,000). To maximize contributions to highly compensated or key employees, Camelot could add to its plan Social Security integration provisions, age-weighted formulas, or cross-tested formulas.

⚄ What does it mean to "integrate" Social Security contributions?

Under the Internal Revenue Code, defined-contribution plans can be *integrated* with Social Security. Congress allowed Social Security integration for a reason: Employees have a Social Security retirement fund based on mandatory contributions in the form of withholding taxes. In 2001, 6.2 percent of every employee's paycheck up to $80,400 of wages was taxed and contributed to the Social Security retirement fund. In addition, the employer must match this payroll tax. In essence, 12.4 percent is contributed toward retirement for every employee on the first $80,400 of income (indexed annually for inflation). Congress feels that since employees who earn more than this wage base do not receive a government-funded retirement to the full extent of their earnings, it is permissible to create disparity in the contribution formula in a qualified retirement plan by allowing a larger percentage contribution and allocation for participants whose wages exceed the Social Security wage base. Strangely enough, Congress has not indexed the percentage allocation up to the 6.2 percent—it is frozen at 5.7 percent. The net result is that participants in retirement plans can have additional contributions made on their behalf equal to 5.7 percent of all wages in excess of the Social Security wage base.

Another requirement for using Social Security integration is that the base contribution for all employees in the defined-contribution plan must be at least 5.7 percent of compensation if the excess contribution is 5.7 percent. Thus, a participant who earned more than $80,400 in 2001 would receive the base plan contribution of 5.7 percent of compensation up to the Social Security wage base *and* an additional contribution of 5.7 percent on compensation in excess of $80,400.

What is an age-weighted formula?

Similar to the formulas used in a defined-benefit plan, *age-weighted formulas* enable employers to proportionately allocate more money to the accounts of older employees. In so doing, they may reduce the total contribution to the retirement plan.

This is based on the premise that to provide comparable benefits at retirement time, a smaller contribution is needed for a younger employee because a dollar contributed today to his or her account has more time to grow than does a dollar contributed to the account of an older employee. Thus, assuming similar interest rates, age weighting enables an employee who is 50 years of age and one who is 25 to receive essentially equivalent benefits at retirement. Because the 50-year-old has only 15 years to accumulate the same hypothetical benefit, significantly higher contributions are allowed. Younger employees will see a gradual increase in the amount allocated to their accounts as they get older, and this could be a good incentive for staying with the company for the long term.

An age-weighted formula in a profit-sharing plan or money purchase pension plan works well for an owner who is older than the rest of his or her employees.

What is a cross-tested formula?

Much like an age-weighted plan, a *cross-tested formula* creates an opportunity for employers to shift a substantial portion of their contribution to key employees.

Under this alternative, the regulations permit a defined-contribution plan to be tested on the basis of equivalent benefits. Cross-testing essentially determines the annuity benefit that each employee's allocation plus future interest could purchase at normal retirement age. It is these hypothetical annuities, rather than the actual allocations, that are tested for nondiscrimination, much as if the plan were a defined-benefit plan.

Participants are aggregated into contribution groups, and a percentage contribution is calculated for each group on the basis of age and salary. Contribution groups can be almost any logical breakdown within the workforce—owners and nonowners, professional and technical, salaried and commission-compensated. For instance, all sales staff could be grouped together and assigned the same rate of contribution based on a percentage of their compensation. As long as the age of the owners' group is at least 5 years more than the average of the other groups, sharply higher contributions can be made on behalf of the owner-employees. The greater the disparity between the ages and incomes of the groups, the more cross-tested plans favor the preferred groups.

Under cross-testing, the same allocation for a younger employee will be projected to earn more interest, and thus convert to a larger annuity, than it would for an older employee. This means that the same rate of allocation for all employees will produce higher equivalent accrual rates for younger employees.

Cross-tested allocation formulas are especially advantageous for employers with discretionary profit-sharing plans because, in great

TABLE 15-3   Combined Retirement Plan

Employer contributions:		
Profit-sharing plan		
$80,400 × 5.7%	$ 4,582.80	
$119,600* × 11.4%	13,634.40	$18,217.20
401(k) 5.7% safe harbor		11,400.00
		$29,617.20
Employee deferral to 401(k)		11,000.00
		$40,617.20

*$200,000 − $80,400.

years, employers can make significant contributions without the burden of having to make a fixed contribution if the business hits a down cycle. Employers can also pair a 401(k) plan with a profit-sharing plan and incorporate the allocation formulas into the profit-sharing portion of the plan. Highly compensated employees can then defer salary to the 401(k) to achieve their maximum deductible contribution limits. However, the IRS is rethinking the rules on cross-testing, so you should consult with your professional advisors to ensure that you are aware of the most current rules.

A Maximizing Example

Can you give an example of a plan that encourages employees to save for retirement and allocates as much as possible to the owners and key employees?

One common design for achieving both these goals involves combining a 401(k) plan with a profit-sharing plan and using a three-pronged approach, namely: employee deferrals to a 401(k) plan up to the maximum, employer matching safe-harbor contributions to the 401(k), and contributions to the profit-sharing plan using the Social Security integration formula.

For example, the employer could install a profit-sharing plan with a Social Security integration formula of 5.7 percent of pay for all eligible employees on all compensation and an additional 5.7 percent contribution on income in excess of the Social Security wage base ($80,400). This essentially allows 5.7 percent contributions on income below the Social Security wage base plus 11.4 percent contributions on income above the Social Security wage base up to the maximum covered compensation limit of $200,000, in 2002, as indexed. This formula results in an allocation of $18,217.20 to a business owner whose income is at least $200,000. (See the calculation in Table 15-3.)

This business owner could also install a 401(k) plan with a 5.7 percent safe-harbor matching contribution for all employees (in addition to the 5.7 percent contribution to the profit-sharing plan). This 5.7 percent contribution results in $11,400 for owners earning $200,000 a year or more in 2002.

For the third prong of the approach, the owner-employee defers the maximum amount allowed, $11,000 (in 2002), to the 401(k), bringing his or her total to $40,617.20.

The employee deferral to the 401(k) is not subject to any non-discrimination testing because of the 5.7 percent safe-harbor matching contribution made to all employees in the 401(k). The business owner (and, presumably, other highly compensated employees as well) receives the $29,617.20 at an employer cost of 11.4 percent (5.7% + 5.7%) for providing the benefits to all participants.

PART FOUR

Benefits for Key Employees

I N PART THREE WE DISCUSSED FRINGE BENEFITS THAT EMPLOYERS must make available to all employees on a nondiscriminatory basis. Now, in Part Four, we explain methods that employers frequently use to compensate and motivate key employees—including owner-employees—on a "discriminatory" basis. These methods generally involve "nonqualified" retirement and incentive compensation plans. *Nonqualified plans* are so called because they do not have to meet the rigid Internal Revenue Code and ERISA requirements governing qualified retirement plans.

Employers use nonqualified plans because annual contributions are not limited as they are with qualified plans; there are no rules for pre-age-59½ distributions as there are with qualified plans; loans are more easily taken from nonqualified plans; and these plans are a means of providing additional benefits for select employees who are already receiving maximum benefits under a qualified plan. In return for this flexibility, however, some of the favorable attributes of qualified plans (tax deduction for employer contributions, income tax deferral for employee-participants, tax exemption for income and gain inside the plan) may *not* be available in a nonqualified plan.

Each alternative should be measured using the following questions as a guideline:

- How is the value of the benefit determined or measured?
- When does a sponsoring employer realize an income tax deduction for a contribution?
- When does a participating employee incur an income tax liability for the benefit?
- Is the benefit taxable to an employee at ordinary-income tax rates or at capital gain rates?
- Who pays the income tax on earnings and capital gains on assets held in trust for future distribution to an employee-participant?

Chapter 16 presents methods for designing deferred-compensation plans and explains the tax impacts of these methods. The promise to pay deferred compensation may be "funded" or "unfunded." Funding the promise to pay may be accomplished through a salary reduction plan, a rabbi trust, or a secular trust. The chapter also examines assets used to fund a plan, such as life insurance and tax-free bonds.

As our contributors discuss in Chapter 17, incentive stock options and nonstatutory stock options may be awarded to employees as inducements to continue employment with the business. Planning with stock options is not limited to large companies. Incentive stock options and nonstatutory stock options are tax-sensitive, and it is important to understand the tax consequences of each alternative, especially in light of the 2001 tax act. Making bonus payments to a key employee in the form of the employer's stock is another strategy that has special merit, particularly when an exit strategy or business succession plan involves an ultimate transfer of control to key employees.

In Chapter 18, our contributors explain how employers can use life insurance as an important benefit for key employees. Life insurance is often provided to, or for the benefit of, a company executive as a Section 162 bonus plan or a split-dollar life insurance plan.

It is important to understand the income, gift, and estate tax consequences of each benefit and to identify tax-efficient opportunities.

chapter 16

Deferred-Compensation Plans

≼ What is a deferred-compensation plan?

A *deferred-compensation plan* is an agreement by an employer to make future payments to an employee as compensation for services to be rendered. This is a nonqualified retirement plan, so it is exempt from most of the rules that apply to qualified plans. For this reason, employers have a great amount of flexibility in structuring deferred-compensation plans. In almost all cases, these plans are "top-hat" plans that benefit a select group of managerial or highly compensated employees.

In addition to deferring a portion of an employee's salary and the attendant income tax until after retirement, a deferred-compensation plan usually provides that the deferred compensation will be paid to the employee if he or she becomes disabled or to the employee's heirs if he or she dies before receiving all the compensation that was deferred. The most common deferred-compensation plans are the salary reduction plan and the salary continuation plan.

321

≼ *What is a salary reduction plan?*

A *salary reduction plan* is a contractual agreement between the employee and the employer in which the employer agrees to provide income to the employee after retirement. As the plan name implies, the employee defers receipt of compensation from the current year to his or her retirement.

For example, assume that Merit Corporation, a closely held medium-size manufacturer in Ohio, wants to hire Jane Dexter as its chief executive officer. Jane is 45 years old and has a distinguished record of leadership and accomplishment in Merit's industry. Merit knows that it must offer Jane a premium compensation package to motivate her to leave her current position with a large publicly held company. The proposed compensation package includes:

- A base annual salary of $350,000
- A profit-sharing plan to which Merit will contribute the maximum amount allowable each year
- An annual bonus compensation equal to 2 percent of any increase in Merit's sales revenue that is realized after Jane becomes CEO
- A salary reduction plan that allows Jane to defer the bonus compensation and the tax on it until she retires, at which time she will probably be in a lower tax bracket (Merit's obligation to pay Jane the deferred compensation may be funded or unfunded.)

≼ *What is a salary continuation plan?*

A *salary continuation plan* is a contractual agreement between the employee and the employer in which the employer promises to pay future compensation to the employee for services yet to be rendered by the employee.

We can again use the example above, but in this case Merit's offer to Jane consists of:

- A base annual salary of $350,000
- A profit-sharing plan to which Merit will contribute the maximum amount allowable each year

■ A continuation of Jane's base salary for 20 years after she retires if she serves as CEO for 20 years or a continuation of 1.2 times her base salary if she serves as CEO for 25 years (Merit's obligation to continue Jane's salary after her retirement may be funded or unfunded.)

⚑ What is an unfunded deferred-compensation plan?

In both of the above examples, if Merit's obligations are *unfunded*, Merit simply promises to make the payments to Jane on her retirement. Merit must make the payments from its annual revenues, not from a special fund set aside for the purpose.

⚑ What is a funded deferred-compensation plan?

In a *funded* plan, the company's promise to pay is secured by property set aside for the purpose of paying the future benefits.

⚑ What difference does it make whether a plan is funded or unfunded?

Whether a plan is funded or unfunded has major implications for both employer and employee. In each of the above examples, if the plan is unfunded, Jane must determine whether Merit will have the financial ability to pay the compensation during her retirement years. She can enforce the promise to pay, but will a company of Merit's size be able to continue the payments?

Whether and how a plan is funded also has tax consequences for both employee and employer. As discussed later in the chapter, certain methods give the employee some assurance of receiving the promised payments and do not cause the employee to prematurely realize income and income taxes.

⚑ What are the disadvantages to the employee of a salary reduction or salary continuation plan?

Under an unqualified deferred-compensation plan, a portion of the compensation and the income taxes usually is deferred until after the employee retires, when he or she will likely be in a lower tax bracket. In order to avoid current income tax and ERISA requirements (including funding, participation and vesting, and fiduciary responsibility), the employer's promise to pay the future compensation must be an unfunded and unsecured promise. This poses the following risks to the employee:

- The employer might not have the funds to pay the benefit when it is due.
- The employer, for various reasons, might refuse to honor its agreement at the time the deferred benefit is to be paid.
- If there is a change of control in the business by the time the employee becomes eligible to receive the deferred compensation, the new control group might refuse to pay the benefit.
- If the employer becomes insolvent or bankrupt before the benefit is due, the company's assets will be confiscated by creditors.

⊴ When must I pay income tax on deferred-compensation payments?

With a properly structured deferred-compensation plan, the employee does not pay income tax on the deferred amount until he or she actually receives the compensation. To avoid immediate taxation, the deferred-compensation agreement must be an unsecured promise to pay by the employer; impose "substantial restrictions or limitations" on the employee's immediate right to the funds; and ensure that the employee does not receive any current economic benefits under the plan (i.e., generally, the benefits cannot be assignable or immediately convertible into cash).

The simplest example of a plan that meets these requirements is a totally unfunded plan, because it consists of nothing more than the employer's promise to make the payments. In the salary continuation example, Jane is not entitled to receive salary continuation payments unless she works as CEO of the company for 20 years—a substantial limitation on her right to receive the payments.

For salary reduction plans, it is important that the employee agree to defer receipt of the income *before* it is due. Many companies that have salary reduction plans require that eligible employees elect to participate in the plan before the first day of the year in which the election is used. For example, employees electing to defer their 2003 bonuses must make that election before the end of 2002.

When the employee receives payments from the deferred-compensation plan, the payments are subject to income taxes and FICA and FUTA withholding.

⚹ When does the employer receive a deduction for the payments under a deferred-compensation plan?

Generally, the employer is entitled to a deduction in the year that the compensation is included in the employee's gross income. In either of the unfunded arrangements above, Merit is entitled to a tax deduction for Jane's salary in each year in which the company actually pays postretirement compensation to her.

⚹ How does an unfunded deferred-compensation plan affect the value of the corporation?

It is an accrued liability. This liability for the future payment of deferred compensation can reduce the value of the company's equity. As liabilities increase, equity value decreases. This "negative" may work in favor of shareholders who want to transfer stock to next-generation family members at the least possible value.

⚹ May an employee contribute to a deferred-compensation plan?

An employee can contribute to a secular trust (discussed later in the chapter). Employee contributions usually entail a salary reduction plan. In one popular arrangement, the employer matches the employee's contributions. If the employee dies before normal retirement age, the employer pays the benefit, or *sum certain,* to the employee's family. Otherwise, the employee is entitled to the benefit over a period of years after his or her retirement.

⚹ How are postretirement benefits usually paid to an employee?

There are three primary distribution, or payout, methods used with a deferred-compensation plan:

1. A lifetime payout (or a payout that lasts the joint lifetimes of the employee and the employee's spouse)
2. A payout over a given number of years
3. A payout with a specific dollar benefit for as long as the unpaid balance permits

⚄ *What can the employer do to secure the promise of the future payment while avoiding the disadvantages you've mentioned?*

The most common way to secure a deferred-compensation obligation is to use a rabbi trust or a secular trust.

ACCUMULATING FUNDS

Rabbi Trust

⚄ *What is a rabbi trust?*

A *rabbi trust* is an irrevocable trust that an employer establishes and funds to provide a source of income for the future payment of benefits to designated key employees. It is called a "rabbi" trust because, in the early 1980s, a synagogue received a watershed IRS letter ruling that confirmed the favorable tax consequences of using a trust to fund and secure the payment of postretirement benefits to its rabbi. The following basic rules apply to a rabbi trust:

- For income tax purposes, the employer is the owner of the trust and its property, and the employee is the beneficiary of the trust.
- The employee recognizes *ordinary income* only when, and to the extent that, he or she receives payments from the trust.
- To avoid triggering an immediate income tax, the employee may not assign, transfer, sell, or otherwise alienate his or her interest in the trust as prescribed by the trust instrument.
- To avoid an immediate income tax, the employee cannot have the right to control or direct the investment of trust assets.
- The trust's assets must remain subject to the claims of the employer's general creditors. Because the trust is exposed to the

creditors, the deferred-compensation plan is still an "unfunded promise to pay."

- The trustee of the rabbi trust must be an independent third party.
- The employer's board of directors and president must have an affirmative duty to inform the trustee of the employer's insolvency or bankruptcy.
- Upon notice of the employer's insolvency or bankruptcy, the trustee must suspend payments to the employee and must deliver the trust's assets and accrued income to the bankruptcy court for payment to the employer's creditors.
- The employee must be a general unsecured creditor with respect to the promised benefits. A rabbi trust *cannot* protect the employee from the risk of loss associated with an employer's bankruptcy or insolvency.

⅍ *What are the income tax consequences for the employer of using a rabbi trust?*

As the owner of the trust, the employer must pay tax on all income and capital gains produced by the trust fund. The employer realizes an income tax deduction for payments actually paid to the employee-beneficiary in the year the trust makes the payments. Any forfeiture (e.g., early termination of service) continues to be owned by the employer. Forfeitures may be returned to the employer from the trust.

⅍ *If the rabbi trust fund is subject to claims of an employer's creditors, how is it more secure, from the employee's point of view, than an unfunded promise to pay?*

A rabbi trust protects employees from a change in company control. For example, suppose a company creates a rabbi trust for ten key executives, including owner-employees. Fifteen years after formation, as many of the executives are nearing retirement age or have already retired, the existing shareholders sell the company to a third party. The new owner installs its own management, which decides not to honor existing deferred-compensation arrangements. With the rabbi trust under the control of an independent trustee, the new management cannot prevent the retired employees from receiving their benefits. New owners and their management-level employees must honor previous contractual agreements.

The rabbi trust agreement usually contemplates a change in company control or ownership. It may provide, for example, that the trust assets be released to participating employees if there is a change of control. When the trust assets are transferred to the participating employees, the employees are considered to be in actual or constructive receipt of the trust assets and must recognize income.

⚎ What are the disadvantages to the employer?

The company cannot access funds contributed to the trust, nor can it use the funds in an emergency or invest them in new business opportunities. Also, the employer must include the income generated from the trust fund in its income.

Secular Trust

⚎ What is a secular trust?

A *secular trust* is another means of accumulating funds to be paid to an employee under a deferred-compensation plan. Unlike a rabbi trust, a secular trust is designed to protect the trust fund from the claims of the employer's creditors. The participating employee is treated as the owner of the trust and its property for income tax purposes. (With a rabbi trust, the employer is the owner for income tax purposes.) Employer contributions usually are fully vested in the employee and must be fully vested (nonforfeitable) to protect the trust fund from the claims of the employer's creditors.

⚎ If the secular trust is a secured promise to pay, doesn't that mean the employee must recognize income?

Yes. As a general rule, the employee pays income tax on the value of the employer's contribution to the trust in the year in which the contribution is made. Subsequent distributions from the trust to the employee generally are tax-free. Items of trust income, gain, loss, deduction, and credit "pass through" to the employee-owner of the trust.

The employer realizes a corresponding income tax deduction for the value of property contributed to the trust. From a tax standpoint, a secular trust has the same effect as a direct payment of current compensation that the employee invests on his or her own behalf. That is the price of shielding the trust from the employer's creditors.

⌐ *Are there exceptions to the general rules for the timing of income tax recognition by the employee and deductibility by the employer?*

Yes. An employer may design a secular trust to allow for various tax ramifications, all of which are based on different variables and goals. These very technical designs are beyond the scope of this book. We recommend that you discuss these exceptions with your tax advisor if you are interested in establishing a secular trust.

FUNDING

⌐ *Should I use life insurance to fund a deferred-compensation plan?*

Life insurance has merit in funding a deferred-compensation obligation in a rabbi trust. In the least complicated case, the employer buys a life insurance policy on the life of a key employee. The company pays all the policy premiums. The purchase of the policy is not a tax-deductible expense but an investment. The premium dollars are not taxable income to the key employee. The policy is owned by the employer, so the cash value accrues tax-free inside the life insurance policy. Death proceeds are not taxable as income to the company.

Proceeds accumulate as part of the company surplus. Over time, the policy builds tax-deferred value and a tax-free life insurance benefit. Eventually, this tax-deferred buildup will serve as the source of the deferred income proceeds.

Policy cash values accrued over the term of the key employee's service may be withdrawn from the policy to help fund the company's payment obligation to the employee. The company realizes a tax deduction when it makes a payment to the retired employee; but to the extent the payment is made from tax-free accumulations of principal within the policy, the company does not realize income when it withdraws cash from the policy.

If the employee dies before retirement or before complete payment of his or her retirement benefit, the death proceeds may be used to pay a lump-sum or deferred benefit to the employee's beneficiary.

≥⁣ *What are the disadvantages of using life insurance to fund deferred-compensation plans?*

There are several potential disadvantages:

- An employee may not be insurable because of his or her medical history.
- The company may be unable to recover the initial cost of the policy if the employee becomes permanently disabled or separates from service within a few years of the policy's acquisition.
- Premium payments are not tax-deductible for the employer.
- Though increases in the policy's cash value and the death benefit are not subject to regular income tax, they may be subject to the alternative minimum tax for some employers, particularly a small corporation that purchases a large policy.

≥⁣ *Will investing in securities exempt from income tax reduce the continuing tax burden of the owner of a rabbi or secular trust?*

Yes. Any financial or investment product that produces tax-exempt income or tax-sheltered income (such as municipal bonds or life insurance) can reduce or eliminate the income tax burden.

≥⁣ *Can a tax-deferred annuity fund a rabbi or secular trust?*

The Internal Revenue Code limits tax-deferred treatment to certain *individual* owners. A secular trust may be a tax-qualified owner because the employee is considered the owner of the trust. A rabbi trust will probably not qualify for the favorable tax deferment because the company is the owner of the trust.

chapter 17

Stock Bonus and Stock Option Plans

STOCK BONUS PLANS

≥ *Should a corporate employer consider rewarding key employees with stock in the corporation?*

Company stock can be an effective and powerful means of awarding additional compensation to selected key employees through a *stock bonus plan*. Ownership gives the employee a personal stake in the success or failure of the company, so it frequently, but not always, increases an employee's commitment to the company and motivates a dedicated effort to work toward company growth. In addition, the company can issue stock as bonus compensation for dedicated, loyal, and exceptional employee performance. And it can do all this without diminishing its cash and cash flow.

Stock bonus plans do, however, have a downside. The company must disclose certain financial information to shareholders. Majority shareholders, officers, and directors have fiduciary obligations to all shareholders, including employee-shareholders. Many states permit shareholders to sue for an accounting and to petition the court to have an officer or director removed for acts of dishonesty and self-dealing. In addition, the number of shares issued to employee-shareholders may shift the balance of power. This could limit the ability of existing owners to manage the business in the manner they prefer.

⚹ *Is the size of a company important?*

Yes, in almost all cases. Microsoft Corporation has a history of paying very low salaries supplemented by significant stock bonuses or stock options. Employees receive something they can sell, that is, liquidate for cash. The stellar increase in the value of Microsoft's stock has made many of its management-level employees very wealthy. But Microsoft stock is publicly traded with a known value.

Many large privately owned companies also reward key employees with company stock as bonus compensation, but what is the value of that stock to an employee? There is no market for privately held stock. Many closely held companies restrict the sale or other transfers of employee-owned stock. Most privately held companies do not pay dividends to stockholders. So, for a key employee, what is the value of a very small minority interest in a large company *if* there is no market for the stock and *if* the transfer of stock is contractually restricted and *if* the company does not pay dividends?

To compensate for the absence of a market and for other restrictions, the company gives the employee limited *put* rights, which allow the employee to require that the company repurchase his or her shares upon retirement or disability. In many cases, the company retains a *call* right—an enforceable right to reacquire the shares from the employee if he or she separates from the company before a specified retirement age.

⚹ *Considering the issues you've just mentioned, can stock bonus plans work for a small company?*

Yes, most definitely. Small companies can benefit from using nonqualified stock bonus plans to attract and retain key employees, to supplement retirement benefits for key employees, and/or to use in succession planning.

For example, an orthopedic group may want to include Sarah, an outstanding younger performer, in its group of older owners as an inducement for her to continue with the group. The owners could allow Sarah to buy into their group, but she may have insufficient savings early in her professional life to finance this buy-in. As an alternative, the group could issue a percentage of ownership to Sarah as bonuses over a 3- to 5-year period. Sarah must include the value of her equity acquisition as taxable income, and the group realizes a reciprocal income tax deduction. When it comes time for the older members of the group to retire, Sarah may be in a position to purchase their remaining stock.

A stock bonus plan can be an excellent tool in an owner's exit strategy by giving an ownership position to a key employee who may or may not be a member of the owner's family. (We discuss exit strategies and succession planning in more detail in Part Five.)

◣ Can we use S corporation stock as bonus compensation?

Yes. Usually, the employee must be an individual or a qualifying trust. The number of shareholders permitted for an S corporation is limited. While a C corporation might not pay dividends to its shareholders, a shareholder of an S corporation may realize income or cash flow from his or her ownership position. Remember, however, that earnings are allocated to the taxable income of S corporation owners even if the income is not distributed.

◣ How are the shares of a closely held company valued for income tax purposes?

If there is no market for the shares, the value must be determined by a business appraiser. Valuation by a business appraiser is also required on the exercise of put and call rights under a stock bonus plan.

STOCK OPTION PLANS

⚖ *What is a stock option?*

A *stock option* is a right to acquire stock in a company at some future time. Options and other derivative investments are available to the general public, but publicly traded stock option contracts are not germane to a discussion of employee stock options granted by an employer.

In an employer-employee relationship, the employer gives an employee the right *(option)* to purchase its stock at some future time at a stated price (the "strike" price), either below or at current value. The expectation is that the value of the stock will rise and the employee will eventually be able to sell the stock for a profit. The employee is not obligated to exercise his or her option. If the price of the stock goes down, the employee need not purchase the stock, so he or she does not risk any out-of-pocket loss.

Corporations use stock options as a means of retaining key employees, as part of a business succession program, as part of a company's benefit package, or for a combination of these purposes.

⚖ *How does a stock option work?*

Let's look at an example: Gary's Distributing Company (GDC) grants its key employee, Harold, $90,000 worth of stock options in each of the first 3 years of a 10-year period. GDC could allow Harold to exercise the stock options all at once when the options are granted, or it could require that the options vest over a period of years. In this example, let's say GDC allows Harold to exercise his stock options any time after year 5 of the 10-year period. In year 6, Harold exercises $180,000 of options. When Harold does this, he pays GDC $180,000 for the number of shares he is buying.

The company must set the strike price of the stock the day it grants the option. Normally, a publicly traded stock is set at the market value on that day; private companies obtain a valuation of the stock. An option works to the employee's advantage if the value of the stock increases between the time the company grants the option and the time the employee exercises it. For example, if the value of GDC's stock at the time it grants the option to Harold is $10 (the strike price) and its stock increases in value to $20 by year 6, Harold pays only $10 for stock valued at $20, and he could then sell the stock for $20 per share.

⋈ Are there different types of stock option plans?

There are two types of employee stock option plans, statutory incentive stock options (ISOs) and nonstatutory stock options (NSOs). Each option has different requirements for establishment, and each is taxed differently to the employee. Stock options issued by employers to employees are often called "incentive" stock options, whether statutory or nonstatutory, because the future benefit offered by the options encourages employees to continue their employment and to work for the growth of their companies.

⋈ Is it a good idea to have a vesting schedule for stock options?

The answer depends on many factors, but generally companies "stage" stock option rights over a period of years of service. The company may grant an employee an option on January 1 to purchase 1000 shares of stock with vesting to occur 25 percent per year over the next 4 years of service. Each January 1 the company grants another option for 1000 shares of stock with the same vesting schedule. After a number of years, each January 1 anniversary will trigger the vesting of 1000 or more shares from the prior 4 years' grants. If the employee leaves to go to work for a rival company, he or she forfeits all unvested options. Depending on the success of the company and the performance of the stock since the company granted the options, this can be a very costly move. In some cases, the employee simply cannot afford to leave—a situation commonly referred to as a "golden handcuff."

⊀ *Do I have to offer stock options to all my employees, or can I give them just to key employees?*

There are no nondiscrimination rules for stock options. With either statutory or nonstatutory options, the employer is free to pick and choose which employees receive them. However, as discussed below, certain owner-employees are not eligible to receive statutory options.

⊀ *Can a corporation issue both statutory and nonstatutory stock options?*

If the corporation has the authority to grant both types of stock options and the exercise of nonstatutory options does not affect the exercise of the statutory incentive stock options granted, then the corporation can issue both statutory and nonstatutory stock options.

⊀ *I've heard some executives refer to a "phantom" stock option plan. What is that?*

Phantom stock option plans have been used for many years to provide incentive compensation to key employees. The phantom plan is *not* a stock option plan; it is nothing more than an unfunded deferred-compensation plan.

Here's how it works: Assume that McCall Corporation wants to reward a key employee or an independent contractor. McCall instigates an employment agreement (a deferred-compensation contract) with the key employee or contractor in which the individual is recognized as owning the equivalent of 1000 shares of company stock. If the stock increases in value over the period of the contract, McCall will pay to the employee or contractor, as cash compensation, an amount equal to 50 percent of the increase in the value of the phantom stock at the conclusion of the defined period. Taxation of benefits is governed by the deferred-compensation rules.

The phantom stock option plan serves many business owners who simply do not want outsiders, including key employees, as fellow shareholders.

Statutory Incentive Stock Options

Requirements

⚑ *What is a statutory incentive stock option?*

An option may qualify as a *statutory incentive stock option (ISO)* only if:

- The option is not transferable by the employee except at death.
- The option is exercisable only by the employee during his or her lifetime.
- The strike price is not less than the current value.
- The option period does not exceed 10 years.
- The amount of the option granted does not exceed $100,000 of stock value in any one year.
- The employee receiving the option does not own more than 10 percent of the voting stock of the company at the time the option is granted.

The company determines whether an option is a statutory stock option at the time the option is granted. The option remains a statutory stock option thereafter.

The company granting ISOs must be careful to comply with statutory requirements in order to achieve the tax benefits associated with them. Although they offer better tax benefits to the corporation than nonstatutory plans, statutory plans are less popular because of these requirements.

⚑ *Can we award incentive stock options on the basis of performance or other standards?*

According to the National Center for Employee Ownership, there are three types of incentive stock option plans that can require performance as a prerequisite to participation:

PERFORMANCE GRANTS: The company grants options on the basis of specific goals, such as stock price, revenues, or profits.

PREMIUM-PRICED OPTIONS: The options are granted at a price higher than the current price. The employee can benefit only if the stock price goes up.

PERFORMANCE-ACCELERATED VESTING: If specific targets are met, the employee is granted accelerated vesting. An incentive stock option plan may, for example, provide that an employee's right to acquire stock at a strike price of $10 will vest at a rate of 25 percent over 4 years. Vesting could be accelerated to 100 percent if certain production goals are accomplished.

Can a statutory stock option require that the employee be an employee at the time the option is actually exercised?

Yes. In almost all cases, if the employee does not exercise the option before leaving the company, the employee forfeits the option. Even if the terms of the option allow the employee to retain the option after leaving employment, he or she must exercise the option (assuming the employee is otherwise entitled to do so) within a short time after leaving the company to receive favorable tax treatment.

Can existing owners receive statutory stock options?

No. The plan does not qualify as a statutory ISO if an employee who owns more than 10 percent of the total combined voting power of all classes of stock of either the employer corporation, its parent corporation, or any subsidiary corporations is eligible to receive options.

Must a statutory stock option be granted under a written plan?

The option must be granted in accordance with a written plan that meets the requirements of the Internal Revenue Code and is approved by the shareholders of the granting corporation within 12 months before or after the date on which the plan is adopted by the board of directors.

What is the permitted duration for a statutory ISO plan?

An ISO plan cannot last more than 10 years from either the date on which the plan is adopted or the date on which it is approved by the company's shareholders, whichever is earlier.

What is the maximum period during which the employee can exercise his or her option?

Ten years. The option may not be exercised thereafter.

Are there requirements with regard to the option price?

Yes. In general, the option, or strike, price of a statutory ISO must not be less than the fair market value of the stock at the time the company grants the option. The company may determine the option price in any manner as long as the minimum price under the terms of the option contract is not less than the stock's fair market value on the grant date.

There is an exception to this general rule. Even if the option price is less than the fair market value of the stock, the option price requirement will be satisfied if the company has made a good-faith effort to value the stock accurately.

Is there an annual dollar limitation for the ISO?

The aggregate fair market value of stock granted during any calendar year may not exceed $100,000. The value of shares of employer stock that an employee can exercise for the first time in any one year under an ISO cannot exceed $100,000, based on the fair market value of the stock at the date of the ISO's grant. After the first time, there is no limit on the amount the employee can exercise.

Taxation

☆ Does the employee recognize income when the employer issues the statutory ISO to the employee?

The receipt of an ISO will not ordinarily trigger the recognition of income. Since the strike price must be equal to the fair market value of the stock at the date of grant, the option is not a transfer of property or something of value to the employee.

☆ Must the employee recognize income when he or she exercises a statutory incentive stock option?

If the employer transfers a share of stock to an employee on his or her exercise of a statutory option, the following rules apply:

- The employee is not required to recognize income for ordinary-income taxes as the result of his or her exercise of the option.
- The employee must include as income for alternative minimum tax purposes the difference (or "spread") between the price he or she pays for the stock at exercise and the fair market value of the stock at exercise.

For example, Merlin Corporation granted its employee, Arthur, an ISO to purchase 100 shares of Merlin Corporation stock at $50 per share. One year later, when Merlin's stock is valued at $100 per share, Arthur exercises the option and Merlin transfers the 100 shares to him. Arthur is not required to report the $5000 difference between the exercise price and the stock's current value as income, but he is required to include that amount in calculating the alternative minimum tax.

☆ What is the alternative minimum tax?

The *alternative minimum tax (AMT)* is like an entirely separate tax system from our regular income tax. In calculating the AMT on stock options, the employee includes the difference between the exercise price and the fair market value at the time of exercise as income. Once the employee determines the AMT income, he or she can apply the AMT exemption, if any. After the employee has calculated the AMT and the regular tax, he or she is required to pay the larger tax of the two.

In exercising an ISO option, if the value of the stock increases sharply over the option period, the AMT can be very expensive.

⋑ *What are the tax implications for the corporation when it grants the option and when the employee exercises the option?*

No deduction is allowed to the employer corporation when issuing or assuming a stock option or when issuing the stock on the exercise of an ISO.

⋑ *Are there any tax consequences for the employee when he or she sells stock that has been purchased under a stock option?*

There are tax consequences for the employee on the sale of the stock. The consequences vary, depending on how long the employee holds the stock and whether he or she paid the AMT on the exercise of the option:

LENGTH OF TIME HELD: If the employee holds his or her stock for 2 years from the date of the grant or for 1 year from the date of exercise, whichever period is longer, the Internal Revenue Code provides that the employee can treat the gain as long-term capital gain. If the employee does not meet this holding period, he or she must treat the gain as ordinary income for the year in which the stock is sold.

ALTERNATIVE MINIMUM TAX: The sale of stock acquired under a qualified statutory stock option plan is subject to the AMT. If the employee paid the AMT at the time of the exercise, the amount of gain on the sale of the stock is the difference between the market value at the time the employee exercised the option and the amount the employee received for the stock when he or she sold it. If the employee did not pay the AMT at the time of exercise, the amount of gain is the difference between the option, or strike, price the employee paid for the stock at exercise and the amount the employee received when he or she sold it.

If the employee pays the AMT at the time of exercise, that tax qualifies for an AMT credit when the employee sells the stock. An employee should complete IRS Form 8801 to see whether he or she qualifies for the AMT credit.

It is important to keep in mind that because the 2001 tax act has reduced individual income tax rates, more individuals will be subject to the AMT.

Are there any tax consequences to the employer when the employee sells the stock?

If the employee sells the stock before the expiration of the holding period (described above), the employer is entitled to a deduction for the same amount as the amount the employee has to treat as ordinary income.

Can an employee transfer or assign an ISO?

In order to qualify for favorable tax treatment, statutory stock options cannot be transferred or assigned. A limited exception permits postmortem transfers under a will or through a probate proceeding if the holder of the option dies without a will.

Nonstatutory Stock Options

What is a nonstatutory stock option plan?

A *nonstatutory stock option (NSO)* works essentially like a statutory option, but it has fewer qualifying requirements than the statutory ISO. For this reason, NSOs are more popular among corporations.

The major differences between statutory and nonstatutory stock options are:

- There is no limit on the dollar amount that the company may grant each year under an NSO.
- The option, or strike, price may be less than the value of the stock at the time the company grants the NSO.
- The company may grant NSOs to persons who own more than 10 percent of the voting stock.
- The tax treatment of nonstatutory stock options is less desirable but also less complicated than that of statutory ISOs.

Table 17-1 compares the features and taxation of NSOs with those of ISOs.

Taxation

⚔ *What are the tax consequences to the employee when the company grants the NSO?*

If the employer grants the option under an option-employment agreement with the employee and the agreement makes the option subject to forfeiture if conditions of employment are not met, there is no taxable event for the employee on the employer's grant of the option. If there is no option-employment agreement, the employee is required to include as ordinary income the difference between the strike price and the value of the stock at the time of the grant.

For example, Evergreen Corporation grants an option to David Richards permitting David to acquire 100,000 shares of its common stock at a strike price of $10 per share. At the time of the grant, Evergreen's stock is valued by an appraiser (there is no established market for Evergreen's stock) at $10.50 per share—a spread of $.50 per share, or a total of $50,000. David's right to exercise his stock option is based on his providing significant services to the company for 2 years from the date of the grant, and all rights are forfeitable.

TABLE 17-1   Stock Options: ISO versus NSO

	ISO	NSO
Income tax at grant	No	No (unless readily ascertainable value)
Tax at exercise:		
Regular income	No	Yes (or when restrictions lapse)
AMT	Yes	Does not apply
Holding period	1 year after exercise and 2 years after grant	None; exercise and sell anytime after vesting
Capital gain	At sale (subject to normal capital gain holding periods)	After exercise
Transfers permitted	To revocable living trust (other transfers prohibited by IRC 421)	To revocable living trust
Length of plan	10-year maximum	No outer limit
Grant amount	Limited to $100,000 in fair market value, which is "first exercisable"	No limit
Taxation at or after death	Step-up income tax basis at death; AMT on difference between fair market value on date of death and the decedent's basis	Options exercised after death taxed as income to the beneficiary

The services that David is to provide to Evergreen are carefully defined in an option-employment contract. Because the conditions of employment amount to a substantial risk of forfeiture, the stock option has no "readily ascertainable value" at the time of the grant, so there is no taxable event for David at that time.

If the nonstatutory stock option were not subject to the performance of future services (and thus not subject to a substantial risk of forfeiture), David would be required to include $50,000 as ordinary income—the difference between the strike price and the value of the stock at the time of the grant.

⚘ What are the tax consequences to David when he exercises the option?

Two years from the date of the grant, Evergreen's stock is valued at $20 per share. Because David completed 2 years of service to the company, as required under his employment contract, David exercises the entire option at once, paying Evergreen $10 per share, or $1 million, for 100,000 shares.

David will recognize as ordinary income the difference between the strike price of $10 per share and the fair market value of $20 at the time he exercises the option—$1 million—even if he does not sell the stock that year. One million dollars is David's basis in the stock.

⚘ What happens when David sells the stock?

David's basis in the stock is now $2 million, the $1 million he paid for the stock plus the $1 million he included in his income when he exercised the option. If David sells the stock for $30 per share within 12 months of exercising his option, his $1 million gain is taxed at ordinary-income tax rates. If he holds the stock for more than a year, the gain is taxed at the 20 percent long-term capital gain rate.

⚘ Is there anything David can do to limit his income tax liability?

Yes. Currently recognizing a small amount of ordinary income is often an inexpensive way to ensure that future appreciation will be taxed at the lower capital gain rates. David can make what is called an *Internal Revenue Code 83(b) election* to include the present value of the benefit, $50,000, in his gross income at the time Evergreen grants the option, even though the stock is substantially unvested and subject to forfeiture. Once David reports and pays the tax, the stock becomes a capital asset. If David holds the stock for 1 year or more after he pays the income tax, then, when he sells the stock, the gain is taxed at capital gain rates rather than ordinary-income tax rates. David's basis in the stock is the $1 million he actually pays for the stock when he exercises the option. If David makes the 83(b) election and then forfeits the stock in the first 2 years, before it is vested, the forfeiture is treated as a sale or exchange. David will realize a loss equal to the difference (if any) of the amount he paid (if any) for the stock and the amount he realized (if any) upon forfeiture.

◢ Are nonstatutory stock options transferable to family trusts and family partnerships?

Nonstatutory stock options are transferable, depending on federal securities laws and the terms of the stock option contract. Such transactions are replete with various tax consequences that depend on many factors. Business owners who are contemplating the use of NSOs as a succession planning or estate planning technique should discuss these issues in detail with their advisors.

chapter 18

Life Insurance as a Benefit

⅏ *Which life insurance can the employer use in benefit planning?*

All the benefit plans we discuss in this chapter require life insurance with a cash value. As a refresher, *cash values* are amounts inside the policy that result when the premium payments exceed the pure insurance, or "mortality," costs charged by the insurance company. Depending on the type of insurance policy, the cash values are invested in several different ways by the insurance carrier or the policyholder. The owner of the policy can access the cash value through surrenders or policy loans.

The four major categories of cash-value insurance are whole life, universal life, variable life, and variable universal life:

WHOLE LIFE: Whole life is the oldest form of cash-value insurance. The excess premium is invested in the insurance company's general portfolio, which usually consists of fixed-income instruments such as bonds, mortgages, and government securities. The return on the account is tied to the long-term bond rate. There is little flexibility for changing premiums or the amount of insurance protection.

UNIVERSAL LIFE: Universal life invests the cash value into an account that is tied to short-term interest rates. This type of insurance became popular in the high-interest period of the early 1980s, when banks and money markets were paying more than 15 percent. Universal life is flexible in that the customer can change premiums and insurance amounts as needed.

VARIABLE LIFE: Variable life invests the cash value into separate subaccounts. Most carriers offer many choices from conservative money markets to aggressive stock accounts. Variable life is not very flexible and has essentially been replaced by variable universal life.

VARIABLE UNIVERSAL LIFE: Variable universal life (VUL), like variable life, invests the cash value in separate subaccounts that, in turn, are invested in various investments, such as stocks, bonds, mutual funds, and money markets. It is flexible in regard to the amount of premiums and insurance protection. Essentially, VUL combines the best features of the older variable and universal life insurance plans.

For more information about life insurance, we recommend *21st Century Wealth: Essential Financial Planning Principles* (Quantum Press, 2000).

EXECUTIVE BONUS PLANS

⚐ *What is an executive bonus plan?*

An *executive bonus plan,* or *Section 162 bonus plan,* compensates or rewards a key employee by providing the employee with life insurance that he or she cannot otherwise afford. The employee selects a permanent life insurance policy of which he or she is the insured person and the owner—the employer cannot be the owner or the beneficiary of the policy. The employer pays the policy premiums as long as the employee remains employed at the company. The employee recognizes the amount of the employer-paid premiums as compensation, subject to withholding requirements and payroll taxes. The employer realizes an income tax deduction for the premiums it pays.

Can the premium payments include the amount of the taxes?

The employer can provide the funds for paying the policy premiums in a number of ways. The *single bonus* is equal to the policy premium; the employee must have the funds to pay the tax on the bonus. The *"gross-up," or double, bonus* is equal to the premium payment plus the employee's income tax on the bonus. With a *special-schedule bonus,* the schedule typically starts with a single bonus and phases to a gross-up bonus.

What are the advantages of an executive bonus plan?

A bonus plan has several advantages for both the employer and the employee:

For the employer

- The plan is relatively simple to set up and maintain. It can be established, administered, and terminated without IRS approval or government reporting.
- There are no nondiscrimination testing rules. The employer can choose highly compensated employees to participate, exclude others, and choose different coverage for each employee.
- Because the bonus plan can be discriminatory, it is a valuable tool for recruiting and retaining key employees and thus is a valuable benefit for the owner of the company.
- The costs are generally tax-deductible for the employer.

For the employee

- The employee has a benefit that he or she might not otherwise be able to afford.

- If the policy is a variable life or VUL, the employee can direct the investments of the cash value.

- Because the employee owns the policy, it usually is protected from the claims of the employer's creditors.

- Accumulations of value within the policy are tax-free, not just tax-deferred.

- The employee can withdraw cash from the policy (up to the amount of premiums paid) for personal or family needs. Withdrawals and policy loans are generally tax-free (but loans are not interest-free).

- At retirement, the employee can take the cash value in a lump sum or can receive periodic payments.

- The employee's family is financially protected in case of the employee's premature death. Death benefits paid to the employee's beneficiaries are not subject to income tax.

SPLIT-DOLLAR PLANS

What is a split-dollar life insurance plan?

A *split-dollar plan* is not a type of insurance but a technique for providing a life insurance benefit to a key employee. It is the mechanism that allows the employer to help an employee purchase permanent life insurance. The basic features of split-dollar plans are:

- The employee and the employer agree to participate by applying for a life insurance policy on the life of the employee. The plan is documented with a written agreement and the delivery of forms required by the insurer to document the arrangement.

- The premium payment is split between the employee and the employer according to a predetermined formula.

- The employer receives a security interest in the policy.

- Life insurance policy benefits are split between the employer and the employee or a beneficiary that the employee designates. Under the typical split-dollar arrangement, on the employee's death or at the termination of the plan, the employer recovers the cash value of the policy from the death benefit and the balance is paid to the employee's beneficiary.

⚔ *How is the premium payment split?*

The employee's share of the premium is equal to the cost of term insurance for a person of the employee's age and health. The employer's share is the balance of the premium for the insurance in the plan. In most arrangements, the employer pays the employee's share of the premium, but sometimes the plan calls for the employee to reimburse the employer. Historically, the cost of term insurance (the employee's share of the premium amount) was the lesser of the insurance company's premium costs for term insurance or the costs prescribed by the IRS. However, due to a recent IRS change, the employee's share is, in most cases, calculated on rates prescribed by the IRS.

⚔ *How are the benefits split between the employer and the employee?*

Under the traditional split-dollar arrangement, the employer is entitled to either (1) its investment in the policy (its share of the premiums) or, in some cases, (2) its investment or the cash value of the policy, whichever amount is greater. Upon the employee's death, the beneficiary, chosen by the employee, receives the balance of the policy proceeds.

⚔ *What is an equity split-dollar plan?*

In an *equity split-dollar plan,* the employer's recovery is limited to its share of the premiums in the policy. The difference between the employer's share of the premiums and the policy's cash value—that is, the policy's equity—accrues for the benefit of the employee.

Tax Consequences

⚑ What are the tax consequences of a split-dollar plan for the employee?

In early 2001, the IRS announced new rules for the taxation of split-dollar plans. For plans established in 2001 and later years, the employee is taxed under either of two methods:

LOAN APPROACH: Under this approach, the amount of the premiums paid by the employer (less any amount paid by the employee) is treated as a below-market loan to the employee. If the transaction is structured and consistently treated as a bona fide loan, the loan amount is not treated as compensation to the employee but he or she is subject to the tax rules for below-market loans. These rules generally require that an employee recognize income each year in the amount of the forgone interest (based on interest rates prescribed by the IRS). However, the employee does not have to recognize additional income for the economic benefit he or she derives from the plan.

ECONOMIC BENEFIT APPROACH: This approach requires that the employee realize taxable compensation each year in the amount of the "economic benefit" he or she receives under the split-dollar plan. Unless the employee reimburses the employer for its share of the premium, the value of the life insurance protection provided each year is a taxable economic benefit. This amount is typically determined by reference to an IRS table. Any "other benefits" to the employee, including policy dividends, whether paid to the employee or used by the employee to purchase paid-up insurance in which the employer has no interest, are taxable to the extent that the economic benefit exceeds amounts paid by the employee. Also, under an equity split-dollar plan, the employee may realize income at some point for policy cash value above the amount needed to repay the employer for its share of the premium advances.

⚑ What are the tax consequences for an employer who establishes a split-dollar plan?

The employer's share of the premiums it pays in a split-benefit policy is not a deductible business expense. However, if the company pays the employee's portion, that payment generates an income tax deduction of some amount, depending on whether the loan or economic benefit approach is used in structuring the agreement. Repayment of the employer's share of the premiums at the termination of the plan or at the employee's death is a tax-free return of capital.

Creation and Administration

⌐ *Are there any ERISA requirements for split-dollar life insurance plans?*

The employer is not required to file any plan documents with the Department of Labor, but the Department of Labor has the right to request a copy of the plan. The employer must make a summary plan description available to each participant.

⌐ *How does an employer establish a split-dollar plan?*

The plan requires written documentation. The documents should provide specific details about the premium payment obligation and the division of ownership of the death benefit and cash values. Many insurance companies offer sample documents for such plans.

Advantages and Disadvantages

⌐ *What are some of the advantages to an employer of using split-dollar insurance plans?*

- The employer is free to choose which employees to cover and what rights and benefits to provide. The choices are made at the employer's sole discretion; one executive or several executives can be covered, while others are not.
- The extra "compensation" helps attract and keep key employees.
- The plan requires no formal qualification or approval by the IRS, and compliance with ERISA is nominal. The details of the

plan are confidential between the employer and the covered employees.

■ No periodic reports or actuarial plan evaluations need to be provided to state or federal regulatory agencies.

■ If the plan terminates before the employee retires, the employer recovers its investment in the policy.

⅍ What are the benefits to the employee of a split-dollar plan?

The following example demonstrates the benefits of split-dollar insurance: ABC Asphalt has a split-dollar plan for its key employee, John. According to the plan, when John dies, ABC has the right to be reimbursed from the cash value for $10,000 in premium payments, plus realized earnings within the policy. The policy provides a death benefit of $250,000. In a traditional split-dollar plan, ABC receives $10,000, and the employee's beneficiary receives $240,000 ($250,000 minus ABC's portion). Split-dollar planning provides the employee (especially a highly compensated employee) with meaningful life insurance coverage at a reduced cost. Split-dollar plans can provide favorable income tax benefits and other advantages to the employee:

■ The employer can pay the premiums on personal insurance policies for the employee and the employee's family members.

■ The economic benefit, which is taxable to the employee, may be a small portion of the actual premiums paid.

■ The employee controls his or her share of the death benefit.

■ The employee can keep the insurance in force if the employer decides to no longer participate in the plan.

⅍ What are the advantages of a split-dollar plan when used in a small, closely held corporation?

In a small, closely held C corporation, tax planning may be the major concern because the owner is also the employee to be insured. Small companies pay out all profits in salaries and bonuses to the owner-employees to produce a "zero" corporate tax. This prevents "double taxation" but does not take advantage of the difference in tax brackets between the corporation and the owner. Owners of a C corporation can use split-dollar plans to create a greater benefit to themselves at a reduced or bracketed tax cost.

For example, an owner-employee in the 35 percent tax bracket takes bonus compensation. He or she invests after-tax dollars into a stock mutual fund and buys life insurance. The corporation could use a split-dollar plan to take advantage of the corporation's 15 percent corporate tax bracket. (Note: Bracket planning will not work for a professional service corporation.)

⚐ What are the disadvantages of a split-dollar plan?

The split-dollar plan has two disadvantages:

- It produces taxable income to the employee for his or her investment in the life insurance policy.
- It does not provide a deduction to the employer for the share of the premiums the employer pays.

The term cost of insurance increases as the employee grows older. At some point, the term cost, which the employee must pay or report as taxable income, may be too great to continue the plan. The employer and employee should consider an exit strategy as a component of the initial planning.

REVERSE SPLIT-DOLLAR PLANS

⚐ What is a reverse split-dollar plan?

A *reverse split-dollar plan* is similar to a traditional split-dollar life insurance plan except that, under this arrangement, the employer owns all or part of the "at-risk" element of the insurance policy and the employee "owns" the cash-value portion. The *at-risk element* is the difference between the cash value of the policy and the total death benefit. When the employee dies, the employee's beneficiaries receive the portion of the death benefit that is equal to the cash-surrender value and any death benefits attributable to the investment portion of the policy. The employer receives the remaining proceeds.

⚜ What are the tax consequences of a reverse split-dollar plan?

Bonus compensation paid to the employee to help the employee contribute his or her share of the policy premium is taxable compensation to the employee and a tax deduction to the employer. Payment of all the premium by the employer is taxable as compensation, measured by either the economic benefit or below-market-loan approach, as discussed above. The employer cannot deduct its annual cost of the policy but can deduct as compensation any other amounts it pays to the employee in connection with the policy.

As long as the insurance contract does not constitute a modified endowment contract (MEC), the buildup of cash value will not be subject to current income tax to either the employee or employer. A withdrawal of cash value from the policy is a tax-free return of investment capital (up to the amount of premiums paid) and is not subject to income tax or capital gain tax.

The payment of death benefits to the company is tax-free income with a basis adjustment equal to 100 percent of the value of the proceeds paid.

⚜ When are reverse split-dollar plans best utilized?

This model works best under any of the following circumstances:

- The employee (usually an owner) is in a higher tax bracket than the company.
- The company wants a death benefit to help it through troubled times in the event of the loss of a key employee.
- The employee wants to have a supplemental source of retirement funds through the tax-free buildup of the cash value inside the life insurance policy.

PART FIVE

Exit Strategies and Succession Planning

ONLY HALF OF ALL FAMILY-OWNED BUSINESSES LAST MORE THAN one generation, and very few last more than two generations, according to a 1999 article by Steven G. Siegel in *Family Business Succession Planning* (National Law Foundation). The federal estate tax is often criticized as the offending culprit; however, the statistics are similar in nations, such as Australia, that do not have an estate or succession tax. Estate tax "erosion" is certainly a factor; but in the opinions of our contributors, it is certainly *not* the primary factor.

357

After years of experience working with small-business owners, our contributors believe that the major causes are (1) the owners' failure to plan in advance for the succession of the business in the event of their death, disability, or retirement and (2) their failure to train, motivate, and involve the next generation of owners.

An *exit strategy* is a long-range plan for the current owners to divest from the ownership of the business when any of certain events occur. Usually, these events are retirement, disability, and death. An exit strategy is implemented through a succession plan. An exit strategy requires a *vision* of 3, 5, 10, and 20 years into the future. Almost every entrepreneur has the capacity to exercise vision, but many entrepreneurs find it difficult to use this capacity to consider a time when they are no longer in control of the company and are no longer the major force in managing it.

While good, solid tax planning is important in developing an exit strategy and business succession plan, the human equation and the human resource (family, employees, and good management) must always remain considerations.

Chapter 19 is an overview of the most common exit strategies and business succession options. The heart and soul of the entrepreneur may lie within the business that has taken years to build and conserve. The continuation of the business after the entrepreneur's death, disability, or retirement is usually very important to the business owner. Will the business pass in ownership and control to other family members, and, if so, are they qualified to operate the company? Will the business be sold to key employees or to outsiders? Is an ESOP an alternative? If large enough, should the entrepreneur take the company public?

Serious succession planning often involves the participation of professionals who will work with the entrepreneur to design a plan that will best meet his or her objectives.

Chapter 20 presents the essential element relevant to all exit strategies, succession plans, and estate plans: valuation of the business. Almost every business will need, at some time, the services of a business valuation professional. Our contributors discuss the factors that influence the value of a business; the valuation process and the methods of valuation appropriate to various businesses; and valuation discounts and how and when they are applied.

In Chapters 21 through 24, our contributors explain the succession planning options that owners can use for divesting their companies in the event of disability or retirement. Planning for what happens to the company at the death of the owners is also part of a succession plan and is discussed in both this part and Part Six.

In cases of joint ownership, the topic of Chapter 21, a succession plan almost always entails a carefully structured buy-sell agreement in which the terms for purchasing the interest of a deceased, disabled, or retiring owner are agreed to in advance. There are two types of buy-sell agreements. In a cross-purchase agreement, the remaining owners purchase the interest; in an entity purchase agreement, the business buys back the interest. The "promise to purchase" in the buy-sell agreement may be funded, usually by life insurance. This alternative may be crucial to families in preparation for the carryover-basis tax system (see Chapter 1).

A sale of the business to employees, including family members who work in the business, can occur in many ways, as explained in Chapter 22. The desire of the entrepreneur to realize a fair price for his or her business must often be tempered by the limited financial resources available to employees for making the acquisition. A compromise, based in economic necessity, is the entrepreneur's sale to key employees in exchange for an installment promissory note. After the sale, the employees who now control the business may find it necessary to take large bonuses to pay the debt service. Other, very creative, selling techniques have been developed to make the sale as tax-efficient as possible. These strategies include a sale to an irrevocable trust that is treated as a grantor trust for federal income tax purposes, a sale in exchange for a private annuity, or an installment promissory note that cancels on death. Midlevel strategies include the use of an employee stock ownership plan.

Many entrepreneurs make gifts of company stock to family members over time. Eventually, the next generation gains a greater ownership share of the business. As our contributors note in Chapter 23, nontax issues frequently govern the parents' decision to use this method. Is the entrepreneur willing to eventually give up a controlling interest in the company? Are family members qualified to operate the company? Will gifts to children who do not work in the business produce a conflict between participating children and non-participating children? Gifts of S corporation stock in trust require careful planning. A qualified S corporation trust may be necessary to protect the tax-reporting integrity of the company. Estate and gift tax exemptions also require careful planning. Special planning with the grantor retained annuity trust, the family limited partnership, and the charitable lead trust can multiply tax savings.

If business owners do not have co-owners, family members, or key employees but are ready to retire, the only realistic alternative is to sell the business to outsiders. This option is covered in Chapter 24. The sale may be for cash or for part cash and part installment promissory note. If the candidate is a large public or private company, the transaction may be a tax-free stock-for-stock exchange. Special care must be taken in structuring the sale or exchange. The entrepreneur must be careful about making unrealistic warranties and representations. He or she must consider personal exposure to liability claims that have an origin before the sale but are made after the entrepreneur is no longer in control of the business and settlement negotiations. If the sale is for an installment promissory note, the entrepreneur should adopt a pessimistic outlook and structure the default and offset provisions of the promissory note and collateral agreement. One of the most critical aspects of a sale is the effect of taxes on the owner. Because business owners commonly have a very low cost basis in their companies, planning for the effects that capital gain and income taxes will have on the proceeds of the sale is very important. Our contributors have presented a unique alternative that enables owners to divest their companies, reduce the effects of taxes, *and* help their favorite charities in the long run: Give the business to charity through a charitable remainder trust while retaining an income for life or for a term of years.

chapter 19

Succession Planning

EXIT STRATEGY

Why do I need an exit strategy?

No one lives forever, and most people do not want to own and operate a business forever. The only question is whether the transition of your ownership will occur before or after your death. Unlike most people who develop investment portfolios that are (or should be) diversified in many different types of investments, business owners tend to invest the vast majority of their funds in one asset, the business. This makes preparing for retirement and planning for the business at death or disability quite complex.

What are my exit strategy options?

You have a number of alternatives for exiting your business:

361

SELL TO CO-OWNERS: You can structure a *buy-sell agreement* so that the company or your co-owners buy your interest when you are ready to retire. Such arrangements also include provisions for what happens to the business if you become disabled or die while fully involved in the management and operation of the business. If you do not currently have co-owners, you may need to bring co-owners into the business or merge with another company as part of your overall exit strategy. That company may have an owner who could become your co-owner, or you may find another entrepreneur with the financial capacity to become your co-owner and to buy your interest at death, disability, or retirement.

SELL TO KEY EMPLOYEES: If you have key employees, who may be family members, you can structure a sale to them before your retirement. For this type of sale, you can expect to receive a significant portion of the purchase price in installment payments over 5 to 10 years.

ESTABLISH AN EMPLOYEE STOCK OWNERSHIP PLAN: An employee stock ownership plan (ESOP) may allow you to transfer all or part of your ownership of the company to your employees. A "leveraged" ESOP may provide you or your estate with a private market for your stock and much-needed retirement income for you or liquidity for your estate to pay for estate settlement costs and estate taxes.

GIVE THE BUSINESS TO FAMILY MEMBERS: Over time, you can gradually give ownership and control of the company to your children or other family members. This strategy lets you see how well your children run the business and helps reduce estate taxes at your death.

SELL TO OUTSIDERS: You may sell to outside parties, which may include any private investment group, individual investor, or another company anywhere in the country or the world. The investors or other company may ask or require that you continue with the business for a period of time or act as a consultant.

GIVE THE COMPANY TO CHARITY: The charity can sell the business or liquidate its assets over time. If you give the company to a charity outright, you receive an income tax deduction. If you give the company to a charity through a charitable remainder trust, you not only receive an income tax deduction but can receive an annual income for the rest of your life.

GO PUBLIC: If your company is large enough and has a record of annual growth that will attract the attention of an underwriter, a public offering can provide you with the market to sell your stock on your disability, retirement, or death. Similarly, you could merge with a public company on a stock-for-stock basis so that you receive publicly traded stock that you can sell.

LIQUIDATE: You can liquidate the company by selling individual assets.

We discuss these alternatives in the chapters that follow.

BUSINESS
SUCCESSION PLAN

⩗ *What is a business succession plan?*

The *business succession plan* details the steps for implementing your chosen exit strategy. Good business succession planning allows the smooth transfer of management control and ownership of the business so that the business can continue to operate, providing good service to its customers and providing cash flow to the owner and/or his or her loved ones. If the owner wants to sell and retire to a South Seas island, good business succession planning will help the owner position the company for a sale, find the buyer at the appropriate time, and create a smooth transfer of ownership.

⩗ *How do I develop a succession plan?*

After you have chosen an exit strategy, most of the succession plan questions you must consider fall into these five categories:

TIME FRAME: Decide when you will retire so that you know how much time you have to train your successors for taking over the reins and to position your business for whatever exit strategy you choose.

OWNERSHIP: Decide in advance whether you want to transfer management only or whether you want or need to transfer ownership as well. This decision is based mostly on how you plan to retire and whether you will need the proceeds for retirement. You should also consider whether it is important to you that the business continue in its present form after you leave. How important is it that the business keep the same name, the same employees, the same philosophy? Are you willing to sell it to others who may run it differently or dismantle it entirely?

MANAGEMENT SUCCESSION: Identify who you want to control the business if you become disabled, die, or retire. This decision is vital to the survival of the business. Consider how you feel about remaining in control of the business while you are still in the business. Realistically consider your ability to adopt a more passive role and your willingness to actually retire from the business. If you cannot give up some control, it will be more difficult for you to assess the abilities of your successors before you leave.

ESTATE PLANNING: If you decide that you want your family to inherit the business after your death, weigh carefully how it should be divided among your children. Equal ownership or even majority-minority ownership invites disaster if your children don't get along. Leaving the business to the child who is active in it is satisfactory to him or her but may cause bitterness for the child or children who receive little or no inheritance. Be sure to consider, as part of your succession plan, how your family will pay the estate taxes without being forced to sell the business. There are techniques for avoiding all of these problems. Your advisors can help you work through the issues and decide the best ones for your goals.

VALUATION OF THE BUSINESS: Determining the value of your business is a necessity for all exit strategy options. You need a valuation for a purchaser in a sale, and you need a valuation for the IRS for estate planning purposes.

Tables 19-1 through 19-3, at the end of this chapter, list questions to contemplate in choosing your exit strategy, developing a succession plan, and training successors. Use your answers to these questions, and review the relevant methods and options presented in this part of *Strictly Business,* as you and your advisors begin to work through the planning process.

⊰ *My daughter Cynthia is employed by my company and is qualified to take over at my death or disability. Tim and Jackie, my children from a prior marriage, are not involved in the company and have no interest or experience in it. I want to be fair to all three children. Should I divide my stock equally among them?*

Perhaps not. In time, Tim and Jackie may perceive that Cynthia receives all the economic benefits of management and ownership—the big salary, a company automobile, and fringe benefits. If you give each child equal ownership, Tim and Jackie may eventually combine their votes to remove Cynthia and attempt to manage the business themselves. They have no experience for doing so. In the long run, the arguments among them could result in having to sell the company.

Unfortunately, this scenario is common when a business-owner parent wants to be fair to his or her children and seeks nothing more than to treat them equally. However, "equal" is not always "fair," and vice versa.

Parents need to give themselves permission to plan fairly, even though the result produces an unequal economic benefit. There are many ways to create an economic benefit for a nonparticipating family member in order to compensate for the transfer of 100 percent ownership of the family business to a participating child. We discuss these techniques in detail in Chapter 23.

⊰ *I'd like my children to continue my business, but I don't know if they are capable of it. How should I proceed?*

Consult with your children as a group and then individually. You will never know what a child wants and expects without asking.

Assume nothing. Keep an open mind, and do not be critical or judgmental. Family participation is not an option if no one in the family wants to continue the business. If one or more family members are interested in continuing the business, it is critical for you to realistically assess their qualifications, often with an impartial third party serving as a guide and facilitator.

To maintain family harmony, choose your successors very carefully and groom them thoroughly. Talk with each of your children about the decisions you are making and the reasons for those decisions. Contain emotional reactions by fully disclosing the facts. Once you have chosen your successor or successors, begin a succession training program immediately.

⊰ *I'm the owner of a third-generation family-owned business. How do I ensure that the company will pass to my children?*

Start by consulting your advisors to discuss the mechanics and practicality of your succession plan. An impartial third-party opinion might alert you to factors that you've never considered. By starting early, you will have time to evaluate all options and choices.

If your children are already working in the business, you will have time to evaluate how each performs and who is best at marketing, administration, finance, and operations.

If your children are not currently in the business but want to make it a career choice, get them involved as early as possible. Don't wait until your retirement years. Provide them with the necessary experience in the day-to-day workings of the business. Be willing to involve children in nonmanagement positions, and permit them to work up the employment ladder on the basis of merit. You may want them to work for another company in your industry before they are entitled to employment in the family company. Working up the ladder and cross-employment—gaining actual experience—will probably help your company's career employees accept your children more quickly. Provide to all employees advance notice of your plan to involve a child or children in management at a future time. Your entire family, your business associates, and your banker should know of your decisions.

⚑ Is a sale of the business to selected children better than giving the business to selected children?

A gift of the company while you are alive or after your death may be perceived by children not in the business as an unequal and unfair distribution to the children who are employed by the business. A sale to children working in the business may be perceived as fair, but a sale is possible only if the children who are to acquire ownership have the financial resources to make the purchase.

⚑ The thought of selling my business so that I can retire overwhelms me. Its cash is flowing nicely; I've got a good management team, but there's nobody I want to sell to at this time. What should I do?

When you started your business, the idea that you might want to sell it someday was probably unthinkable. Now that you have begun to think seriously about how you will retire and that you might have to sell the business, you're experiencing uncertainty. Your leadership has required enormous energy and more than a little emotional attachment, so putting yourself in the role of a seller is quite distressing.

Deciding when to sell your business will be one of the most important decisions in your life. It not only will have a direct impact on your business life but also will have profound effects on your personal well-being and financial status. With all the effort and sacrifice required to build a business, you are wise now to take extra time to carefully consider your exit plan.

With a good cash flow and a management team in place, continuing to own the business—but not being involved in all the day-to-day operations—can be to your advantage. You can continue to draw a salary, receive fringe benefits, and participate in the retirement plan. Under the right circumstances, the business may pay for some of your travels. You can remain involved in the areas of the business that you most enjoy. You maintain your community connections and stature. Meanwhile, your business may continue to grow in value.

Your reduced involvement in the business may give your management team time to flourish and eventually step up to the plate to buy the business from you. It will also allow potential outside buyers to see that the business can be run profitably and successfully by a new owner, thus enhancing the likelihood of a better offer in the future.

Whom should business owners select as advisors in establishing a succession plan?

Succession planning is a complex process, not a transaction. No one advisor has the expertise in all areas that a business succession plan must cover. Business owners should work with a team of advisors to produce the best options and alternatives. The team should consist of the owner's financial advisor and accountant, an attorney who specializes in business and estate planning, and the company's accountant and attorney. Special expertise may be provided by an insurance professional and a business valuation professional.

TABLE 19-1   Choosing an Exit Strategy: Considerations

- Do I want to retire?
- When will I retire? (Establish a time frame.)
- How much money do I need for retirement?
- Do I want to retain control of the business as long as I am working in the business?
- Do I need to transfer management only and receive income from the business during retirement?
- Can the business continue under different management and control and still provide my retirement funds?
- Do I want to sell the business and use the proceeds for retirement?
- Do I need to sell the business in order to retire?
- Do I want my family to sell the business after my death, or do I want the business to remain in the family?
- Do I want to expand the business?
- Can the business be transferred in its present form? Or must I first convert it to a different ownership structure?
- Is the business well-positioned to be transferred?
- Do I have the resources and the will to see through the transition process?

TABLE 19-2   Developing a Succession Plan: Considerations

Sole owner at retirement or disability:

❑ What do I want to happen to the business, me, and my family if I become disabled and can't participate in the operation of the business?

❑ What do I want to happen to the business, me, and my family if I retire?

❑ How will my absence affect the performance level of my business?

❑ Are there family members who can take over the business now or, with proper training, at some time in the future?

❑ Is there a nonfamily employee (or employees) who is qualified to continue managing the business?

❑ Can power be shared among the key employees?

❑ Will I need to hire and train someone as my successor?

❑ Can the company afford to pay my full salary?

❑ If I no longer earn a salary, how will this affect my family and me?

❑ If I decide to sell the business, how will I find a buyer to pay my price?

Sole owner at death:

❑ How will my heirs pay the estate taxes and other costs to settle the estate?

❑ Can my family readily sell the business?

❑ How will a value be determined for the business or the assets?

❑ Who has the authority to sell or liquidate the business?

❑ Who has the authority to maintain the business until a sale or liquidation is accomplished?

❑ Is the confidentiality of my business affairs important?

❑ Who do I want to inherit the business?

❑ Are there family members who can take over the business now or, with training, in the future? When will I bring them into the business?

❑ What do I leave to my other children to equalize their inheritance?

❑ How will my spouse be taken care of after my death?

Co-owner at retirement or disability:

❑ Can we afford to pay the disabled owner's salary from cash flow?

❑ How will his or her absence affect our ability to continue the business at current levels of performance?

❑ Will we allow the disabled or retiring owner to sell his or her interest to someone outside the existing ownership group?

❑ Will the company or the other owners buy his or her interest?

❑ How will we put a value on the owner's interest?

❑ What are the terms of payment?

❑ Can the company's cash flow tolerate the burden of a buyout?

TABLE 19-2   Developing a Succession Plan, *continued*

Co-owner at death:

- ❏ Will we allow the deceased owner's family to sell his or her interest to someone outside the existing ownership group?
- ❏ Is the business located in a community property state where a nonowner spouse may have an interest?
- ❏ Will the company or the other owners buy the deceased owner's interest?
- ❏ How will we value the deceased owner's interest?
- ❏ What are the terms of payment?
- ❏ Can the company's cash flow afford a buyout?
- ❏ Is confidentiality of our business affairs important?

TABLE 19-3   Identifying & Training Successors: Considerations

- ❏ Which individuals are qualified to succeed me in management? (Is there just one or a group?)
- ❏ Do their interests, skills, and education match the needs of the business?
- ❏ Which family members own interests in the business? What percentages do they control? How old are they? Are any of them key employees?
- ❏ When will I begin to train my successors?
- ❏ Who else will train my successors, and how? (Successors may need both inside and outside professional training and education.)
- ❏ Are my candidates able to preserve and enhance existing banking or other lending relationships?
- ❏ Do my candidates have strong financial backgrounds?
- ❏ Do they have the ability to raise money for invested and borrowed capital?
- ❏ Who is best with vendor relationships?
- ❏ Who is qualified and best suited for human resource management?
- ❏ Are these the same persons I want to take over ownership of the company?
- ❏ Are they financially able to buy the company?
- ❏ Am I willing to help them buy the company?
- ❏ When will I begin to give them control?
- ❏ When will I begin to give them ownership?
- ❏ How much ownership and control will I give them while I'm still working in the business?
- ❏ How much ownership and control will they have after I retire?
- ❏ Who are the other potential buyers of the business?

chapter 20

Business Valuation

PURPOSES OF VALUATION

⚐ *What does a business valuation do?*

A business valuation establishes the value of a business as a whole or the value of a partial interest in a business through quantitative and qualitative analysis. A value is placed on the business assets, both tangible (building, land, and equipment) and intangible (goodwill, trademarks, patents, and customer lists).

⚐ *Why and when is a business valuation report needed or prudent?*

A business valuation report may be produced for any one or more of the following reasons:

BUY-SELL AGREEMENT: As part of the succession planning process, business owners predetermine the price of redeeming an owner's equity interest on his or her death, disability, or retirement or on some other triggering event. A business appraiser conducts a full valuation study and analysis and recommends a valuation formula that is representative, in the years to come, of the present and future value of the business. This formula is then incorporated into a buy-sell agreement among the owners. When the triggering event occurs years later, the remaining owners apply the formula to purchase the interest of the departing owner. The services of the valuation expert are not needed at that time unless the IRS contests the formula.

SALE OF PARTIAL INTEREST TO EXISTING OWNERS: If the owners did not previously enter into a buy-sell agreement to establish a formula for valuing a departing or deceased owner's interest, or the agreement did not include a valuation formula, the valuation expert determines what the equity interest is worth.

SALE OF THE BUSINESS: A valuation expert, or business appraiser, is frequently employed before a sale of the business to help establish a range of values, from high to low, so that the business owner can set an initial asking price. The appraiser can assist in the collection of financial information that potential buyers will want to inspect as part of their "due-diligence" process. An appraiser can also represent a prospective purchaser of a business, examining the books and records of the company, setting the purchaser's bid price, and assisting during negotiations.

SALE OF PARTIAL INTEREST TO A NEW OWNER: When existing owners want to sell equity to a new owner, they often employ a business appraiser to establish a range of values, from high to low, for the sale of a partial interest in the business.

ESTATE PLANNING: Tax value is not always fair market value. The business appraiser must understand and apply the special rules imposed by the Internal Revenue Code and case law that govern the valuation of the various types of closely held business enterprises for transfer tax purposes. A valuation report, at the very least, should protect the business owner from undervaluation penalties if the gift or estate tax return reporting transfers of ownership is audited by the Internal Revenue Service.

Lender applications: Lenders often require valuations to document the business's ability to pay principal and interest from its cash flow.

Stock option plans: Closely held stock that employees acquire under a stock option bonus plan should be valued on an annual basis. Closely held stock contributed to an employee stock ownership plan (ESOP) must be valued annually.

Management control: Management sometimes employs a business appraiser on a regular basis to monitor the progress, growth, and success of the company and to measure corresponding increases in the value of the organization. Companies that are positioning themselves for an initial public offering often get annual valuations.

Are there any special rules for valuing a business for gift tax purposes?

Yes. Special rules apply to tax valuations. For gift tax purposes, the value of the property transferred is measured by what the assignee receives, not what the assignor gives up. For example, if dad is going to give all his shares of stock in a closely held corporation simultaneously to eleven family members, the value of the gift to each family member is determined by considering each gift separately and not by aggregating all of dad's holdings in the corporation immediately before the gift. The application of any discounts would be determined in connection with each separate gift to each family member.

The rule is different for estate tax purposes. All shares or units of ownership of a deceased owner are treated as a single block for valuation purposes.

Are there ways to "fix" the value of a business for buy-sell purposes and for estate tax purposes?

A buy-sell agreement can help determine a value for estate settlement reasons. The owners must agree in advance on a reasonable formula or price per share or unit that reflects the fair market value of the stock at the time it is exercised. We caution you, however, that buy-sell agreements involving members of the same family are scrutinized by the Internal Revenue Service for potential tax abuse. There is a risk that the IRS will perceive a sale to family members as an artificially contrived method of avoiding gift and estate tax. Documentation is important. To avoid unintended gifts to family members in the sale of a business interest:

- The business purchase agreement should be in writing and must be a bona fide business arrangement.

- The terms of the agreement must be comparable to similar transactions between unrelated persons in an "arm's-length" transaction.

- The agreement must not be a device to transfer the business to family members for less than full and adequate consideration.

A business appraiser can assist the family, or other ownership group, to produce a valuation formula that is enforceable and that is tied to the real value of equity now and in the future.

Is an independent business appraisal helpful for avoiding or surviving an audit?

Yes. The IRS tends to challenge the value (price) in a sale or gift of equity by one family member to another. Decisions of the U.S. Tax Court indicate that family members may reasonably rely on the opinion of value produced by an independent appraiser, and they emphasize the importance of involving outside advisors and consultants in negotiating the sale and setting the purchase price. This protects the transaction, at the very least, from undervaluation penalties.

Is it necessary to have a business valuation performed in the case of a divorce?

Almost always. A business valuation is often necessary, and sometimes required by law, to determine an adequate and equitable division and distribution of the marital property between the divorcing parties. Business appraisers may also play a role in mediation.

APPRAISERS

⚐ What guidelines should I use in selecting a business appraiser?

The appraiser you choose should:

- Have experience in appraising businesses in your profession or industry
- Have a good reputation in the business valuation profession
- Be actively associated with one or more professional business appraisal organizations
- Be known for his or her clear writing and ability to provide commonsense, nontechnical explanations for complex matters
- Have the ability to serve as a "teaching" witness in case an issue is a contested matter (A qualified appraiser who provides very technical, difficult-to-understand explanations may do more harm than good in such situations.)
- Insist on independence and on detachment from undue influence of you and your advisors

You should ask prospective appraisers how much time they dedicate to business valuation work, and you should ask your advisors to help you determine whether the appraisers are considered qualified by the professional community.

⚐ How do I determine who is qualified as a business appraiser?

A qualified business appraiser or valuation expert is a person who, through training and experience, has obtained the necessary skill and knowledge to perform business valuations. Such a person usually possesses one or more of the following designations (or is actively affiliated with an accredited group): accredited senior appraiser (ASA), certified business appraiser (CBA), certified valuation analyst (CVA), certified public accountant/accreditation in business valuations (CPA/ABV), and chartered business valuator (CBV). Appendix A provides a description of these designations, requirements for earning them, and their accrediting organizations.

While the designations indicate that the appraiser has completed some level of advanced training and testing, certification or accreditation by a professional association or society does not guarantee that the person has sufficient experience or is appropriate for all assignments. There are cross-discipline professionals who have very significant qualifications. These include certified public accountants who specialize in complex tax issues; business broker/underwriters who know what a business is worth because they are actively involved in selling and acquiring companies or in taking companies public; and attorneys who specialize in tax matters, sales, and acquisitions of companies.

VALUATION PROCESS

⩗ *What are the steps in a business valuation?*

1. The business appraiser and the business owners define the valuation engagement (purpose and scope).
2. The appraiser gathers the necessary information.
3. The appraiser analyzes the information gathered.
4. The appraiser determines the most probable value of the enterprise or equity interest.
5. The appraiser prepares and issues a valuation report. (Many appraisers provide a first draft of the report to the owners for review. The owners have the opportunity to test the appraiser's assumptions and conclusions. The appraiser then produces and delivers a final draft.)

⩗ *What information does the appraiser need for a business valuation?*

The exact information the appraiser needs varies from industry to industry. As a general rule, the appraiser needs at least the following:

1. Financial information (historical and prospective), including financial statements; listings of accounts receivable and aging, accounts payable and aging, and creditors; federal, state, and local tax returns; inventory records; accounting methods used; and details about fixed assets and their values.

2. Factual history of the company, including a tour of the facilities. If inventories and inventory controls are a material valuation factor, the appraiser requires a verification of inventory and needs to observe how fixed assets are used in the business.

3. Information about competitors, comparable companies, and the industry. Trade magazines are very helpful to the appraiser in understanding the industry.

4. Interviews of the company's management team and professional advisors. Interviews help the appraiser determine the variables that influence the performance and growth of the company.

5. An accurate and complete list of owners and the shares or percentage owned by each.

6. Copies of organization documents, transfer restriction agreements, buy-sell agreements, and voting trust agreements in order to determine what restrictions on ownership and transfer of ownership apply.

Valuation Standards

What are the components of a good business appraisal?

The courts have concluded that valuation reports should comply with the Uniform Standards of Professional Appraisal Practice (USPAP) published by the Appraisal Foundation. The appraisal study and report should include:

- A description of the business enterprise, the assets, and/or the equity interest to be appraised
- The purpose and intended use of the appraisal
- The definition of value the appraiser employed

- The effective date of the appraisal and the date of the report
- The methods the appraiser used or didn't use and the reasons why and why not
- An analysis of comparable companies
- An examination of comparable sales
- A site inspection of the company's premises
- Interviews with management
- Information from outside sources such as suppliers, customers, competitors, and financial institutions
- Information about the company's competitors
- Information about the industry in which the company does business
- Sufficient information to support the appraiser's conclusions and to enable the company and its advisors to understand the report and conclusions (Any specific limiting conditions associated with the appraisal assignment and study should be disclosed in the report.)
- A clear and accurate disclosure of any extraordinary assumptions that directly affect the appraisal and indicate the impact of assumptions on value
- A summary of the qualifications of the appraiser
- A signed certificate that the appraiser followed the USPAP requirements (For example, the appraiser must disclose that he or she has no financial interest in the company and that his or her compensation is not contingent on an outcome.)

The report should be clear, accurate, and logically organized and be in a readable format that supports the appraiser's conclusions in a manner that is not misleading.

⅍ *Should management and management's advisors review the report?*

Yes. The benchmark of quality is that management should be able to understand the report.

In reviewing your appraisal report, critically evaluate the data and documentation to be certain that it is relevant to your business circumstances. Assess the similarity of the assumptions to your business, and attempt to discern whether there is any reason why such apparent similarities would not be applicable in your case. In other words, be sure that the information the appraiser used to formulate a conclusion is correct and current and that the appraiser considered all relevant facts and circumstances.

⚘ What is meant by "value"?

In general, *value* is an ascertainable dollar amount that a seller will accept, and a payer will pay, for property or for a service. There are numerous "standards of value" that may or may not govern the appraiser's approach:

FAIR MARKET VALUE: Fair market value, or "market value," is the price at which property would change hands between a willing buyer and a willing seller when neither is acting under a compulsion to buy or sell and both have reasonable knowledge of all relevant facts.

INVESTMENT VALUE: This is generally considered the value of property to an investor on the basis of his or her minimum requirements for return on the investment, as measured by income or annual appreciation in the value of the investment. Investment value may or may not be equal to the fair market value of an asset. It may consider differences in future earning-power estimates, various perceptions of degree of risk, tax status, and synergies of other operations owned and controlled by the investor.

The term "economic value" has a similar meaning. *Economic value* is the present value of all reasonably expected future benefits to be realized by an investor over the holding period of the investment (e.g., dividends and appreciation in the value of the investment asset that the investor can realize on the sale of the investment).

FAIR VALUE: The fair-value standard is frequently dictated by state law for divorce settlements, shareholder litigation, and other controversies. Since ownership in most closely held companies has no market and no fair market value, fair value is (1) investment value, (2) economic value, or (3) intrinsic, fundamental value.

PREMISES OF VALUE: These are assumptions regarding the circumstances under which a sale will occur and what will become of the business in the future. For example, does the buyer need to sell quickly to pay overdue personal loans, does the buyer plan on continuing the business, or does he or she plan on tearing it down and constructing a high-rise condominium project on the property?

GOING-CONCERN VALUE: Valuing a company as a going concern assumes that the business is a viable operating entity and that there is no evidence that the owners intend to liquidate it.

LIQUIDATION VALUE: Liquidation value is the opposite of going-concern value. Liquidation value identifies the net amount the owners will have after termination of the business and a sale of its assets in complete liquidation. In determining a liquidation value, no value is attributable to goodwill or other intangible assets that do not, in fact, have a value apart from the going-concern value of the company. In an *orderly liquidation,* the assets are sold over a reasonable period of time in order to obtain the best price available for each asset. In a *forced liquidation,* the assets are sold off quickly and often all at once in an auction sale.

BOOK VALUE: "Book value" is an accounting term, not a valuation concept. It is almost never the fair market value of a business, although a business's book value is often the starting point for determining its fair market value. Book value for fixed assets is the historical cost basis reduced by depreciation. Net book value is the depreciated value of assets reduced by all liabilities.

Is there one method that can be used for all valuation purposes?

The general valuation standard applied to both tax and nontax valuations is fair market value, that is, the price at which a property would change hands between a willing buyer and a willing seller, neither being under any compulsion to buy or sell and both having reasonable knowledge of relevant facts. A business is worth what someone will pay for it as a whole—a 100 percent ownership interest.

Nonetheless, different valuation standards exist, and the one used will depend on the purpose of the valuation. Different state and federal statutes, regulations, and case law precedents may impose different standards of value and sets of criteria for valuations performed for certain purposes. For example, a valuation for the purpose of buying or selling a business will consider all the forces that affect supply and demand, whereas a valuation for the purposes of estate, gift, inheritance, and income taxes or of divorce will use a fair-market-value standard.

⚴ How do you determine the value of a closely held business?

The value of a closely held business is based on net worth and other relevant factors. The Internal Revenue Service suggests that the following be considered in the valuation of a closely held entity:

- The nature of the business and the history of the enterprise
- The economic outlook in general and the condition and outlook of the specific industry in particular
- The book value and financial condition of the business
- The earning capacity of the business
- The dividend-paying capacity of the business
- Whether the enterprise has goodwill or other intangible value
- The sales of the stock or units of ownership and the size of the block of ownership being valued
- The market prices of stocks of corporations engaged in the same or a similar line of business whose stocks are actively traded in a free and open market, either on an exchange or over the counter

Although these factors are objective, significant variations may result from how they are applied to a specific company and the weight given to each factor.

Valuation Adjustments

You mentioned that appraisers use adjustments. What adjustments are appropriate in valuing a closely held business?

In valuing the stock of a privately held business, several adjustments may be made:

LACK-OF-MARKETABILITY DISCOUNT: This discount reflects the inherent difficulty in marketing a business that is not registered for sale to the general public and is not freely traded on any stock exchange. This difficulty results in a delay between the decision to sell and the completion of the sale and is represented by a valuation discount—the lack-of-marketability discount. Valuation adjustments for lack of marketability vary. Though the discount is based on the facts and circumstances of each case, the amount of a discount for lack of marketability can be substantial, ranging from 20 to 35 percent or more.

LACK-OF-CONTROL, OR MINORITY-INTEREST, DISCOUNT: The lack-of-control, or minority-interest, discount is a reduction in value applicable to the valuation of an equity interest that represents less than 50 percent of the ownership of the company. The rationale for this discount rests on a number of factors, including the inability of a minority owner to control corporate policy, determine compensation or dividend payments, or realize his or her pro-rata share of the business's assets through liquidation. This discount is typically between 10 and 25 percent. It is important to note that the discount is applied to an equity valuation determined on a control basis. If the valuation is based on a market approach utilizing publicly traded securities, the discount is already implicit in the determination and no further reduction would be warranted.

Limited partnership interests inherently have no control. The limited partner cannot control or operate the business, handle investment of the assets owned by the business, or determine when and if distributions of income are to be made. Lack of control can influence the value of an equity interest if management is material to the business's income production and investment growth. A valuation discount for noncontrolling equity interests in a corporation or partnership recognizes that an investor will probably pay more for control and that he or she will pay less in the absence of control.

CONTROL PREMIUM: Conversely, if an owner has more than a 50 percent share of the business and has the right to control the business, a control premium may be appropriate in valuing the block because a buyer will usually pay more for control. This has been confirmed by market studies.

KEY-PERSON DISCOUNT: The death or permanent disability of a key employee can be ruinous to a company that relies on a few key people for the generation of new business and the maintenance of current customers. The key-person discount recognizes the potential reduction in income, and corresponding impairment of equity value, if the business is dependent on a few key people and if company performance truly depends on the continued participation of each one.

SWING-VOTE PREMIUM: A swing vote can best be explained with an example: Assume that a company has three shareholders, two owning 48 percent each and the third owning 4 percent. The third one, with 4 percent, is said to have a "swing vote" because that shareholder can influence the company's decisions in situations where the two larger shareholders disagree. A buyer may pay for a minority equity interest if he or she wants the influence associated with a swing vote. An existing 48 percent shareholder will most certainly pay more to acquire voting control.

How do valuation discounts work?

The term "discount" refers to the percentage reduction in the amount that a willing buyer will pay for a property because of an impairment to the value of the property. For example, assume that five people start a company by contributing $100,000 each. The book value of the company is $500,000. If Ann, one of the initial owners, decides to sell her interest to her child (or any other buyer), the value of that interest may be considerably less than $100,000 because the one-fifth interest gives Ann's child little or no actual control over the company. The valuation expert applies a 25 percent discount for lack of control and applies a 10 percent discount for lack of marketability. Discounts are applied sequentially, so $100,000 is first discounted by 25 percent, leaving $75,000, which is then discounted by 10 percent. A one-fifth interest in this company would be worth $67,500.

⚐ What factors affect the size of a discount for lack of marketability?

Significant distributions of cash to owners increase value and decrease the time it will take to find an interested buyer (time to market). Owners who receive little in distributions will find it difficult to locate an interested buyer. Time to market is long-term in nature, and the seller will probably be required to substantially discount his or her asking price to interest a potential buyer.

Other factors that may affect the discount for lack of marketability include the potential pool of buyers who have the financial ability to make the acquisition; the size of the block of stock or units of ownership; the prospect of an initial public offering, buyout, or merger; and restrictive transfer provisions such as buy-sell agreements.

Financial Factors

⚐ What is capitalizing?

The *capitalization rate* is generally a market rate of return for investment instruments (or companies) that are similar and comparable in nature, risk, and return. This rate is used to convert or capitalize a stream of dollars to a present value. You can capitalize historical, current, or expected future levels of returns on virtually any stream of dollars, such as revenues (gross or net), earnings, cash flow, dividends, distributions, and interest.

⚔ What financial ratios are used in a business valuation?

Business appraisers use all the financial and operating ratios that we discussed in Chapter 3. The main types of ratios are profitability, growth, cost control, asset utilization, liquidity, and debt utilization. Financial ratios are an integral tool for analyzing trends. They enable the appraiser to compare a company's own ratios over time and to establish appropriate capitalization rates, identify the company's strengths and weaknesses, and make comparisons with other companies' and industry averages.

⚔ Will the appraiser use the financial statements we prepare?

Since most closely held businesses have actual values (true economic reality) that differ from what is recorded on the financial statements (GAAP/tax basis), adjustments are required to "normalize" the statements so that they more closely reflect the business's true financial position and results of operations on a historical and current basis. It is important to understand that the type of historical financial statements produced by management may have a significant effect on the number and type of economic adjustments that need to be made. Examples include:

ALLOWANCE FOR DOUBTFUL ACCOUNTS: The appraiser must challenge reasonableness as applied to trade accounts and notes receivable by comparing estimated current write-off to historical.

INVENTORY: The appraiser must consider the valuation method used (LIFO versus FIFO), the company's write-down and write-off policies, and the industry's standard costing policies.

MARKETABLE SECURITIES: These may require adjustment to market value.

DEPRECIATION METHODS: A review of the company's depreciation methods and estimated useful lives for the depreciable fixed assets should be performed. Included in the review would be a comparison with industry practice.

LEASES: All leases must be properly classified and accounted for either as capital or operating leases.

CAPITALIZING VERSUS EXPENSING POLICY: It should be ascertained whether the company has taken a reasonable position regarding the expensing of certain fixed assets and inventory items or whether capitalizing adjustments are necessary.

INCOME RECOGNITION TIMING: Especially in a business that accounts for long-term contracts and installment sales, income recognition times need to be understood and, if necessary, adjusted for reasonableness.

ACCOUNTING FOR TAXES: If a company uses different accounting methods for financial statement purposes and for tax purposes, a deferred tax liability most likely will be recorded. A review is necessary to determine whether the deferred liability will result in an actual liability; otherwise, it may need to be removed. Key tax items often encountered include amounts for tax credits and net-operating-loss carryovers.

EXTRAORDINARY OR NONRECURRING ITEMS: A requirement of normalized financial statements is to reflect earnings on a consistent basis. Therefore, any amounts reported as extraordinary or nonrecurring should be removed in order to properly reflect a normalization of operating results. Examples include litigation settlements, gains or losses on the sale of assets, gains or losses on the sale of business segments, and insurance proceeds on key-person or property casualty claims.

COMPENSATION OF OWNERS AND MANAGERS, INCLUDING PERQUISITES: Since many officers and owners compensate themselves on the basis of what the business can afford, and not necessarily on the true economic value of the services performed, adjustments may be necessary to bring the compensation more in line with what the market is paying for similar services. Fringe benefits must also be reviewed in determining the full effect of officers' and owners' compensation.

CONTINGENT LIABILITIES: Contingent liabilities, which are both probable and estimable, should be shown and accrued in the financial statements. Contingencies most commonly encountered are pending lawsuits, unrecorded product liabilities, unrecorded past-service liabilities, unrecorded accrued warranty liabilities, environ-mental liabilities, and permanent impairment of a long-lived asset.

OPERATING VERSUS NONOPERATING ITEMS: If nonoperating items (items that are not used in the operation of the business, such as stocks and mutual funds) are included in the financial statements, they should be reviewed and valued separately from the company's operations.

Assets

⅏ What are intangible assets?

The earning ability (capacity) of a company is partly attributable to the value of intangible assets. These assets may or may not be carried on the company's books. The most common intangible assets are:

- Goodwill (generally thought of as a business's identity, reputa-tion, customer satisfaction and loyalty, and similar positive qual-ities that enhance its profitability)
- Trademarks, patents, copyrights, registered trade names, and registered marks
- Location, customer lists, covenants not to compete, franchise agreements, license agreements, leasehold interests, relation-ships, and software codes

⅏ How are intangible assets valued?

There is no exclusive method for valuing intangibles; each case must be viewed on its own merits. Three commonly used approaches are:

- The *market approach,* based on guideline listings of or actual sales of the same or similar intangible property in a primary or secondary market. This method is difficult in application because intangibles are generally not sold separately from other business assets.

- The *income approach,* based on the capitalization of the projected income that could be realized from the use, forbearance, license, or rental of the asset.
- The *cost approach,* which estimates the present value of the asset on the basis of the principle of substitution. For example, the value of an intangible asset is no more than the investment a prudent businessperson would make to replace the asset with a comparable substitute.

How are tangible assets valued?

Tangible assets are usually adjusted to market values. Several measures are utilized for the adjustments. The *used replacement cost* is the price at which used equipment in comparable condition can be purchased on the open market, plus the cost of transporting and installing the equipment. The *depreciated replacement cost* is the cost of replacing the item with new equipment, minus an allowance for the length of time the item has been in service.

The *orderly liquidation value* is the net amount expected to be received if the assets are sold off in an orderly manner (one at a time, obtaining the best price available per piece on the open market). In contrast, the *forced liquidation value* is the net amount expected to be received if the assets are sold off immediately. This often occurs in an auction, and the best price is rarely obtained.

VALUATION FORMULAS

Is there more than one valuation formula that can be used in valuing a business?

Yes, numerous formulas can be used in valuing a business. They typically fall into four categories: market, income, asset, and hybrid.

Market Formulas

⚓ What are the market approaches to valuation?

VALUATION OF THE WHOLE: The entity value of a company can be determined by considering and weighing the selling price of the same or similar businesses. Some professional business appraisal organizations (such as the Institute of Business Appraisers) maintain a database that records and reports sales and selling variables (price to assets, price to revenues, price to earnings). Information from prior transactions may indicate whether a company in the industry customarily sells at a multiple of sales, a multiple of asset values, or a multiple of earnings and within a range of values.

VALUATION OF EQUITY: A market approach uses publicly traded stock prices for similar companies as a guideline for calculating the freely traded value of equity in a closely held company, assuming that the closely held company is a publicly traded company, not a private one. The estimate of value is determined by using value multipliers such as price to earnings, price to cash flow, and market value of invested capital divided by book value of invested capital. Market-derived discounts are then used to adjust the price of closely held equity for lack of marketability and for minority, noncontrolling ownership. This process, called the *guideline company method,* has merit for companies large enough to actually support an initial public offering. The guideline company may produce unsupportable values for small closely held companies that are not comparable to a public company in size, management depth, and capitalization.

DISCOUNTS AND CAPITALIZATION RATES: To develop a risk-adjusted capitalization rate and a discount rate for the closely held business valuation, appraisers may use market rates of return on comparable investments in the public marketplace. This is a component of a market approach analysis for a company of any size. Greater investment risk (and operating risk) is associated with less-capitalized operating companies than, for example, with a closed-end corporate bond fund. The risk is reflected by historical rates of return. Investments in publicly traded less-capitalized companies have more risk of loss and failure than does a bond fund investment.

☙ *What procedures must be followed in comparing one company to another?*

Can a company with a fiscal year that ends in June be compared to a company with a calendar-year fiscal year? Can a company that calculates earnings before tax be compared to one that calculates earnings per share on an after-tax basis? Can a cash-basis company that does not report accruals for accounts receivable and accounts payable be compared to a company that reports on an accrual basis? A realistic comparison to industry averages usually requires that the analyst adjust a company's financial records to the method reported for its industry. Such adjustments usually include the following components:

- Normalize the balance sheet and income statement. The statement should exclude nonrecurring revenues, such as proceeds from the sale of a subsidiary or other capital asset. Financial statements should be adjusted to an accrual basis if industry statistics are derived from accrual adjustment statistics.
- Collect comparative financial data for an average company of similar size in the industry.
- Calculate the financial ratios available for the company's industry.
- Calculate the balance-sheet items as a percentage of total assets.
- Calculate the income-statement items as a percentage of total revenues.
- Compare the common-size balance sheet to industry norms.
- Compare the common-size income statement to industry norms.
- Compare the financial ratios to industry norms.
- List and evaluate the subject company's strengths and weaknesses compared to industry statistics.

≈ *My wife owns a company that manufactures ten automobiles per year. Should we use the stock market values of the big auto companies as comparables?*

The danger with using the market-value approach is that you must use companies that are truly comparable both in size and industry to get a fair valuation.

Income Formulas

≈ *What are the income approaches to business valuation?*

There are six common income approaches that appraisers use:

CAPITALIZATION OF EARNINGS AND REVENUES: This method emphasizes the value of income and cash flows in a valuation of the company and in a valuation of fractionalized interests for any company or partnership as a going concern. The method is often used for operating companies whose value as a going concern is greater than the liquidation value of the company. Value is expressed as a multiple of gross earnings, net earnings, or net cash flow. Different valuation multiples may be applied to minority-shareholder interests and controlling-shareholder interests. For example, the buy-sell agreement of an operating company requires that the equity interest of a minority shareholder be redeemed at a value equal to a multiple of 35 percent of the prior year's gross revenues divided by the percentage of ownership to be acquired. Multiples of gross revenues have an advantage. The multiple recognizes the significance of earnings to the equity value in an operating company. Gross revenues are not subject to manipulation. Net revenues may be understated in a closely held company because of tax-planning and aggressive compensation policies.

MULTIPLE OF DISCRETIONARY EARNINGS: This method is commonly used to value smaller businesses. The method can provide a valid indication of value for small to midsize companies and is particularly useful when owner compensation and perquisites represent a significant portion of total company earnings, the business is managed by owners, and a range of values is desired and appropriate. Variable multiples are applied to discretionary cash flow to produce a range of values. The appraiser selects a value from the range that is most probably applicable to the value of a majority interest or, in the alternative, a minority ownership interest in the business.

DISCOUNTED EARNINGS: This method is also referred to as the *discounted-cash-flow method* because cash flows, not book earnings, are important in this approach. The method is favored when future cash flows are not consistent from year to year.

PRICE-TO-EARNINGS RATIO: The present value of an equity interest is determined by multiplying earnings per share by a multiple. The multiple may be market-derived and adjusted for control or lack of control and for marketability or lack of marketability.

DIVIDEND-PAYING CAPACITY: Most closely held C-class corporations do not pay dividends. The capitalization of zero earnings (dividends) produces a zero value of equity. This method examines adjusted cash flows actually available for distribution to owners and uses all or a part of the cash flow available for distribution to owners as a substitute for dividends. The term "discretionary cash flow" indicates an amount in excess of reasonable deductions, a reasonable deduction for compensation to owner-managers, debt service, and working-capital requirements that management may, in its discretion, distribute to owners as dividends or may retain, all or in part, for reinvestment in the company. A business appraiser must be careful in the application of this method. There is a potential for an overvaluation of equity if the dividend-paying capacity is considered without a reciprocal adjustment to net worth for "deemed" distributions.

EXCESS EARNINGS: This method is often encountered in divorce valuations. It calculates a reasonable return on invested assets. The excess of value (capitalization of earnings or discounted-cash-flow value) is excess earnings. The excess-earnings value represents the goodwill value of the business or professional practice. This method, however flawed, considers both asset values and income values of a company on a going-concern basis.

≱ *In using a capitalization-of-earnings method, should past, present, or future earnings be considered?*

Past earnings can indicate trends and potential growth. Present and reasonably projected future earnings should be considered in applying a capitalization-of-earnings multiplier. Past performance should be based on at least the last 5 years of financial statements, including balance sheets and incomes statements.

Asset Formulas

≱ *What is the asset approach to the valuation of a business?*

An *asset approach* calculates the value of a company's assets minus its liabilities. Valuations of the company's receivables, inventory, fixed assets, investments, and intangibles are considered:

NET BOOK VALUE: This formula is simple to apply and many owners prescribe book value as the applicable buy-sell standard. Values are based on the most recent financial statement with no adjustments. No adjustments are made for minority interests or the absence of marketability. The "net" in net book value requires that asset values reported on the financial statement be reduced by "booked value" of liabilities reported on the financial statement. For cash-basis companies, no adjustment is made for accrual items such as accounts payable and accounts receivable. The formula usually undervalues equity interests in an operating company and may undervalue or overvalue an equity interest in an investment holding company or partnership.

ADJUSTED NET BOOK VALUE: This formula usually requires that all tangible assets of a company be adjusted to fair market value as of a prescribed buy-sell valuation date (date of death or date of termination). The present value of accounts payable, accrued expenses, notes payable, and other expenses is subtracted. This produces one measure of adjusted net book value. This method does not permit valuation adjustments for lack of control or lack of marketability. It overstates the value of a noncontrolling interest in an investment holding company and can understate the value of an equity interest in an operating company. Adjusted net book value may be useful in calculating the alternative value of the whole of an asset-heavy firm such as a timber company.

ADJUSTED NET ASSETS: The value of the assets owned by a business is given more weight than would be the case in a valuation based on a prospective income stream.

Hybrid Formula

⚐ *What is the hybrid approach?*

Some appraisers use a hybrid version of the discounted-cash-flow model that blends the income and the asset approaches. It produces a present value for any given year of both assets and income, considering growth and the risk of investment (or, in the valuation of the whole, the business risk). Cash flows are increased from year to year by a justifiable growth rate, and the residual value of principal is adjusted from year to year by a justifiable growth rate for asset values.

chapter 21

Selling
to Co-owners

BUY-SELL AGREEMENTS

*⋈ My partner and I are not seeing eye-to-eye on business operations,
and it's becoming difficult to get anything accomplished. What
can we do?*

Hindsight isn't very helpful at this point, but your situation is exactly why experts recommend that business owners implement a buy-
sell agreement early in their relationship. The agreement establishes
a method for one of the owners to exit the business or, at the very
least, for all the owners to resolve disagreements before they become
debilitating.

Fifty-fifty ownership produces very special problems. For instance, if one 50 percent owner wants to separate from the other,
who is entitled to the business name, address, telephone number,
customer lists, and business records? A buy-sell agreement, contem-

plating the possibility of future separation, can provide binding particulars.

⚞ What is a buy-sell agreement?

A *buy-sell agreement* is an exit strategy for business owners to use in the event of death, disability, disagreement, or retirement (often known as *triggering events*) to protect both the departing owner and the integrity of an ownership group. A buy-sell agreement documents the owners' decisions regarding:

- Restrictions on the sale or transfer of ownership interests to parties outside the current ownership group
- Which triggering events will require that an owner sell, and the business or other owners buy, the owner's interest in the business
- How the business interest is to be valued on a triggering event
- How payment is to be made (lump sum or installments)

⚞ Is the triggering event in a buy-sell agreement limited to the death of an owner?

No. Triggering events can include other events, such as retirement or other termination of employment, disability, divorce, bankruptcy, and so on.

⚞ What kind of entities can use buy-sell agreements?

Buy-sell agreements are used by all multiple-owner entities: corporations, general and limited partnerships, and limited liability companies.

⚞ What are the most important objectives of a buy-sell agreement?

A buy-sell agreement should have several tax and nontax objectives, as shown in the following list:

Tax objectives

- Minimize income tax for the seller (capital gain versus ordinary income).
- Maximize the tax basis for the buyer.
- Fix the value of an owner's interest for estate tax purposes.

Nontax objectives

- Provide cash to the owner's estate for paying estate taxes and other costs.
- Control the voluntary transfer of an owner's interest during his or her lifetime and avoid the introduction of outsiders (e.g., a divorced spouse, the estate of a deceased spouse, or a business competitor) into the ownership group.
- Delineate a clear method of determining the value of the deceased or departing owner's interest, such as a specific sale price or a formula to determine the price.
- Provide the remaining owners or the company with the liquidity needed to fulfill the obligation and prevent forced liquidation of the company.
- Provide a market to a business owner for his or her interest, which is otherwise not marketable.
- Provide for an orderly transition of ownership, management, and control.

Types of Agreements

What types of buy-sell agreements are available?

Three types of agreements commonly used in buy-sell planning are the cross-purchase agreement, the entity-purchase (redemption) agreement, and the hybrid agreement.

What is a cross-purchase agreement?

A *cross-purchase agreement* is a buy-sell agreement in which the remaining co-owners agree to purchase the interest of a deceased or departing owner. A *solo-purchase agreement* permits one owner, to the exclusion of all other owners, to acquire the business interest of a deceased or departing owner, thereby possibly changing the control structure of the business.

Cross-purchase agreements are favored when there are only two or three business owners. The cross-purchase agreement is overly complex and expensive to administer if there are more than three owners, especially if the obligation is to be paid ("funded") with life insurance.

⚜ What is an entity-purchase agreement?

In an *entity-purchase,* or *redemption, agreement,* the business agrees to purchase (redeem) the interest of a deceased or departing owner. After redemption, the ownership percentage of the remaining owners increases. For example, suppose a company has four owners who each own a 25 percent interest. On redemption of the equity interest of owner A, owners B, C, and D will each have a 33 percent ownership interest.

⚜ What is a hybrid agreement?

The *hybrid agreement* is also called a *two-tier agreement.* Both the individual equity owners *and* the company itself may have rights, duties, and/or obligations within the same agreement to acquire the interest of a deceased, disabled, or retiring owner. The hybrid agreement provides a "wait-and-see" opportunity that permits remaining owners to individually purchase the equity interest or to shift the acquisition burden to the company. A hybrid agreement may permit a partial redemption by the company and a partial acquisition by the remaining owners.

⚜ How do we decide which agreement to use?

Selection of the appropriate type of arrangement depends on several considerations, such as:

- How many owners have an interest in the company?
- Are all the owners employees of the company?
- Are the owners related to one another?
- Who will buy out the deceased or departing owner—the company or one or more remaining owners?
- How will the company or the remaining owners pay the obligation?
- Is it likely that the business will be sold during the lifetime of existing owners?

Valuations for Agreements

Is the IRS obligated to honor a valuation formula agreed to in a buy-sell agreement if all the business owners sign the agreement?

As a general rule, the IRS is not bound by the value prescribed in a buy-sell agreement, especially in the case of a family-owned and -controlled company. The IRS frequently takes the position that the pricing under a buy-sell agreement is designed to reduce the federal estate tax burden to the family. The Internal Revenue Code states that the IRS has the right to ignore the buy-sell agreement for transfer tax valuation purposes unless the agreement:

- Is a bona fide business arrangement
- Is not a device to pass property to other family members for less than full and adequate consideration in money or money's worth
- Is comparable, regarding the terms of the agreement, to similar arrangements entered into by other, unrelated persons in a arm's-length transaction

A business valuation appraisal can provide substantiation for these issues by showing that the price is not artificially contrived but fairly represents the value of equity and that the terms of the buy-sell agreement are comparable to those of similar arrangements entered into by unrelated persons in an arm's-length transaction. A business attorney or business advisor can document that the agreement is a bona fide arrangement and can also show that it is comparable to similar agreements among unrelated persons in an arm's-length transaction.

Chapter 20 provides detailed information about business valuations.

FUNDING
THE AGREEMENT

❧ *We're considering a buy-sell agreement for our business, but neither of us has the cash to buy out the other if anything happens. How can we get the cash to pay the obligation?*

In an increasing number of cases, life insurance is used to fund a buy-sell agreement. This approach can be effective in almost any type of buy-sell arrangement. Life insurance is the preferred means of funding the buyout at the death of an owner, since the premium payments often are affordable and thus ensure the availability of a lump-sum cash payment to the owner's family. Accumulated cash values are also a source of payments to the owner after his or her retirement or disability.

However, there may be instances in which life insurance is not available or affordable due to the age or health of the owners. And life insurance may not provide sufficient cash on an owner's disability, retirement, or departure. Therefore, a buy-sell agreement usually includes some combination of the following funding solutions to ensure payment under the agreement:

- Individual savings or personal borrowing or, in a redemption arrangement, capital surplus or debt financing
- Cash-value life insurance contracts

- Owner-financed payout using an installment note
- Disability insurance

✍ *My partner has agreed to purchase my interest in our business in the event of my death. How can I make sure that she can afford to do so?*

The triggering events in a buy-sell agreement—most notably death and disability—are typically unexpected. Your concern for your partner's ability to fulfill her agreement to purchase your interest in the business is a serious one. How much cash will she have at the time of a triggering event? What other debts may she have then? Will purchasing your interest in the business render her insolvent or force liquidation of the business? Meeting these concerns is typically best addressed through a combination of insurance and thoughtful consideration of the needs of the departing owner and his or her family.

Both life insurance and disability insurance are ready funding mechanisms if the triggering event is death or disability. They provide a known source of capital whether the death or disability occurs 6 months or 20 years from now. They assure the departing owner's family that the needs of the business will not interfere with the remaining owner's ability to fulfill his or her purchase obligation. And they allow the owners to structure reasonable terms for payment of the balance of the purchase price not covered by insurance.

Company Assets

✍ *Are there drawbacks to leaving a redemption agreement unfunded and using the company's assets to pay the obligation?*

Yes. The payment obligation may consume business capital and cash flow. A deferred-payment obligation must be booked as a liability, which may limit the company's ability to borrow for working capital. Some businesses create a "sinking fund" to fund future redemption obligations. For corporations, state law may prohibit a corporate redemption if, at the conclusion of the redemption process, the assets of the business are less than its liabilities.

⚄ What is a sinking fund?

A *sinking fund* is a fund of assets accumulated during the life of the buy-sell agreement to pay the redemption obligation. Normally, the business agrees to create the fund by making periodic cash deposits, which the company invests in order to increase the fund. A sinking fund appears on the balance sheet of the business as a long-term investment, making it available to the company's creditors. The fund's earnings appear on the business's income statement, making them subject to income taxes.

Life Insurance

⚄ What types of life insurance can be used to fund buy-sell agreements?

The insurance may be term life, whole life, universal life, or variable life.

⚄ Who owns and pays for a life insurance policy?

The answer depends on the type of buy-sell agreement:

- *Cross-purchase agreement:* Each owner owns, pays for, and is the beneficiary of a life insurance policy on each co-owner.
- *Entity-purchase agreement:* The business owns, pays for, and is the beneficiary of a life insurance policy on each of the owners.
- *Hybrid agreement:* The owners or the company, or both, can own, pay for, and be the beneficiary of a life insurance policy.

Cross-purchase plans can, and hybrid plans often do, employ split-dollar life insurance planning.

How does the ownership work in a cross-purchase plan?

In a cross-purchase agreement, where the remaining owners purchase the deceased owner's interest, each owner of the business (referred to here as a "contract owner") acquires a life insurance policy on the life of each co-owner. The contract owner owns, pays for, and is the beneficiary of the policy.

On the death of the insured owner, the contract owner collects the proceeds, which are not taxable for income tax purposes, and buys the deceased owner's interest from his or her estate. The estate of the deceased owner gets a step-up in income tax basis, so the sale by the estate is usually free of capital gain tax. If the policy proceeds exceed the buy-sell obligation, the contract owner realizes a tax-free benefit.

Are there any downsides to owning life insurance in a C corporation?

Yes. The corporation is subject to the alternative minimum tax (AMT) on the life insurance proceeds paid on the death of a shareholder. The corporation is also subject to the AMT on the cash-value buildup in the policy. And the policy's cash value is available to the corporation's general creditors.

Can a partnership own life insurance on the life of a partner? Is there a risk that the entire policy proceeds will be included in the estate of the insured partner upon his or her death?

If the partnership is both the owner and the beneficiary of the policy, the life insurance policy will not be included in the estate of the insured partner. Under case law, the proceeds of policies payable to a partnership are not included in a partner's estate merely by virtue of his or her control of the partnership.

There are five owners in our company, and we'd like to have a cross-purchase agreement. Is there any way to avoid having to purchase twenty life insurance policies?

One way is to create an insurance trust with an independent trustee.

The trustee can purchase one policy on the life of each owner, so you would have only five policies. This approach reduces the premiums and administrative costs. An insurance trust also guarantees that the death benefit will actually be used to purchase a deceased owner's interest in the business and will not be used for some other purpose by a co-owner.

◀ How can a split-dollar arrangement be used with a cross-purchase or hybrid buy-sell agreement?

Each contract owner enters into a separate split-dollar agreement with the company to share in the premium payment and death benefit on the other owners. The contract owner must pay for the economic benefit of the insurance, that is, the term insurance cost of the policy. The company pays for the balance of the premium. Each contract owner assigns the company the right to collect from the death benefit the amount of the premium it paid, or the cash value. At the insured owner's death, the company is reimbursed and the contract owner receives the balance of the death benefit, which he or she pays to the deceased owner's estate to purchase that owner's interest in the business.

In a hybrid plan, the contract owners use the death benefit to buy the interest of a deceased owner, and the company uses its cash-value payment to redeem a portion of the deceased owner's stock. The company can also use the cash value in the policy to purchase a disabled or retired owner's stock. (See Chapter 18 for details on split-dollar arrangements.)

◀ Can we use existing policies and just change the ownership?

For a cross-purchase agreement for a corporation, the use of existing policies is not recommended. If shareholders A and B own policies on their lives and "swap" policies, the IRS considers this a "transfer for value." On the death of either shareholder, the insurance proceeds paid to the surviving shareholder are *taxable income*. To avoid this tax problem, each shareholder should purchase a new policy on the life of each other shareholder. Likewise, if a trust is formed to own and administer the life insurance policies, the policies should not be acquired by each individual owner and then transferred to the trust; the trustee should acquire new policies.

⚐ Do transfer-for-value rules apply to other entities?

There are five safe-harbor exceptions to the transfer-for-value rules:

- A transfer for "love and affection," that is, purely a gift
- A transfer to the insured person
- A transfer to a partner of the insured person
- A transfer to a partnership in which the insured person is a partner
- A transfer to a corporation in which the insured person is a shareholder or officer

⚐ Can business owners and their company use a partnership to hold life insurance policies for funding a stock redemption plan?

As an alternative to having the corporation acquire the life insurance policies, a general or limited partnership can be formed to own and protect the life insurance policies as a source of liquidity for funding the obligations of the stock redemption agreement.

This is how it works: The corporation and its shareholders are the partners of the partnership. The partnership acquires the life insurance policies. The partnership agreement provides that no partner may unilaterally withdraw from the partnership or force liquidation of the partnership but that any partner may withdraw from the partnership within 60 days after the death of any other partner. Each partner is to make an annual contribution to the partnership in proportion to each one's percentage of ownership and in an amount sufficient to cover the partnership's obligations. In a "corporation-pay-all" plan, the corporation makes the total contribution to the partnership. In this plan the contribution attributable to each partner's percentage interest in the partnership is taxable income from the corporation to the partner.

The corporation and the shareholders enter into a stock redemption agreement. The stock redemption agreement should *not* require that the corporation use the proceeds from the partnership to pay the redemption obligation; if it did, the arrangement might appear to be a "step" transaction.

The corporation does not own an interest in a life insurance policy; it owns an interest in a partnership, so the alternative minimum tax should not apply. The shareholders of the corporation can transfer existing policies to the partnership under the transfer-for-value exceptions.

Disability Insurance

⚞ *How do we fund a disability buyout?*

A buy-sell agreement may provide for a buyout of an owner's interest when he or she becomes permanently disabled. The business can purchase a disability policy with payment to the business for funding a redemption of the disabled owner's interest.

Otherwise, in an unfunded arrangement, a redemption agreement may provide that the company will pay fair value for the ownership interest over an extended period of time. A lump-sum payout on disability is almost impossible for a small company.

ADVANTAGES
AND DISADVANTAGES

⚞ *What are the advantages and disadvantages of a cross-purpose buy-sell agreement?*

Advantages

- Funds accumulated by the business owners are usually protected from the claims of business creditors.

- Funding can be implemented through the payment of additional compensation to owners if the compensation is not excessive for tax purposes.

- Funding may cost less if the individual owners are in a lower tax bracket than that of the business.

- Control can be reallocated on an elective basis if some, but not all, owners want to purchase the interest of a deceased or departing owner.

- The acquiring owners realize a step-up in the income tax basis for the interest acquired.

Disadvantages

- Cross-purchase agreements are often underfunded because life insurance for funding the obligation may entail numerous policies and the cost of each policy may not be (in fact, never is) equal.

- They are cumbersome in companies with more than two or three owners because of the multiple policies.

- For owners in high tax brackets, accumulating the necessary funds to cover the purchase obligation may be difficult and expensive because after-tax dollars are used to fund the agreement.

⅍ *What are the advantages and disadvantages of an entity-purchase buy-sell agreement?*

Advantages

- Funding is provided by the business rather than by the individual owners.

- The tax cost of funding may be less if the business has a lower tax bracket than the individual owners do.

- Plans funded with life insurance require only one policy per owner.

Disadvantages

- There is no new cost basis in the acquired interest.
- Accumulated funds to pay the obligation may be subject to the claims of business creditors.
- Funding may cost more if the business has a higher tax bracket than the individual owners do.
- The corporate accumulated earnings tax may be a problem.
- There is no flexibility for reallocating control.
- Under the law of many states, a redemption can be made only from corporate surplus.

chapter 22

Selling to Employees

SALE TO KEY EMPLOYEES

I have no family to take over the business, but I do have two key employees who might want it. What methods could I use to sell my business to them?

A sale to nonfamily key employees is almost always motivated by the desire to reward them for years of loyal and unselfish service. Your employees will probably be unable to pay for the business in a lump sum, so depending on your time frame before retirement, you might consider other methods for accomplishing the sale. For instance, you can compensate the employees with stock bonuses and stock options. This will increase the employees' ownership stake in the business over time, during your active administration of the business. A buy-sell agreement can provide for the purchase of your remaining shares in the company.

Another possibility is to have your company sponsor an employee stock ownership plan (ESOP) for all employees. Owners can use an ESOP to achieve retirement and business continuation goals because it is a qualified retirement plan that is permitted to own shares of the company's stock. We discuss ESOPs later in this chapter (see also Chapter 13).

⚜ *I've decided to retire and sell my business to my key-employee children. I want the income from the sale to provide for my spouse and me during our retirement. Our children agree with the plan but don't have the money to purchase the business outright. Plus, if they did purchase it outright, I'd have a big capital gain problem. What do you suggest?*

The four most commonly used planning techniques for selling a business to children are (1) installment sale to the children, (2) installment sale to an intentional grantor trust, (3) sale for a self-canceling installment note, and (4) sale in exchange for a private annuity. Table 22-1 compares the main features of these techniques.

Installment Sale

⚜ *What is an installment sale?*

In an *installment sale,* the owner sells his or her property in exchange for an installment note that requires at least one principal payment per year, other than the year of the sale. This technique is frequently used to finance the purchase of a business or an owner's share of a business.

Installment sale reporting, as provided under the Internal Revenue Code, can offer the seller the flexibility of timing capital gain recognition, either deferring capital gains over time or electing to recognize such gains immediately. Keep in mind that marketable securities are not eligible for installment reporting.

Special rules apply to installment sales between members of the same family. It is important that you understand and apply these rules.

TABLE 22-1   Comparison of Sales Techniques

Feature	Install-ment sale	Inten. grantor trust	SCIN	Annuity	ESOP
Sale to key employees only	Yes	Yes	Yes	Yes	No
Seller recognizes capital gain	Yes*	No	Yes*	Yes[†]	Yes[‡]
Seller pays income taxes	Yes*	Yes[§]	Yes*	Yes[†]	No
Seller freezes value of business at date of sale	Yes	Yes	Yes	Yes	Yes
Value of business is removed from seller's estate	Yes	Yes	Yes	Yes	Yes
Seller makes gift	No	Yes	No	No	No
Obligation must be secured by mortgage instrument	Yes	Yes	Yes	No	Yes
Principal payments are deductible expenses	No	No	No	No	Yes
Interest payments are deductible	Yes	No	Yes	No	Yes

*Over the note term. [†]Over the annuity term. [‡]Can be deferred. [§]On trust income.

ᴁ *When is an installment sale appropriate?*

An installment sale is appropriate if the owners want to use it not only as a succession planning technique but also as an estate planning technique. If the property is likely to appreciate in value, the installment sale can "freeze" the value of the company, for estate tax purposes, to its value at the time of sale. The greater the appreciation potential, the more profound the estate tax–reduction results.

The installment sale works best if the cash flow from the business is sufficient to help meet the debt-service requirements. An important factor is the human element. The current owner is no longer involved in operating the business but is dependent on the success of the business to receive his or her retirement income.

The installment sale is considered to be a sound tax planning procedure. There are no expected changes in the law that would limit the application of this tool.

◢ Do I need the formality of a promissory note?

Yes. Even though an installment sale is a friendly transaction, it needs to be formalized with a promissory note. The note should:

- Clearly state the selling price, based on a formally appraised value
- State a fair market rate of interest on the note
- Specify the term of the note and the payment amounts
- Be secured by an interest in the business or some other asset

◢ What would be considered a fair rate of interest?

The minimum interest required on an installment sale note is the applicable federal rate (AFR). The federal government publishes AFRs each month for short-term notes (not over 3 years), midterm notes (greater than 3 but not more than 9 years), and long-term notes (greater than 9 years).

◢ What if I don't charge a high-enough rate of interest?

If the rate of interest is not at least equal to or greater than the AFR, the IRS will do two things:

- Consider part of the transaction to be a gift rather than a sale, so the seller may be liable for gift taxes
- Recalculate the interest payment difference between the actual rate charged and the AFR and allocate the difference as taxable income to the seller

Some practitioners suggest a conservative interest rate of 120 percent of the AFR in a family transaction. Note, however, that the

AFR is often lower than what local lenders charge on similar loans. It is possible to give a "break" on the interest rate and still be within the guidelines that will prevent an unintentional gift.

Financing the purchase

⚐ *Where do my children or other key employees get the money to make the installment sale payments?*

Quite often, children or other key employees don't have enough money of their own to make the payments on an installment sale— especially if the business is very valuable. However, there are a number of solutions to this problem. The most common solution is to have the payments come from the profits of the business itself. This works especially well with a pass-through entity, such as an S corporation, a partnership, or a limited liability company that has elected partnership status. The business may distribute earnings to its owners (now the children or other key employees), who can use the distributions to pay the installment note's principal and interest.

If the business is a C corporation, however, this presents an obstacle. The dividends would be taxed at both the corporate and the individual levels when distributed to the key employees. Most business owners want to avoid this double taxation.

An alternative solution, for a C corporation and any other entity, is to pay bonuses to the key employees or simply raise their salaries enough to allow them to make the installment note payments. This compensation would be taxable income to the employees but would be tax-deductible to the business.

Tax effects

⚐ *What are the tax effects of the installment sale for the buyer?*

If the entity is an S corporation or partnership, the characterization of interest is determined by the nature and use of the business assets.

For example, if you acquire stock in an S corporation that conducts an active trade or business and you materially participate in the company's business, you may deduct the interest as a business expense.

The interest on an installment obligation to acquire a C corporation, however, is considered investment interest. Investment interest is deductible only to the extent of net investment income, so it is subject to the 2 percent floor on miscellaneous itemized deductions. This can present a problem for a buyer of C corporation stock, because there is no offsetting pass-through income unless the C corporation pays dividends.

The buyer's basis in the business is the sales price.

✍ *What are the tax effects of the installment sale for the seller?*

As the seller receives payments, each payment will consist of return of the original cost basis not subject to income tax, part capital gain, and part interest income. There are three major tax effects on the seller:

INCOME TAX: Each payment will include interest on the sale price that is taxed as ordinary income.

CAPITAL GAIN TAX: If the selling price is greater than the owner's basis in the business, a capital gain occurs. Since family businesses are often started from nothing, the actual basis in the stock may be close to zero. Thus, the whole selling price could be subject to federal and state capital gain taxes. However, the IRS allows you to pay the capital gain tax over the life of the promissory note. In other words, the gain is recognized and taxed one piece at a time, when you receive installment note payments. That makes it a little easier to deal with.

There are two exceptions to this capital gain arrangement: (1) If you decide to sell or dispose of the promissory note, you will have to recognize the gain immediately; and (2) if your children sell the business to another buyer within 2 years, you will have to recognize the gain immediately. The purpose of these exceptions is to discourage the practice of selling the property on an installment sale simply to get a step-up in cost basis and then reselling it to avoid the capital gain tax. In such cases, the IRS holds that the first sale wasn't legitimate, and it will therefore levy taxes on the whole value.

ESTATE TAX: One of the biggest benefits of the installment sale has to do with estate taxes. Once you sell the business to your children or other key employees, it is no longer in your estate for estate tax purposes. You do not own the business any more—the children or other key employees do.

Of course, you still own the promissory note, and its value will be included in your estate. If the loan is paid in full before your death, any money from the sale that you haven't spent will be included in your estate.

However, the value of the promissory note is locked in at the time of sale. Thus, if the value of the business increases, the value in your estate will not go up. It will be the same as the value at the time of sale or even less if you are spending the payments (e.g., on your retirement).

Advantages and disadvantages

⋈ *I see how an installment sale can enable my children or other key employees to buy the business and can provide my spouse and me with ongoing income for retirement. Are there any other advantages of an installment sale?*

From the family's perspective, the biggest benefit is being able to keep the business in the family. You may also use the proceeds from the installment sale to provide nonbusiness assets that will pass to those of your children who are not involved in the business.

⋈ *Are there any disadvantages of an installment sale?*

Yes, there are some disadvantages, depending on your point of view:

- Once the business is sold to children or other key employees, you have given up control (assuming you sold at least a controlling interest). For some, this is a very difficult adjustment to make. For others, they can hardly wait to be rid of the burden.

- The sale of the business results in the recognition of a capital gain.

- You now have perhaps your largest investment tied up in one asset—a promissory note. If something goes wrong and you don't get paid, this could be disastrous to your financial well-being. If you sell the promissory note or otherwise dispose of it, this will accelerate the capital gain that you may be hoping to spread out over a long period of time.

- You might outlive the payments under the installment sale.

- There is no liability protection. The installment note is an asset subject to attachment by your creditors.

Intentional Grantor Trust

≱ What is an intentional grantor trust?

A very effective technique is to sell a business that is growing rapidly in value to a special kind of grantor trust, called an *intentional grantor trust,* of which the business owner is the grantor. The significant feature of this kind of trust is that income generated by the trust is attributable to the grantor for income tax purposes, but the trust property is not included in the grantor's estate for estate tax purposes. The intentional grantor trust is an irrevocable trust, and assets transferred to it are subject to gift taxes when applicable. But the income generated by transferred assets is taxed to the grantor. So far it doesn't sound like a very good deal, does it?

If you create an intentional grantor trust, however, and then sell your company to the trust, perhaps taking back a note rather than cash, you will not recognize any capital gain on the transaction. This is because for income tax purposes the trust assets are considered your assets. You receive annual or more frequent loan payments designed to return principal and interest calculated at a rate the government considers a market rate. Because this is a sale for fair market value, there is no gift and thus no gift taxes, yet a highly appreciating asset has been removed from your estate for gift and estate tax purposes.

This is a sophisticated transaction that requires significant coordination with the rest of your estate and succession planning, but under some circumstances this technique can be very effective.

Self-Canceling Installment Note

What is a self-canceling installment note, and how can I use it to transfer my business to a family member?

The *self-canceling installment note (SCIN)* is very similar to the installment sale—the owner sells his or her business to a family member, taking back a promissory note. It also has most of the same advantages and disadvantages of the installment sale. However, there is one major difference between the two: The SCIN provides that the entire note balance is forgiven if the seller dies before the note is paid in full. This means that there is no taxable value to be included in the seller's gross estate upon his or her death. For a SCIN to be valid, however, the buyer must pay a premium for the self-canceling attribute.

As an estate planning tool, the self-canceling installment note has significant potential for reducing estate tax (but not income tax) if the seller dies before the note is paid.

Are the formalities for the SCIN the same as those for a regular installment sale?

Yes. The self-canceling installment note must:

■ Clearly state the selling price, based on a formally appraised value

- State a fair market rate of interest on the note
- Specify the term of the note and the payment amounts
- Be secured by an interest in the business or some other asset

⇗ *Do I have to specify anything special in the promissory note for the sale of the business, other than saying that the debt is forgiven on my death?*

Yes. The note should specifically state, "For additional consideration, the payment obligations of this note, both as to principal and interest, will terminate on the death of the note holder." The "additional consideration" is a premium the children (the buyers) must pay for the cancellation feature of the note; without it, the transaction may be considered a taxable gift to the children. The premium, or extra payment, may be a higher purchase price for the business or a higher interest rate.

⇗ *What is the term of the SCIN?*

As a general rule, the term of the note should not exceed the seller's actuarial life expectancy. The premium the buyer pays for the self-canceling feature is determined by the term of the note and the seller's age—the longer the term, the higher the premium. Thus, the buyer may want to repay the note as quickly as possible. Also, both parties typically want the note paid off as soon as practical.

⇗ *What are the tax consequences of a SCIN?*

The capital gain consequences of a SCIN are the same as those of an ordinary installment sale. However, the addition of the premium increases the amount of income the seller will recognize over the term of the note. If the seller dies before the note is repaid, the deferred gain is accelerated and the seller's estate must pay capital gain tax on the unrecognized gain, even though the note payments have ceased.

The primary benefit of a SCIN is that if it is properly structured, neither the value of the business that was sold nor the promissory note itself is subject to estate tax when the seller dies. Remember that with an ordinary installment sale, the unpaid amount of the note is included in the seller's estate. With a SCIN, the note is canceled and so has no value at death. And if a proper premium was paid, no gift results either.

Private Annuity

⚐ What is a private annuity?

With a *private annuity*, the seller sells the business to a buyer (or buyers), who is usually a member of the seller's family, in return for the buyer's promise to pay a fixed amount to the seller for the rest of the seller's life. The property sold in exchange for the annuity is not included in the seller's estate for federal estate tax purposes. The annuity is "private" because the buyer of the property is not in the business of writing annuity contracts.

⚐ How is the annuity payment calculated?

The present value of the annuity is the fair market value of the company. There are specific formulas for calculating a payment schedule that will create a net present value equal to the purchase price on the basis of your statistical life expectancy. The payment obligation terminates on your death. If you die before your statistical life expectancy, your children will pay less than the business is worth at the time of sale. However, if you live longer than the statistical life expectancy of someone of your age, your children have to continue the fixed payments over your lifetime and will pay too much for the company.

Thus, private annuities are sometimes recommended when the actual life expectancy of the seller is less than the average life expectancy of the seller's statistical age group. You must live more than 1 year after the transaction, however, or the IRS may ignore the actuarial tables and treat the transfer as a gift.

⚄ *What if I want to provide an income stream not only for my own life but also for my husband's life?*

The private annuity will allow that. You can require that the annuity payment be made for your life and for the life of your husband. The result is that the buyers will make smaller payments but over a longer period of time.

⚄ *When is an annuity an appropriate means for selling the business to children?*

An annuity is appropriate in any of the following situations:

■ The owner's estate will be subject to gift tax at his or her death.

■ The transferor wants to exchange the burden of ownership for a fixed payment amount payable over his or her life.

■ The family history of the seller suggests that it is unlikely the seller will live to his or her actuarial life expectancy.

■ The business is likely to appreciate in value.

■ The business produces an annual cash flow equal to or greater than the required annuity payment, or the buyer has sufficient other resources to make the annuity payment.

⚄ *What rules have to be followed so that the private annuity isn't considered a gift?*

If you abide by certain rules, chances are strong that you can avoid making a taxable gift in setting up a private annuity. The rules include:

■ Do not tie the payments in any way to the amount of income earned by the business after the sale.

■ Do not retain any interest whatsoever in the property exchanged for the private annuity, not even a security interest. The seller has no right to control or manage the property, to vote stock or a partnership interest, to sell the property, to mortgage the property, or to exchange the property for another asset. This limitation is absolutely critical.

■ Make sure that the children are personally liable for the payments, regardless of how well the business does, and that the payments are *not* secured by the business or any other assets— the seller must rely only on the payer's promise to make the life-time annuity payments.

■ Use the IRS annuity tables to calculate the amount of the annuity payment.

■ Death cannot be imminent when you arrange the private annuity.

■ Don't set up a private annuity with your children if they have no way of making the payments without your gifts to them. Be sure the business provides enough cash flow to make the payments, and avoid setting up a private annuity with children who are not involved in the business.

❧ *How do my children make the annuity payments?*

As with an installment sale, the business itself will usually generate enough income to make the payments. Either the income is distributed to the children as dividends or distributions or the children's salaries are raised to accommodate the payments.

Tax effects

❧ *How are my spouse and I taxed on the income we receive from this transaction for the rest of our lives?*

The IRS views each payment that you receive as two parts: the capital part and the annuity part. The capital part is considered a return of your basis (the amount you paid for the business) plus any capital gain you earned. The annuity part is taxed as ordinary income, and the capital gain is subject to capital gain tax.

⚱ *What are the estate tax results of this transaction?*

Generally, neither the annuity nor the business is included in your estate (or your spouse's estate) at death. However, if you do not follow the rules in establishing the annuity, it could be seen as a gift in which you retain a lifetime interest, and thus it would be at least partially includible in your estate.

Advantages and disadvantages

⚱ *What are the advantages of using a private annuity to sell an interest in a closely held business?*

There are a number of advantages to an owner's selling a business interest by way of a private annuity:

- The seller retains income for life.
- The value of the annuity is not includible in the seller's taxable estate.
- Provided that the annuity's payment equals the fair market value of the property sold, the private annuity is not deemed to be a gift.
- The future appreciation of any assets sold via the private annuity is kept outside the seller's taxable estate.
- Because the private annuity calls for payments to be made over the lifetime of the seller, any gains from the sale can be spread over the seller's life expectancy (or over the seller's and his or her spouse's life expectancy).

⚱ *What are some of the disadvantages of a private annuity?*

Some of the disadvantages are:

- The sale and the private annuity contract must be irrevocable.
- The buyer runs the risk that the seller may outlive his or her

scheduled life expectancy. Consequently, the buyer may pay more than the original value of the business.

■ The buyer is not allowed a tax deduction for the annuity payment or the interest on the payment; the payment is treated as a capital expenditure.

■ The seller risks nonpayment, since the buyer's promise is unsecured; if the business fails or the buyer has other financial difficulties, the money for paying the annuity may not be there. If the seller is depending on the annuity payments for financial support, the private annuity may not be the best approach.

SALE TO
ALL EMPLOYEES

Employee Stock Ownership Plan

Is there an exit strategy that will create a market for my stock and provide a retirement plan for my employees?

Yes. If your company is a C or an S corporation, consider using an *employee stock ownership plan (ESOP)*. ESOPs are qualified retirement plans that are useful tools of corporate finance. An ESOP can help a company provide an excellent qualified retirement benefit for all long-term employees and can enable owners to accomplish a number of business succession planning objectives. Benefits to owners include:

■ Creating a market for the privately held stock

■ Creating a tax-deductible method of financing the buyout

■ Enabling a key-employee group to borrow the money for a buyout through leverage opportunities available in a specially designed variation of the ESOP

■ Receiving tax-favored treatment if at least 30 percent of the stock is sold by a C corporation business owner

How does an ESOP work?

First, the company establishes an ESOP as a qualified retirement plan for its employees. The shareholders sell their stock to the ESOP trust at an appraised value. The ESOP either borrows funds to purchase the stock all at once or buys the stock over time with the funds contributed each year by the company (a tax-deductible contribution). Each year the ESOP allocates the stock among the participants in a manner similar to the way a profit-sharing plan does. When employees leave the company, they receive their vested ESOP shares, which the company or ESOP will buy back. One major benefit of the ESOP is that it allows the company to repurchase shares with pretax dollars; this generally saves thousands of dollars. Employees who sell their shares back to the ESOP also win, as they can defer capital gain taxes by reinvesting their gains in stocks of other companies.

When should a business owner consider an ESOP as an exit planning strategy?

Generally, ESOP planning experts can make a case for this planning technique for businesses as small as $500,000 in value. The major benefit of an ESOP is the ability of an owner to sell part, or eventually all, of the business without recognizing any immediate gain for tax purposes.

What factors should I consider in determining whether my company should implement an ESOP?

Some of the factors you want to consider are:

- Do you have middle managers who are progressing in their ability to run the company without you?
- Is your company growing and in a trade or industry that will continue to grow during the next decade?
- Can you or should you convert your company to a C or an S corporation to establish an ESOP?

- Is your payroll at least $500,000 per year?
- Is your company a U.S. domestic company?

⚛ Which companies should not implement an ESOP?

A company should select another alternative if it has a poor record of earnings and is not likely to improve its earnings in the future. A company is not a candidate if it does not have sufficient payroll to service an ESOP loan and to generate tax savings.

⚛ Can an S corporation be 100 percent owned by an ESOP?

Since January 1, 1998, S corporations have been allowed to adopt ESOPs. An S corporation that becomes 100 percent owned by an employee stock ownership plan can effectively be a tax-exempt entity since the earnings of the company are not subject to corporate income tax but "pass through" to its shareholder, the ESOP. Because the ESOP is tax-exempt, the dividends are not taxed until distributed at a later date to retired employees.

⚛ How does an ESOP get the money to buy company stock?

There are two basic types of ESOPs, a regular ESOP and a leveraged ESOP. In a *regular ESOP,* the company makes cash contributions to the ESOP (as with any retirement plan), and the trust then buys the stock from a shareholder. If the plan is new and does not have the cash to purchase all the shares immediately, the ESOP can purchase the stock over time or can buy all the stock in exchange for a promissory note, either way using the company's annual contributions to pay.

In a *leveraged ESOP,* the trust formed to administer the ESOP borrows money from a lender to buy the shares, and in most instances the shareholders guarantee the loan or the company cosigns or guarantees repayment of the loan. Alternatively, the company borrows the money and makes a loan to the ESOP trust.

Sources for loans to ESOPs are the same as those for any business loan, including banks, the Small Business Administration, and other lending institutions.

Tax effects

≱ *How does the company reduce its income taxes by implementing an ESOP?*

If the company contributes to the ESOP to purchase the shares, the contributions are fully deductible (within limits). Contributions of newly issued stock are tax-deductible. If the ESOP borrows money to buy the stock, the loan will be repaid from contributions to the ESOP, making both interest and principal payments deductible.

≱ *How does the selling shareholder avoid capital gain on the sale of shares to an ESOP?*

Under the Internal Revenue Code, if a selling shareholder of a C corporation sells at least 30 percent of the company stock to the ESOP, the shareholder will not recognize a capital gain on the sale if he or she invests the proceeds in "qualified replacement property" within 12 months. The selling shareholder must own the stock for at least 3 years before the sale to qualify. (This "rollover" technique is not available for S corporation shareholders.)

≱ *What is qualified replacement property?*

Qualified replacement property (QRP) is defined as securities of domestic corporations not controlled by foreign companies. The corporation must use more than 50 percent of its assets in the active conduct of a trade or business to qualify, and it must not have passive income (rents, royalties, dividends, interest, etc.) that exceeds 25 percent of its gross receipts.

Mutual funds, real estate investment trusts (REITs), and government bonds do not qualify.

⊿ *What happens when I sell the qualified replacement securities?*

When you sell the QRP, the unrecognized capital gains on your original sale of stock to the ESOP will be taxed along with any capital gain from appreciation on the QRP since you purchased it. Also, if you die owning replacement securities, your beneficiaries receive a step-up in basis to the fair market value of the QRP at the date of death, just as with other property. This ability to defer capital gain taxes on the sale of the company stock can be a major factor in an owner-seller's decision of whether to use an ESOP.

Formalities

⊿ *How expensive is an ESOP to begin and to maintain?*

There are several cost considerations. Legal fees vary. The National Center for Employee Ownership estimates a cost of $5000 to $10,000 for a small firm. A business valuation for a small company can add additional, sometimes substantial, expenses because it must be performed annually. An ESOP requires diligent administration. Loan origination fees and costs apply if the ESOP borrows money.

⊿ *What are the rules for an ESOP?*

The primary requirements for a qualified ESOP are that the plan must:

- Be in writing and provide all the information necessary for qualification
- Be established by the employer and intended to be permanent
- Be communicated to employees in the form of a summary plan description
- State who can make contributions: the employer, the employee, or both
- Be for the exclusive benefit of the participants and their beneficiaries, with the primary benefits for the participants

- Meet ERISA's minimum vesting, participation, and coverage standards
- Not discriminate in favor of highly compensated employees
- Meet the minimum funding rules of a defined-benefit plan and comply with the maximum contribution and benefits under the Internal Revenue Code
- Include a clearly definable statement of the benefits

What happens to ESOP stock when the employee retires or terminates from the company?

The ESOP must be able to redeem shares from retiring or terminated employees. The company or the ESOP trust can pay the employee either in a lump sum or over a period of 5 years with a reasonable interest rate. The obligation of the company to purchase the shares of the employee is typically referred to as the company's "repurchase liability."

It is important that an analysis of this liability be completed before establishing the ESOP. This issue underscores three major factors for the company to consider:

- The company will want a valuation of its stock price performed by a reputable outside firm to avoid any hint of manipulating prices for its own benefit.
- The ESOP needs to maintain sufficient liquidity to cover the redemptions.
- If the stockholders have to guarantee loans made to the ESOP and the ESOP does not have sufficient liquidity to repay the loans in addition to its repurchase liability, the stockholders may be compelled to honor the guarantee.

chapter 23

Giving to Family Members

CONSIDERATIONS

> ⚜ *After weighing all the pros and cons of giving versus selling the business to family members, I've decided to give it to my children and grandchildren. What should I be thinking about before I do that?*

For parents, gift giving is the simplest, most frequently used, and often the most powerful method for transferring the business itself or the wealth it represents to children and other family members. There are several techniques for giving the business to members of the next generation, so it is important that you consider all the issues and define your goals in order to select the appropriate technique for your situation. Your advisors can help you establish your goals, recommend the best technique, and prepare the required documents to implement it as part of your overall exit strategy and succession plan. In giving the business to family members, business owners usually want to achieve goals in the following categories:

FAMILY SUCCESSION PLANNING: The business represents the family heritage, and the owners want it to continue for future generations, protected from the loss of its current leadership, as well as from creditors and ex-spouses. Parents or grandparents want to begin the formal transition process while they are still present to give the younger generation the benefit of their skills, experience, and knowledge. They want to ensure that the business is owned by the family members they choose, not by family members who do not want to run the business or lack the ability to do so. Owners want to facilitate the family culture represented by the business and to promote family values with regard to wealth and its creation.

ESTATE TAX PLANNING: One reason people make gifts is to remove the value of the assets from their estates and thus reduce the amount of estate taxes when the donor dies. Giving assets away also transfers to the recipient all postgift appreciation in the value of those assets. For example, if an ownership interest has a value today of $1 million but grows to $2 million in 15 years, a gift today of that interest removes the $1 million of appreciation from the donor's estate and puts it in the recipient's hands. Even if the estate tax is repealed in 2010, a giving program may still make sense for estate and income tax reasons until then.

INCOME TAX PLANNING: If business owners want to shift excess income to other family members, giving income-producing shares to family members may be wise.

ASSET PROTECTION: Business owners want to ensure that the business interests they are giving to children and other family members are not subject to the claims of the recipients' creditors or entangled in divorce proceedings.

VALUATION ADJUSTMENTS: Gifts of partial ownership interests made during the life of the donor often produce lower valuations than will be the case if the total asset is valued for death tax purposes; such gifts result in a lower gift and estate tax for the donor. For example, three gifts of a one-third interest in a business will have a total value, for gift tax purposes, of less than 100 percent of the business held by one owner at death.

❧ What other issues should I consider?

In establishing your goals and choosing the best method for giving the business to your children, consider the following factors:

TYPE OF ENTITY: Your current ownership structure will determine how you transfer the business or whether you must change the entity in order to make the transfer.

CONTROL: The type of entity and your desires for giving up or maintaining control of the business go hand in hand. For example, if your company has only one class of ownership, such as a general partnership, adding a new owner would generally mean giving up significant control.

INCOME NEEDS: When you give away an asset, the assumption is that you are willing and financially able to give up all rights to that asset. You must consider the cash-flow consequences of giving business interests to family members. If you need the income generated by the company, consider all the aspects of the transfer before making your gift. Giving a gift with "strings" attached (e.g., the continued right to receive income from the asset you gave away) is ineffective in removing the asset from your estate.

OTHER ASSETS: If your business is the greater part of your estate and you plan to give it to just some of your children, you need to consider what you will give or leave to the other children to "equalize" your estate, as well as how you will care for your spouse after you are gone.

ESTATE AND GIFT TAXES: Each of the techniques for giving the business to your children produces different results for purposes of estate and gift taxes. It is important that you understand the basic concepts of the "unified" gift and estate tax system, as it exists today and as it changes in the near future, in order to make appropriate choices over time.

Despite the impact that taxes can have on the decision of whether to make a lifetime or a testamentary gift of the business to children and family members, taxes may not always be the most important consideration. Some parents may place more weight on the nontax reasons for choosing one technique over another.

⚮ *Can you elaborate on the family succession issues?*

All the techniques we discuss in this chapter presume that the family members who receive the business become active participants in its operation. Proper implementation of giving the business to family members begins well before the actual transfer. It is crucial that parents discuss their goals with their children and everyone else who will be affected by the decision. Particularly important are discussions of the nontax reasons for the decision.

If they haven't begun the process already, parents should guide children or grandchildren to gradually take on more responsibility in the family business and should reward the ones who do well with greater responsibility. Numerous studies reflect the disadvantageous effects of unearned wealth on children. This is a tremendous concern for family business owners, many of whom built their businesses from the ground up and want to give a successful enterprise to children who haven't yet earned it. A system of training and guiding provides continuous opportunities for passing values to the next generation.

Type of Entity and Control

⚮ *What issues are involved in giving away different entities?*

Owners always have the option of converting existing entities into new entities to facilitate giving the business to children or other family members. In general, however, each ownership structure poses certain problems:

SOLE PROPRIETORSHIP: In a sole proprietorship, there is no business "interest" to give away, only assets. To give the business to family members, the owner would have to create a different ownership structure. Professional advisors can help the sole proprietor determine which business structure would be best for achieving his or her goals.

Partnership: Giving an interest in a partnership means adding a new partner. If it is a general partnership, the owner loses some control over the business. If it is a limited partnership and the owner does not want to dilute his or her control, the owner can give only limited partnership interests.

C corporation: In a corporation, control rests in the hands of the majority stockholder, so that owner probably will not want to give away more than 49 percent of the voting interest. However, some states protect minority shareholders in ways that might cause more control to shift to the minority family shareholders than the majority stockholder desires. The majority stockholder of a C corporation also has the option of issuing different classes of stock with different rights assigned to each.

S corporation: The S corporation creates special challenges for and limitations on gift-giving strategies. With a few exceptions, S corporations must be owned by individuals, thus excluding the use of certain types of trusts, family limited partnerships, and other means of passing ownership interests in the business to family members or others. Also, S corporations can have only one class of stock. While they can issue both voting and nonvoting common shares, no other distinction between the two types of stock is allowed. An S corporation is limited to seventy-sive shareholders, and that may also limit your planning opportunities. There are a few techniques available (discussed later in the chapter), but if a majority stockholder of an S corporation wants to give stock to family members, he or she may be forced to relinquish the S corporation tax status.

Professional corporation: In general, a professional corporation must remain in the hands of licensed professionals. Therefore, you would be able to give the stock only to family members who are licensed in your profession.

⋈ If I own a corporation, can I give away some of the stock while retaining the right to vote the stock?

The Internal Revenue Code provides that, in many circumstances, if a stockholder of a closely held corporation gives away stock but directly or indirectly retains the right to vote the shares given away, the stock that was transferred will be included in the donor's taxable estate.

This rule will likely apply if a taxpayer transfers closely held stock to a family limited partnership (FLP) and retains the right to vote the stock by virtue of being the general partner. To be safe, closely held stock should not be placed in an FLP without thorough consideration of this point.

⋈ Is there any way for me to retain control of the corporation if I give ownership interests to my family?

If you are a C corporation owner, you may want to investigate recapitalizing your stock to provide for voting and nonvoting shares. You can create two classes of stock, one with voting authority and one without. You retain the stock with the voting control and give your children the other class, with no voting authority. In this way, you remain in control of the company but your children have a substantial portion of the ownership interest.

For example, X Corporation is recapitalized to authorize 10,000 shares of voting common stock and 100,000 shares of nonvoting common stock. The nonvoting shares are distributed as a nontaxable stock dividend to the existing owners of common stock. A parent transfers his or her nonvoting shares to a family partnership, to family members, or to family trusts. The holders of the nonvoting shares cannot vote to remove or replace the existing management.

You should also consider the effect of this restriction on the value of the gifts you are making. If you retain too much control and income, you may also be retaining much of the value even though you own only a small percentage of the outstanding shares. This would be considered a "control premium" (discussed in Chapter 20).

≥∆ *You said that only certain types of trusts can own S corporation stock. Which trusts can do so?*

Because only individuals can own S corporation stock, only trusts that the Internal Revenue Code essentially "ignores" for income tax purposes can hold S corporation stock. These trusts include revocable living trusts, demand trusts, grantor retained annuity trusts, certain other grantor trusts, certain charitable lead trusts, qualified subchapter S trusts (QSSTs), and electing small-business trusts (ESBTs). Some of these trusts are described in this chapter or elsewhere in the book.

Gift and Estate Taxes

≥∆ *What is the "unified" gift and estate tax system?*

The federal gift and estate tax is a *unified tax* in the sense that it is imposed on the cumulative transfers made during life (lifetime gifts) and on death (testamentary gifts). A transfer tax is assessed on every item that you transfer to another individual, minus the amount that the IRS says is exempt from the transfer tax. You can transfer, or give, property to another person either while you are alive or on your death.

The *federal estate tax* is assessed against any assets owned or controlled by a person at the time he or she dies. The *gift tax* is assessed against gifts made during the person's lifetime. Whether transfers are made by gift during life or by will or trust at death, the transfers are taxed at the same rate. Under the 2001 tax act, the IRS will annually publish a schedule of the rates. For 2002, the rates essentially start at 37 percent and increase to 50 percent on transfers over $3 million (for subsequent years, see Chapters 1 and 27).

Even though the tax rates are the same for transfers during life or at death, the economic effects of making taxable gifts during life and those of transferring property at death can be substantially different.

⫸ *Can you give me an example of what you mean by different economic effects?*

The techniques presented in this chapter have varying results on income, capital gain, gift, and estate taxes. Here are two examples:

Income and capital gain taxes: When you make a lifetime gift, the recipient of the gift takes your cost basis in the gift for purposes of computing capital gain. So if you give your business to your children during your life and they later sell the business, they will pay capital gain tax, just as you would if you sold the asset.

Alternatively, if you leave the business to your children at your death (before 2010), they receive a "step-up" in your cost basis to the current market value at the date of your death. If your children sell the business at a later time, they will pay capital gain tax on the difference between the value at your date of death and the amount they receive on the date of sale.

For example, Dad's basis in his company is $50,000 and in 2002 it is worth $700,000. If Dad gives the business to his son, Bill, today, Bill's cost basis is $50,000. If Bill sells it tomorrow, he is responsible for the capital gain tax on $650,000. In contrast, if Dad dies today and leaves the company to Bill, Bill's interest receives a step-up in basis to the $700,000 date-of-death value. If Bill sells the company tomorrow for $700,000, there is no capital gain.

Federal estate taxes: When you make a gift of an asset, the value of the asset at the time of the gift and all appreciation on that gift are removed from your taxable estate, thus reducing the potential estate tax obligation. Let's assume that over the years Dad's business appreciates to $2 million and he leaves it to Bill at death. As Dad's heir, Bill owes estate taxes on the $2 million estate. However, if Dad gives the business to Bill today, while it is still valued at $700,000, Dad removes the $700,000 business plus the $1.3 million in appreciation from his estate, thereby avoiding all estate taxes.

These are just simple examples of the economic effects of giving the business during the owner's lifetime or leaving it at death. They do not take into consideration the exemptions that are available, but they do demonstrate the issues that owners should consider. Many business owners have a very low cost basis in their businesses, so the effects of capital gain taxes and estate taxes are important considerations in the decision of giving during life or at death.

◢ What are the exemptions you mention?

There are four major tax exemptions, but only two apply to the issue of giving business interests to family members:

GIFT TAX CREDIT: The 2001 tax act created a $1 million lifetime gift tax credit for every individual that is applied to gifts made during lifetime. This credit is separate from the estate tax exemption (also called the *applicable exclusion amount*). However, even though they are delineated in the act as two separate exemptions, they are applied in a unified manner. For example, in 2004, the estate tax exemption is $1.5 million and the gift tax credit is $1 million. If you give your business, valued at $1 million, to your child in 2004 and then die in the same year, the estate tax exemption of $1.5 million is reduced by the $1 million gift tax credit that you used to make the lifetime gift. Thus you have only a $500,000 estate tax exemption left for passing other assets to your family. If you don't make any lifetime gifts and you die in 2004, you do not have $2.5 million to use as an estate tax exemption; you have only the $1.5 million estate tax exemption.

For purposes of this chapter, we will refer to these two exemptions as the "unified gift and estate tax exemptions." It is important for you to understand that the gift tax credit is constant at $1 million through 2010 and that the estate tax exemption starts at $1 million in 2002 and increases through 2009. So, under the current law, between now and December 31, 2009, you can transfer $1 million gift tax–free during your life and then pass the difference between $1 million and the amount of the estate tax exemption at death. If the estate tax is repealed as scheduled, you can transfer $1 million gift tax–free during your lifetime and not worry about the estate tax at all in 2010.

ANNUAL GIFT TAX EXCLUSION: The annual gift tax exclusion allows individuals to give away tax-free a certain amount of money per year per person to as many persons as they want. This exclusion is indexed annually for inflation but only in increments of $1000. In 2001, it was $10,000, and it is not expected to reach $11,000 until 2004 or later, on the basis of the current rate of inflation. You can remove assets and their appreciation from your estate during your lifetime by using this annual exclusion.

We discuss all the tax exemptions in Part Six.

⚄ What type of property is best to give away in order to minimize federal estate taxes?

Because a gift of property totally removes the value of the property from an individual's estate, it is most beneficial to give property that is expected to substantially appreciate in value in the future. By transferring property in this manner, the donor can use the unified balance of the gift and estate tax exemptions against the transfer of other property more advantageously than using it to transfer highly appreciated property at death.

⚄ If the estate and gift tax rates are the same and I'm not concerned about income tax and capital gain tax issues, does it really matter if I give the business to my child during my life or at my death?

With passage of the 2001 tax act, whether lifetime giving makes sense depends on a variety of factors: In 2010 the federal estate tax is to be repealed, and in 2004 taxpayers will have a larger credit for estate taxes ($1.5 million) than for gift taxes ($1 million).

However, until at least 2004 and maybe beyond, lifetime giving can matter. The maximum gift tax rate is actually less than half the maximum estate tax rate, even though the same tax rate and table is used for both. For someone who has a taxable estate, it is less expensive to make lifetime gifts to loved ones than it is to make testamentary gifts to them.

For example, let's say that you want your child to have $1 million. If we assume that you have already used your unified gift and estate tax exemptions, that you are in the 50 percent unified tax bracket, and that you give the $1 million to your child in 2002 while you are alive and well, you can write a check to the IRS for $500,000 in gift tax after you write the check to your child for $1 million. In other words, it costs you $500,000 to make a $1 million gift to your child. On the other hand, if you want your child to have the $1 million at your death and, again, assuming no exemptions, you'll have to leave the child $2 million to start with because the estate tax on a $2 million testamentary gift is $1 million in 2002. So it will cost you $500,000 more to leave a full $1 million to your child at your death than it costs to give the same amount to him or her during your lifetime.

Annual gift tax exclusion

⚖ *Is it possible to give partial business interests using the annual exclusion amount?*

Certainly. Business interests are frequently part of a giving strategy in business succession and estate planning. If you have one child to whom you want to give the business, you may give him or her $10,000 each year. Together, you and your spouse could give $20,000 each year to this child. The only difficulty with this approach is that each year you will have to get the business appraised so that you know exactly how much of the business is worth $10,000.

⚖ *My wife does not own an interest in my business. Do I have to give her an interest in order for her to make gifts of the business to our child?*

If your wife does not own an interest in the company, you may want to give her an interest to meet other objectives. However, for purposes of a gift strategy to transfer the business to your child, you and your wife can use a technique called *gift splitting*, which is the opposite of what it sounds like. Spouses can join together to make gifts each year and double the annual exclusion amount, no matter which one of them owns the property. Thus, if your wife approves, you may use her annual exclusion to give $20,000 worth of business interests each year to your child. It doesn't matter that she does not own an interest in the company.

Unified gift and estate tax exemptions

≱ *What if I want to give more than the $10,000 annual exclusion amount?*

Not all techniques for giving ownership of the business to your children will allow you to use the annual exclusion, or you may choose to give more than the annual exclusion in any one year. In either event, you can use some or all of your unified gift and estate tax exemptions to avoid gift taxes on gifts of business interests during your lifetime. For example, let's say that you give shares of your company's stock valued at $30,000 to your daughter in 2002 and that the annual gift tax exclusion is $10,000. The first $10,000 of the gift is free of gift tax (you are single, so cannot use gift splitting); the balance of $20,000 is subject to gift tax. However, you do not pay gift tax on the $20,000. Instead, your $1 million gift tax credit (and later the amount of your estate tax exemption) is reduced by $20,000.

≱ *Is this a good use of my unified gift and estate tax exemptions?*

Whether you use any or all of your exemptions during your lifetime depends on the size of your estate, your overall business succession and estate planning goals, and your family's personal and financial situation. If you don't have a better use for your estate tax exemption and if the value of your business is growing, then by giving an interest today that will be worth more in the future, you leverage your gift.

For example, if you give 49 percent of a company that is worth $1 million today, you may use as much as $490,000 of your unified gift and estate tax exemptions. If the company is worth $2 million when you die, your family will already hold $980,000 worth of the company, and that amount is excluded from your taxable estate.

Your estate planning attorney and financial advisor can project the actual economic hazards or benefits of using this technique in your specific situation.

TECHNIQUES

⚜ *What are the techniques for giving business interests to my family?*

The most common techniques for giving businesses to family members are outright gifts of business interests to family members, gifts through "demand" trusts, gifts through irrevocable grantor retained annuity trusts, family limited partnerships, and charitable lead trusts. Each of these techniques achieves different goals, as we discuss below.

Outright Gifts of Business Interests

⚜ *What is the simplest way of giving ownership interests to family members?*

The least complicated method of giving business interests to your family members is to simply give them the interests outright by assigning the interests to them or issuing stock in their names. Your attorney can help you with the documentation.

⚜ *Are there any drawbacks to giving the ownership interests outright to my children?*

The most common drawbacks are that the owner may not want to give up control or may want to retain the income rights to the ownership interests. Beyond that, there may be important business continuity reasons that would discourage outright gifts of ownership interests. For example, an equity interest owned outright by a child may be subject to attachment by the child's creditors or an exspouse. As long as the interest is not S corporation stock, using certain types of trusts or a family limited partnership to give ownership interests to children would protect against these problems.

⚞ *What can I do to reduce the risks of having gift interests involved in the personal problems of the donee?*

Consider giving your business interests to a trust or series of trusts of which your children are the beneficiaries, instead of giving the interest outright to the children. A properly drafted trust can insulate trust assets from the claims of the beneficiaries' creditors and, in most states, may protect trust assets from the claims of spouses in a divorce proceeding.

Demand Trusts

⚞ *Can you give an example of how I would use a trust to provide creditor protection and still use the annual exclusion amount?*

Assume you want to give your three children equal interests in your corporation. Also assume you want each child to have significant control over the interests transferred:

■   You establish three separate trusts. Each child is the beneficiary of and the trustee of his or her trust.

■   Because you want your gifts to the trusts to qualify for the annual gift tax exclusion, your children, as the beneficiaries of the trusts, must have a *present interest,* or current right, to enjoy the gifts. If you make a gift to a trust in which the beneficiary's interest doesn't fully vest until much later, the IRS considers it a gift of a future interest, and such gifts of business interests will not qualify for the annual gift tax exclusion. To accomplish your goal, your attorney drafts the trusts so that the children have a current right to enjoy each gift even though the property remains in the trust. This type of trust is often referred to as a *demand trust.*

■ You and your spouse transfer $20,000 worth of ownership interests to each child's trust every year using your annual gift tax exclusion. If you and your advisors determine that you should use part or all of your unified gift and estate tax exemptions, you can increase the value of the transfers at any time.

■ The children, as trustees, hold legal title to the trust assets and have all rights attendant to the ownership interests you transferred to the trusts, such as voting rights.

■ The children take your income tax basis in the ownership interests that you transfer, but they do not recognize capital gains until they sell the business interests.

■ Profits are distributed to the trusts and become trust income. You may provide in the trust agreements that the trustees distribute this income or that they reinvest it in other assets.

■ The business interests are now trust assets and enjoy protection from most creditors' claims. If one of your children is involved in a lawsuit or falls subject to a creditor's judgment, the shares in the trust are protected.

⩗ *That example assumes that I want to give control to my children. What if I want to keep control?*

The technique also works well if you want to retain significant control over the ownership interests that you give to your children through the trusts. Naming someone other than your children to be the trustees and having a good owner-shareholder agreement can keep you in control of the business during your life. Special classes of ownership interests and compensation arrangements can control cash flow. A friendly trustee can provide for the children's needs separately.

Grantor Retained
Annuity Trusts

⊰ *What is a grantor retained annuity trust, and how is it used?*

A *grantor retained annuity trust (GRAT)* is an irrevocable split-interest trust. "Split interest" refers to the fact that the grantor (the trust maker) retains a current interest and gives away a future interest. The present interest is in the form of an annuity that the trust pays to the trust maker. The future interest is given to *remainder beneficiaries,* usually family members. Because this is a gift of a future interest, the gift does not qualify for the annual gift tax exclusion. Instead, the trust maker must use all or part of his or her unified gift and estate tax exemptions.

The owner of the business, as the grantor-maker of the trust, gives the business to the trust. The trust receives the income from the business and uses it to pay the trust maker an annuity for a specified term of years. After the specified term expires, the remaining trust property is distributed or held in trust for the family members.

⊰ *How do I determine the amount of income I will receive from the GRAT?*

As its name implies, the GRAT pays an annuity. The trust pays a fixed rate of return (e.g., 8 percent) on the value of the gift asset as established when the trust maker transferred the asset to the trust, regardless of the actual income realized by the asset in the trust. The returns generated by the business in excess of the amount needed to pay the annuity are added to the trust principal for eventual distribution to the remainder beneficiary.

⊰ *Is the value of the gift to the trust the value of the business?*

No. Because the beneficiary is required to wait for a term of years before receiving any benefit from your gift, the value of the business is reduced by the recipient's opportunity cost of having to wait for the benefits. The IRS publishes monthly *applicable midterm rates* for determining the present value of the remainder interest, or the opportunity cost, for the value of the gift.

For example, let's assume that Jessica, age 50, gives her business valued at $1 million to a grantor retained annuity trust that is going to pay her an annuity equal to 7.5 percent of the trust property for a period of 12 years. Assuming the applicable midterm rate for valuing the remainder interest is 8.2 percent, the value of the gift for gift tax purposes is $459,370. If Jessica has enough of her $1 million gift tax credit available to offset the gift, she owes no gift tax.

Not only has Jessica removed the $1 million business from her estate at no tax cost, but she has also removed all future appreciation of the business from her estate. If the business grows at the rate of 10 percent annually, at the end of 12 years, Jessica's children will receive property having a value of over $1.5 million with no additional estate or gift tax on the appreciation. If the value of the property in the trust is increasing faster than the rate the IRS uses to calculate the value of the gift, Jessica will transfer significant property to her children at greatly reduced gift tax costs.

Can you give an example of how you would set up a GRAT so that an owner can pass the business to a child?

Let's assume Joe owns a $4 million company and wants to transfer it to his daughters, Julie and Jill. Joe is 60 years old and has a significant retirement account, but he would rather work until he's about 70. We'll further assume that the company is profitable enough for Julie and Jill to retain Joe as an employee, after he transfers the ownership to them, for as long as they need him or as long as he wants to work. Joe's accountant tells him that his estate tax liability will be approximately $1.6 million if Joe continues to own the company without doing any planning.

Joe begins by placing some restrictions on the sale and other transfer of company interests in order to ensure family control. He then transfers 90 percent of his interest to two GRATs, one for each daughter, and he retains 10 percent. The term of the payout in each trust is 10 years. At the end of the 10-year period, each GRAT distributes the business interests to two separate trusts that he has already established for his daughters as beneficiaries.

Joe hires a valuation expert who values the company and the 45 percent ownership interest Joe is transferring to each GRAT; with a combined marketability-minority discount of 40 percent, the resulting value is $2,160,000 (see Table 23-1). Joe transfers the 90 percent interest in his company to the trusts and retains the annuity income interest, which is $251,986 annually, for 10 years. The only value subject to gift tax is the present value of the remainder interests in the trusts for Julie and Jill. Applying the IRS midterm rates to the $2,160,000, minus the present value of Joe's payments for the 10 years, the present value of the remainder interests is $548,000. The gift of $548,000 is less than Joe's gift tax credit amount for 2002, so no gift tax is due.

By using this technique, Joe has preserved the family business for Julie and Jill, provided a nice stream of income for himself until it is time to start distributions from his retirement account, and eliminated the estate and gift taxes on the transfer to his daughters.

⚑ *What are the advantages of using a GRAT to give my business to my children?*

A grantor retained annuity trust is a popular device in business succession planning when the business owners want to achieve the following:

■ Create an ongoing income stream from a business.

■ Remove the value of the business from their taxable estates.

■ Remove appreciation on the business from the owner's taxable estate, especially when the business has the potential for significant capital appreciation.

■ Maintain management control of the business until the expiration of the term and then distribute it to the family-member beneficiaries of the trust.

■ Realize significant valuation discounts (generally 35 to 60 per-

TABLE 23-1   Valuation for Joe's GRAT

Fair market value of company	$4,000,000
90% interest	3,600,000
Less: 40% discount	1,440,000
90% value transferred to trusts	$2,160,000
Value of the remainder interest	$ 548,000

cent) on the value of the gifts, thereby allowing the owners to leverage their ability to give away more.

■ Protect the business from family members' creditors and exspouses.

■ Give S corporation stock to family members.

⋈ *Are there any disadvantages of using a GRAT for succession planning?*

Yes. If the business owner–trust maker dies before the termination of the trust term, a portion of the value of all assets transferred to the trust becomes includible in the maker's estate.

In addition, if the business does not generate sufficient income to make the required payments, property of the trust must be distributed "in kind" to meet the payment obligation. As a result, the property will have to be valued annually to determine the in-kind distributions and equity interests being transferred back to the trust maker.

⋈ *Is there any way to mitigate the damages that can occur if the trust maker dies before the end of the trust term?*

A GRAT is especially useful when the business owner has a long life expectancy, no significant health problems, and a family history of longevity. However, if the owner wants to protect his or her estate plan against premature death, the owner can purchase a life insurance policy to cover the amount of taxes that will have to be paid if the property is included in his or her estate. To ensure that the life insurance proceeds are kept out of the estate, he or she will purchase the policy through an irrevocable life insurance trust (see Chapter 28).

Family Limited Partnerships

≱ *Why would I want to form a limited partnership to give my business to my children?*

Family limited partnerships (FLPs)—limited partnerships in which all the partners are family members—are used mainly for business succession and estate planning purposes. An FLP is one of the most effective means for senior generations to transfer wealth to junior generations yet maintain control over the underlying assets. When properly created, an FLP provides an opportunity for both generations to receive the benefits of wealth transfer at a reduced tax cost, insurance, management, creditor protection, and discounting. When an FLP is used properly, significant wealth can be passed to junior generations with reduced estate and gift taxes. In addition, the FLP provides more flexibility than other techniques in this chapter because it is an entity that partners can change to adapt to changing situations. The grantor retained annuity trust and the charitable trusts are irrevocable trusts that do not permit amendments.

≱ *If I own an S corporation, can I still form an FLP?*

Limited partnerships are not eligible owners of S corporation stock, and the transfer of S stock to a limited partnership would terminate the S election. However, the owners of an S corporation are not precluded from using an FLP as part of their overall planning. For example, land owned by the corporation may be transferred to the partnership in exchange for partnership interests. The partnership can then lease the assets back to the S corporation. You need to consult with your tax professional to ensure that such transactions do not create an unforeseen tax liability.

I'm interested in transferring part of my company and other assets to my children and grandchildren, but I'm not ready to turn over control of the company. Who controls a family limited partnership?

Remember that family limited partnerships are just limited partnerships in which all partners are family members. All the laws regarding limited partnerships apply. Thus, the general partners control the FLP. Because you (or you and your spouse) would normally be the general partner of your own FLP, you have 100 percent control. You are the only one who has the right to control the business of the partnership and, therefore, the right to control how its assets are used and invested.

You can include provisions in the partnership agreement that increase your degree of control as the general partner. For example, the partnership agreement can provide the following:

- It takes a "supermajority" or even a unanimous vote to change the general partner. (This ensures that you remain the general partner, notwithstanding your percentage ownership of the partnership.)
- You decide whether to make distributions of income and, if so, when.
- You have the right to control the operation of the business, including how, when, and where you invest assets.
- You, as the general partner, control whether or not to admit new partners to the partnership.
- You can be reasonably compensated for your services, and the limited partners are not compensated except in their increased share of partnership assets, which equates to their increased participation in management.

You can include whatever provisions you want in the limited partnership agreement so that you, as the general partner, have the desired amount of control. However, be aware that having the right to vote stock of a controlled corporation, in your capacity as general partner, may cause that stock to be included in your gross estate at death (see the discussion above).

≱ How can an FLP provide me with an income?

As the general partner, you can authorize distributions of partnership assets, and you are entitled to receive a reasonable fee for management. The compensation amount must be reasonable considering the time required to manage the partnership and its investments and the responsibility assumed by the general partner. Trust company fees for managing a trust of similar size are often used as a guideline in setting the compensation of a general partner. Excess compensation or distributions to the general partner could damage the integrity of the partnership for transfer tax purposes.

≱ How does an FLP reduce gift and estate taxes?

The value of the limited partnership interests is subject to a discount in calculating their fair market value. The following example shows how an FLP usually works.

Ellen Barnes wants to give her children and grandchildren her sole proprietorship, which is worth $1 million, and not pay gift tax to make the transfer. Ellen and her husband Joseph form the EJB Limited Partnership. Ellen becomes a 1 percent general partner, and Joseph becomes a 1 percent general partner. (For asset protection purposes, they could also form a corporation or limited liability company, of which they are the controlling owners, to be the general partner.) Each of them becomes a 49 percent limited partner. Ellen and Joseph want to give away the 98 percent limited partnership interests as follows: to each of their three children, a 26 percent interest; to each of their two grandchildren, a 10 percent interest.

The Barnes hire a valuation expert to value the partnership

interests. Because the limited partnership interests have no control and are generally not marketable under the partnership agreement, the appraiser discounts the value of the 98 percent limited partnership interests by almost 40 percent. For gift tax purposes, the amount the Barnes are giving away is $588,000.

Using their annual exclusion amount, they give $20,000 a year in limited partnership interests to each of the five children and grandchildren; over a period of approximately 6 years, they give away the 98 percent limited partnership interests. Alternatively, they could use $588,000 of their combined gift tax credit and give the full 98 percent partnership interests to the children and grandchildren in 1 year.

During and after the gift, Ellen and Joseph still have full control of the FLP because they are the general partners. The children and grandchildren own a total of 98 percent of the FLP, but they have no control and cannot give away or sell their limited partnership interests.

Ellen and Joseph removed $980,000—98 percent of the value of the business—plus all future appreciation on the business from their estates, but they used discounts to reduce the gift tax value to $588,000.

By the time Ellen or Joseph dies, their 2 percent general partnership interests will likely be subject to additional lack-of-marketability discounts for estate tax purposes.

⚛ How do we make the gifts of the partnership interests?

Using your annual exclusion amount or your gift tax credit, you make gifts of the fractional limited partnership interests to your children or other family members or to trusts for the benefit of your children or other family members.

Essentially, making a gift of a limited partnership interest is merely a paper transaction. You are giving away not an interest in specific assets but an interest in the partnership itself. A common method of making the gift is to draft a *memorandum of gift*. You state in the memorandum that you are making a gift of a certain percentage of the specifically named family limited partnership, and you state the value of that gift.

The recipient of the gift usually signs the memorandum, indicating that he or she acknowledges receipt of the gift on a particular date. Thus, a completed gift has occurred because both the giver and the receiver acknowledge making and receiving the gift. A better practice is to have the signatures acknowledged, or at least the signature of the donor.

How does the FLP reduce our income taxes?

The FLP does not pay income taxes on its profits. A limited partnership is a pass-through tax entity. Income, losses, and deductions flow through to each partner on the basis of his or her percentage of ownership. In most families, the children are in lower income tax brackets than their parents are, so the results are a lower tax for the parents and a lower tax for the family unit.

Can you summarize the advantages of using an FLP to give the business to our children and grandchildren?

■ General partners can still receive income for managing the business.

■ For estate tax purposes, the fair market value of the asset and all future appreciation on the asset are removed from the parents' estates.

■ For gift tax purposes, significant valuation discounts (generally 35 to 60 percent) on the limited partnership interests are available.

■ Discounted values of the gifts leverage the donor's ability to give away more. Even greater leverage is available if the limited partnership interest is transferred to a grantor retained annuity trust or is held by another entity that is subject to discounting.

■ Mom and dad maintain control of the assets and business through their ownership of the general partnership interest. The limited partners have a voice in management only to the extent specified in the partnership agreement.

- With appropriate buyout provisions in the partnership agreement, assets remain in the family for future generations.

- Limited partnership interests are protected from the FLP's creditors' claims.

- The general partners can protect themselves by using an entity with creditor protection, such as a corporation or limited liability company, as the general partner.

- The partnership agreement can be amended, so it is more flexible than a GRAT.

- The income and losses of the partnership pass through to the partners, thus shifting income to partners in lower tax brackets.

⅍ *What are the disadvantages of the family limited partnership?*

There are several disadvantages:

- Setting up a family limited partnership is expensive.
- The currently favorable tax law could change.
- The currently favorable state law, which offers strong asset protection, could change.
- Business owners must have the partnership's property appraised periodically to calculate the value of the limited partnership interest gifts.

Like many opportunities in life, your family partnership has the potential for enormous benefits to you and your family, but it is also expensive and carries a degree of uncertainty in terms of what future tax laws may say. However, no one knows what tax laws will be in the future; we cannot avoid planning because of that uncertainty. As to expense, you have created a wonderful estate for yourself and your family, and the potential estate tax savings to your family may far outweigh the expense of the FLP.

Charitable Lead Trusts

⚖ *What is a charitable lead trust?*

Like the grantor retained annuity trust, a *charitable lead trust (CLT)* is also an irrevocable split-interest trust. "Split interest" in the case of the CLT refers to the two types of beneficiaries who benefit from the trust. The present interest is in the form of income that the trust pays to a charity, and the remainder interest is given to remainder beneficiaries, usually family members.

The owner of the business, as the maker of the trust, gives the business to the trust. The trust receives the income from the business and uses it to pay the charity an income for a specified term of years. After the specified term expires, the remaining trust property is distributed or held in trust for the family members.

Charitable lead trusts can be either inter vivos or testamentary. An *inter vivos CLT* is one created during the donor's lifetime. A *testamentary CLT* is one created at the donor's death. Either way, the donor is creating a split-interest trust with the income going to one class of beneficiary for a certain period of time and the remainder interest going to a different class of beneficiary.

There are two types of charitable lead trusts, which differ only in how the income stream is calculated and paid: the charitable lead annuity trust and the charitable lead unitrust.

⚖ *How can I benefit from using an inter vivos charitable lead trust to give the family business to my children?*

- You are entitled under the Internal Revenue Code to a charitable income tax deduction equal to the present value of the income interest to be paid to the qualified charitable organization.

- You remove the value of the business and all future appreciation on the property from your estate.

- You will enjoy seeing your favorite charity use the funds for causes you support.

■ You are able to transfer the business to your children.

⚜ Should the maker of the trust be the trustee?

As a general rule, no. The charitable lead trust is very tax-sensitive: if the maker is the trustee or even indirectly controls the "beneficial use and enjoyment of the payment" to the charity, this may cause the entire principal of the trust to be included in the maker's estate. To be absolutely sure of a favorable tax outcome, the trustee of the trust should be independent.

⚜ Who controls the business during the trust term?

The trustee holds legal title to the trust assets and has all rights attendant to the ownership interests you transferred to the trust, such as voting rights. You would draft owner-shareholder agreements in conjunction with the trust agreement to delineate the trustee's rights and obligations as an owner-shareholder and as the trustee so that you can retain day-to-day management of the business.

⚜ What is a charitable lead annuity trust?

A *charitable lead annuity trust (CLAT)* pays a fixed amount to the charitable income beneficiaries as determined by the valuation of the trust assets at the time the maker contributes the assets to the CLAT. For example, a parent contributes a $1 million business to the CLAT, and the trust is to make annual payments of $60,000 to Duke University for a term of 10 years. Duke will receive the same annuity payment each year even though the value of the trust's assets fluctuates over time.

⚜ What if the trust property does not earn enough money to meet the annual payment obligation?

The trustee must make up the difference. This can be done by selling trust property to generate the needed cash or by distributing trust property in kind to make up the income payment deficiency.

ᴁ What is a charitable lead unitrust?

A *charitable lead unitrust (CLUT)* pays a fixed percentage to the charitable income beneficiaries on the basis of a yearly valuation of the trust assets. For example, a parent contributes a $1 million business to the CLUT, and the trust is to make annual payments of 7.5 percent of the trust's assets to Duke University for a term of 10 years. Each year the trustee determines the value of the trust's assets and pays Duke 7.5 percent of that value. Since the value of the assets will likely vary from year to year, so will the annual payments to Duke.

ᴁ What if the trust earns $80,000 and its payment obligation is only $60,000. Who pays the tax on the difference?

The charitable lead trust is *not* exempt from taxation, and income tax rates for trusts are higher than those for individuals. If all its income during the charitable term is not required to be distributed to a charitable organization, the trust is responsible for the tax, but it also takes the charitable income tax deduction for the payments it makes to the charity.

A charitable lead trust can be formed in such a way as to make all income taxable to the trust maker and provide the maker with a very large charitable income tax deduction in the year he or she funded the trust. However, the trust maker may have a problem with paying personal income tax on income that he or she does not actually receive and will never receive.

ᴁ How is the value of the lead and remainder interests in a CLAT calculated for tax purposes?

The present value of the charity's annuity interest and the value of the remainder interest are calculated in the same manner as they are for a GRAT (described earlier in the chapter). The trust maker receives either an estate tax or a gift tax deduction for the value of the charity's interest, and the value of the remainder interest to the children is subject to estate or gift tax. If the trust maker establishes the CLAT while living, he or she may or may not receive an income tax deduction equal to the present value of the charity's interest, depending on how the trust is created.

⊰ Can we use our annual exclusion amounts with this trust?

No. Since the remainder beneficiaries do not benefit from the trust for several years, the annual exclusion cannot be applied toward gifts to this trust.

⊰ Is stock in an S corporation a suitable asset for a charitable lead trust?

It is suitable only if the trust is formed so that the trust maker recognizes the income from the trust and if the term of the trust does not exceed the trust maker's realistic life expectancy.

⊰ Is stock in a C corporation a suitable asset for a charitable lead annuity trust?

Generally, yes, but there are some tax drawbacks. If a company distributes dividends to the charitable lead trust so that the trust can make the annuity payments, the company's profits may be taxed twice. The company pays taxes on its income and distributes the after-tax profits to its shareholders as dividends. Dividend payments are not tax-deductible by the corporation, and the dividends are taxable income to the shareholder, the trust; thus the company's profits are taxed a second time. The dividend payments are deductible by the trust to the extent that the dividends are used to make a distribution to charity, so the second round of taxation may be avoided or at least reduced.

There are other alternatives that can be used to create cash flow for a charitable lead trust. If you are interested in using a charitable lead trust to give your business to your children, your advisors can help you analyze the best methods for achieving this.

⚜ *Are there any drawbacks to transferring an interest in an ongoing business to a charitable lead trust?*

Charitable lead trusts are subject to the general private-foundation rules and thus are prohibited from owning "excess business holdings." If the business interest transferred to the charitable lead trust is actively engaged in a trade or business, as opposed to investing in passive assets, the trust must generally dispose of the business interest within 5 years or significant penalty taxes will apply. There are several exceptions to the excess-business-holding penalty. One exception is that as long as the actuarial value of the charitable lead interest is no more than 60 percent of the value of the trust's assets, the charitable lead trust is *not* subject to the excess-business-holdings rule.

Therefore, careful consideration and consultation with your attorney and tax advisors are necessary before you transfer an interest in a closely held business to a charitable lead trust.

⚜ *Who should consider the use of a charitable lead trust?*

- Persons who have surplus income taxed in very high tax brackets.
- Those who already make large charitable gifts. The charitable lead trust changes the form of the transaction while passing a future benefit to family members.
- Those who need a very large charitable income tax deduction to offset lump-sum proceeds from a sale of the business, lump-sum distributions from a qualified retirement plan, and the like.
- Those who have large to very large estates and need to multiply the power of their unified gift and estate tax exemptions.

chapter 24

Selling
to Outsiders

PREPARING FOR A SALE

How do I maximize the value of my business for eventual sale?

This is a common question. As an entrepreneur, think in terms of what *you* would want if you were buying a business. Most business buyers are looking for a consistent income stream and an investment that will increase in value. They will be concerned about any economic uncertainty or disruption that might arise from a change of ownership. Consider the following strategies to enhance the value and marketability of your company:

- Create systems and build a staff so that the business can function effectively while you are gone. If you must be there constantly to keep things running smoothly, you really have not built the business to its full potential value. Remember, investors with the most money to invest are not "buying a job."

- Build a sufficient asset base as needed for your business, but do not overinvest since doing so will diminish the profitability and attractiveness of the business. Eliminate financial statement "trash" represented by assets that are not productive, uncollectible accounts receivable, and obsolete inventory.

- Maintain good, reliable financial records and a well-documented history of business operations. (Proper documentation is discussed later, under "The Marketing Plan.")

- Promote efficiency by maintaining customer lists and documenting customer loyalty.

- If location is important, be sure that ownership and leasing arrangements protect the ability to continue operations in a given location.

- Do not treat the business as a personal tax shelter. Tax-saving tactics of limiting the reported profits by deducting personal expense items through the business produce the appearance of inadequate profits. Now is the time to restate the financials in order to accurately reflect the real profitability of your company.

- Spend more time working *on* your business and less time working *in* your business! Michael Gerber's outstanding best-seller, *The E Myth Revisited* (HarperCollins, 1995), is required reading for any business owner who wants to increase business value and get more out of life while owning the business.

⅍ *No family member wants to take over my business, so I'm going to sell it. What's the first thing I should do?*

You need to understand that the best deal isn't likely to fall into your lap. Your success will come from the implementation of a systematic approach to properly presenting and marketing your company for the highest value. You are going to do this only once, so it is vitally important that you do it correctly.

You should gather together the same team of advisors who helped you create your exit strategy, business succession, and estate plans: your accountant, attorney, financial advisor, valuation expert, and industry specialist if you have one. Ask them to recommend a sales professional or broker who specializes in sales and mergers of closely held companies. This person will be the project manager for creating the systematic approach for the sale, but he or she will not be successful without the help and advice of you and your regular team of advisors in regard to establishing the plan of sale and recommending the best method for your situation.

What things should I think about before meeting with my team?

Your advisors will ask you to consider some of the same questions you thought about when you were developing your exit strategy and succession plan. The most important of these are, "Where do I personally want to be after the sale?" and "What do I need to net from the sale after all transaction expenses are paid, including income taxes?" As the Chinese proverb says, "If you don't know where you're going, you won't know when you get there." Your answers to these questions will set the stage for your advisors to recommend the best options and develop the sale approach.

The Marketing Plan

What is involved in developing a marketing plan?

The following issues are important:

ASSET OR GOING-CONCERN SALE: You have to determine what it is that you are selling. You can sell your business as a "going concern" (i.e., you sell all your stock or other ownership interests), or you can sell just the assets of the business. These are completely different transactions that require different approaches to the sale and have different tax results.

YOUR LEVEL OF RISK ACCEPTANCE: You have to ask yourself how much you are willing to accept and how long you are willing to wait to get it. Your answers to these questions tell your advisors whether you are willing to take stock or notes in payment or whether you will accept only full, immediate payment.

FORMS OF COMPENSATION: If you are willing to accept some risk and take something other than full cash on the sale, you should determine which forms of compensation are acceptable. Will you accept stock, a secured note, an annuity, a share of future earnings, a consulting agreement, or a royalty or licensing agreement?

TAXES: Remember, there are always three parties involved in the transaction: the buyer, the seller, and the IRS. Taxes affect the form of the transaction, the structure of the sale, the price, and the timing of the payments for both the investor and the seller. Often, tax savings are the key to closing a gap between the seller's price expectations and the buyer's ability to pay.

PROFIT: What will you do with the profit from the sale? You may have in mind that you will retire and live off the proceeds from the sale; however, these proceeds present both financial and estate planning opportunities and challenges. If the majority of your assets were previously invested in your business, you did not have a great deal of cash to invest in other places; after the sale you will have such cash, so you need to determine how and where to invest it. If your current estate plan provides that the business passes to your family or that your family is to sell the business in the event of your death, you now need to update the plan so that the proceeds of the sale are passed to your family in the amount and manner of your choosing.

✍ *What are some mistakes that business owners make when they're selling their businesses?*

Some of the most common mistakes business owners make are:

NOT UNDERSTANDING THE BUYER'S MOTIVE: Rather than emphasizing the business's growth potential, owners often dwell on past performance. Buyers are looking to the future for return on investment and growth potential. Remember: Buyers seldom buy what sellers think they are selling.

NOT HAVING PROPER COUNSEL: Without professional help, owners are prone to taking advice from the wrong people.

TRYING TO SELL TO THE WRONG PEOPLE: One of the biggest mistakes is thinking that the best purchaser of the business is a competitor, customer, or supplier. If the sale doesn't happen with one of these parties, and most sales don't, a great deal of confidential information about your company has been needlessly disclosed. Suddenly, a lot of people know more about your company's profits and operations than they should. Keep your intentions confidential unless you're ready to sell immediately and at a rock-bottom price.

ASSUMING THAT THE BEST PURCHASER IS LOCAL: Most sellers naturally assume that the market for their business is the immediate surrounding area. We are now in a global economy: the world is your marketplace, and the best purchaser may be anywhere in the country or the world. Thousands of very quiet private investment groups and offshore investors are interested in acquiring profitable, U.S.-based privately held companies.

PRESENTING IMPROPER DOCUMENTATION: Investors are evaluating the purchase primarily on the basis of future growth potential and expected return on investment. They want to see what the profits would have been if you had run the business as a public company. They also want you to prepare 3- to 5-year pro-forma financial projections, backed by solid market research, substantiating the future potential of the business. Simply stated, create a presentation that *explains the past and sells the future.*

NOT PLANNING FOR THE SALE: Many business owners have not thought about what their real personal financial needs will be. If you're willing to wait for some of the payments, investors have more flexibility to pay a much higher price. If you insist on an all-cash deal, savvy investors discount their offering price by 35 percent or more.

BEING THE FIRST TO MENTION PRICE: One cardinal rule of negotiating is to never be the first one at the table to mention price. An experienced acquirer who sees a big future potential may have a higher price in mind. Value is very subjective. You will always regret "leaving money on the table" if you make this pricing mistake.

⍦ *What is proper documentation for the sale?*

The documentation should include an updated business plan, including the information we detailed for expanding a business, and a professionally prepared valuation report (see Chapters 2, 4, and 20). This presentation is used to document and establish an increased future value for a potential investor while objectively substantiating all the underlying assumptions needed to arrive at that value. The report should include both a quantitative value assessment and realistic recommendations for the future growth of the business.

QUANTITATIVE VALUE ASSESSMENT: Most owners of closely held businesses suppress profits to reduce taxes, so the company's financial statements do not reflect the true value of the business. The harder it is for investors to see the overall profit and realistic cash-flow picture, the less likely it is that they will buy. Financial recasting is a crucial element in understanding the real earning history and potential of a business. You should restate or recast the financial statements for the past 3 to 5 years so that you will be able to show the investor the "adjusted" available cash and profits from the business:

- Remove all direct and indirect owner compensation, and substitute fair market salaries for professional managers.
- Eliminate debt service, since the financing considerations will vary with the type of buyer.
- Eliminate all historical nonrecurring, extraordinary, or personal expenses.
- Establish realistic market values for all understated (book-value) assets.
- Apply different depreciation schedules to reflect actual rather than tax considerations.
- Eliminate assets that are nonproductive, not essential, or of greater value outside the business (e.g., real estate and excess cash).

- Identify the appropriate growth strategies for showing the profit, cash, and net worth that prospective investors will realize as they apply their capital.

In short, the financial statements should reflect what profits would have been had your company been run as a public company. The restated financial history of your business needs to be presented in a way that investors understand.

FUTURE RECOMMENDATIONS: The true value of any business is based in large part on its prospects for the future. Even a company in a marginal position today may grow tremendously in the future due to economic, business, or market developments. Anticipate this growth and document it as part of your overall current business value.

Research industry leaders, similar-size competitors, and overall national industry averages to determine conditions and prospects in your industry and their effect on your company's value. Analyze trends to determine future growth, and prepare 3- to 5-year pro-forma income statements taking all these factors into account. Make sure that your updated business plan or presentation package addresses the following:

Your current environment

- How do you describe your business?
- What products or services do you currently sell?
- Who buys your products or services, and who else could?
- Who are your major customers?
- What percentage of your sales do your major customers account for?
- Why do people buy from you?
- Whom do you compete with for business?
- Are there any geographic limits?
- How do you sell (bid for work, company salespeople, distributors, etc.)?

- Do you advertise? If so, how much do you spend?
- Do you use product sales literature?

New sources of income

- How do you see the future of your industry?
- What major factors can influence the future of your business?
- What additional products or services can you make and sell?
- How will you increase sales for each major revenue source?
- Do you think new markets will open to you? If so, which ones?
- Do you think there will be new products to sell?

Current production versus maximum capacity

- Given additional business, how much more can you produce with what you have?
- Who are the key people you now have, and who will need to be added as you grow?
- What other ideas or plans have you thought about that can be implemented?
- Will new business come from new customers?
- Will new business come from increasing sales to existing customers?
- What exactly will it take to expand the business for maximum value?

COMPARISON OF YOUR COMPANY WITH OTHERS IN THE INDUSTRY: The business must provide the investor with a return on the purchase that compares favorably to returns from other investment options. An analysis of a number of key financial ratios in the recast statements will measure your business against other available opportunities. If the business does not compare favorably on the key ratios, your advisors may suggest corrective action.

What does the sales and marketing process consist of?

The process has six main components:

Preparing a presentation package: This selling document, or offering memorandum, for your business describes your company in detail to prospective qualified investors. Buyer prospects see objective proof of not only what your business has actually done but, more importantly, what it is capable of doing.

Identifying qualified investor prospects: Locate likely prospects on the basis of acquisition criteria of publicly traded corporate investors and private and public investor groups throughout the world. Only parties that have a genuine interest in buying or have the appropriate synergy should be approached as prospects.

Confidentially approaching each target prospect: Secure a written "nondisclosure" agreement. Early contacts with prospects should be made at the highest possible level, beginning with the chairperson or CEO. The initial contact should provide enough information to determine the investor's level of interest without revealing your identity or the intensity of your interest in selling. In order to maintain confidentiality, preliminary discussions should take place away from your business's location.

Meeting with the prospective investors: In the first meeting, you and the prospective purchaser become acquainted and set the tone for future dealings.

Beginning negotiations: A properly structured deal accomplishes your needs, meets the investor's objectives, and balances the risk of the transaction.

Performing due diligence: While negotiations are in process, a prospective buyer signs a letter of intent, at which point the *due-diligence process* begins. Unquestionably, this is the most distressing and most dangerous phase of a business sale. The prospective buyer and the buyer's legal, accounting, and other experts will gather additional information, examine records, and speak with key members of your staff. You should insist that confidentiality be maintained at this early stage in order to avoid upsetting customers, competitors, suppliers, and any employees you haven't told about the sale.

⚐ *What role does each of my advisors play in this process?*

Your team of advisors should help you find an experienced business sales professional (an intermediary) and a valuation expert. In addition, each advisor performs specific functions:

- The sales professional conducts interviews; studies the strengths, weaknesses, and potential of the existing business; helps you advise the valuation expert in regard to the purpose of the valuation or the updating of your existing valuation; presents you with options for structuring the sale transaction; and prepares the business offering summary.
- Business or industry specialists can provide industry-specific information to the sales professional and perhaps suggest additional prospects from the industry.
- Your attorney and accountant advise you of the tax consequences of various sale options so that you can decide which options to eliminate, and they help you prioritize the remaining options on the basis of tax consequences so that you can maintain flexibility during negotiations.
- Your attorney drafts and/or reviews all the documents needed throughout the entire sales process.
- Your financial advisor anticipates and projects the financial and tax impacts of the sale on your overall financial situation. Considering the enormous impact of the sale, it may be necessary to create an entirely new financial plan for you.

Someone has to provide financial and other information to the prospective purchaser during the due-diligence process. Depending on who is working with you in your existing business, you can delegate these responsibilities to either your team of advisors or trusted managers.

Value versus price?

⚐ *You haven't mentioned anything about the actual selling price.*

Isn't it important for me to decide on the price I want before I meet with my advisors?

The factors that contribute to determining the actual selling price are:

PROFESSIONAL VALUATION: In order to sell your business for the most favorable price and under the best terms, a professional opinion of its value is a logical and essential baseline for informed decision making before you approach the market. This opinion offers potential acquirers enough credible information to make a sound decision and to economically justify the purchase. The longer it takes someone to understand and appreciate the real opportunity, the more likely it is that the sale won't happen. Simply stated, time kills deals.

Many owners have an unrealistic price in mind. Recent surveys indicate that few companies have a current business valuation available. Not surprisingly, then, half the time owners are unrealistically high in their asking price, and the other half of the time they are low. Whether you think your business is worth $5 million or $50 million, until you have a formal valuation by a professional business appraiser, you can't begin to discuss or justify a selling price that makes sense.

PREMIUM VALUE: The actual marketing process, if properly implemented and managed, will provide the best determinant of value. Even though you may have a very good professional opinion of your business's value, that figure may not be the actual selling price. Remember, standard valuation approaches do not attempt to address the premium value a synergistic buyer may pay. A synergistic corporate buyer may be able to expand sales by using its existing sales force or may save costs by eliminating duplicate functions. Such prospects should be at the top of the list because they have a very real justification for paying more. Depending on many factors, including the investor, the structure, the marketplace, and the approach, the actual selling price can sometimes be a great deal more than the valuation. Consider the valuation, but recognize that "the market is smarter than all of us."

Warranties

⊠ *What else do I need to know about the due-diligence process?*

It is critical that the information you give to the purchaser be accurate "to the best of your knowledge." Even an unintentional bookkeeping error just before a sale can expose the most honest seller to liability when the buyer discovers the mistake. A sale contract includes your statement that what you say about the history and condition of the company is, in fact, true and complete. In legal terms such written and unwritten promises and statements are called *warranties* or *representations*.

Even if you earnestly believe that what you promise to be true is true, you can be liable to the purchaser, after the sale, if such "good-faith" promises turn out to be not true.

⊠ *I have a friend who sold his corporate shares in a business and was then sued by the purchaser. The purchaser got to return the shares and get his money back. How can this be?*

Most states have "blue-sky" laws. A purchaser of corporate shares can sue for a return of his or her money (plus interest and attorneys' fees) on the basis of alleged misrepresentations made by the seller or the seller's failure to disclose material facts. The purchaser's right to undo the transaction is called a *recision*. Honesty, integrity, and a full disclosure of all known facts may not be enough to protect the seller. For this reason, it is very important that anyone selling shares of a closely held corporation be represented by a lawyer who can diminish the risk of liability under a blue-sky law.

⊠ *I want to sell my business without the risk of being liable to the purchaser for warranties or representations. What happens if I refuse to give such statements and the sale agreement states that the purchaser is taking the business "as is and with all faults"?*

A purchaser who requires that you give warranties or representations is likely to offer you a higher price and more favorable terms than a purchaser who does not insist on such statements. If you refuse to give representations or warranties, you should expect that the purchaser will resist giving you the price and terms that you want. Consider the reverse: When you buy something "as is," you'll almost always pay less.

Financing

✍ *What are the possible ways that I can be paid for my business?*

You can be paid through any one or a combination of the following:

Investor's equity: In a structure of this kind, the buyer gives you stock in another company in return for your ownership interests or assets. As a general rule, you should not consider a stock-for-stock sale if the acquiring company is closely held and if you will not have the ability to actively participate in its management and control. If the buyer is offering stock in a public company, the stock-for-stock arrangement could be a bonanza because you can sell the stock. You will have liquidity, probably for the first time in your business life.

Your business: The buyer may want to make periodic payments from the business cash flow. As long as the business is profitable, you're in good shape. But you are clearly sharing with the buyer the risk that the business will not succeed in the future. Until the installment note is paid off, your financial situation remains tied to the company, even though you no longer control it.

Lenders: In this structure, the buyer will obtain financing from banks, financing institutions, and other sources.

✍ *Is a stock-for-stock trade with a public company the best deal for a sale?*

The answer depends on whether or not there are restrictions on your ability to immediately sell the stock. If there are, you have to consider the strength and profitability of the acquiring company. Public stock having a value of $10 million may decline to $8.5 million in value by the time you can actually sell the stock free of restrictions.

✍ *Is there a way for me to merge my closely held corporate business with a publicly traded corporate business?*

Yes. Most states allow two corporations to merge by adopting a mutual plan of merger agreed to by a vote of the shareholders of each corporation. Because the shares of your existing corporation are closely held—not registered under federal and state securities laws—your corporation's shareholders may find it difficult to sell their shares. With a merger, you could exchange your unregistered shares for registered and publicly traded shares in the other corporation. Estate and financial planning is much less complicated if what you own can be sold, and it is far more complicated if your primary estate asset is a nonmarketable interest in a closely held company.

Security

✍ *What can I do to make sure I get paid?*

Security is possibly the most misunderstood aspect of a transaction and certainly the greatest cause of a sale's breaking down or totally falling apart. Once attorneys begin doing their best to protect their clients, the degree of security required becomes a question of how much the parties will compromise and how reasonably each can approach the subject.

The parties must agree on which investor obligations should be secured and how they should be secured (e.g., promissory notes, lease payments, consulting fees, and covenants not to compete). If the seller is going to carry back debt and is expecting to receive periodic payments for noncompete or consulting agreements from the investor, it is important that the security for such debt consideration be reviewed and mutually agreed on in advance.

To enhance security, the seller should consider two very important issues:

FINANCIAL QUALITY OF THE BUYER: It is just as important for the seller to require a full disclosure of all financial information about the acquiring company as it is the other way around. Send in an army of accountants and advisors to be absolutely sure that you know everything you need to know about the acquiring company. You will never have an increased risk of loss by acquiring too much information. It is the information you do not have and did not discover that may produce an unanticipated loss. Be sure to document representations of fact in your sales contract. Obtain warranties that the information is true and correct. If it is a closely held company that is to acquire your company, seek personal owner guarantees and warranties. If you are in fact a lender in an installment-sale acquisition, act like a lender. Require security for the repayment of a purchase money obligation.

INTEGRITY OF THE BUYER: The buyer's integrity, competence, industry knowledge, business experience, and so on, are important. Almost all entrepreneurs have a gift for assessing these characteristics. Lenders often say that the real value of a repayment obligation is based on the integrity of the obligor, not the property he or she provides as loan collateral. A person of questionable character will find a way to take advantage of you or to renegotiate the purchase price after it has been fixed. Beware if you, the seller, have an intuition that the persons who control the acquiring company are questionable in any way. Hindsight will usually prove your intuition to be correct.

The following, in order of their practical importance to a seller, are additional means of security:

- A lien on the assets of the business, usually against accounts receivable, inventory, equipment, and real estate. Most often this will be a second lien, subordinated to any existing or planned bank borrowing.
- Default provisions in the loan agreement incorporating financial operating ratios, monthly statements to the seller, and remedies within a specified period of time. These enable the seller to quickly recognize a problem, go to court for a judgment if the

default is not fixed, and repossess the business before erosion has taken place.

- Pledge of stock of either the selling or the buying corporation.

- Decreasing term insurance on the buyer during the period of obligation to the seller, for the amount of the decreasing obligation.

- Limitations on bank borrowing for the buyer while obligations to the seller exist.

- Limitations on compensation for the buyer while obligations to the seller exist.

- Contracts with key employees that, if broken, trigger immediate payment of any remaining obligations to the seller.

- The personal guarantee of the buyer (a last resort in collateral priorities because a suit in the courts is costly and could take 1 to 3 years, and the assets of the buyer would probably be eroded in that time).

- A comprehensive and detailed sales contract.

What are my rights if the buyer defaults on the installment note?

Your rights are governed by contract law and the specific remedies that you prescribe in your sales agreement. You may be limited to repossessing the company assets, or you may have recourse against the buyer personally.

Postsale Liability

I've spent many years building my business. The purchaser I have in mind insists that I agree not to compete with my old business after she buys it. What are your thoughts?

A purchaser almost always wants to bar competition by the seller. If the seller makes a contractual promise not to compete, a breach of that promise can make the seller liable to the purchaser for damages. If, during a breach, the seller is still expecting payments from the purchaser for the promise not to compete, the purchaser could be expected to interrupt those payments. A court can order a breaching seller to stop competing.

A wise seller will consider:

- Whether he or she really wants to promise not to compete
- Whether the payments for the sale should be required periodically over the life of the noncompete
- Whether the purchaser is likely to interrupt installment payments in the event of breach of the noncompete
- Whether the price and terms of payment will meet the seller's expectations if there is no interruption because of competition
- Whether the noncompete is sought by the purchaser only to make the installment payments income tax–deductible

If my C corporation sells its assets, what protection from liability will my corporation and I have?

If your corporation continues to exist after the sale of its assets, it will be liable for debts in existence as of the date of the sale. It will also be responsible under contracts it entered into before the date of the sale, as well as be liable for contingent liabilities that arose before the date of the sale. And, because a corporation has perpetual existence, it will have to continue meeting its corporate formalities and tax obligations until it is dissolved. Dissolution may not be a practical option for many sellers as it would require the acceleration of recognition of installment-sale income and could result in the transfer of contingent corporate liabilities to the shareholders and directors of the corporation.

However, if the buyer of the assets is using them in conducting the same business as your corporation was, it must be doing so as a new entity. Thus, even if the buyer is operating the business under a trade name associated with your corporation, you and your corporation are insulated from liability for debts and claims arising from the use of the sold assets by their new owner.

Taxation

⋈ *What did you mean when you said that tax savings are the key to closing a gap between the seller's price and the investor's ability to pay?*

A seller may focus on the gross selling price, not after-tax value. Shift the focus to after-tax net. By structuring the transaction so that it is governed by capital gain tax rather than ordinary-income tax, often the after-tax net return to the seller is acceptable to the seller and approximates what the buyer is willing to pay. Bottom-line planning may produce win-win solutions that facilitate the sale of a company.

⋈ *How is an asset sale taxed?*

For tax purposes, the sale requires the allocation of the overall purchase price among the tangible and intangible assets sold. The amount and characterization of the gain (or loss) resulting from the sale are based on each specific asset rather than on the fact that the asset was used in a business activity. To that end, each asset has its own tax characterization, adjusted tax basis, and holding period. Asset sales produce long-term or short-term capital gains or losses as well as ordinary income, making price allocation an important consideration. The buyer has similar, but often contrary, interests in allocating the purchase price to particular assets. It may be advantageous for the buyer to allocate more of the purchase price to inventory and other rapidly depreciable assets. The allocations must follow rules specified by the Internal Revenue Service to ensure that the purchase price is reasonably allocated among all transferred assets.

⋈ *What are the tax consequences of selling the assets of my C corporation instead of its stock?*

The sale of your business assets generates a taxable gain to your corporation. If the sale proceeds are then distributed to the shareholders as a partial or complete liquidation of the company, the shareholders are subject to tax on the difference between the basis in their stock and the amount received in the liquidation. Ordinarily, this gain is treated as capital gain.

🔶 *How is the sale of intangibles, such as goodwill or "going concern," taxed?*

The business community treats goodwill and going-concern-enterprise values as valuable business assets. The Internal Revenue Service also recognizes the value of such intangible assets. The sale and purchase of intangible assets often results in frequent controversies among the government, seller, and buyer. This is because there is, without proper documentation, difficulty in placing a reliable value on intangible assets. The controversy is complicated because a seller and a purchaser often have conflicting interests in the allocation of the purchase price.

Regulations adopted for 1986 and subsequent years require that the allocation of a sales price to goodwill and "going concern" be measured by subtracting the combined fair market value of all other purchased "hard" assets from the total purchase price. A business that does not establish a value for intangible assets cannot amortize the assets for tax purposes. An allocation to intangible goodwill in the purchase contract can allow the purchaser to establish a cost basis in intangible assets. Since 1993, purchasers have been permitted to amortize and deduct the cost of intangible assets over a 15-year period.

🔶 *A prospective buyer has offered to continue my annual compensation of $250,000 for 5 years in exchange for occasional consulting services and my promise not to participate in any competitive company. What are the tax consequences of my covenant not to compete?*

The $250,000 compensation payment for your covenant not to compete is taxable to you as ordinary income in the year received. The buyer gets to deduct the operating expense for the compensation payment, thereby saving income tax on that amount of operating income.

⩗ *I'm the sole proprietor of an engineering consulting company, and over the years I've acquired several patents. How will these patents be treated for tax purposes?*

The sale or exchange of a patent by the original holder produces a capital gain or loss. Patent rights (trademarks, intellectual property rights) must be held for at least 1 year.

REDUCING TAXES IN A SALE

⩗ *Is there any way to structure the sale of my business so that there is no tax?*

There are basically three techniques for reducing or eliminating the taxes on the sale transaction:

- Noncorporate shareholders may exclude from gross income 50 percent of any gain from the sale or exchange of qualified-small-business stock.
- In a tax-free exchange, you exchange your stock for the buyer's stock. Your tax basis for the buyer's stock that you receive is the same as your basis for the stock of the company you are selling, so there is no capital gain or income tax.
- You can transfer the business to a charitable remainder trust.

With the right help your tax bite can be reduced and you may net a great deal more than you thought.

Qualified-Small-Business Stock

⩗ *I own a corporation that I acquired approximately 5 years ago. I'm considering selling it and understand that there are special tax benefits for sales of certain small-business stock. How do I determine whether my stock qualifies?*

Noncorporate—individual—owners may exclude from gross income 50 percent of any gain from the sale or exchange of qualified-small-business stock (QSBS) held more than 5 years. To qualify for this favorable tax treatment, the corporation must meet the following requirements:

■ The corporation must be a domestic C corporation.

■ The stock must have been originally issued after August 10, 1993.

■ The stock must be issued directly by the corporation or through an underwriter to the taxpayer.

■ The stock must be issued for money or property or as compensation for services.

■ The aggregate gross assets of the corporation cannot exceed $50 million at any time on or after August 10, 1993, and cannot exceed $50 million before and immediately after the issuance of the stock to the taxpayer.

■ The corporation must be an *active business,* which generally means that at least 80 percent of the corporation's assets are used in a qualified trade or business.

≥▲ *What are the tax benefits of owning qualified-small-business stock?*

The maximum amount of a taxpayer's gain that may be excluded, with respect to each issuing corporation, in any taxable year, is limited to the *greater* of (1) $10 million (minus the amount of gain previously excluded by the taxpayer with respect to the issuing corporation) or (2) ten times the aggregate adjusted basis of the stock of the issuing corporation

If the sale of the stock qualifies for the 50 percent exclusion, the remaining 50 percent of gain, which is included in income, is not eligible for the 20 percent long-term capital gain rate; rather, it is subject to tax at the 28 percent rate. In addition, 42 percent of the excluded gain is treated as a preference item for alternative minimum tax (AMT) purposes. For qualified-small-business stock acquired after December 31, 2000, the AMT preference amount is reduced to 28 percent of the amount excluded. The preference is treated as a permanent difference for AMT purposes. There will be no related AMT credit to be used in the future.

Can I sell my qualified-small-business stock and avoid income taxes by reinvesting in new qualified-small-business stock?

Yes. An individual taxpayer may elect to roll over capital gain from the sale of qualified-small-business stock held more than 6 months by purchasing other small-business stock during a 60-day period beginning on the date of sale. In addition, the tax law does not limit the replacement stock to stock in just one corporation. Therefore, you can diversify your investments in multiple small-business corporations or purchase another small-business corporation without present gain recognition.

What happens if, after selling my qualified-small-business stock, my only option is to reinvest a portion of the proceeds? Can I take advantage of the 50 percent gain exclusion with respect to the remaining gain?

The two provisions regarding qualified-small-business stock are not mutually exclusive. You can purchase replacement stock to shield part of the gain, and if the stock has been held for 5 years, you can utilize the 50 percent exclusion to decrease the taxes on the balance of the taxable gain.

Charitable Remainder Trust

My business is free of debt and worth about $1 million. I want to sell it so that I can invest the $1 million to provide for my retirement. My accountant says that my basis in the business is so low that I'll have to pay a sizable capital gain tax. What can I do?

Because you have a low basis, if you sell the business, you will have to pay capital gain tax to the Internal Revenue Service in the year of the sale. You might also have to pay income tax of some kind on the same gain to your state government. The combination of these taxes can severely reduce your sale proceeds for investment.

It is possible for you to contribute your business to a charitable remainder trust and defer the immediate taxation of the sale.

⅏ What is a charitable remainder trust?

A *charitable remainder trust (CRT)* is another type of irrevocable split-interest trust. The business owner–trust maker transfers his or her business to the trust, retaining a current interest in the form of income payments and giving to a charity a future interest in the form of the "remainder" of the principal or assets in the trust. The term of the trust can be for a life or lives or for a specified number of years. At the end of the term of the trust, the remainder of the trust property is transferred to the charity.

After the owner transfers the business to the trust, the trustee of the trust sells it and the purchaser pays the proceeds to the charitable remainder trust. The trustee invests the proceeds and pays the income beneficiary. There is no taxable capital gain to the trust when the trustee sells the business. The principal will be kept intact to earn more.

It is often better for owners to contribute stock or other business interests to a charitable remainder trust. Many business owners would rather have a million-dollar income-generating base inside a CRT than have a smaller after-income-tax income-generating base outside the trust.

⅏ I've heard that there are many situations where giving my business to charity should be considered as an exit strategy. Why would I want to do this?

Giving the business to charity through a charitable remainder trust:

- Provides the owner–trust maker with an income tax deduction to the extent of the remainder interest that will pass to charity, valued under the government's valuation tables.

- Provides the owner-maker with estate and gift tax charitable deductions to the extent of the remainder interest that will pass to charity, valued under the government's valuation tables.
- Allows the owner-maker to spread the capital gain recognition over a period of years because a charitable remainder trust is exempt from capital gain tax.
- Enables philanthropic business owners to give to charity while retaining the right to income from the donation for a period of years

A charitable remainder trust allows a business owner to divest himself or herself of the business by converting it to lifetime income without paying an immediate capital gain tax when the business is sold. It reduces the business owner's income taxes now and reduces estate taxes at the owner's death. And it lets the owner give significant amounts to a charity of his or her choice.

⚜ Can I contribute S corporation stock to a charitable remainder trust?

Unfortunately, most of the benefits of using a CRT are not available with S corporation stock. There are techniques for getting around this limitation to some extent, so ask your advisor to help you if you own S corporation stock.

⚜ If I have a buyer for my company already, how would I use the CRT?

Let's use an example: Betty and David Sinclair own all the stock of Twilight Ventures Corporation, which they started 25 years ago. The company is valued at $10 million. David and Betty have almost no income tax basis in their stock. SunMark Corporation, a publicly traded company, has expressed an interest in acquiring all of Twilight's stock for $10 million cash. Before negotiation for the sale begins, Betty and David create a charitable remainder trust and transfer their stock to it.

The charitable remainder trust is tax-exempt; it does not pay income taxes or capital gain taxes when it sells the stock. David and Betty retain the right to receive from the trust a payment of $900,000 every year for life (a 9 percent annuity interest). After David and Betty die, the trust assets will go to the Greater Cat's Gap Area Foundation. The community foundation is to apply the income from the endowment for education and youth sports. David and Betty realize a large charitable income tax deduction for the present value of the remainder interest that will ultimately pass to charity.

Will the income payable by the charitable remainder trust to David and Betty be tax-free income? No. The annuity payments will first be treated as ordinary income and then as capital gains to them, depending on the amount of ordinary income the trust earns during the year. Betty considers the deferral of the tax liability on the sale to be more preferable than a lump-sum payment of the tax for the year of sale. Some of the income from the annuity payments will be off-set by the charitable income tax deduction that she and David can take for year 1 and thereafter, over the 5-year carry-forward period.

≥\ *If I want to liquidate my corporation, can I get any tax benefit from using a CRT?*

Yes. Using our example of David and Betty again, let's assume that no one is interested in buying Twilight Ventures and so they decide to liquidate it over time. Because Twilight is a C corporation, it will pay capital gain tax on any gain from the sale of capital assets and David and Betty will pay capital gain tax on liquidating distributions of cash and property in kind from the corporation. If David and Betty contribute the stock to a charitable remainder trust and the trust liquidates the assets, they defer the second level of capital gain tax.

≥\ *Can we contribute partial interests to a CRT as part of a buy-sell arrangement? If so, how will this create an income for us?*

Let's say that Twilight Ventures Corporation is owned 80 percent by David and Betty and 20 percent by their son, Trey. David is ready to retire from the business, but he and Betty have no meaningful retirement assets to provide them with an income. They contribute their 80 percent of Twilight's stock to a charitable remainder trust.

Twilight puts out a call to redeem the stock of all shareholders. The trustee of the CRT accepts the offer to redeem part or all of the stock in the CRT. The value for the redemption has to be based on the $10 million fair market value. Twilight then redeems the shares owned by the trust in exchange for a promissory note. The note payments are sufficient to permit the trustee to make the annual annuity payments to David and Betty.

In order to use this strategy, it is essential that your CRT have an independent trustee to decide whether to accept the offer to redeem the stock. Since the offer will allow the trustee to diversify the trust portfolio for future growth, almost all trustees would view it as a prudent transaction and accept the offer.

◢ How does a CRT increase my income?

Income is increased when the trust maker holds highly appreciated assets that generate low income. In creating a charitable remainder trust, the trust maker transfers the highly appreciated assets to the CRT. The CRT can sell the appreciated assets without triggering the capital gain that would have been levied if the trust maker sold the assets in his individual capacity. The proceeds can then be invested in income-producing securities that pay a predetermined percentage to the trust maker.

Table 24-1 shows how income can be increased through a CRT. It assumes a 9 percent return on investments, a 30 percent tax rate, and annuity payments at the same rate as the return on investment each year.

Taxation

◢ What are the gift tax results of the charitable gift?

The transfer of property to a charitable unitrust or a charitable

TABLE 24-1   Increased Income through a CRT

	Without a CRT	With a CRT
Stock sale	$750,000	$750,000
Capital gain taxes	187,500	0
Net proceeds	$562,500	$750,000
Return on investments/annuity payment (9%)	$50,625	$67,500
Less: Maker's income tax (30%)	15,188*	20,250
After-tax cash	$35,437	$47,250

*Rounded to nearest dollar.

annuity trust is a gift, and a gift tax return is required. A charitable gift tax deduction is allowed for the value of the remainder interest that is to pass to charity. The value of the gift to the charity is the present value of the remainder interest, which is calculated by deducting from the property's fair market value the payments that you are to receive over the term of the trust (on the basis of the Internal Revenue Service's assumed rate of return).

⩕   *What are the limits of the charitable income tax deduction?*

Certain limitations are placed on income tax deductibility for lifetime charitable gifts. The amount of the deduction is determined by such factors as the value and tax basis of the property given, the type of charity the gift is given to, the timing of the gift, and the income of the donor. In general, the deductions are:

- A 50 percent deduction against your adjusted gross income (AGI) for gifts of cash and short-term capital gain property
- A 30 percent deduction against your AGI for gifts of appreciated long-term capital gain property
- A 5-year carryover for unused deductions

⊲⟩ *What are the estate tax consequences of a charitable remainder trust?*

The value of the trust must be included in the donor's estate. This is offset by the estate tax charitable deduction or by the estate tax marital deduction if the surviving spouse is the only remaining non-charitable beneficiary and the trust is to continue for his or her life. The net effect is that the CRT does not increase the donor's estate taxes but, in fact, reduces them.

⊲⟩ *If I serve as trustee for the investments in my CRT, are there any tax consequences?*

While it is possible for you to act as your own trustee for your charitable remainder trust, this may not be advisable. If the trust maker serves as trustee, great care must be taken to prohibit or limit the retention of any power that might cause him or her to be taxed on all the trust income under Internal Revenue Code rules. The general rule, a safe harbor, is to provide for the service of an independent trustee, especially with a unitrust, which must be valued annually, and especially if the trust principal is an interest in a partnership or in a corporation that the maker manages and controls.

⊲⟩ *How are the annual payments taxed?*

How the payments are taxed depends on the character of the income earned by the trust. Under the current rules, the income is treated first as ordinary income, then capital gains, then tax-free income, and finally as a return of capital. No matter how the funds are invested inside the trust, there will be capital gains to be distributed from the initial sale.

Income payments

⊲⟩ *Can a charitable remainder trust pay out for the lives of more than one income beneficiary?*

A charitable remainder trust can benefit more than one person; usually this is done for a husband and wife. Remember, though, that the longer the trust is estimated to pay out to the income beneficiaries, the less the income tax deduction is to the donor.

✍ Are the payments the same each year?

The answer depends on the type of charitable remainder trust you create. There are three types of CRTs: charitable remainder annuity trust, charitable remainder unitrust, and charitable remainder unitrust with net income makeup provisions.

✍ What is a charitable remainder annuity trust?

A *charitable remainder annuity trust (CRAT)* is a charitable remainder trust that pays a fixed amount to the beneficiary (at least 5 percent and not more than 50 percent) during the term of the trust (whether for life or for a number of years). The present value of the remainder interest going to charity must be at least 10 percent of the value of the property contributed to the trust. This may dictate how much the annuity amount can be.

The trust maker cannot make additional contributions to a CRAT once it is established, and the trustee must make the specified payments to the beneficiary even if the trust did not earn enough income during the year to pay the annuity amount. For example, if the trust maker sets up a CRAT with a gift of $1 million and specifies that the income beneficiary is to receive $100,000 each year, the trustee must pay the beneficiary $100,000 each year even if the trust earned less than 10 percent in any year. If the trust income is not sufficient to make the annuity payment, the trust maker cannot contribute more property to make up the deficiency; the trust must liquidate trust property to make a cash payment or must distribute in-kind property having a value sufficient to make up the deficiency.

✍ What is a charitable remainder unitrust?

A *charitable remainder unitrust (CRUT)* is a charitable remainder trust that pays a fixed percentage (at least 5 percent and not more than 50 percent) of the principal to the income beneficiary during the income term of the trust. The present value of the remainder interest going to charity must be at least 10 percent of the value of the property contributed to the trust.

With a CRUT, the trust maker *can* make additional contributions to the trust once it is established. The fixed percentage amount is applied annually to the trust assets as valued each year. Thus, the payment amount can vary from year to year and provide the income beneficiary with a hedge against inflation. For example, if the trust maker sets up a CRUT with a gift of $1 million and specifies that the income beneficiary is to receive 10 percent of the value of the trust each year, the trustee must pay the beneficiary 10 percent of whatever the value of the trust is at the beginning of each year of the trust's income period. As the value of the trust property increases, the payment to the income beneficiary increases a corresponding amount.

⚜ *Once I've chosen a payout rate, can I change it?*

In general you cannot change the payout rate. However, you can have the CRT drafted in such a way that the rate automatically increases in the future. The regulations provide that the rate can increase each year but the change cannot exceed 120 percent of the previous year's rate. If you want this option, you need to inform your attorney so that he or she will include the appropriate provision in your CRT document.

⚜ *What is a charitable remainder unitrust with net income make-up provisions?*

A *charitable remainder unitrust with net income makeup provisions (NIMCRUT)* allows the income beneficiaries to take less than the required payout percentage if the trust assets make less than that amount in a given year. The trust then holds what is considered an "IOU" for the amount it was supposed to pay to the income beneficiaries. Generally, the IOUs, or makeup amounts, can be satisfied in future years, at the beneficiary's discretion, but only from available net income. Trust principal may not be used to satisfy a deficiency.

Because of the income deferral and makeup attributes of a NIMCRUT, it is sometimes used as a nonqualified retirement plan strategy. For example, if a NIMCRUT holds $1 million in bonds and is supposed to pay 7 percent, or $70,000, during a period when its earnings are only 5 percent, or $50,000, there is an annual deficiency of $20,000. The deficiency may accumulate until the income beneficiary is ready for retirement. At that time, the trustee sells the bonds and invests in a financial product that will provide a return in excess of the 7 percent amount. All the accumulated makeup income may be distributed to the income beneficiary during his or her retirement years.

⚑ Which is better, a CRAT or a CRUT?

The answer depends on your goals and situation:

- The unitrust requires an annual revaluation of the trust property. This can be very expensive if the trust owns an interest in a closely held company or partnership. The annuity trust requires only an initial valuation; thereafter, the payments are fixed.

- With the annuity trust, there is a limit on the annuity payments in order to comply with the 10 percent remainder requirement. The unitrust does not have this requirement.

- The annuity trust does not "inflation-protect" the income beneficiary over a period of time, whereas the unitrust does.

- The annuity trust is not complicated to administer. The NIMCRUT, with its deficiency account, is more complicated and expensive to administer.

- Additional contributions cannot be made to an annuity trust, but they can be made to a unitrust.

Qualified charities

🙠 *Can I name any charity to be the remainder beneficiary of a charitable remainder trust?*

Basically, you can name any charity or organization that qualifies as a tax-exempt organization under Section 501(c)(3) of the Internal Revenue Code. Such organizations do not have to pay income taxes, and contributions to them are tax-deductible by the donors. Most churches, hospitals, medical research institutions, educational institutions, zoos, museums, community orchestras, and organizations such as the Red Cross, the Salvation Army, the Boy Scouts, and the Girl Scouts are qualified charities.

🙠 *You said the trust is irrevocable. What happens if I want to change the charity that's the beneficiary of the CRT?*

The trust instrument can be drafted in such a way as to allow the trustee to change the remainder beneficiary. This change must be done before the death of the last income beneficiary. Any change of charitable beneficiary must be done in compliance with Internal Revenue Code requirements and with preferences that you delineate in the trust instrument, such as a list of charities that the trustee must choose from.

Advantages and disadvantages

🙠 *What are some of the advantages of transferring my business to a charitable remainder trust?*

The use of a charitable remainder trust:

■ Removes the value of the business from the business owner's estate

■ Qualifies for a charitable deduction on the owner's federal income tax return

■ Allows the trust maker to retain an income stream on the entire value of the trust, not just the value of the asset after the payment of income taxes

❧ What are the disadvantages of using a charitable remainder trust?

For the business owner, the major disadvantage of the charitable remainder trust is that after the death of the trust maker, the property in the trust goes to the selected charity rather than to his or her heirs. Parents who use CRTs often create *wealth replacement trusts* to maximize their children's inheritance and make up for the value of the assets they gave to charity.

❧ I don't like the idea that my heirs won't receive my business wealth on my death. Is there any way around this if I use a CRT?

You must consider the value of all attributes: the present value of your retained income interest over your lifetime, the present value of your charitable income tax deduction, and the present value of probable transfer tax savings. The combined economic benefit may be greater than the value of the property you contribute to the CRT. The remainder interest will pass to charity at your death, but you can use a wealth replacement trust to provide your children with an equivalent economic benefit.

For example, assume that you sell your small business for $1 million and that your capital gain tax will be $200,000. The CRT saves you from a lump-sum capital gain tax in the amount of $200,000. In addition, your accountant estimates that you will realize a charitable income tax deduction in the amount of $180,000, which will reduce your income tax by $86,000 over a period of 4 years. How much life insurance can you buy with the $86,000 you save in income taxes? The wealth replacement strategy involves the purchase of an insurance policy to replace the wealth your children would have received had you not opted to use a charitable remainder trust. The policy is owned by a trust you establish for the long-term use and benefit of your children. Properly designed and funded, the trust will keep the value of the policy out of your taxable estate at the time of your death.

Depending on your philanthropic desires, the charitable remainder trust combined with a wealth replacement trust may provide you with sufficient economic benefit to make the donation worthwhile.

PART SIX

Estate Planning

IDEALLY, ESTATE PLANNING IS A WELL-INTEGRATED ELEMENT OF THE overall business planning that the business owner has engaged in throughout his or her lifetime. The purpose in developing an estate plan is to have it augment lifetime succession planning or be the sole mechanism for accomplishing the nondisruptive transfer of the business at an owner's disability or death

Let's assume a business owner has arranged the disposition of his or her business interest by giving it away during his or her lifetime or by having someone purchase it upon retirement, disability, or death. The business owner's revocable living trust or last will and testament handles the transfer of whatever the business owner receives as proceeds from the sale of the business, triggered by disability or death, and the transfer of all the owner's nonbusiness assets.

More frequently, business owners have not given their entire business interest away during their lifetime and have not entered into any type of binding arrangements to sell the interest at their disability or death. In these cases the pure estate planning element becomes the last opportunity for accomplishing the smooth transition of the business on the owner's disability or death.

In Part Six we address estate planning with both these scenarios—and everything in between—in mind. It is very important that estate planning for business owners be coordinated with all other business planning that has been accomplished for the owners.

The questions and answers in Chapter 25 provide an overview of the issues facing owners as they contemplate the future of their businesses after they are no longer in control (as a result of their disability or death). Emphasis is placed not only on business goals and objectives but, more importantly, on family planning issues unique to business owners, as well as those issues that are common to all of us.

In Chapter 26, our contributing authors submitted a number of questions and answers on revocable living trusts. It is not surprising that we received so many questions and answers on this topic, because many of our contributors are very well versed on this subject. It is critical that business owners have a revocable living trust as the centerpiece of a well-coordinated overall plan. When a business owner has funded his or her business interest into a properly drafted living trust, the trust provides a mechanism for continued management of the business upon the disability or death of the business owner without the delay imposed by a court-administered guardianship or probate process. A will cannot provide these benefits and is, therefore, an inferior tool for the business owner.

The questions and answers about the federal estate and gift tax system in Chapter 27 cover the tax costs associated with the lifetime or testamentary transfer of a business. This chapter details many of the special tax benefits that are available to business owners who carefully structure their businesses.

Chapter 28 begins with general strategies to optimize the use of credit shelter planning with a family trust and optimal marital deduction planning with a marital trust. Chapter 28 also presents sophisticated and exciting opportunities for business owners to pass significant value to their families, and sometimes to favorite charities, while significantly reducing estate taxes. Chapter 28 ends with strategies for using life insurance, valuation adjustments, testamentary charitable lead trusts, testamentary charitable remainder trusts, and other techniques to leverage available deductions and credits to reduce taxes.

chapter 25

Estate Planning Overview

THE ESTATE

⚰ *What is an estate?*

In estate planning, *estate* describes everything you own. Often the media use the term "estate" only for wealthy individuals. However, whether rich, poor, or somewhere in between, we all have estates comprising the assets we own.

⚰ *What is included in my estate for estate tax purposes?*

Everything that you own at the time of your death is a part of your estate for estate tax purposes. "For estate tax purposes" means the assets are valued to determine whether any estate tax is owed and, if so, how much. Your estate includes tangible and intangible property. Examples of tangible property are real estate, household goods and furnishings, and automobiles. Intangible property includes life

497

insurance, retirement accounts, stocks, bonds, interests in closely held businesses, and notes or other claims. Monies such as interest, rents, shareholder dividends, and partnership distributions that are payable to you but uncollected at the date of your death are also part of your estate.

⚖ *I hear different answers when I ask if life insurance is included in an estate. Is it or isn't it tax-free?*

Yes and no. It comes as a great surprise to many beneficiaries that the life insurance proceeds they receive can be subject to an estate tax. If the insured owned the policy at the time of his or her death or had any "incidents of ownership" in the policy, the death benefit of the policy is included in the insured's estate and is subject to estate tax. Of course, during 2010 when the estate tax is repealed (and possibly thereafter), life insurance proceeds will not be subject to federal estate tax. However, due to the uncertainty over the future of the estate tax, at this point it is wise to continue planning to keep life insurance out of the insured's estate.

Life insurance death benefits are generally *income tax*–free to the beneficiaries of the policy. Therefore, when beneficiaries receive the proceeds from the insurance company, they are not required to include the amount in their taxable income in the year of receipt.

⚖ *What is an incident of ownership?*

An *incident of ownership* is the ability to do any one or more of the following: surrender or cancel the policy, pledge the policy for a loan, obtain a policy loan, change the beneficiary, or assign the policy. If you have any incidents of ownership in any insurance policy on your life on the date of your death, the entire value of the death benefit will be included in your estate. Furthermore, if you gave up all incidents of ownership in a policy less than 3 years before your death, the value of the death benefit is still included in your estate. There are several ways to avoid the inclusion of life insurance proceeds in your estate, which we discuss later in Part Six.

⅏ *Are stock options that I received from my employer included in my estate?*

Yes. If you die owning stock options, they are included in your estate. The IRS has ruled that the value of the stock options for estate tax purposes is the "spread"—that is, the difference between the option price (strike price) and the market price on the date of death.

⅏ *How is my estate valued, and at what point in time is it valued?*

The assets you own at the time of your death are valued at their fair market value at the date of your death. Some assets may not have a readily ascertainable market value and will need to be appraised by a certified appraiser who is qualified to value the type of asset in question. Other assets, such as marketable securities, have an easily ascertainable fair market value.

In certain cases, an alternate valuation date, which is 6 months after the date of death, may be used, rather than the date of death. This alternate valuation date may be used only if the value of the gross estate is less on the alternate valuation date than it was on the date of death and the accompanying estate taxes are less at the alternate valuation date. Once the valuation date is selected, all assets must be valued on the same date; thus we can't use a date-of-death value for some assets and the alternate valuation date for others.

ESTATE PLANNING
FOR THE BUSINESS OWNER

⅏ *What is estate planning?*

Robert A. Esperti and Renno L. Peterson, cofounders of the National Network of Estate Planning Attorneys and the Esperti Peterson Institute, created a wonderful working definition of estate planning. In essence, it says that "I want to control my property while I am alive and well; plan for my loved ones and myself in the event of my disability; and then give what I have to whom I want, when I want, and the way I want; and to do so at the lowest possible overall cost to myself and those I love."

Estate planning is the creation and implementation of a plan that will care for you, your loved ones, and your property if you become disabled and that will provide an orderly transition of your property, including your business, upon your death, so that all or many of these transactions occur with a minimum of delay, court intervention, publicity, cost, and taxes.

✄ *Why is estate planning important for the business owner?*

The business is often the major value of the business owner's entire estate. A significant challenge is presented when the owner wishes to pass the business intact (that is, undiminished by the cost of paying estate tax) to members of his or her family at death.

Studies have shown that less than 50 percent of all businesses will pass to the second generation and less than 20 percent of all businesses will pass to the third generation. One cause of the problem is estate taxes, which can take away up to 50 percent (2002 top rate) of the assets of a small business upon an owner's death. The situation can be exacerbated by the tendency of the IRS to overvalue small businesses, which may result in tax disputes. Interestingly, the average settlement value for business valuations that go to trial is less than half of the IRS's initial valuation.

Estate taxes are a well-known adversary. Less well understood is that they are often not the biggest barrier to a successful transfer of the business to the next generation. Most studies show that about 25 percent of key shareholders in closely held businesses have any estate planning in place and that most business owners do not have succession plans. A business owner will spend tens of thousands of hours creating a successful business and often less than a day planning its transition.

✄ *Why does estate planning seem to be such a difficult process for business owners?*

Business owners don't have proper succession or estate planning because, first, business owners tend to be entrepreneurial and therefore eternally optimistic. They may perceive estate planning to be a pessimistic undertaking because it involves discussions of disability, death, and giving up control of a business that has been their life for many years. These are difficult topics to the business owner.

Second, business owners tend to be incredibly busy. Proper succession and estate planning is a process, not a transaction. Like any process, it takes time. And time is a scarce resource for many business owners.

Proper estate planning is not just tax planning. It is not a plan for giving up control. It is lifetime planning that will ensure continued control and allow the business owner not only to enjoy a life of success but also to leave a legacy of significance.

⋑ What are the challenges business owners face in estate planning?

Effectively maintaining and passing control of a business can be even more important than tax or legal issues. Table 25-1 is a checklist, derived from comments made by our business-owner clients, that shows estate planning challenges facing many business owners. You may use the checklist in preparation of your own planning. Throughout Part Six we discuss these and other issues and highlight a number of methods that can help you and your advisors accomplish your goals.

⋑ As a business owner, what should my primary estate planning concern be?

Liquidity is a primary concern. There is often not enough cash to pay all the taxes and expenses and to take care of beneficiaries who may need cash today. Because many families of business owners don't have enough liquid assets to easily pay the estate taxes when they come due, the owner's estate may need to sell the family business to raise capital to pay the estate taxes.

Proper planning is based on a firm foundation, with husband and wife at the base of the pyramid, then family, wealth preservation, wealth expansion, and, at the peak of the pyramid, saving

TABLE 25-1   Business Owner's Estate Planning Checklist

❑ The value of my business is the largest portion of my estate. If my succession plan called for a sale or gift of my business to one child active in the business, what's left in my estate to pass along to my spouse and other children?

❑ My succession plan calls for the sale of my business to an outside party. What's left in the estate to pass along to my spouse and children?

❑ How will my family pay the estate taxes?

❑ Do I have sufficient other assets so that I can treat my children equally: give my business to one child and give equal value to my other child?

❑ What does my spouse get if my business is going to the children?

❑ What happens if I don't have a succession plan for the business during my lifetime but just leave it to my family at my death?

❑ What happens if there are four children in the family and they all work in the business?

❑ What happens if there are multiple children but some don't work in the business?

❑ What happens if no one in the family works in the business but there is a key employee who expects to be able to purchase the business?

❑ I want to be sure my spouse and I are taken care of in the event of a death or disability.

❑ I want to maintain control of my affairs and my business.

❑ I don't want to impoverish myself and live an austere lifestyle simply to save taxes for my children and grandchildren.

❑ I do not want my children or grandchildren living off inherited money.

❑ I want to encourage a strong work ethic in my descendants.

❑ I feel it is very important to conserve funds for college or other post-high school education.

❑ I feel strongly about my child being encouraged to pursue a particular career.

❑ After my child graduates from a 4-year college, I want my trustee to follow specific instructions in providing for my child.

❑ I want to pass on the things that are important to me that are not material, such as family values, history, and heritage.

❑ I want to leave a legacy.

❑ I want to protect the wealth I've already created from creditors and predators.

❑ If I can, I'd like to expand my wealth to be sure that I have enough to carry me through retirement.

❑ I'd like to make a difference in my community by contributing to causes that I care about.

❑ I'd like to save taxes.

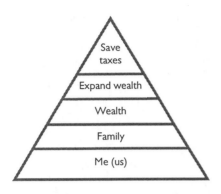

Save
taxes

Expand wealth

Wealth

Family

Me (us)

Figure 25-1 Planning pyramid. Copyright © 1989 by the National Network of Estate Planning Attorneys, Incorporated. Printed with permission.

taxes, as shown in Figure 25-1. Once the foundation is properly laid, tax savings are fairly easy to accomplish. But if we build our pyramid on the point of tax savings, it is likely to topple over!

☙ *I hear that estate taxes have been repealed. Why should I plan for estate taxes?*

We described in Chapter 1 the changes to the federal estate and gift tax system brought on by the 2001 tax act. In essence, the act calls for a gradual decrease in estate taxes between 2002 and 2009, followed by a total repeal of the estate tax in 2010, and followed by a return of the estate tax the next year. Quite honestly, no one knows what the estate tax laws will be in the future, but there's no question that estate taxes can have a devastating effect on small-business owners. Throughout Part Six, we assume that a federal estate tax of some form will exist at your death. Prudent planning dictates that we hope for the best but continue to plan for the worst.

☙ *You keep telling me that I need a team to coordinate my estate planning. Why do I need so many professionals?*

The field of estate planning is becoming more and more complex. As families become more aware of the various options available to them for planning that involve both lifetime goals and after-death goals, it also becomes apparent that a number of qualified professionals are needed. This group includes most of the same professionals you used for succession planning, if you chose to do any.

These individuals would generally include an estate and tax planning attorney, a financial advisor, an accountant, a life insurance professional, a business valuation appraiser, and a trust officer.

Planning for Children

I'm concerned that if I die today, my boys would decide not to work. Do you have any suggestions for handling this issue?

For parents with this concern, it often makes sense to include a get-a-job clause in the trust for the unmotivated child. Such a clause might essentially say that "I give to my son, on a monthly basis, an amount equal to what he earns in the workplace."

This language may help prevent the traditional "trust-fund-kid syndrome." If your son, at the age of 25, chooses to be a couch potato, then he would receive no money to buy potato chips. On the other hand, if your son goes to work at McDonald's and earns $1000 per month, his trust would match it. When he becomes a manager of McDonald's and earns $2000, the trust matches that amount. Hopefully, this financial opportunity will be an incentive to the beneficiary to be a productive member of society.

I have three children who don't work in the business, so I'll probably sell it to two key employees. What should be my estate planning goals?

You need to consider how you want your assets to pass on your death. Even if you no longer own your business at your death, you will have the proceeds from the sale of your business, including, perhaps, a promissory note you accepted as part of the purchase price for the business, and all the other assets you own. These assets will fund the estate planning "vehicles" that you and your estate planning attorney create for the benefit of your three children.

If dividing my business equally among my children is not appropriate, what can I do to treat them equally and fairly?

The first thing is to determine if there are enough other assets, such as stocks, bonds, or real estate, that you can give to your child or children who are not involved in the business to equalize the value of your business passing to the child or children active in the business. Keep in mind that some of those relatively liquid assets may be needed for estate taxes so that the business does not have to be sold at a discount to a nonfamily member.

One of the best ways to solve an equalization and/or a liquidity problem is with life insurance. You can equalize your estate with the proceeds, or your heirs can use the proceeds to pay the estate taxes. Insurance policies are usually purchased inside an irrevocable trust to provide an estate tax– and income tax–free death benefit.

⚖ *What do I need to consider when leaving my business or the balance of my estate to my children or grandchildren?*

Leaving a business at your death to your children and or grandchildren is a challenge. As famed investor Warren Buffet once said, "I want to give my children enough money so that they can do anything, but not so much that they do nothing." Large outright gifts and inheritances might be appropriate in a few cases, but most of the time other arrangements for your family might work better for them. Here are some things to consider:

AGE: Minors can only receive property under the control of a custodian, and they cannot have absolute control over it until age 18 or 21, depending on which state you live in. Without proper arrangements in a trust, they get all of it at a rather young age. Could you have handled a substantial inheritance at that age?

WEALTH MATURITY: Some children and adults are good business and financial stewards. Others are not. Either they spend too much, have no business judgment, are financially illiterate, or become easy prey to friends, relatives, and "gold diggers."

MARRIAGE: Not all marriages last forever. Without your careful planning, an inheritance can go outside your bloodlines through a divorce. Some marriages are great, and you may even want to provide for the surviving in-law spouse.

INDIVIDUALITY: Children and grandchildren have a way of enhancing and complicating our lives! At young ages, it is difficult to predict how they will turn out. Your provisions need to have enough flexibility to accommodate change. Some adult children become very successful, while others will always struggle. No two siblings are alike. Consider these factors: mental and physical health (do any of them have "special needs"), employability, education, work ethic, chemical dependency, personal problems, and marriage stability.

EQUAL TREATMENT VERSUS EQUAL DISTRIBUTION: Most parents do not keep a ledger on how much they spend on each child. They spend according to each child's individual needs. Yet at death, parents often feel compelled to divide everything equally. Sometimes, equal isn't always equal and equal isn't always fair. In our experience, we have observed that adult children are much more understanding than their parents are about the need for unequal distributions among themselves when the circumstances warrant such treatment.

YOUR VALUE SYSTEM: Most families would actually like some guidance on what to do with an inheritance or, more specifically, what you would like them to do with the inheritance you left them.

Once you have considered the above criteria as they apply to your children or grandchildren, it is much easier to give guidelines to an estate planning attorney.

   I don't want to give my children outright ownership of my business at my death. What options do I have for distributing my business and my other assets to my children?

HELD IN TRUST: You can include in your estate planning document that, at your death, your assets will be "held in trust" and that the income and principal can be used for the beneficiary, including funds for college, medical expenses, and the like.

DISTRIBUTIONS AT DIFFERENT AGES: Your can include in the document when each of your beneficiaries is to receive the business interests and other assets. Many people feel that even 21 years of age is too young and prefer age 25. Others, depending on the beneficiary and amount involved, prefer to instruct the trustee to give the beneficiary staggered distributions at stated ages (for example, one-third at age 30, one-third at age 35, and the balance at age 40). You can include any special instructions you desire, including that the trustee make mandatory distributions for the health, maintenance, and support of the children or that the trustee make discretionary distributions based on whether the children appear financially responsible, are behaving in a socially desirable manner, or meet any other guidelines that you provide.

VALUE GUIDELINES: Let your trustee and guardian know what you think is important to you. Here are a few of the guidelines we have had some clients give to their trustees:

- I do not want my children or grandchildren living off inherited money.
- I feel it is very important to conserve funds for college or other post-high school education.
- I want my children raised with a strong Christian influence.
- I want my children raised with a strong Jewish influence.
- I feel strongly about my child being encouraged to pursue a career in medicine.
- Upon my child's graduation from a 4-year college, I direct my trustee to provide my child with a 3-week fully paid trip to anywhere in the world of his or her choice.

The point is that you can do almost anything you want to within your trust as long as it is not illegal or against public policy. Your estate planning attorney can probably make even more suggestions on how to draft trusts to provide the proper incentives and motivations for your children and grandchildren.

Planning for Minors

Can I leave my business to my minor child?

Generally, minors cannot take title to or convey property. If you name your child as the beneficiary of your estate and you die while your child is still a minor, the trustee of your revocable living trust or personal representative of your will winds up holding the business in trust for the benefit of the minor. All the administration and distribution opportunities discussed in the previous answer apply when considering the terms of the trust to hold your minor child's interest in your business.

⊰ *If I give my business via a trust to my child who is a minor, how long should I leave it in trust?*

There are two considerations to discuss in this situation. First, let's assume you create a revocable living trust today and name your minor child as the beneficiary. You can be the trustee of this trust and control when and how much training, protection, and control you give to your child as he or she ages and matures.

However, you also have to make provision in the trust agreement for the possibility that you will not be there to perform these functions. In this second consideration, you have to tell your successor trustee what to do in your absence. How long do you want to protect the child? As a parent you have a feel for the maturity of your own child. For most parents, the danger is that they turn over control to a child too soon. If you are concerned with erring too strongly to the other side and not turning control over soon enough, you can remedy this by giving more liberal distribution instructions to the trustee and, perhaps, even giving your child some discretion in removing and replacing the trustee as well. It is not uncommon to see a child given increasing amounts of involvement and control as he or she matures. One idea is to make the child a cotrustee and vest voting rights in him or her over time. In any event, the business should remain in trust until the child is mature enough to handle it.

If you are trying to protect your child against a possible divorce or creditors, it is best to leave the business in trust for the life of the child so long as you clearly articulate in the trust the standards under which distributions are to be made to him or her.

chapter 26

Foundation Documents

REVOCABLE LIVING TRUST

⊰ *What are the best options to transfer my business to those of my choosing upon my death?*

Although there are several methods to transfer your business and all your other property at your death to your intended recipients, the two most effective are a will or a revocable living trust.

For most small-business owners, a revocable living trust is the better of the two foundation estate planning documents.

Features

⊰ *Would you identify briefly why I should consider a revocable living trust as a planning tool?*

A *revocable living trust* is a contract between the trust maker (sometimes called a *grantor* or *settlor*) and the trustee who manages the assets in the trust. The trust maker transfers assets to the trustee of the trust. The trust contains the maker's instructions about the management and control of the maker's property while he or she is alive and the distribution of the maker's estate after his or her death. The trustee of the trust must follow all the trust maker's instructions. The individuals who benefit from the revocable living trust are called the *beneficiaries*. You will be the primary beneficiary of your trust while you are living.

You can, and normally should, serve as the initial trustee. You can name others as trustees, either to serve as cotrustees with you now or as successor trustees after you decide you do not want the job anymore or after your death or disability.

A revocable living trust is the central document of a well-coordinated estate plan and offers many technical and practical opportunities. A well-drafted trust is usually no more difficult to follow than a road map is. It can clearly state (often in your own words) your reasoning and purposes for doing things a certain way. The trust is very easy to change as needed, which gives you great flexibility. It gives you an excellent method for organizing your affairs, which affords tremendous value to you and to those who will be following the instructions you leave.

Once you create your revocable living trust, all your assets should be retitled to the name of the trust. When this process is completed, you, as an individual, will no longer technically own any property. Your revocable living trust will be the legal owner, but you will retain complete control of your trust and the assets in it because you will act as the initial trustee and have the ability to remove and replace any other trustees. Additionally, you have complete control because you have retained the right to amend your trust at any time, to take out assets or to add assets at any time, and to completely revoke the trust, if you so desire, for any reason.

᠕ *Can you summarize what a living trust can do?*

AVOIDS LIVING PROBATE: If you become disabled or are unable to manage your financial affairs, your living trust can eliminate the need for a court-appointed guardian or conservator to take control of your assets. This living probate process can be very expensive and time-consuming. If you have transferred all your assets to your living trust, it will control how those assets, including your business, are managed during your incompetency. Your living trust should provide a set of detailed instructions to guide your successor trustee on how to care for you and your family and how your business should be managed during the time of your incapacity.

AVOIDS DEATH PROBATE: Your assets can go directly to your beneficiaries after your death without court interference.

DISTRIBUTES ASSETS: After your death, all property in your living trust is distributed according to your precise written instructions. You can leave assets to your beneficiaries outright on your death or instruct that the assets be held in the trust and distributed over time. You can treat each beneficiary individually by creating a separate trust for him or her with different provisions spelling out the terms of distribution customized for the special needs of each one.

IS EASY TO CREATE AND MAINTAIN: An attorney experienced in living trust planning can easily create a trust document to fit your needs. If you want to change a particular provision because of a change in circumstances, you and your attorney can accomplish this with a simple amendment. If the law changes, your attorney can prepare an amendment to bring your trust up to date.

HAS NO ADVERSE LIFETIME INCOME TAX CONSEQUENCES: Because your living trust is revocable, you report and pay tax on the income generated by the trust assets on your personal income tax returns. This means that your personal income tax situation is exactly the same after you create your living trust as it was before. You have the same income tax exemptions, deductions, credits, and liabilities. You will even continue to file your income tax returns using your Social Security number.

IS VALID IN EVERY STATE: The laws of every state recognize the validity of a living trust. Your living trust can freely cross state lines with you without any need to redraft its terms to comply with local law if you decide to move to another state.

IS DIFFICULT FOR DISSATISFIED HEIRS TO ATTACK: You have probably heard the stories about bitter contests over the validity of a will submitted for probate. A living trust is not part of the public probate process, which invites and encourages disputes. It is also not governed by the archaic and complex rules surrounding a will, and this makes a living trust less prone to attack by dissatisfied heirs.

AVOIDS PROBATE IN MULTIPLE STATES: If you own real estate in multiple states, you can avoid the "ancillary" probate in each state as long as that real estate is titled in the name of your trust.

IS PRIVATE: One of the most important benefits of a revocable living trust to a business owner is the privacy it offers his or her surviving family members: it does not subject the family's business affairs to the public living or death probate process as would a will.

BRINGS PEACE OF MIND: When your living trust is completed, you and your loved ones can relax, knowing you have taken every step to protect them in the event of your disability or death.

⚐ *Does a revocable living trust allow any savings from estate taxes?*

The revocable living trust does not in itself provide any greater savings from estate taxes than can be accomplished with proper will planning. However, a commitment to establishing, funding, and maintaining a living trust makes it far more likely that planning with a revocable living trust will provide maximum tax savings.

If you are married, the trust for you and the trust for your spouse can be designed to automatically establish a family trust (also called a *credit shelter, B,* or *bypass* trust) and a marital trust upon the first death. The family trust functions to preserve the estate tax exemption amount (also called the *applicable exclusion amount*) of the first spouse to die. The surviving spouse and your children can be given the use of the assets in the family trust during the surviving spouse's lifetime without having those assets included in his or her taxable estate upon his or her death. It is important to note that the assets in the family trust may appreciate to an unlimited amount and still not be subject to estate taxes when they are ultimately distributed to your children.

Disability Planning

⨺ *What do you mean by "disability planning"?*

Proper estate planning is not just planning for the disposition of your property at your death. It is also planning for the care of you, your business, and loved ones if you are alive but unable to make decisions due to mental or physical incapacity. For example, when you must be absent from your business for a period of time, you designate a manager in your absence to handle things for you. Just as parents of young children leave a set of instructions for the baby-sitter, you need to leave instructions for your "managers" about what to do under different situations, even down to the names and telephone numbers of whom to call for advice.

A properly drafted revocable living trust is your set of instructions for the disability trustee—the manager or the baby-sitter—to do what you would have done.

⨺ *I'm worried that if I become disabled or die, my family business will be all tied up in court and red tape for a while. If my children can't move quickly to run the business, the interruption could damage it irreparably. What can I do?*

Business owners should create a succession plan for the business in the event of disability or death. If the business is owned by more than one individual, a buy-sell agreement or a shareholder's agreement with the other owner or owners is often an effective means for dealing with disability, especially if it is long-term or permanent. If the business is owned by one individual, perhaps a buy-sell agreement can be established with a key employee. In both instances, part or all of the purchase price may be funded with disability insurance.

For short-term disability a shareholder's agreement can address who will take over the management functions of the disabled owner. If there is only one owner, the owner's revocable living trust will play a key role. The successor trustee should be given the power in the trust agreement to take all actions the owner could have taken to run the business during the owner's disability. For example, if you have transferred ownership of your business—stock or LLC or partnership interests—to your trust, then upon your disability or death, your successor trustee can take all the actions necessary, such as directly managing the business or to selecting others to do so.

Trustees

ᐧᐧ *If for any reason I can't act as trustee of my revocable living trust, who will?*

You will initially act as your own trustee. In your trust document, you will name one or more successor trustees to act in your stead in your absence or incapacity. Naming these individuals is very important. It is through these trustees that you will be able to remain in control of your person and your property and, perhaps, run your business with the instructions you've outlined in your living trust.

ᐧᐧ *Whom should I select as successor trustee to handle my business?*

You will want to select someone who has the knowledge and expertise to run your business or whom you trust to hire someone else to take over the operation of your business. The criteria that make one individual ideal for running your business may not make that person ideal for making decisions regarding the personal affairs of you and your loved ones. You may decide to select several successor cotrustees to cover the personal and the business aspects. However, if you have family members active in your business, they may be ideally suited to handle all the trustee duties.

ᐧᐧ *Are friends and advisors good choices for trustees?*

Friends, colleagues, and advisors are frequently named as successor trustees. However, if they are close personal friends of many of your family members, they may be subject to pressures from family beneficiaries and find it more difficult to make the tough financial decisions. To minimize these concerns, it makes sense that before you name them, you ask them if they will agree to the job. Educate them about living trusts and what yours provides. You should encourage them to ask questions so that they understand what you want.

≜ *Shouldn't our kids be the successor trustees of our living trusts?*

Most clients assume that one or more of their children should be their trustees. This is not always the best choice. You cannot predict the effect their serving alone or together will have on the family unit. It may be an accident waiting to happen. Even with the best intentions, many family members are not suited for or capable of serving in this position. A better choice may be to name your child or children to serve as cotrustees with the individual or institution you select to handle your business interests.

≜ *Should we consider a corporate trustee?*

A corporate trustee is often a good choice as a trustee or a cotrustee. A corporate trustee has experience managing the administration of trusts and investing trust assets. A corporate trustee also has "deep pockets" and thus the financial wherewithal to reimburse the trust for any mistakes it makes.

A corporate trustee, however, may not be a good choice for running your business. If you select a corporate trustee, you may also wish to name a cotrustee who has the expertise to run your business.

FUNDING

Importance of Funding the Trust

≜ *What does "funding a trust" mean?*

Funding a trust is simply the retitling of assets from the individual owner's name to the name of the owner's revocable living trust. For example, John Smith owns his house in his individual name. His lawyer drafts a living trust for John, who signs the trust on July 10, 2001. To fund John's house into his trust, his attorney prepares and records a deed showing the new owner as "John Smith, Trustee, or his successors in trust, under the John Smith Revocable Living Trust dated July 10, 2001, and any amendments thereto."

Be aware that, as simple as this process sounds, estate plans can fail because people do not take the time or hire professionals to fund their trusts.

⚜ *Why is funding a trust so important?*

If nothing is funded to the trust, the trust will contain nothing and have nothing to control. The trust's instructions become virtually worthless—until a court transfers the assets into the trust. If assets are not properly funded into the living trust, upon disability or death of the trust maker, a court-administered guardianship or probate proceeding will be required.

Funding Business Interests

⚜ *My accountant has suggested that I create a revocable living trust and transfer all my assets to it. What should I consider in deciding whether or not to transfer my business interests to my trust?*

TYPE OF ENTITY: The type of entity that you own an interest in is critical because there may be some restrictions on certain types of ownership interests being held by a trust.

TRANSFER RESTRICTIONS: If you determine that your trust may legally hold your ownership interest, you have to determine whether there are any transfer restrictions contained in any agreement, such as a shareholders' agreement or a partnership agreement.

TRUSTEES: Bear in mind that if the trust becomes the owner of the business interest, most likely the trustee of the trust will "vote, manage, and control" the business interest that is in the trust. In addition, you will want to be certain that the trust agreement adequately addresses the management of the business interest and possible disposition of the business in the event of your disability or death.

RETIREMENT PLANS: Another consideration is the impact that this transfer may have on an owner-employee pension or profit-sharing plan, or another qualified plan, interest. While the business ownership interest and the pension, profit-sharing, or other qualified plan interest may be mutually independent of one another, this issue should be assessed.

OTHER DISPOSITION: You and your advisors should consider your overall estate planning goals and other techniques that you may use to reduce estate taxes. You may transfer your ownership interests to another type of trust agreement instead of the living trust.

Do I lose control by transferring my business to a living trust?

No. If you are the trustee of the living trust, you are entitled to make all decisions as to the assets in the trust. Any business interest in the trust is managed by you, the trustee.

Can I transfer my sole proprietorship to my living trust?

Yes. However, since you own all the business assets in your individual name, it is necessary to transfer each business asset individually to your living trust just as you would any other property.

Can I transfer my limited partnership interest at my death to my children by using a living trust?

You must review the limited partnership agreement to make sure that this type of transfer is permissible. Generally, all transfers of limited partnership interests require the approval of the general partner. The general partner, however, should have no problem allowing you to engage in sound estate planning and transfer your partnership interest into your living trust. The general partner has no desire to have your interest tied up in a guardianship or probate proceeding any more than you do.

Once the partnership interest is titled in the name of your living trust, the terms of the trust can leave the partnership to your children upon your death, either keeping it in trust for their benefit or transferring it to them outright.

Can I transfer my limited liability company to my living trust?

You need to review the LLC operating agreement to make sure that this type of transfer is possible. If there is no provision for such a transfer or it is prohibited, the operating agreement can be amended to permit the transfer. Usually the consent of the other members or of the member manager is required for all transfers. Some forward-thinking agreements freely permit transfers to an owner's living trust without requiring approval by the members.

Assets Requiring Special Attention

❧ I am the sole shareholder of a minority-owned business. If I transfer my shares into my revocable living trust, my company will lose its minority-owned business status. What should I do?

Many states allow you to own assets with a *transfer-on-death (TOD)* or *payable-on-death (POD)* designation. If your state has adopted either of these, you can designate that upon your death a named beneficiary becomes the sole owner. In many states you can use the TOD or POD designation to name your living trust as the beneficiary at your death. This allows you to maintain the minority-owned business status until your death and still keeps it out of probate even though you couldn't fund it to the trust during your lifetime.

Corporate stock

❧ Can I transfer shares of a closely held business for which the stock certificates are subject to transfer restrictions?

Closely held stock often presents special challenges when funding a revocable living trust. Certain types of closely held stock may be subject to various state statutes or shareholders' agreements which restrict the stock's transferability. Any transfer in contradiction to an underlying agreement or in violation of state statute may create unintended consequences. Because revocable living trusts are now the standard for good estate planning, shareholders' agreements often allow transfers to the owner's revocable living trust. If your agreement doesn't permit such a transfer, consider having a shareholders' meeting to discuss the benefits to all shareholders of amending the agreement to allow such transfers.

✺ Can my living trust own my subchapter S stock?

Yes. During your lifetime, your revocable living trust can own your S corporation stock because a revocable living trust is a permissible S corporation shareholder. Your trust will continue to qualify as an eligible S corporation shareholder for 2 years following your death. Your estate planning attorney can also draft the trust in a manner that will allow the trust to be an eligible S corporation shareholder after the 2-year period. As we have discussed throughout this book, it is important to select a knowledgeable estate planning attorney to draft your trust to meet your specific needs, including special drafting if you own stock in an S corporation.

✺ Can I transfer my stock in my professional corporation to my revocable living trust?

The problem with transferring stock in a professional corporation to a revocable living trust is the potential for a trustee not licensed in the profession to gain control of the corporation. Therefore, in some states the transfer of professional corporate stock to a revocable living trust is prohibited. On the other hand, when a professional dies without a revocable living trust, his or her estate will be administered through the probate process. The executor, who is unlikely to hold a professional license, will have authority under the state's probate code to operate the business until it is sold, which is usually within 6 months.

It seems contradictory that an executor who is not a licensed professional can operate a professional business but a trustee cannot. There is a movement to allow the transfer of professional stock to a revocable living trust so long as there are appropriate restrictions placed upon a trustee who is not a licensed professional, such as the business will be sold within 6 months and the services will be provided only by licensed professionals. Consult your attorney regarding the recommended treatment of the stock of your professional corporation in your state.

Retirement plans

⅍ *Should I fund my qualified retirement plan into my trust?*

No. The ownership of qualified retirement plans, IRAs, and most annuities may not be titled in the name of a trust. If you were to transfer the ownership of your IRA or other qualified plan into the name of your living trust, the transfer would be classified as a distribution. As such, it would be completely taxable in the year you made the transfer and would create negative income tax consequences.

However, for many business owners, qualified plans, IRAs, and annuities are a significant asset in their estate and should not be ignored. It is very important to consult a trusted advisor on coordinating such assets within your estate plan, so that estate tax and the income tax savings are optimized upon your death. Expert assistance is highly recommended in this area.

⅍ *Whom should I name as the primary and contingent beneficiaries of my qualified retirement plan or IRA?*

You can name primary and contingent beneficiaries of qualified retirement plans and IRAs so that the proceeds avoid probate and pass directly to the named beneficiary by operation of law. However, determining the beneficiary of your qualified plans has personal planning implications as well as tax implications, and you must consider these within your overall estate planning goals and objectives. Once again, ask your estate planning advisors for specific guidance in your particular situation.

ANCILLARY DOCUMENTS

⅍ *What other documents should accompany my living trust for me to have a complete estate plan?*

At a bare minimum you should have (1) a pour-over will and (2) health care documents including a living will, health care power of attorney, and durable power of attorney, which are very important in protecting your assets in the event of disability.

⚖ *Why do I need a will if I have a revocable living trust?*

A simple pour-over will must be prepared along with your living trust. The purpose of the pour-over will is to allow your personal representative to "pour over" to your living trust those assets which may not have been transferred to your trust during your lifetime. If you do not have a pour-over will, those assets will pass by the laws of *intestacy,* which are state laws that determine who receives the property of people who die without a will. A pour-over will allows you to control this property. If you have minor children, you can name guardians for them only in a will.

⚖ *What is a living will?*

A *living will* is a document that contains instructions about the continuation or withholding of life-sustaining medical treatment if you are terminally ill or in a permanent vegetative state. Your feelings about how you should be treated under these circumstances become important when you are incapable of making these medical decisions for yourself. The exact form and content of a living will are regulated by state law and vary significantly from state to state.

⚖ *What is a health care proxy?*

A *health care proxy,* or a *health care power of attorney*, is more broad than a living will in that in it you name a close relative or friend to make health care decisions for you if you are not mentally or physically able to make those decisions. These health care decisions include long-term care, surgery, or other medical procedures. A health care proxy is much like a financial power of attorney except it is limited to health care issues. Health care proxies are also regulated by state law and vary from state to state.

⚖ *Why do I need a durable power of attorney?*

Powers of attorney are documents that name an agent (or attorney-in-fact) to make decisions and act on behalf of the grantor of the power. A regular power of attorney will become invalid (when it may be needed most) on the incapacity of the grantor—unless it is "durable." *Durable powers of attorney* are very important because they remain valid even when you become disabled, and they continue to be valid until you revoke them or until your death. Powers of attorney may be general and cover all decisions, or they may be limited and cover only specific actions. A power of attorney may also become effective at one of two different times, depending on the terms of the agreement: immediately (an immediate power of attorney) or upon incapacity (a springing power of attorney). Estate plans centered around a revocable living trust also include a general durable power of attorney to provide the agent with the ability, upon the incapacity of the trust maker, to transfer assets to the revocable living trust that may not have been titled in the name of the trust.

ESTATE PLAN REVIEW

When should I consider reviewing or revising my estate plan?

Once you have set up a comprehensive estate plan and have fully funded your revocable living trust, you should review or revise your estate plan after any of the following occurrences:

- Deaths: Spouse, child, other beneficiary, guardian, executor, and so forth
- Births: Child or grandchild
- Marriages: Yours, a child's, or other beneficiaries'
- Divorces: Yours, a child's, or other beneficiaries'
- Changes in estate value
- Changes in tax laws
- Changes in your goals and objectives

chapter 27

Taxes,
Deductions,
and Payments

TAXES

⚘ *What is the federal estate tax?*

The *federal estate tax* is a tax on the value of all assets owned by a person at the time of death. The *federal gift tax* is a tax on the value of gifts made during a person's lifetime. The federal estate tax and gift tax make up a "unified estate and gift tax system." The tax rate is the same whether the transfer of property is made during life or at death.

⚘ *What are the estate and gift tax rates?*

The estate and gift tax rates for the period before passage of the 2001 tax act are shown in Table 27-1. Starting in 2002, the tax rates will change each year as the maximum rate drops (Table 27-2). For 2010, the estate tax is repealed, but the gift tax remains with a top rate of 35 percent. Under current law the federal estate tax will return in 2011, using the brackets shown in Table 27-1.

TABLE 27-1   Unified Federal Estate and Gift Tax Rates before the 2001 Tax Act

If value of taxable estate is		The tax is	Of the amount over
Over	But not over		
–	$ 10,000	18% of amount	
$ 10,001	20,000	$1,800 + 20%	$10,000
20,001	40,000	$3,800 + 22%	$20,000
40,001	60,000	$8,200 + 24%	$40,000
60,001	80,000	$13,000 + 26%	$60,000
80,001	100,000	$18,200 + 28%	$80,000
100,001	150,000	$23,800 + 30%	$100,000
150,001	250,000	$38,800 + 32%	$150,000
250,001	500,000	$70,800 + 34%	$250,000
500,001	750,000	$155,800 + 37%	$500,000
750,001	1,000,000	$248,300 + 39%	$750,000
1,000,001	1,250,000	$345,800 + 41%	$1,000,000
1,250,001	1,500,000	$448,300 + 43%	$1,250,000
1,500,001	2,000,000	$555,800 + 45%	$1,500,000
2,000,001	2,500,000	$780,800 + 49%	$2,000,000
2,500,001	3,000,000	$1,025,800 + 53%	$2,500,000
3,000,000*		$1,290,800 + 55%	$3,000,000

Note: These rates will be in effect again when the 2001 tax act ends in 2011.

*For estates between $10 million and $17,184,000, the benefit of the graduated rates is phased out, resulting in an additional 5 percent tax on the estate.

⚄ *What is the generation-skipping transfer tax, and why should I care about it?*

In the past, wealthy individuals could often avoid paying more than one estate or transfer tax when transferring property from generation to generation by placing the property in special trusts for the benefit of their children, grandchildren, and more remote descendants. The transfer tax was imposed only on the initial transfer into the trust. To eliminate this opportunity, in 1986 Congress enacted the present version of the federal *generation-skipping transfer (GST)*

TABLE 27-2   Top Federal Estate and Gift Tax Rates under the 2001 Tax Act

Year	Rate, in %
2002	50
2003	49
2004	48
2005	47
2006	46
2007	45
2008	45
2009	45

tax. Any property which escapes the gift or estate tax at any given generational transfer may be subject to the GST tax, which is imposed on the transferred property at the top rate in effect that year for estate taxes. This tax is in *addition to* all other estate or gift taxes imposed on the transfer. Under the 2001 tax act, the GST tax is scheduled to go away in 2010, only to return in 2011 at a flat rate of 55 percent.

⚜ *What is a step-up in basis, and why is it important in estate planning?*

The *basis* is the value of an asset for income and capital gain tax purposes and, generally, is the amount the owner paid for the asset. The basis is the starting value from which a gain or loss can be computed upon the sale or exchange of the asset. For example, let's assume you own an asset that you purchased some years ago for $10,000 (your cost basis) and that is now worth $50,000. If you sell the asset today, you have a capital gain of $40,000, on which you would owe income tax.

   Suppose you give this asset to your daughter. Since you are still alive when you make the gift, your daughter "steps" into your shoes, takes your cost basis ($10,000) as her cost basis, and has the same taxable gain ($40,000) if she sells the asset today.

Now let's assume instead that you die and leave the asset to your daughter today. Her cost basis in the asset is stepped up to $50,000, the market price as of your date of death. If she were to sell the asset today, your daughter would owe no income taxes. If she sells it later, she will owe income taxes only on the gain above the $50,000 stepped-up value.

The 2001 tax act eliminates step-up in basis in 2010 when the estate tax is repealed. As we discussed in Chapter 1, this poses a new complication in estate planning, particularly for small-business owners who have buy-sell agreements. We present a planning option for this situation in Chapter 28.

CREDITS AND DEDUCTIONS

⤴ *Are there any exemptions for the gift tax?*

Yes, there are two gift tax exemptions:

1. The 2001 tax act created a $1 million lifetime *gift tax credit* for every individual to make gifts during his or her lifetime.
2. There is an *annual exclusion* of $10,000 (indexed for inflation) per person per year for gifts made during the gift maker's life.

⤴ *How does the annual exclusion work?*

You can give the annual exclusion amount to as many different individuals as you desire. For example, if you have a son who is married and has four children, you could give $60,000 in annual exclusion gifts in any year ($10,000 to your son, $10,000 to your daughter-in-law, and $10,000 to each of the four grandchildren). If you are married, your spouse could do the same as well, making a total of $120,000 in gifts from both of you in a given year. As you can see from this example, large amounts can be removed from your estate without using any of your lifetime gift tax credit or paying any gift taxes.

⚖ *Can I give away part of my business each year to my children by using annual exclusion gifts?*

Yes, you can. Even if you decide not to transfer your entire business in one transfer to your children during your lifetime as part of a succession plan, you can still take advantage of reducing your estate by making annual exclusion gifts of interests in your business to your children. If you and your wife jointly make these gifts, you can transfer substantial amounts over time as illustrated in the previous answer. One burdensome aspect of giving small interests in your business every year is the need to have an appraisal done each year to accurately value the interests you give away. We discuss valuation issues and giving your business to children and other family members in more detail in Part Five.

⚖ *What is the estate tax exemption, and how does this work with the new gift tax credit?*

The estate tax exemption is the dollar amount that an individual can transfer at death free of estate taxes. If the total taxable estate is less than or equal to the estate tax exemption, no federal estate tax is due.

Even though the estate tax exemption and the gift tax credit are delineated in the 2001 tax act as two separate exemptions, they are applied in a unified manner. For example, in 2006, the estate tax exemption is $2 million and the gift tax credit is $1 million. If you give your business valued at $1 million to your children in 2006 and then die in 2006, the estate tax exemption of $2 million is reduced by the $1 million gift tax credit, leaving only a $1 million estate tax exemption to pass other assets to your family. If you didn't make any lifetime gifts and died in 2006, you would not have $3 million to use as an estate tax exemption; you would have only the $2 million estate tax exemption.

The gift tax credit is constant at $1 million through 2010, and the estate tax exemption starts at $1 million in 2002 and increases as shown in Table 27-3 until the estate tax is repealed in 2010. Under the current law, it is important to understand that you can transfer $1 million gift tax–free during your life and then pass the *difference* between $1 million and the amount of the estate tax exemption at death. If you plan to give away $1 million during your lifetime, this difference is what you have available to pass other assets tax-free at death to your heirs between now and December 31, 2009. When the estate tax is repealed in 2010, you still have the $1 million gift tax credit available. When the federal estate tax returns in 2011, the estate tax exemption amount will drop back to $1 million.

With proper planning, a married couple is able to shield two full estate tax exemption amounts from taxation no matter which year it is. We discuss this in more detail in Chapter 28.

◢ *I understand that there is no estate tax no matter how large my estate if I leave everything to my spouse. Is this true?*

This is called the *unlimited marital deduction*. The law allows an individual to leave an unlimited value of assets to his or her spouse free of estate tax, as long as the surviving spouse is a U.S. citizen. The theory is that the marital deduction is just a postponement of the estate tax event until the second spouse dies. If the surviving spouse is not a U.S. citizen, this unlimited marital deduction is not available unless a special trust is established for the assets passing to the surviving spouse.

◢ *Are there any exemptions for the generation-skipping transfer tax?*

There is a very important GST tax exemption. The GST exemption allows every individual to shelter up to $1,060,000 (indexed annually for inflation) of his or her estate from the GST tax at each generation. From 2004 through 2009, the GST exemption will equal the estate tax exemption amount in effect for the year in question (see Table 27-3). This is a marvelous and little-understood opportunity to preserve assets for multiple generations.

◢ *What are estate tax charitable deductions?*

The taxable estate may be reduced by the value of any transfer to or for the use of any organization which meets specific requirements

**TABLE 27-3   Schedule of
the Estate Tax Exemption Amounts**

Year	Amount
2002–2003	$1,000,000
2004–2005	$1,500,000
2006–2008	$2,000,000
2009	$3,500,000
2010	Estate tax repeal
2011	$1,000,000*

*The 2001 tax act ends.

and which is organized and operated exclusively for religious, charitable, scientific, literary, or educational purposes. The amount of the allowable charitable deduction may not exceed the value of the property. Planning with inter vivos (lifetime) charitable lead trusts and charitable remainder trusts to obtain charitable tax deductions is discussed in Part Five.

Estate tax charitable deductions are also available for the charitable portion of any charitable lead trust or charitable remainder trust established at your death (i.e., testamentary trusts).

⚜ *Are there any exemptions available for the new carryover basis beginning in 2010?*

As we explained in Chapter 1, beginning in 2010, the previous step-up-in-basis system is replaced with a carryover-basis system which dictates that the beneficiary take the asset with the same basis as the decedent had prior to his or her death. The 2001 tax act provides that, beginning in 2010, a decedent's administrator can increase by $1.3 million the basis of property owned by a decedent at his or her death. Also, property left to a surviving spouse that is qualified spousal property is entitled to an additional $3 million increase in basis. *Qualified spousal property* is defined as property passing outright to a spouse and any property passing in trust that would have qualified for the marital deduction (e.g., property in a qualified terminable interest property marital trust).

BREAKS FOR
SMALL BUSINESSES

What estate tax breaks are available to business owners?

Over the years, Congress has enacted several pieces of legislation in an attempt to reduce the estate tax burden and to allow greater opportunity for a small business to survive an owner's death. Here are some examples of Congress' lessening of the tax bite for family business owners:

- Alternatives to valuing real property for purposes of calculating estate taxes (i.e., special-use valuation)
- A deduction from an individual's gross estate whenever an interest in a qualified family-owned business is included in the estate
- Certain changes that benefit owners of corporations
- Installment option for the payment of estate taxes

Special-Use Valuation

What is "special-use valuation"?

Typically, in determining the fair market value of real property for estate tax purposes, value is based on the property's "highest and best use." *Special-use valuation* is intended to provide an alternative when the property is actually being used for farming, ranching, or other small-business purposes which may not have been the property's highest and best use. The goal is to value the property based on its actual use, which most often will produce a lower value and thereby provide a means by which the decedent's family may avoid a forced sale of real estate in order to pay estate taxes.

The market value reduction available with a special-use valuation was, however, limited to $800,000 in 2001 (but is indexed annually for inflation).

For example, a 500-acre farm located several miles from a popular ski area may have a value of $500 per acre for agricultural purposes ($250,000) but a value of $3000 per acre if valued for its highest and best use—in this case, development of condominiums for sale and lease to skiers ($1.5 million). If the decedent's estate consisted mostly of this real property used in farming but was valued at $1.5 million, the surviving family members would probably have no option but to liquidate the property to pay the estate taxes. Application of the special-use valuation would permit a reduction of the real property's value by $800,000 and, perhaps, allow the family to continue the farming operation.

⚄ Without all the technicalities, can you describe the general requirements of the special-use valuation?

The major Internal Revenue Code requirements for the real property to qualify for special-use valuation are:

- The decedent must have been a U.S. citizen or resident.
- The net value of the property in question (real and personal) must equal at least 50 percent of the gross estate.
- The real property portion must be at least 25 percent of the gross estate.
- The real property must have been *owned* by the decedent (or family member) for 5 of the last 8 years prior to the decedent's death.
- The decedent or a member of the decedent's family must have materially participated in the operation of the farm or business for at least 5 of the last 8 years prior to the decedent's death.
- The property must pass to a qualified heir, that is, someone who is a parent, spouse, ancestor, or lineal descendant of the decedent's spouse or parent.
- Special-use valuation must be elected on the original estate tax return even if filed late.
- The special-use valuation is irrevocable.

⅍ *Does the special-use valuation apply if the real property is owned or leased by the family corporation or partnership?*

Special-use valuation for a decedent's estate is available to property owned by a corporation or partnership (or an LLC taxed as a corporation or partnership) only if either (1) there are fifteen or fewer partners or shareholders or (2) the decedent's gross estate holds at least 20 percent of the capital interest in the partnership or corporate voting stock.

The amount of the partnership or corporate real estate and personal property (qualifying for the use valuation) which can be used by the estate to satisfy the 50 percent and 25 percent requirements in the previous answer is determined by multiplying the qualifying property's respective values by the decedent's business interest percentage. For example, if the decedent owns 50 percent of the corporation that owns the real estate, this satisfies the requirement that the estate hold at least 20 percent of the capital interest. If the real estate owned by the corporation is valued at $1 million and the estate is $2 million, then 50 percent of $1 million is $500,000, or 25 percent of the gross estate, which satisfies the requirement of the real property portion.

a   What do you mean by "material participation"?

Material participation is defined as active employment on a substantially full-time basis: 35 or more hours per week or fewer hours if sufficient to personally and fully manage the business. While no single factor determines whether a family member is materially participating in the business, physical activity and participation in management are the principal factors. The IRS will find material participation if the individual performed activities which indicate, overall, that he or she was significantly involved in the business. There is generally an emphasis on periodic inspections and active consultations in which management decisions are relied on to establish material participation, and sole reliance on truly fundamental decision making generally will not, of itself, meet the standard.

Even if day-to-day operations of the business are performed by nonfamily employees or agents, material participation can be established if a qualified heir meets one of several tests allowed by the IRS. Also, if the qualified heir is the surviving spouse or a full-time student or is under age 21, the IRS imposes an active-management standard that requires less involvement than material participation. *Active management* means making the management decisions of a business (other than the daily operating decisions).

⚜ *Are there any restrictions on the use of the property after my death?*

Beginning any time within a 2-year grace period of the decedent's death, the real property must be devoted to the special-use business with a qualified heir's material participation in managing the property, and this must continue for 10 years. If it is not devoted to the special use or if the property is disposed to someone other than another qualified heir within those 10 years, the qualified heir and all other persons who have an interest in the property are subject to personal liability for a recapture tax. This tax is essentially equal to the estate tax difference between the fair market value and the special-use value. The recapture tax is due within 6 months of the event triggering the recapture and may trigger an additional state tax as well.

Every individual who has an interest or who may reasonably obtain such an interest in the real property during the recapture period must consent to the terms of the election and sign an agreement, which is filed as an attachment to the estate tax return.

⚜ *With all the compliance involved, should my heirs make the special-use election?*

As you may have gathered from the previous answers, it may be difficult to initially qualify for the special-use valuation, and qualification requires constant monitoring by the estate planning attorney or accountant. If the family ceases to use the premises for qualified purposes or ceases to materially participate in the use of the property, the initial estate tax savings are lost. However, as long as the family is willing to deal with the estate tax recapture uncertainties, this provision can save a substantial amount of estate tax. It is critical that the family and the team of advisors thoroughly discuss the pros and cons before making this election.

Qualified Family-Owned Business

⚜ *Are there any special estate tax credits for family-owned businesses?*

Families of decedents who owned and operated family businesses may take advantage of an exclusion called the *qualified family-owned business interest* (QFOBI) deduction. The maximum QFOBI deduction is $675,000, but the deduction will no longer be available after 2003.

⚜ *What is a qualified family-owned business interest?*

An interest in a family-owned business is qualified if the business meets any of the following three conditions:

1. The business is a sole proprietorship (100 percent ownership).
2. The decedent and members of the decedent's family own 50 percent of the business.
3. The members of two families own 70 percent or the members of three families own 90 percent of the business. (Under the 70 and 90 percent rules, at least 30 percent of the interest must be owned by the decedent and members of the decedent's family.)

⚜ *What's the difference between the qualified family-owned business interest deduction and the special-use valuation?*

Special-use valuation reduces the value of only the real property in an estate. The QFOBI deduction applies to any type of qualifying assets in an estate. The legislation establishing the QFOBI deduction was passed several years after the legislation for special-use valuation, and as a result, many provisions of the QFOBI deduction refer to the rules for special-use valuation. However, even though the qualifying criteria are very similar, they are not identical.

Of special note is that the two tax provisions can be used in conjunction with each other, and if real property is valued for estate tax purposes using the special-use valuation, that valuation is used to determine qualification for the QFOBI deduction.

How do the QFOBI deduction and the estate tax exemption amount work together?

The two exemptions combined cannot exceed $1.3 million. The executor may elect to deduct the maximum QFOBI deduction of $675,000 in any given year, and an estate tax exemption amount may also be claimed but only up to $625,000—unless the QFOBI deduction is less than $675,000.

For example, in 2002, John dies while owning a business that qualifies for the QFOBI deduction. If the business is valued at $700,000 and his total estate is $1.4 million, the QFOBI deduction is $675,000 and the estate tax exemption amount is $625,000.

Provisions for Corporations

Are there any special options available for corporations?

Yes. Section 303 of the Internal Revenue Code permits a corporation to redeem from a deceased shareholder's estate an amount of stock equal in value to the deceased owner's funeral expenses, administration costs, and death taxes. In essence, it provides an infusion of cash into the estate to pay these expenses.

For a Section 303 redemption to work, the value of all the stock owned by the deceased shareholder in the corporation must exceed 35 percent of the decedent's adjusted gross estate. The benefit of meeting the Section 303 requirements is that the redemption will be income tax–free to the estate because it is treated as a sale of stock rather than a taxable dividend to the estate.

Practically speaking, however, liquidity in the business is still a key factor in determining whether the stock can be repurchased.

≤\ I suppose that capital gain taxes apply on the sale of the stock?

Since the stock is part of the shareholder's estate, the deceased shareholder's basis will be stepped up to its date-of-death value. There will be capital gain on any amount by which the stock's purchase price exceeds its date-of-death value.

Installment Payments of Federal Estate Tax

≤\ My estate consists largely of my interest in a closely held business. Are there any breaks that let families of small-business owners pay taxes over a period of time instead of being forced to pay them in full within 9 months?

Yes, there is some relief. The estate taxes may be paid over a 14-year period as long as the estate meets the qualification requirements. Internal Revenue Code Section 6166 was enacted to prevent the hardship that results when surviving family members are forced to sell a family business to pay estate taxes.

≤\ How do we know whether we qualify for this special treatment?

In order to qualify for Section 6166 treatment, the following conditions must be met:

- The decedent must have been a U.S. citizen or resident at his or her death.
- The decedent's business must be a sole proprietorship or an

interest in a partnership, LLC, or corporation that meets various ownership requirements of a closely held business.

- The business must be an active trade or business.
- The value of the ownership interest must be more than 35 percent of the decedent's adjusted gross estate.

✍ *You said that it has to be a closely held business interest. How does the Internal Revenue Service define "closely held business interest"?*

The following are *closely held business interests* for Section 6166:

- An interest as a sole proprietor in a proprietorship carrying on a trade or business
- An interest as a partner in a partnership carrying on a trade or business if (1) the partnership has forty-five or fewer partners or (2) the deceased partner owned at least 20 percent of the partnership
- Stock in a corporation carrying on a trade or business if (1) the corporation has forty-five or fewer shareholders or (2) the deceased shareholder owned at least 20 percent of the voting stock of the corporation

As a result of the above requirements, any interest in a sole proprietorship will qualify as a closely held business interest as long as it carries on a trade or business.

Even if a business has more than forty-five partners or owners, it may still qualify as a closely held business interest. For example, an interest owned jointly by a husband and wife is generally considered to be owned by one owner. So even though forty-five married couples owning stock as joint tenants represent ninety people owning stock, the business still qualifies as being owned by forty-five people.

Also, stock and partnership interests owned by the decedent's brothers, sisters, spouse, ancestors, or lineal descendants are deemed to be owned by the decedent. This rule conceivably would allow a corporation owned by a hundred people to qualify—although the value of the ownership interest included in the decedent's estate must still exceed 35 percent of the adjusted gross estate and the deceased shareholder must have owned at least 20 percent of the corporation.

⚜ Can an estate qualify for a special-use valuation and pay the taxes under the installment method?

It is possible to take advantage of the special-use valuation and elect to pay the tax in installments. The estate must qualify separately for each election, and the elections must meet their respective deadlines. The special-use valuation can be elected on the original estate tax return, even if it is filed late, whereas the installment election must be made on a timely filed estate tax return. Also, any recapture taxes that become due upon revocation of a special-use valuation are not eligible for payment by installment.

⚜ Can farm property qualify for Section 6166 installment payments?

The key issue is whether the decedent's activities satisfy the trade or business requirement. If the decedent was actively involved in the farming operation, the farm will qualify. For example, the IRS held in one instance that a decedent was engaged in farming because his income was based on farm production rather than on a fixed rental and he participated in important farming decisions. The IRS held in another instance that a decedent was not engaged in farming because he was a 96-year-old who leased his land and gave away his livestock to his children.

⚜ What interest rate is charged on the deferred tax?

The main reason Section 6166 is so attractive is the reduced interest rates available. In 2001, the first $1,060,000 of taxable value (adjusted annually for inflation) of a closely held business was eligible for a 2 percent interest rate. The interest rate for the estate tax attributable to the value of a business which exceeds that amount is 45 percent of the rate which the IRS charges for underpayment of tax.

⅍ *Is the interest paid under Section 6166 tax-deductible?*

Unfortunately, neither your estate nor your heirs are entitled to deduct the interest paid under Section 6166.

⅍ *Assuming my estate qualifies for installment payments, can the election be terminated by the IRS?*

Yes, the election can be terminated by the IRS for a number of reasons. This is why the election must be made and closely watched by an estate planning professional. The occurrence of any of the following gives the IRS the authority to revoke a Section 6166 election:

- If 50 percent or more of the value of the closely held business interest is disposed of
- If a withdrawal of money or other property totaling 50 percent or more of the value of the closely held business interest is made
- If the estate misses an interest or principal payment by more than 6 months
- If the estate has undistributed net income for any year in which a Section 6166 principal payment is due and does not use that income to reduce the balance of the unpaid installments

PAYMENTS

⅍ *How much time after my death does my family have to pay my federal estate tax?*

The federal estate tax return, Form 706, must be filed within 9 months of a decedent's death. The tax is due with the return. The Internal Revenue Code imposes a penalty for each month of delinquency, unless the person responsible for filing the return can show that the delay was due to reasonable cause. Upon a showing of good cause, an extension, usually limited to 6 months, can be obtained for filing the return. If the estate tax is not paid in full within 9 months of death, interest occurs on the outstanding balance until paid.

≱ *Most of the value of my estate is in my business. How will my estate come up with the cash to pay the taxes?*

This is a challenge many owners of closely held businesses face. Options include selling, using cash on hand, and borrowing.

Sell: The family may have to sell the business or its assets. However, any forced sale generally results in receipt of a lower value.

Use cash on hand in the business: Even if there is that much cash inside the business, using it for estate taxes may hurt the company's cash flow at the worst time, the loss of the owner. Once again, distribution of the cash from the corporation to the estate may create taxable income to the estate.

Borrow funds: If a loan can be arranged by the company, the interest rates will most likely be higher than normal, due to the uncertainty of the future success of the business with the owner out of the picture. Also, if a distribution of the cash is made to the estate, and not as a loan to the estate, the loan *must* be repaid with profits from the business.

≱ *Is there any way to plan in advance for the money my family will need to pay the estate tax?*

Often the only viable solution is the purchase of life insurance on the business owner. If you feel your family will be faced with a terrible financial loss at your death, you can use life insurance to provide liquidity. By your structuring the ownership of life insurance through an irrevocable trust, the life insurance supplies liquidity to your estate without being included in your estate for estate tax purposes. For details on planning with irrevocable life insurance trusts, see Chapter 28.

chapter 28

Techniques
to Reduce Taxes

⚐ *If the federal estate tax is going to be repealed, why do I need any
techniques?*

As this book goes to press, there is still a federal estate and gift tax until 2009, and the federal estate tax will be repealed only for 1 year:
2010. The following year it returns exactly as it was in 2001 before
President Bush signed the 2001 tax act. Unless Congress makes the
estate tax repeal permanent, you cannot afford to ignore planning.
You must assume that there will be an estate tax of some sort when
you die. For purposes of this chapter, we assume that a federal estate
tax will exist when we die, we assume that there is a gift tax on lifetime gifts, we assume that there will be no step-up in basis on the assets we leave to our heirs, and we advise you to make the same assumptions. There are few, if any, downsides to planning now, and
doing so greatly increases the chances that your children will receive
the maximum inheritance possible at your death, whenever that
might occur and under whatever law is in existence at the time.

MAXIMIZING DEDUCTIONS
AND CREDITS

Marital Deduction
and Estate Tax Exemption

If I can transfer an unlimited amount to my husband, why should I be concerned about planning? Couldn't I just transfer the business to him on my death?

Very often the first-to-die spouse leaves everything to the surviving spouse, taking full advantage of the unlimited marital deduction. However, this type of planning can create an estate tax trap for the family. Leaving all the property to a spouse wastes the deceased spouse's available estate tax exemption amount. As a result, a couple will have only one estate tax exemption to use when the surviving spouse subsequently dies and the property goes to their children, causing additional, unnecessary estate tax at that time.

Let's look at what happens to John and Jane, who don't plan to use both their estate tax exemptions. John and Jane are married with two children. They own assets with a combined value of $1.4 million. Either spouse dies in 2002 or 2003, and for simplicity, we will assume the second spouse also dies in the same year and that the estate value remains the same. Figure 28-1 shows the effect of estate taxes on their children as a result of no planning, that is, the first to die leaving all assets outright to the survivor. The survivor can pass on only his or her estate tax exemption amount tax-free, and the estate tax exemption of the first spouse to die is wasted.

How do I make certain I am taking advantage of the estate tax exemption to save on federal estate taxes?

If you are single, you will automatically be able to preserve the estate tax exemption amount, regardless of the estate plan you adopt.

In Figure 28-2, we've shown the effects on John and Jane's estate when they accomplished proper planning. Upon the death of the first to die, their will or living trust establishes a *marital trust* and a *family trust* (sometimes called a *credit shelter, B,* or *bypass trust*). The purpose of the family trust is to shelter the decedent's estate tax exemption amount while allowing the surviving spouse to receive economic benefits of the decedent's assets during the survivor's lifetime. The family trust holds the estate tax exemption of the first spouse to die. As a result, that amount is sheltered from tax not only at that spouse's death but also at the surviving spouse's subsequent death because that amount is *not* included in that spouse's estate. When the second spouse dies, his or her estate tax exemption can be applied against entirely different assets. As you can readily see in Figure 28-2, with John and Jane planning properly for the estate tax exemptions, they were able to pass the entire $1.4 million estate tax–free to their children.

⨎ *Since the estate tax exemption amount changes, how can I be sure that we will use all of it?*

It is common for attorneys to draft wills and living trusts with language, technically known as a *formula clause*, that will automatically compensate for any increases in the estate tax exemption or any decreases that are a result of prior taxable gifts you made. These clauses tend to be rather complex because the attorney needs to take into account a number of factors to maximize the overall planning benefits to you and your family. If your goal is to take maximum advantage of the estate tax exemption, the formula clause says "to transfer to the family trust the maximum amount of my assets that can be transferred without creating an estate tax. The balance of my assets is to be transferred to my marital trust."

As long as the amount of your assets equals or exceeds the estate tax exemption amount at the date of your death, the formula clause will ensure full use of your available estate tax exemption.

⨎ *I am marrying for the second time, and I would like to protect my children from my first marriage. Can I make sure that my children and my new wife are provided for after my death yet still maximize the marital deduction and estate tax exemption?*

Yes. You can still create marital and family trusts to use the marital deduction and your estate tax exemption amount. The difference is

Either John or Jane dies in 2002 or 2003

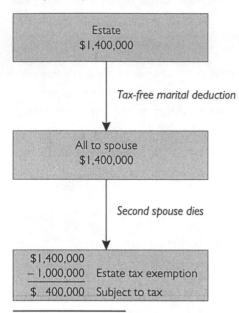

Figure 28-1   Effects of not planning.

that you will include special provisions in these trusts to achieve your other goals. You will use a special type of marital trust called a *qualified terminable interest property (QTIP) trust* that will provide income to your new wife for her lifetime.

A QTIP provision drafted into a revocable living trust or a will can be very useful in your situation since you would like to ensure the welfare of your wife if she survives you but you want to control who will ultimately receive the property upon her death. The QTIP provisions ensure that the remaining marital trust assets will go to the children of your first marriage. In addition, depending on your situation and whether you are trying to preserve as much of the family trust for the benefit of your children as you can, you would instruct the family trust trustee to use those funds only for your children and not for the benefit of your wife.

Either John or Jane dies in 2002 or 2003

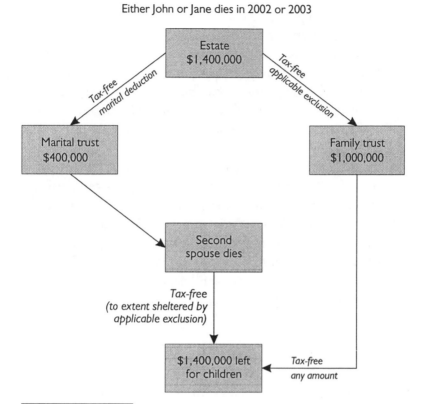

Figure 28-2 Effects of planning.

Generation-Skipping Transfer Tax Exemption

🖎 *What is the technique to deliver exempt property to generation after generation while avoiding the generation-skipping transfer tax?*

Within your revocable living trust you can establish a trust that benefits your grandchildren or your children and grandchildren. This trust is funded at your death with property, to which your trustee is directed to apply all or a portion of your generation-skipping transfer (GST) tax exemption. You and your spouse can each establish a GST trust in your revocable living trusts to maximize the amounts that will be exempt from GST tax. Once exempted, property transferred to this trust, including all appreciation in value and all accumulated income, remains free from additional federal estate tax as long as it remains in the trust. (It is not protected from income tax.)

Transfering your business to this trust may allow the business to remain in trust for many generations without incurring transfer tax. Trust income and principal (depending on the trust terms) can be available to future generations undiminished by estate or generation-skipping taxes. Not subjecting the business to estate tax as its benefits are passed from generation to generation should dramatically increase its value. Reinvesting some of the income or appreciation each year would make the trust increase in value. The compounding process over the decades and generations could result in a stunning increase in value.

How long can this generation-skipping trust last?

For a long time all states had laws which prevented property from remaining in trust in perpetuity—simply speaking, forever—without being subject to transfer taxes. Within the last few years a number of states have abolished this "rule against perpetuities." If you live in a state that has abolished the rule against perpetuities, you and your attorney can easily create a GST trust to last indefinitely. If you reside in a state that has not yet abolished the rule, your attorney can assist you in establishing a GST trust under the laws of a state that has abolished the rule.

Does this planning favor grandchildren over children?

One misconception is that this type of planning skips children in favor of grandchildren. The children can still receive tremendous benefits from the trust. These trusts can be set up so that the trustee pays income and principal for the health, education, maintenance, and support of all the children and grandchildren beneficiaries.

With such a setup, the trustee would have broad latitude to make payments to your children.

⊲ *Can you summarize the advantages of generation-skipping trusts?*

For parents with sufficient assets, it makes sense to have their trust arrangements for children structured to include GST provisions for the following reasons.

REDUCTION OF BENEFICIARIES' ESTATE TAXES: The total amount of assets in a GST trust, including accumulated earnings and appreciation from the date the trust is created, is exempt from death taxes in the child's estate.

FLEXIBILITY: Children can act as trustees of the trust and, in that capacity, can manage the investment of the trust assets and determine to whom the income and principal will be distributed. You can give a special power of appointment, so that the child can make provisions for a spouse to receive income or change the distribution among grandchildren or great-grandchildren following his or her death.

ASSET PROTECTION: The trust can contain provisions which help protect the assets in the trust from creditors or a divorcing spouse.

As with any estate planning tool, GST trust provisions should be tailored to the family's circumstances and should probably not be used if the children are not comfortable with the arrangements.

Carryover-Basis and Step-Up-in-Basis Exemptions

⊲ *Since the new carryover-basis system that you spoke of doesn't begin until 2010, is it necessary to plan for this now?*

This is an issue you need to discuss with your advisors in terms of your personal goals. If an individual dies between now and Decem-

ber 31, 2009, and leaves assets to his or her surviving spouse in a
standard marital trust, that property will receive a step-up in basis to
the value as of the decedent's date of death.

However, under the 2001 tax act, if the surviving spouse dies in
2010, none of that spouse's property remaining in the marital trust
will be eligible for any of the $1.3 million basis increase as it passes
to his or her heirs. The 2001 tax act does not allow an allocation of
basis to a surviving spouse's interest in marital trust property because
it does not treat the marital trust property as "property owned by the
surviving spouse."

For example, in 2010 a surviving husband individually owns
assets with a fair market value of $1.5 million and an aggregate basis
of $1.2 million and is the lifetime beneficiary of a marital trust with
$2 million of assets that have an aggregate basis of $1 million. If the
surviving husband died in 2010, his individually owned assets
would be stepped up in value to $1.5 million, an increase in basis of
$300,000 (using $300,000 of the $1.3 million available). However,
the remaining $1 million basis increase to the surviving husband's
estate would be wasted, because it could not be used for the property that remained in the marital trust. So if the beneficiaries were to
sell all the marital trust assets, there would be a taxable gain of $1
million on the sale, generating significant federal, and perhaps state,
tax liability.

One technique advisors and their clients should consider is giving the trustee of the marital trust, perhaps in consultation with the
remainder beneficiaries, the ability to distribute assets outright to
surviving spouses, at which time they will be the owners of the
assets, so that they can fully allocate basis to the property that they
own. However, if the trustee of the marital trust distributed the $2
million in assets out of the marital trust assets before the surviving
spouse's death, then on his or her subsequent death the excess $1
million basis increase could be allocated to those assets. This technique shelters the full date-of-death fair market value from gain at a
later sale by the heirs. Furthermore, the children inheriting the
property will be able to depreciate it based upon its new stepped-up
value.

For those who already have estate plans or are thinking about estate plans to establish marital trusts for their surviving spouses upon their deaths, they need to consult with their legal advisors to consider modifying or creating their initial plans to take advantage of planning opportunities to minimize the carryover-basis problem.

REDUCING ESTATE VALUE

⚖ *Why would I want to reduce the value of my estate?*

The primary factor that determines the amount of estate taxes is the value of your estate at the time of your death. Therefore, if you can reduce the value of your estate, you can reduce the amount of estate taxes assessed against your estate.

⚖ *Which strategies do you recommend for reducing the value of my estate to save estate taxes?*

There are many effective devices for reducing the value of all sizes of taxable estates in order to save estate taxes. The techniques that we discuss in this chapter are valuation planning, irrevocable life insurance trusts, family limited partnerships, and charitable trusts. (Giving your business or interests in your business to family or charity also reduces the value of your estate. We discuss those techniques in Chapters 23 and 24, respectively.)

Valuation Planning

⚖ *How does valuation planning reduce the estate and gift tax value of a business property?*

Valuation planning reduces the value of a business for lifetime or testamentary transfers. This results in smaller gift taxes due on the lifetime gifts and/or lower estate taxes due at the death of the business owner. This result occurs because of how the Internal Revenue Service and the courts determine the estate and gift tax value of property. (See also Chapter 20.)

⚐ *How is the estate and gift tax value of a business property determined?*

The estate and gift tax value of a business property is defined as the price that a willing buyer would pay a willing seller, with both having reasonable knowledge of the facts and being under no compulsion to buy or sell. It is assumed that the competing interests of the hypothetical buyer and seller will result in determining the fair market value of the property. The fair market value is used to establish the estate and gift tax value of the donor or decedent's interest in the property, including his or her interest in a business.

⚐ *How do discounts affect the concept of willing buyer, willing seller?*

Planning for discounts is accomplished in the context of the willing buyer, willing seller definition of fair market value. Reducing the desirability of the property will often reduce the amount that a buyer will pay a seller. When the fair market value of property is reduced, by definition, the estate and gift tax value is reduced.

⚐ *How does this work?*

Essentially, the technique involves dividing the ownership of property among several people. Here are two examples:

1. John owns 100 percent of a 1-acre parcel. He transfers one-third ownership of the parcel to Mary and one-third to Jim, and John keeps one-third.
2. John owns 100 percent of the stock in Acme Corporation, and he transfers one-third of the stock to Mary and one-third of the stock to Jim and keeps one-third himself.

In both cases a willing buyer would typically pay John, Mary, or Jim separately less than one-third of the price he or she would pay for the whole acre or corporation.

ᴥ *Why do such changes in the ownership structure of an item of property reduce its value?*

The typical willing buyer wants at least three things from a purchase of property: (1) the ability to freely sell the asset at any time so as to change investments, (2) complete access to the cash flow generated by the asset, and (3) the ability to control management decisions regarding the asset.

ᴥ *How do the changes in ownership affect those factors?*

In the case of changing to fractional ownership interests, a willing buyer must be able to purchase all the ownership interests to obtain the desired ownership features described in the preceding answer. If the buyer can purchase only a partial interest in the asset, he or she is forced to deal with another owner on all matters relating to the property, including sale, access to cash flow, and management. This means that the willing buyer will not pay a pro-rata price for a partial interest in the property.

For example, Susan owns 100 percent of a parcel of real property that is worth $1 million and transfers a 50 percent interest to her son. A prospective buyer would not pay $500,000 for Susan's remaining 50 percent interest because the buyer will not have absolute control of the property and access to cash flow. Therefore, Susan's 50 percent fractional ownership of the property is worth less than its pro-rata share of the entire property. For the same reason, a buyer would not pay Susan's son $500,000 for his interest in the property either, unless he was buying Susan's interest at the same time for the same price.

The result is that the value of Susan's gift to her son is less than $500,000, and the value of what she kept is now less than $500,000. This "discounted" value saves both gift taxes, on the initial transfer of 50 percent to the son, and estate taxes, on the 50 percent included in Susan's estate at her death. There are cases in which the tax courts allowed discounts as small as 15 percent for a 50 percent share of property and as high as 44 percent for a 50 percent interest.

Irrevocable Life Insurance Trust

⅏ *What is an irrevocable life insurance trust?*

Irrevocable life insurance trusts (ILITs) have been used by estate planners for many years. Generally, an ILIT consists of an irrevocable living trust (which is established and operates while the maker is alive) whose only asset during the lifetime of the trust maker is an insurance policy on the trust maker's life. The trust maker makes gifts to the trust, and the trustee uses the gifts to pay the premiums on the life insurance policy.

An ILIT removes the value of the proceeds from the trust maker's estate, and upon the death of the trust maker, the trustee uses the proceeds as directed in the trust agreement.

Transferring an existing life insurance policy to an ILIT reduces estate tax liability by removing the insurance from the insured's estate but only if the insured trust maker survives at least 3 years after making the transfer of all rights in the policy. If the trust maker dies within this 3-year period, he or she is still considered to be the owner of the policy. This 3-year rule does not apply to new policies purchased directly by the trustee of the ILIT.

An ILIT is a highly technical trust document controlled not only by trust law but also by the Internal Revenue Code and various other regulations, rulings, and court cases. Nevertheless, if the technical requirements are met, the client with a $1 million life insurance policy may save up to $550,000 in estate taxes with this important planning tool, because it will keep the value of the policy out of the insured's estate.

⅏ *Why do I need to remove life insurance proceeds from my estate?*

Any life insurance policies on your life that *you* own are included in your taxable estate and will increase your estate tax liability. Typically people purchase life insurance to provide financial protection for their survivors. If that is the reason for insurance, it would make sense to prevent the insurance proceeds from being included in the insured's estate; otherwise, the proceeds not only are subject to estate tax but also increase the value of the estate, potentially moving into a higher estate tax bracket.

For example, Tim wants to provide his two children with $1 million of insurance proceeds at his death so he purchases a policy. If Tim's estate were in the 50 percent estate tax bracket, he actually needs to purchase a $2 million policy to provide $1 million, after estate taxes, to his children.

⌁ *So how does Tim remove the life insurance proceeds from his estate?*

He needs to make sure that he does not own the life insurance policy. The most common and effective way of doing this is to establish an irrevocable trust designed especially to own life insurance. The trustee of Tim's trust purchases a $1 million death benefit policy—half the coverage at half the cost of Tim's buying the policy himself. Tim's children, as the trust beneficiaries, are the recipients of $1 million in insurance proceeds at his death.

Using a properly drafted ILIT to own insurance policies keeps the insurance proceeds out of your estate because you don't own the policy at your death.

⌁ *Instead of using an ILIT, why can't I just give the money to my son and daughter to pay the premiums and let them own the policy? Doesn't that keep it out of my estate?*

Yes. If your children owned the policy, it would keep it out of your estate. This method may work for you if you have a small number of children who are responsible adults and who tend to agree with each other to act decisively and in a coordinated way.

On the other hand, as owners of the policy, your children are free to name anyone as a beneficiary, withdraw cash from the policy, or even cancel it. Furthermore, you would have no say over when and how the cash values are spent or how the death proceeds are spent after your death, and ultimately the insurance proceeds may be subject to your children's creditors or could end up in the wrong hands. For these reasons, an irrevocable life insurance trust works better.

∗ If I am making gifts to the trust so that the trustee can pay the premiums, do these gifts qualify for the annual exclusion?

The ILIT document contains specific provisions intended to optimize the tax benefits of the trust. Such provisions include the use of a beneficiary demand right, or a "Crummey" power, so that most, if not all, of the gifts the maker makes to the trust for the annual premium payments qualify for the annual $10,000 gift tax exclusion.

∗ Can you tell me how I would set up an ILIT and how it would work?

As the maker of the trust, you create the irrevocable trust and decide on its terms. You direct in the trust that the trustee is to purchase the life insurance policy and use the gifts to pay the insurance premiums. The trustee is also directed as to how the trust assets, including insurance proceeds, are held, administered, and distributed for the benefit of your spouse and/or children.

The trustee applies for a life insurance policy on your life only or for a joint policy on the lives of both you and your spouse.

You make gifts of cash to the trust in the amount of the annual insurance premium and take full advantage of the available annual exclusions.

The trustee notifies the trust beneficiaries (in a prescribed writing) of their right to withdraw that gift, and when the trust beneficiaries don't withdraw the gift within the appropriate deadline, the trustee uses the cash to pay the premiums for the life insurance policy.

∗ How can an ILIT work with my business succession planning?

You can include provisions in the ILIT to allow your trustee to use the proceeds to purchase your business interest from your estate or from your revocable living trust so that the estate has cash to pay estate taxes or cash to pay capital gain taxes under a carryover-basis system. Your family members, as your beneficiaries, will own and keep the business.

For example, John James has an estate valued at $6 million, which includes an LLC valued at $4 million. All his assets are titled in the name of his revocable living trust. John has also established an ILIT in which his two daughters are the beneficiaries, and his trustee purchased a $4 million insurance policy on John's life.

When John dies, his estate owes $2.5 million in estate taxes, plus other amounts for settling his affairs and debts. Without the ILIT, the only choice his daughters would have would be to sell the business, probably at a fire sale price, to pay the estate tax bill. However, the ILIT trustee (after collecting the policy proceeds) purchases the business from the revocable trust for $4 million, and the revocable trust trustee uses the cash to pay the estate tax liability and other expenses. Since John's daughters are equal beneficiaries of the ILIT, they will be equal owners of the business and will not be forced to sell it just to pay the taxes. His daughters also receive, through the living trust, what remains of the $4 million after the taxes and expenses are paid. This would essentially work the same way if John died under the carryover-basis system with capital gain taxes being due instead of estate taxes.

Life insurance owned in an ILIT has many benefits: reducing the value of your estate, providing the liquidity to pay the estate tax and yet not be subject to estate tax on your death, and keeping the business in the family for another generation. An alternative benefit is providing the liquidity to pay the capital gain tax if a buy-sell agreement requires the family to sell the business to the other owners when a carryover-basis system is in effect.

⬥ *I have heard of a joint life insurance policy. What is that?*

There are several variations on a joint policy, the most common of which is a *second-to-die* policy (sometimes called a *survivor life* policy) insuring the joint lives of a husband and wife. It is a life insurance policy that pays the death benefit only after the second spouse dies. Remember, good estate planning can defer estate taxes at the death of the first spouse by using the unlimited marital deduction (discussed in Chapter 27). However, marital deduction planning alone only defers the tax until the second death. Therefore, the second-to-die policy is ideally suited for estate planning situations because it pays the benefit when the money is needed the most—to pay the estate tax liability which is due after the second spouse dies.

Because of the strong likelihood that one spouse will live longer than the other, second-to-die policies cost substantially less than single-life policies. Furthermore, if one spouse is not healthy or even "uninsurable," it is typically less expensive to obtain joint insurance on the couple instead of single coverage on the healthy spouse, because adding that uninsurable spouse increases the chances that the insurance company will not have to pay the death proceeds as soon as it would with an individual policy.

Family Limited Partnership

⚵ Why use a family limited partnership for estate planning?

A family limited partnership (FLP) can hold all assets that are appropriately held by any limited partnership. Even if there is no formal business being operated or owned by an FLP, the business of the FLP could be to manage and invest *other* family assets. (See Chapter 5 for how to create an FLP and Chapter 23 for using an FLP to give the business to family members.) Remember all the reasons we previously discussed for creating an FLP:

- Has a management mechanism whereby parents may give their children ownership interest in investment assets while maintaining absolute control over management decisions
- Provides income to children, thereby allowing parents to teach their children the value of money so that they do not suffer the negative effects of receiving "unearned" wealth
- Provides a system for parents to train their children in good stewardship and pass family values to them

- Has more flexibility than other techniques do for passing assets to children, because it is an entity that partners can change to adapt to changing situations
- Takes advantage of valuation discounting
- Protects family assets from creditors
- Keeps assets in the family in the event of a failed marriage by restricting transfers of interests in the event of divorce, effectively preventing "nonfamily" spouses from raiding the family wealth

⊀ If I didn't use the FLP to transfer our family business, why would I use it as part of my estate plan?

In Chapter 25 we presented many issues that our business-owner clients considered when they were creating their estate plans. The FLP can be used in a variety of situations. For instance, if you have sold or will sell your business to an outside party as your exit strategy, your estate will consist of the proceeds of the sale. You could establish an FLP to pass those proceeds in the form of other investments and your other assets to your spouse and children.

Suppose you have four children, only one of whom works in the business. If you are giving or selling the business to the child who works in the business, you could form an FLP to hold the other assets in your estate and give those assets to the other three children. This not only gives you an opportunity to do all of the things mentioned in the previous answer but also gives you a mechanism for equalizing the estate for your children. All four can feel equally important because they are managing the family business.

The FLP can allow you to achieve the other goals of encouraging a strong work ethic, passing on aspects that are important to you, such as family values, history, and heritage, and leaving a legacy.

⊀ How does the FLP save estate taxes?

The rigid transfer restrictions and lack of control that come with the ownership of a limited partnership interest result in valuation discounts that apply to lifetime or testamentary transfers of those interests. Thus, the fair market value of a limited partnership interest is deemed to be worth less than the fair market value of the actual assets owned by the partnership. This is a fundamental concept that needs to be understood clearly. The application of this concept in the estate planning arena encourages accelerated gifts of limited partnership interests by parents during lifetime to their children and a reduction in the size of a parent's estate, which in turn reduces the estate tax liability upon a parent's death.

A limited partnership is a business with two classes of partners: general partner, usually mom and dad, and limited partners, initially mom and dad. The general partner has unlimited liability, but mom and dad can form another entity with liability protection to be the general partner. The general partner is responsible for managing the business and has total control over the decisions of the partnership. The limited partners have no control over the partnership.

Mom and dad own a nominal general partnership interest, such as 2 percent, and, initially, own the limited partnership interests of 98 percent. Mom and dad give limited partnership interests each year to the children up to their annual exclusion amounts or even use all or part of their estate tax exemption amount.

Because a limited partnership interest in the FLP lacks control and usually lacks free transferability, a discount can be obtained for the limited partnership interests with a qualified appraisal. Thus, more actual value is transferred on a discounted basis. Whatever limited partnership interests mom or dad give away during their lifetime reduces the value of their estates. If mom and dad still own any limited partnership interests at their death, those will also be subject to discounts in value, which reduce the size of the estate and therefore the amount of the estate tax liability.

⊰ *How does the family limited partnership provide asset protection?*

Since the family members don't have access to the underlying assets in the FLP, neither do their creditors. A creditor cannot become a partner against the family's wishes. If a creditor wins a judgment, the most the creditor can have is the right to the income distributed from the partnership for the partnership interests in question. But the general partners have full discretion to decide whether they wish to make any distribution of income. This protection may deter or prevent lawsuits and promote settlements.

⚔ *If I want to use a partnership for creditor protection purposes, should I be the general partner of my family limited partnership?*

You can, although it is not recommended. The general partner is personally liable for all partnership debts and claims against the partnership. One of the goals is to protect you from personal liability. It is better to create an entity, such as a limited liability company, a corporation, or a trust, to be the general partner. This gives you a shield against personal liability. In some instances, a limited liability company can be used instead of a family limited partnership with the same positive results, plus the added benefit of no personal liability for anyone.

Testamentary Charitable Trust

Testamentary charitable lead trust

⚔ *I don't want to create a charitable lead trust while I am alive but I would be interested in creating one at my death. Can I do that and, if so, how?*

Testamentary *charitable lead trusts (CLTs)* are commonly established by individuals with philanthropic goals. As we discussed in Chapter 23, when establishing a lifetime (inter vivos) CLT, you must immediately part with the assets you wish to donate to it, even though your heirs eventually end up with them. By waiting to establish a CLT until your death, you retain the full use and enjoyment of the assets during your lifetime. (See Chapter 23 for using lifetime charitable lead trusts as a technique for giving the business to family members.)

≩ *Can I use a testamentary charitable lead trust to reduce estate taxes?*

A testamentary CLT is a wonderful estate planning technique to reduce and, if desired, even eliminate estate taxes. Yes, believe it or not, you can *eliminate* federal estate taxes by incorporating a testamentary CLT in your will or revocable living trust.

For example, John Smith dies in August 2003 and is survived by a 15-year-old son and a 12-year-old daughter. John's revocable living trust contains $10 million in assets, all of which flow into his testamentary *charitable lead annuity trust (CLAT)*. The CLAT pays 10 percent of its initial value to the Red Cross for 19 years. Thus, the trustee pays $1 million per year to the Red Cross for 19 years. At the end of 19 years, when the children are 34 and 31, respectively, the remaining CLAT assets pass to the children free of federal estate tax. If the assets appreciate at 10 percent per year, after 19 years the children would receive approximately $10 million totally free of estate taxes. The beauty of the charitable lead trust is that the estate tax can be eliminated for any size estate.

If you are married and have a revocable living trust which takes advantage of the estate tax exemption amount and the unlimited marital deduction at the death of the first spouse, there is no tax at the first death. At the second death, the balance of the assets in the trust plus the surviving spouse's individual assets can be allocated to a CLT structured to pay an income to charity for a term of years that results in a 100 percent charitable estate tax deduction.

≩ *How can a testamentary CLT be used in conjunction with my business succession plan?*

Suppose you currently have a buy-sell agreement which at your death requires your partner to purchase your business interest for a promissory note. The sale price in the buy-sell agreement must be the fair appraisal value of the business. You create a testamentary CLT under the terms of your living trust or will with a formula that provides for a percentage payout for a term of years, at the end of which your children receive the remainder of the assets in the CLT.

At your death, your partner executes the promissory note to your will or revocable living trust. The note should have a reasonable maturity date and interest rate (i.e., the current rate at the time of execution) and annual payments. There is little or no capital gain tax on this transaction, because the basis of your ownership interest is stepped up to the date-of-death value. The note is then transferred to the CLT. When the CLT receives the payments, it will use the money to make the required CLT payment to the charitable income beneficiary. When the CLT terminates, your children receive the balance remaining in the CLT.

This technique can result in the CLT remainder beneficiaries' receiving a significant asset, at a greatly reduced or eliminated estate tax, while you provided a benefit to your favorite charity.

⚖ Does the testamentary CLT work the same as the inter vivos CLT in most respects?

Yes, a testamentary CLT is very similar in operation to a CLT established and funded during the lifetime of the trust maker.

Testamentary charitable remainder trust

⚖ I'm not interested in using an inter vivos charitable remainder trust now, but it does sound like something I might want to create after my death. Can I create a testamentary CRT?

If you desire to have your business and/or other assets held in trust for a period of time with a fixed percentage paid out to one or more individuals and at the end of the term have the remaining assets paid to a charity, you can include provisions in your will or living trust to establish a testamentary *charitable remainder trust (CRT)* at your death. The income from the business can be paid to your family members during the term of the trust, and then the business passes to the charity upon their deaths. Your estate will be entitled to a favorable estate tax treatment. (Lifetime charitable remainder trusts are discussed in Chapter 24 as a technique for selling the business to outsiders.)

⅏ How do testamentary charitable remainder trusts help save estate taxes?

Estate tax savings are achieved with a testamentary CRT because the portion of the value of the asset that qualifies for the estate tax charitable deduction is removed from the deceased donor's taxable estate.

⅏ Can you give us an example of how a testamentary charitable remainder trust works?

A typical scenario for a testamentary CRT would be as follows: Theresa owns all of the stock of a C corporation, worth $2 million, which generates an annual dividend income of $200,000. Let's assume Theresa's estate is in the 50 percent estate tax bracket. If she left the stock outright to her 55-year-old son, the estate tax generated by the company would be $1 million.

Instead, let's say that Theresa created a testamentary *charitable remainder unitrust (CRUT)* and the stock was transferred to it at her death. If the trustee of the CRUT sold the stock immediately following her death for its date-of-death value, there would be no taxable gain. The CRUT allows her son to receive 5 percent of the fair market value of the testamentary CRUT assets determined on a yearly basis (paid in quarterly installments) for the remainder of his life.

In the first year, Theresa's son would receive $25,000 per quarter. Assuming the federal rate for determining the amount of the charitable deduction in the month of her death was 8 percent, the estate tax charitable deduction would be approximately $675,000.

In this scenario transferring the stock of the business into a testamentary CRT established within the business owner's revocable living trust reduced the estate tax on the business from $1 million to $325,000. At the son's death, the remaining testamentary CRT assets are paid to the charity named by the trust maker in the CRT.

A testamentary CRT has many of the same characteristics as lifetime CRTs. A testamentary CRT is tax-exempt, so all the income that flows into a CRT from the business is not taxed to the CRT. Instead, income is taxed to the income beneficiary as distributions are made from the CRT.

⚶ How is the income from a testamentary CRT paid?

Just as with an inter vivos CRT, a testamentary CRT can be either a charitable remainder *annuity* trust (CRAT) or a charitable remainder *unitrust* (CRUT). A CRAT pays a fixed amount to the income beneficiaries as determined by the valuation of the trust assets at the time the assets are contributed to the CRAT. A CRUT pays a fixed percentage to the income beneficiaries based on a yearly valuation of the trust assets.

⚶ Can my income beneficiary change the charity that is the charitable remainder beneficiary of the CRT?

The testamentary CRT instrument can be drafted in such a way as to allow the CRT income beneficiary to change the charitable remainder beneficiary. This change must be done prior to the death of the last income beneficiary. Any such change of charitable beneficiary must be done in compliance with the requirements set out in the trust.

⚶ Who should consider creating a testamentary CRT?

A testamentary CRT is best suited for a business owner who does not want to give up the business or other assets during his or her lifetime, has no family or key employees to take over the business, wants to make a significant charitable transfer, but also wants or needs to provide a "guaranteed" income stream to a child or children for life. The testamentary CRT will accomplish these objectives very nicely.

᠔ *What are the disadvantages of using a testamentary CRT as an estate planning tool?*

■ Your beneficiary does not receive your business interests or the proceeds from the sale of the business but only a fixed payment from the CRT.

■ A testamentary CRT does not eliminate all estate taxes attributable to the property transferred into the CRT at your death.

■ The age, as well as the number, of income beneficiaries greatly affects the amount of the deduction.

■ The property used to fund the CRT cannot be used to pay any of the estate taxes.

■ CRTs only work with C corporation stock and some partnership interests.

᠔ *Is there a way that I can give my business to a charity through a testamentary or lifetime charitable remainder trust but pass the value of my business to my family?*

Most individuals who create a testamentary or lifetime CRT take the additional step to replace the wealth of the remainder interest which they have given or will give to charity. They do this by creating a *wealth replacement trust* during their lifetime. The wealth replacement trust is just another term for the irrevocable life insurance trust, which is specifically designed to own a life insurance policy on the trust maker's life. When a life insurance policy is purchased by an irrevocable life insurance trust, it is not only income tax–free upon the trust maker's death but also estate tax–free.

At the death of the ILIT trust maker, the proceeds from the life insurance policy in the ILIT are given to the beneficiary to replace the value of the remainder interest in the charitable remainder trust that he or she "lost" as a result of its being given to charity.

Additionally, the life insurance proceeds in the ILIT can be used to provide liquidity for the estate tax liability that cannot be satisfied with assets in the CRT. Earlier in this chapter we discussed how ILIT funds can be used to pay estate taxes without causing the insurance proceeds to be included in the insured's taxable estate.

Conservation Easements

⚜ *I am a retired farmer, and the economic boom has resulted in more and more of the family farms in my area being taken over by developers. Because of the changing economics in our region, the price of farmland has significantly increased in value. My children are now adults and have moved away from the farm to pursue their own careers. Is there a way I can save my farm from confiscatory estate taxes?*

You may want to consider a conservation easement. A conservation easement restricts future development of the property. The easement is donated to a local government or preservation organization, which has the right to enforce the development restrictions. Even though you have to donate the easement, you still retain ownership of the property. Your ownership rights may include disallowing public access, continuing farming operations, and transferring the property by sale, gift, or bequest. You may even want to retain some limited development rights that allow you to produce income from the property for you and your heirs.

Creation of a conservation easement will result in a lower valuation of the property for purposes of estate planning. The easement can generate an immediate income tax deduction, based on the loss in valuation, if you make the gift of the easement during your lifetime or generate an estate tax deduction if the conservation easement is established at your death in your revocable living trust or will. Depending on local rules, the easement may also reduce your property taxes.

appendix A

Information for Business Owners

TABLE A-1   Small-Business Resources

Resource	Services
General information	
Small Business Administration (SBA) 409 Third St., SW Washington, DC 20416 800-U-ASK-SBA www.sba.gov	Provides programs, services, training, counseling, & information on a wide range of topics. Website includes small-business start-up kit, free software, & extensive guidance.
Service Corps of Retired Executives 409 Third St., SW, Sixth Fl. Washington, DC 20024 800-634-0245 www.score.org	Offers mentors, e-mail counseling, & workshops. (affiliated with SBA)
U.S. Business Advisor www.business.gov	Lists links to federal government information & services.
Small Business Taxes & Management www.smbiz.com/sbrl041.html	Lists links to office of each state's secretary of state.
Business plans	
Bplans.com www.bplans.com	Includes sample business plans plus information, advice, consultant referrals, etc.

566

Resource	Services
"The Business Plan: Road Map to Success" www.sba.gov/starting/ indexbusplans.html	Includes outline & tutorial from SBA.

Consumer protection	
U.S. Consumer Product Safety Commission Washington, DC 20207 301-504-0000 www.cpsc.gov	Aims to minimize injuries & deaths from consumer products.
Federal Trade Commission 600 Pennsylvania Ave., NW Washington, DC 20580 202-326-2222 www.ftc.gov	Promotes competitive marketplace & consumer protection. Website covers sales, warranties, legislation, etc.

Employee relations	
Occupational Safety and Health Administration (OSHA) U.S. Department of Labor 200 Constitution Avenue, NW Washington, DC 20210 202-693-2000 www.osha.gov	Aims to reduce workplace fatalities, injuries, and illnesses.
U.S. Department of Labor Office of Public Affairs 200 Constitution Ave., NW Washington, DC 20210 202-693-4650 www.dol.gov	Prepares workers for jobs & ensures adequacy of workplaces. Website includes labor laws, wage standards, federal acts (e.g., COBRA & ERISA), & *Small Business Handbook*.
U.S. Equal Employment Opportunity Commission 1801 L St., NW Washington, DC 20507 202-663-4900 www.eeoc.gov	Promotes equal opportunity in employment through law enforcement, education, & technical assistance. Website includes federal acts & discrimination issues.
U.S. National Labor Relations Board 1099 14th St., NW, Rm. 9820 Washington, DC 20570-0001 202-273-1960 www.nlrb.gov	Addresses relations between employers & unions. Website explains what to expect in cases before NLRB.

TABLE A-1   Small-Business Resources, *continued*

Resource	Services
Import/export	
Foreign Trade Information System Sistema de Información al Comercio Exterior (SICE) Organization of American States www.sice.org	Promotes free trade in the Americas. Website includes NAFTA reports.
International Trade Administration (ITA) Trade Information Center U.S. Department of Commerce Washington, DC 80230 800-USA-TRADE www.ita.doc.gov	Supports exporters & U.S.-based international companies; protects against harmful import practices. Website covers NAFTA rules.
U.S. Customs Service 1300 Pennsylvania Ave., NW, Rm. 6.3D Washington, DC 20229 www.customs.ustreas.gov	Provides advice, protection, & control of merchandise shipped into the country.
U.S. International Trade Commission 500 E St., SW Washington, DC 20436 202-205-2000 www.usitc.gov	Controls harmful import practices; protects patents, trademarks, and copyrights.
Export-Import Bank of the United States (Eximbank) 811 Vermont Ave., NW Washington, DC 20571 800-565-3946 www.exim.gov	As the official export credit agency of the U.S. government, offers loans, guarantees, & insurance.
Insurance	
Life & Health Insurance Foundation for Education (LIFE) 2175 K St., NW Washington, DC 20037 202-464-5000 www.life-line.org	Provides information & education on life, health, & disability insurance.
U.S. Department of Labor www.dol.gov/dol/pwba/public/ pubs/cobra99.pdf	Provides information on Consolidated Omnibus Budget Reconciliation Act (COBRA).

Resource	Services
Patents, trademarks, and copyrights	
U.S. Patent and Trademark Office General Information Services Division Crystal Plaza 3, Rm. 2C02 Washington, DC 20231 800-786-9199 www.uspto.gov	Provides information, forms, services, & documents.
U.S. Copyright Office Library of Congress 101 Independence Ave., SE Washington, DC 20559-6000 202-707-3000 www.lcweb.loc.gov/copyright	Processes & protects copyrights.
Retirement plans	
U.S. Department of Labor www.dol.gov/dol/asp/public/ programs/handbook/erisa.htm	Explains Employee Retirement Income Security Act (ERISA).
Taxes	
Internal Revenue Service 1111 Constitution Ave., NW Washington, DC 20224 800-829-1040 www.irs.gov	Website includes special assistance for small businesses & the self-employed.
SBA Hotlist: Taxes www.sba.gov/hotlist/taxes.html	Provides information & advice, with links to state tax & revenue agencies.
Small Business Taxes & Management www.smbiz.com	Includes free online journal providing information on tax issues affecting small businesses.
Social Security Administration 6401 Security Blvd. Baltimore, MD 21235-0001 800-772-1213 www.ssa.gov	Provides information & assistance. Website covers Social Security for employers & Medicare.

TABLE A-2   Referral Organizations

Organization	Services
Alliance of Merger & Acquisition Advisors (AMAA) 3100 Bristol St., Ste. 390 Costa Mesa, CA 92626 800-320-4604 www.advisor-alliance.com	Provides member referrals, including accountants, attorneys, & other corporate financial advisors who work with business owners on exit strategies, business succession, & sales transactions.
American Academy of Estate Planning Attorneys 9360 Towne Centre Dr., Ste. 300 San Diego, CA 92121 800-846-1555 www.estateplanforyou.com	Provides member referrals.
American Institute of Certified Public Accountants (AICPA) 1211 Avenue of the Americas New York, NY 10036-8775 888-862-4272 www.aicpa.org	Provides member referrals, including CPAs, PFSs (personal financial specialists), & CPA/ABVs (CPAs accredited in business valuation).
American Society of Appraisers (ASA) 555 Herndon Parkway, Ste. 125 Herndon, VA 20170 703-478-2228 www.appraisers.org	Provides member referrals.
Canadian Institute of Chartered Business Valuators (CICBV) 277 Wellington St. West Toronto, Ontario, Canada M5V 3H2 416-204-3396 www.businessvaluators.com	Provides directory of members by region.
Certified Financial Planner (CFP) Board of Standards 1700 Broadway, Ste. 2100 Denver, CO 80290-2101 303-830-7500 www.cfp-board.org	Makes CFP referrals.
Esperti Peterson Institute (EPI) 1605 Main St., Ste. 700 Sarasota, FL 34236 941-365-4819 www.epinstitute.org	Maintains registry of masters & fellows in estate & wealth strategies planning.

Organization	Services
Financial Planning Association (FPA) 3801 E. Florida Ave., Ste. 708 Denver, CO 80210 800-322-4237 www.fpanet.org	Provides referrals of CFP practitioners & offers free information about financial planning & choosing a financial planner.
Institute of Business & Finance (IBF) 7911 Herschel Ave., Ste. 201 La Jolla, CA 92037-4413 800-848-2029 www.icfs.com	Makes CFS referrals. (formerly Institute of Certified Fund Specialists)
Institute of Business Appraisers (IBA) P.O. Box 17410 Plantation, FL 33318 954-584-1144 www.instbusapp.org	Maintains member directory by state & specialty.

International Association of
  Registered Financial Consultants
  (IARFC)
P.O. Box 42506
Middletown, OH 45042
800-532-9060
www.iarfc.org
	Provides referrals of registered financial consultants.

National Association of Estate Planners and Councils (NAEPC) 270 S. Bryn Mawr Ave. P.O. Box 46 Bryn Mawr, PA 19010-2196 610-526-1389 www.naepc.org	Maintains member directory by state & specialty.
National Association of Family Wealth Counselors (NAFWC) P.O. Box 308 Franklin, IN 46131 888-597-6575 www.nafwc.org	Provides directory of members by name, state, & status.
National Network of Estate Planning Attorneys (NNEPA) 1 Valmont Plaza, Fourth Fl. Omaha, NE 68154-5203 800-638-8681 www.netplanning.com	Provides member referrals; offers continuing education & tools for estate planning attorneys.

TABLE A-2   Referral Organizations

Organization	Services
Society of Financial Service Professionals (SFSP) 270 S. Bryn Mawr Ave. Bryn Mawr, PA 19010-1295 888-243-2258 www.financialpro.org	Provides member referrals. (formerly American Society of CLU & ChFC)

TABLE A-3   Licensing and Regulatory Agencies

Agency	Functions	Area regulated
Federal Trade Commission (FTC) 600 Pennsylvania Ave., NW Washington, DC 20580 202-326-2222 www.ftc.gov	Enforces federal antitrust and consumer protection laws; ensures that the nation's markets function competitively, efficiently, & free of undue restrictions; eliminates practices that are unfair or deceptive; conducts activities such as consumer education.	U.S. marketplace
Financial Accounting Standards Board (FASB) 401 Merritt 7 P.O. Box 5116 Norwalk, CT 06856-5116 203-847-0700 accounting.rutgers.edu/ raw/fasb	Consisting of 9 members, sets the accounting rules of the U.S. under the auspices of the SEC; also establishes the standards of financial accounting & reporting for the private sector. (The SEC has statutory authority to establish these standards for publicly held companies but has relied on the private sector for this function to the extent that the private sector does so in the public interest.)	Financial accounting and reporting standards

Agency	Functions	Area regulated
Internal Revenue Service (IRS) 1111 Constitution Ave., NW Washington, DC 20224 800-829-1040 www.irs.gov	"Enrolled" means licensed by the federal government; "agent" means authorized to appear in place of the taxpayer at the IRS. (Only EAs, attorneys, and CPAs may represent taxpayers before the IRS.)	Enrolled agents (EAs)
National Association of Securities Dealers (NASD) Regulators 1735 K. St., NW Washington, DC 20006 800-289-9999 www.nasd.com www.nadsr.com	Self-regulates the securities industry & the Nasdaq stock market through registration, education, & examination of member firms & their employees, creation & enforcement of rules designed for the protection of investors, surveillance of markets operated by Nasdaq, & cooperative programs with government agencies and industry organizations.	Registered broker/dealers, investment advisors/ advisory firms, & representatives; various series licenses
National Association of State Boards of Accountancy (NASBA) 150 Fourth Ave. North, Ste. 700 Nashville, TN 37219 615-880-4200 www.nasba.org	Serves as a forum for the nation's state boards of accountancy, which administer the Uniform CPA exam, license CPAs, & regulate the practice of public accountancy in the U.S.; sponsors committee meetings, conferences, programs, & services to enhance the effectiveness of its member boards.	CPAs
Securities Investor Protection Corporation (SIPC) 605 Fifteenth St., NW, Ste. 800 Washington, DC 20005-2215 202-371-8300 www.sipc.org	Protects customers of SEC-registered broker/ dealers against losses caused by the financial failure of a broker/dealer (but not against a change in the market value of securities); funded by its member securities broker/ dealers.	Broker/dealers

TABLE A-3   Licensing and Regulatory Agencies, *continued*

Agency	Functions	Area regulated
State insurance commissions	Administer and enforce state insurance laws.	Insurance sales
U.S. Securities and Exchange Commission (SEC) 450 Fifth St. Washington, DC 20549 800-732-0330 www.sec.gov	As an independent, quasi-judicial regulatory agency, helps establish & administer federal securities laws; regulates firms engaged in the purchase or sale of securities, people who provide investment advice, & investment companies.	Registered investment advisors/ advisory firms, broker/dealers, & representatives

TABLE A-4   Professional Licenses and Designations

Designation	Accrediting institution and requirements
ABV: Accreditation in Business Valuation (available to CPAs)	AICPA: meet experience requirements, pass exam, be member of AICPA; maintain involvement in business valuation & meet continuing ed requirements.
AEP: Accredited Estate Planner (available to estate planning practitioners who have completed certain graduate estate planning courses)	NAEPC & American College: pass exam in trust banking, insurance, accounting, law; meet NAEPC's continuing ed requirements.
ASA: Accredited Senior Appraiser	ASA: pass exams, submit appraisals for peer review, meet ethical standards.
Broker/dealer (one that is licensed to buy & sell investment products for or to clients: "dealers" sell securities they own; "brokers" buy & sell securities on behalf of investors)	SEC

Designation	Accrediting institution and requirements
CBA: Certified Business Appraiser	IBA: pass exam (or hold similar certification from another organization), submit 2 business appraisal reports.
CDP: Certified Divorce Planner	ICDP: take class, pass exam.
CEBS: Certified Employee Benefit Specialist	International Foundation of Employee Benefit Plans: complete study program, pass exams, abide by principles of conduct.
CEP: Certified Estate Planner	Liberty Institute: complete course, pass exams.
CFA: Certified Financial Analyst (available to experienced financial analysts—securities analysts, money managers, & investment advisors focusing on analysis of investments & securities of company or industry groups)	Association for Investment Management and Research: complete course, pass 3 annual exams, fulfill AIMR ethics requirements, submit to regulatory authority of AIMR.
CFP: Certified Financial Planner (available to those with a bachelor's degree who have completed a financial planning curriculum at a U.S.-accredited college or university & have 3 years of financial planning experience, or 5 years without a degree)	CFP Board of Standards: pass exam, adhere to CFP Board code of ethics, periodically disclose investigations or legal proceedings related to professional or business conduct, take 30 hours continuing ed every 2 years, complete biennial licensing requirement with CFP Board, submit to regulatory authority of CFP Board.
CFS: Certified Fund Specialist (available to financial services professionals)	IBF: complete course, pass exam, adhere to IBF code of ethics, take 15 hours continuing ed per year, register annually.
ChFC: Chartered Financial Consultant (for accountants, attorneys, bankers, insurance agents, brokers, and securities representatives with 3 years of business experience)	American College: complete 10-course curriculum, pass exams, adhere to code of ethics, take 60 hours continuing ed every 2 years.

TABLE A-4   Professional Licenses and Designations, *continued*

Designation	Accrediting institution and requirements
CIC: Chartered Investment Counselor (available to those employed by an ICAA member firm who have 5 years' experience in an eligible occupation)	ICAA: complete the CFA exam, provide work & character references, endorse ICAA Standards of Practice, complete an ethical conduct questionnaire.
CIMA: Certified Investment Management Analyst (the only advanced designation specifically for investment consultants; must have 3 years' experience in investment management consulting)	IMCA: complete program, pass exam, adhere to code of ethics, recertify every 2 years by taking 40 hours continuing ed.
CIMC: Certified Investment Management Consultant (for financial consultants)	Institute for Investment Management Consultants: meet ethical, experience, and continuing ed requirements, pass 2 levels of NASD-administered exams.
CLU: Chartered Life Underwriter (for insurance & financial services professionals with 3 years' business experience)	American College: pass 10 college-level courses, abide by the college's code of ethics.
CMA: Certified Management Accountant	IMA: have experience, take classes, abide by ethics standards, meet continuing ed requirements.
CPA: Certified Public Accountant	Licensed by states: pass Uniform CPA exam, satisfy work experience & statutory & licensing requirements of the state(s) in which one practices.
CPCU: Chartered Property Casualty Underwriter	American Institute for CPCU: take classes, pass exams, have experience, abide by code of ethics.
CPMA: Certified Professional Management Advisor (available to CPAs)	Quantum Institute for Management Advisors: take classes, pass exam, meet continuing ed requirements.

Designation	Accrediting institution and requirements
CSA: Certified Senior Advisor	Society of CSAs: attend 3-day program or complete correspondence course & testing; take home-study exams to maintain certification.
CTFA: Certified Trust and Financial Advisor	ICB: have experience, take self-study course, pass exam.
CVA: Certified Valuation Analyst (available to CPAs)	NACVA: be member of NACVA, take classes, submit references, complete exam.
Fellow of the Esperti Peterson Institute (EPI) (for financial advisors & accountants who have technical knowledge of financial, estate, insurance, & investment tools)	EPI: complete program, attend classes annually, participate in monthly conference calls, prepare case design book for a hypothetical client.
J.D.: Juris Doctor, or Doctor of Jurisprudence (the basic law degree; replaced the LL.B. in the late 1960s)	Accredited law schools: complete required studies, pass exam.
LL.M.: Master of Laws (an advanced law degree)	
LUTCF: LUTC Fellow	LUTC: complete classes, pass ethics exam, belong to a local life underwriters association.
M.B.A.: Master of Business Administration	Certain colleges and universities: complete required studies, pass exam.
MS: Master of Science (in taxation) (graduate-level study in financial planning, wealth management, tax planning, retirement planning, and estate planning)	College for Financial Planning: complete 12 courses with 3.0 (B) grade-point average.
MSFS: Master of Science in Financial Services	American College: complete 36 course credits, including 2 residency sessions.

TABLE A-4   Professional Licenses and Designations, *continued*

Designation	Accrediting institution and requirements
M.S.T.: Master of Science in Taxation	Certain colleges and universities: complete required studies, pass exam.
PFS: Personal Financial Specialist (available to CPAs)	AICPA: meet experience requirements, pass exam, be member of AICPA; meet ongoing experience & coursework requirements.
RFC: Registered Financial Consultant (for those with a securities/insurance license or one of the following: CPA, CFA, CFP, CLU, ChFC, J.D., EA, or RHU)	IARFC: meet education, examination, experience, & licensing requirements, take 40 hours continuing ed per year, abide by IARFC code of ethics.
RFP: Registered Financial Planner (for members of RFPI)	RFPI: complete study course, have experience in field.
RHU: Registered Health Underwriter (available to those involved in the sale & service of disability income & health insurance)	American College: complete 3-course curriculum, meet experience, ethics, & continuing ed requirements.
RIA: Registered Investment Advisor (one who recommends stocks, bonds, mutual funds, partnerships, or other SEC-registered investments for clients)	SEC and/or state securities agencies: file an ADV (Advisor) form detailing educational & professional experience & a U-4 form disclosing any disciplinary action.

TABLE A-5   Professional Organizations

Organization	Functions
Alliance of Merger & Acquisition Advisors (AMAA) 3100 Bristol St., Ste. 390 Costa Mesa, CA 92626 800-320-4604 www.advisor-alliance.com	Provides informational, educational, business, development, & transaction resources for accountants (CPAs), attorneys, & other corporate financial advisors.
American Bar Association (ABA) 750 N. Lake Shore Dr. Chicago, IL 60611 312-988-5522 www.abanet.org	Ensures the continuation of programs promoting quality legal services, equal access to justice, better understanding of the law, & improvements in our justice system; provides members with information & tools; sponsors workshops, seminars, CLE sessions, & publications.
American Institute of Certified Public Accountants (AICPA) 1211 Avenue of the Americas New York, NY 10036-8775 888-862-4272 www.aicpa.org	Provides resources, information, & leadership focusing on advocacy, certification, licensing, communications, recruiting, education, standards, & performance.
American Society of Appraisers (ASA) 555 Herndon Parkway, Ste. 125 Herndon, VA 20170 703-478-2228 www.appraisers.org	Fosters professional development through education, accreditation, publications, & other services.
Association for Advanced Life Underwriting (AALU) 2901 Telestar Ct. Falls Church, VA 22042-1205 703-641-9400 www.aalu.org	Proposes & monitors legislation & regulation regarding advanced life underwriting; provides education & leadership in improving the business environment for advanced life insurance professionals.
Esperti Peterson Institute (EPI) 1605 Main St., Ste. 700 Sarasota, FL 34236 941-365-4819 www.epinstitute.org	Provides information, research, instruction, publications, & speakers bureau for estate planning professionals.

TABLE A-5   Professional Organizations, *continued*

Organization	Functions
Estate planning councils	For those who specialize in tax, estate, & business planning, provide opportunity to interact, exchange ideas, & pool knowledge; organized at local level.
Financial Planning Association (FPA) 3801 E. Florida Ave., Ste. 708 Denver, CO 80210 800-322-4237 www.fpanet.org	Embraces the principles of the International Association for Financial Planning (IAFP) & Institute of Certified Financial Planners (ICFP); open to everyone affiliated with the financial planning profession. (formerly IAFP & ICFP)
Institute of Business Appraisers (IBA) P.O. Box 17410 Plantation, FL 33318 954-584-1144 www.instbusapp.org	Provides professional education & accreditation, technical support, & market data on all aspects of appraisal of small & midsize businesses.
Institute of Certified Bankers (ICB) 1120 Connecticut Ave., NW Washington, DC 20036 800-433-9013 www.aba.com	Sponsored by the American Bankers Association, provides professional education & certification programs.
Institute of Certified Divorce Planners (ICDP) 6395 Gunpark Dr., Ste. W Boulder, CO 80301 800-875-1760 www.institutecdp.com	Provides professional education, certification, & tools.
Institute of Management Accountants (IMA) 10 Paragon Dr. Montvale, NJ 08645-1718 800-638-4427 www.imanet.org	Keeps members up to date on changes affecting management accounting & financial management professions, provides new insights & ideas, gives ethical guidance.
International Association of Registered Financial Consultants (IARFC) P.O. Box 42506 Middletown, OH 45042 800-532-9060 www.iarfc.org	Fosters professional development through education, provides industry information, distributes information on legislation affecting financial planning, including taxes.

Organization	Functions
Investment Counsel Association of America (ICAA) 1050 17th St., NW, Ste. 725 Washington, DC 20036-5503 202-293-4222 www.icaa.org	Represents the interests of federally registered investment advisor firms, lobbies Congress & government agencies, promotes standards among investment advisors.
Investment Management Consultants Association (IMCA) 9101 E. Kenyon Ave., Ste. 3000 Denver, CO 80237 303-770-3377 www.imca.org	Develops standards for investment consultants, promotes the interests of the profession, provides education, & fosters information sharing among members.
Life Underwriters Training Council (LUTC) 7625 Wisconsin Ave. Bethesda, MD 20814 888-260-5882 www.lutc.org	Provides training & certification.
Million Dollar Round Table (MDRT) 325 W. Touhy Ave. Park Ridge, IL 60068-4265 847-692-6378 www.mdrt.org	Provides members with resources for improving technical knowledge, sales skills, & client service while adopting high ethical standards; comprises top 6% of life insurance producers worldwide.
National Association of Certified Valuation Analysts (NACVA) 1111 Brickyard Rd., Ste. 200 Salt Lake City, UT 84106 www.nacva.com	Provides training, certification, & continuing ed in business valuation, litigation consulting, & fraud prevention, offers tools & technical support.
National Association of Enrolled Agents (NAEA) 200 Orchard Ridge Dr., Ste. 302 Gaithersburg, MD 20878 301-212-9608 www.naea.org	Promotes professionalism & interests of members, acts as advocate of taxpayer rights.
National Association of Estate Planners and Councils (NAEPC) 270 S. Bryn Mawr Ave. P.O. Box 46 Bryn Mawr, PA 19010-2196 610-526-1389 www.naepc.org	Provides education & designations for estate planners & estate planning attorneys.

TABLE A-5   **Professional Organizations,** *continued*

Organization	Functions
National Association of Family Wealth Counselors (NAFWC) P.O. Box 308 Franklin, IN 46131 317-736-8750 www.nafwc.org	Provides opportunities for education & networking.
National Association of Insurance and Financial Advisors (NAIFA) 2901 Telestar Ct. Falls Church, VA 22042-1205 877-866-2432 www.naifa.org	Serves as advocate for insurance agents & consumers; encourages legislation to protect policyholders, develops policy, advances its position with lawmakers & regulators; enhances skills of members, promotes ethical conduct, & offers education; organized at state & local levels. (formerly National Association of Life Underwriters)
National Association of Personal Finance Advisors (NAPFA) 355 W. Dundee Rd., Ste. 200 Buffalo Grove, IL 60089 888-FEE-ONLY www.napfa.org	Helps fee-only professionals enhance skills, market services, & gain a voice with government & consumers; publishes monthly *NAPFA Advisor* & offers educational opportunities to members.
National Association of Tax Practitioners (NATP) 720 Association Dr. Appleton, WI 54914-1483 800-558-3402 www.natptax.com	Serves professionals working in all areas of tax practice, provides assistance with federal & state tax questions, & presents workshops.
Planned giving councils & roundtables	Promote the concept of planned giving; organized at local level, but many are associated with the National Council on Planned Giving.
Registered Financial Planners Institute (RFPI) 2001 Cooper Foster Park Rd. Amherst, OH 440-282-7176 www.rfpi.com	Provides training & certification.

Organization	Functions
Risk and Insurance Management Society (RIMS), Inc. 655 Third Ave. New York, NY 10017 212-286-9292 www.rims.org	Provides products, services, & information for managing all forms of business risk; offers member publications, education for the ARM designation, & other services.
Societies of CPAs	Promote the accounting profession within government & to the public; provide members with education, information, & opportunities to interact with colleagues & participate in community service projects; organized at local level.
Society of Financial Service Professionals (SFSP) 270 S. Bryn Mawr Ave. Bryn Mawr, PA 19010-1295 888-243-2258 www.financialpro.org	Sets & promotes standards of excellence for professionals in financial services; supports members' commitment to advanced education & high ethical standards. (formerly Society of CLU & ChFC)

appendix B

The Contributory Book Series and Protocol for *Strictly Business*

Eileen Sacco, Managing Editor

History of the Contributory Book Series

With the publication of *Wealth Enhancement and Preservation* in 1995, the Institute established its Contributory Book Series, in which fifty-two highly regarded professionals from across the United States participated to create a comprehensive book on financial planning. Subsequent research projects included a second edition of *Wealth Enhancement and Preservation* (1996), with research from ten additional contributing authors; *Legacy* (1996), with a select group of eighty-seven members from the National Network of Estate Planning Attorneys who focused on the most commonly asked questions about estate, business, and tax planning; and *Generations* (1998), a reconceptualization of *Legacy*, with forty-nine new contributors adding comprehensive questions and answers.

Ways and Means (1998) became the Institute's first cross-discipline text, and it brought together the legal and financial planning professions to assist the public in understanding how to plan properly for retirement and how to coordinate the results of that effort with estate planning.

21st Century Wealth (2000) drew on research from fifty-one expert financial planning professionals to present sophisticated financial planning strategies made available by the Taxpayer's Relief Act of 1997 and the IRS Restructuring Act of 1998, new rulings issued by the Department of the Treasury and the

IRS, and the excitement of the new millennium. This book also launched the Institute's new publisher, Quantum Press.

The Institute and Quantum Press expanded the multidisciplinary collaboration by including accountants with attorneys and financial advisors on the *Strictly Business* project, begun in 1998, to help business owners understand and plan for their unique situations. Ninety-one professional authorities contributed their experience, knowledge, and skills to this text.

Each book has the following objectives:

- To be the most professional research project of its kind and be recognized as unique in both its focus and scope
- To ascertain the critical planning questions that clients are asking their professional advisors nationwide and the precise answers of those advisors
- To publish meaningful text that will assure the readers that they can get immediate assistance from professionals on the basis of the planning concepts and strategies learned from the book
- To heighten the public's understanding of the knowledge and contributions that highly experienced financial advisors, attorneys, and accountants bring into the lives of their clients
- To improve the quality of financial, estate, and business planning services offered by professionals to clients by sharing the ideas and techniques of a number of authorities in a highly condensed, user-friendly form
- To be recognized as a major contribution to the financial, estate, and business planning literature

The Institute staff invested many hundreds of hours developing protocols for the first *Wealth Enhancement and Preservation* research project. The Institute and, now, Quantum Press have added elements to the protocols and have diligently adhered to these protocols in all subsequent contributory book projects.

Protocol

Definition of Authority or Expert

The Institute defines an "authority" or "expert" as an outstanding professional who is technically competent, is an effective communicator, and has, at a minimum, a 5-year record of meeting his or her clients' needs.

Research Protocol

As with all previous contributory books, the first step in following the protocol was to create the "Research Questionnaire" for *Strictly Business,* which is an outline of potential topics for the final book, organized in a cohesive chapter format. However, every contributing author is encouraged to provide his or her own input outside the parameters of the "Research Questionnaire." Time, demanding schedules, and the need to eliminate as much repetition as possible led the Institute and Quantum Press to a protocol of a minimum of forty questions and answers from each contributing author.

Qualifying Professionals: The Application Process

When originally developing the protocol for the first research project, the Institute submitted its definition of *expert* and the objectives of the research project to trusted financial planning colleagues and asked them to design the criteria that would help the Institute not only identify potential contributors but also judge the level of their expertise and credentials. On the basis of the input of these colleagues, the Institute established criteria for an authority and an expert and developed an extensive "Application and Profile" for the financial planning professionals and the criteria for evaluating each applicant, which are weighted according to the input received from our colleagues and established by Bob Esperti, Renno Peterson, and the Institute staff prior to the first research project. Before contacting prospective contributors for *Strictly Business,* Quantum Press staff asked several of the Institute's fellows in Wealth Strategies Planning to review and update the criteria, application, and requirements, especially in light of inviting accountants into a project for the first time.

Applicants had to provide a completed "Application and Profile," along with ADV Part II if they are registered investment advisors with the Securities and Exchange Commission and U-4 forms if they are registered with the NASD. After receipt of this information, Quantum Press carefully reviewed and graded each professional under the established evaluation procedures. Depending on the discipline in which each applicant is licensed, Quantum Press checked the NASD website, state securities division, state insurance commission, state board of accountancy, or state bar association for disclosures (arbitrations, claims, lawsuits, etc.). Before Quantum Press finally accepted an applicant for *Strictly Business,* editors David Cahoone and Larry Gibbs reviewed the "Application and Profile" and conducted telephone interviews of each applicant they did not know personally.

The telephone interviews allowed the editors to determine the level of each applicant's knowledge of business, succession, and estate planning and to satisfy themselves that the applicant was committed to the project and understood all its parameters. The interviews also allowed the applicants to ask any questions about the individuals who would be editing their research.

Quantum Press then mailed to each applicant a letter of either nonacceptance or acceptance. In addition to an acceptance letter, Quantum Press mailed a "Contributing Expert and Authority Agreement," a "Research Question-

naire," and specifications for submitting a photograph, a personalized introduction, and biographical information.

The applicants who were ultimately accepted into the *Strictly Business*
project submitted a total of 3640 questions and answers, amounting to over
1000 manuscript pages.

Research Editing Protocol

The Quantum Press staff combined and organized the research from all the
contributing authors by "Research Questionnaire" category. The managing
editor reorganized and outlined the research into a standard book structure
and delivered the manuscript to the senior legal editor, who eliminated those
questions and answers that were *not* common to a majority of the contributors. The remaining research *and* the eliminated questions and answers were
delivered to David and Larry. They read the research questions (and confirmed
whether the eliminated research was not applicable), combined similar material, and edited the remaining questions and answers into the cohesive and
understandable questions and answers that appear in this text.

The managing editor and senior legal editor reviewed the resulting working manuscript for clarity and technical accuracy. Quantum Press provided a
working manuscript to each contributing author for review. In this way,
Quantum Press ascertained the validity of the responses and added to the quality of the final text, and contributors were able to increase the level of their
participation in the research project. A number of contributing authors supplied additions to the working manuscript.

The logistics of a Contributory Book Series project is daunting, to say the
least. The process of initiating the project; creating the materials for the invi-
tees, applicants, and contributing authors; following up on all the invitations;
checking the applications and credentials; collating all the necessary information and paperwork, including the questions and answers; and turning the
material into a book calls for extraordinary organization and commitment
from the contributors, editors, Quantum Press, and its staff. In fact, this brief
overview of the process does not do justice to the 20 months of work simply
because the volume of information and protocol developed for these projects
consists of hundreds of pages of material and thousands of hours of effort. The
Institute and Quantum Press are proud of the degree of professionalism dis-
played by all participants in the creation and completion of *Strictly Business*.

appendix C

Contributing Authors

Robert H. Acker, CLU, ChFC
5680 North Littlefield
Weidman, MI 48893
517-644-2532 fax 517-644-3288

Jack Anderson, CEP
The Normandy Group
1675 Larimer Street, Suite 675
Denver, CO 80202
303-893-8700 fax 720-946-0226
jack@rgsnormandy.com

Bradley C. Baldridge, CFP
Morgan Kenwood Ltd.
5130 West Loomis Road
Greendale, WI 53129-1424
414-423-4020 fax 414-423-4035
brad@bradbaldridge.com

Michael R. Bascom, J.D.
Michael R. Bascom, PC
Estate & Business Planning Attorneys
1203 Macy Drive
Roswell, GA 30076-6350
770-594-2288 fax 770-594-2285
mbascom@mindspring.com

Gary J. Boecker, J.D.
Boecker & Co., LPA
4000 Embassy Parkway, Suite 430
Fairlawn, OH 44333
330-665-5000 fax 330-665-4365
gboecker@boecklaw.com

Robert D. Bond, J.D., CPA
Smith-Moore & Associates
333 North Belt East, Suite 1230
Houston, TX 77060
281-448-4100 fax 281-445-3101
bond44@flash.net

Kevan Boyles, J.D.
Law Office of Kevan Boyles, P.A.
350 Royal Palm Way, Suite 405
Palm Beach, FL 33480
561-833-2472 fax 561-837-6611
kevanboyle@aol.com

Francis K. Brown II, CPA, M.S.T., CVA
Vance, Cronin & Stephenson, P.C.
195 State Street, 6th Floor
Boston, MA 02109-2602
617-720-2600 fax 617-720-4468
fbrown@vcspc.com

Margaret E. Brown, J.D.
The Brown Law Firm, P.C.
40 Lake Bellevue, Suite 100
Bellevue, WA 98005
425-451-2403 fax 425-451-2492
margaret@brownlawfirmpc.com

Steven W. Brown, J.D.
Brown & Vogel, Chartered
2035 East Iron Avenue, Suite 101
P.O. Box 2177
Salina, KS 67402-2177
785-826-2525 fax 785-826-2588
steve@brownvogellaw.com

Philip J. Bryce, J.D., CPA
Bryce, Crandall & Coleman, PLLC
212 South Peters Road, Suite 101
Knoxville, TN 37923
865-690-5566 fax 865-690-4967
pbryce@bcc-law.com

Curtis A. Burr, CPA, ABV, CVA
Burr, Pilger & Mayer
600 California Street, Suite 1300
San Francisco, CA 94108
415-421-5757 fax 415-288-6288
cburr@bpmllp.com

Stanley R. Byrd, J.D., CFP
Stanley R. Byrd, Inc., P.S.
2150 North 107th Street, Suite 150
Seattle, WA 98133-9009
206-363-0123 fax 206-363-0216
stan@stanbyrd.com

David K. Cahoone, J.D., LL.M. (Tax)
Esperti Peterson & Cahoone
A National Estate Planning Law Firm &
   Partnership of Professional Corporations
1605 Main Street, Suite 700
Sarasota, FL 34236
941-365-4819 fax 941-366-5347
dkcahoone@aol.com

Stephen G. Chapman, CLU, LUTCF
Advent Wealth Strategies Group, LLC
2735 East Parleys Way, Suite 305
Salt Lake City, UT 84106
801-303-0700 fax 801-303-0701
spokrock@aol.com

Michael Cherewka, J.D.
Cherewka & Radcliff, LLP
624 North Front Street
Wormleysburg, PA 17043
717-232-4701 fax 717-232-4774
mc@cherradlaw.com

Paul T. Coleman, J.D., LL.M. (Tax)
Bryce, Crandall & Coleman, PLLC
212 South Peters Road, Suite 101
P.O. Box 30107
Knoxville, TN 37923
865-690-5566 fax 865-690-4967
pcoleman@bcc-law.com

Dennis C. Cook, J.D.
Cook & Associates, P.C.
505 South 3rd Street, Suite 200
Laramie, WY 82070
307-745-7320 fax 307-745-6120
cook@cookandassociatespc.com

Neil R. Covert, J.D.
Covert & Black, LLC
311 Park Place Boulevard, Suite 360
Clearwater, FL 33759
727-449-8200 fax 727-450-2190
ncovert@covertlaw.com

John L. Csenge, CIMC, CFP
Csenge Advisory Group
4755 East Bay Drive
Clearwater, FL 33764
727-437-6000 fax 727-437-6650
jcsenge@fscorp.com

Richard F. DeFluri, CIMC, RFC
Abundance Wealth Counselors, LLC
270 Walker Drive
P.O. Box 106
State College, PA 16804
800-253-3760 fax 814-231-2276
richardd@abundancellc.com

Jeffrey R. Dundon, J.D., LL.M. (Tax)
156 East Spring Valley Road
Centerville, OH 45458
937-438-3122 fax 937-291-5491
jrdundon@erinet.com

Brian A. Eagle, J.D.
Eagle & Fein
8500 Keystone Crossing, Suite 555
Indianapolis, IN 46240
317-726-1714 fax 317-475-1270
baelegal@aol.com

Sidney Eagle, J.D., LL.M.
Eagle & Fein
342 Madison Avenue, Suite 1712
New York, NY 10173-0098
212-986-3211 fax 212-986-3219
sidney@eaglefein.com

Kyle S. Enright, M.B.A., CFA
Enright Financial Consultants
21515 Hawthorne Boulevard, Ste. 1050
Torrance, CA 90503
800-272-2328
310-543-4559 fax 310-316-0401
kenright@enrightfinancial.com

Stephanie V. Enright, M.S., CFP
Enright Financial Consultants
21515 Hawthorne Boulevard, Ste. 1050
Torrance, CA 90503
800-272-2328
310-543-4559 fax 310-316-0401
senright@enrightfinancial.com

David Etherington, J.D., M.B.A.
2830 N.W. 41st Street, Suite L-1
Gainesville, FL 32606
352-377-1351 fax 352-380-9096
etherington@dbe-law.com

Jeffrey J. Febbo, CFP
C. J. M. Planning Corp.
801 Walnut Avenue
Easton, PA 18042
610-252-0455 fax 610-252-0900
jeff@febbo.com

Jeffrey A. Forrest, MSFS, MS, CFP, ChFC
Wealth Enhancement & Preservation, LLC
1177 Marsh Street, Suite 200
San Luis Obispo, CA 93401
805-547-1177 fax 805-547-1625
jeff.forrest@wealth-enhancement.com

Donna L. Freeman, CLU, CFP, CEBS, MSFS
Resonate, Inc.
4750 Ashwood Drive
Cincinnati, OH 45241
513-605-2500 fax 513-605-2505
dfreeman@resonatecompanies.com

John E. Freiburger, ChFC, CFP, AEP, MSFS
Partners Wealth Management
1700 Park Street, Suite 200
Naperville, IL 60563
630-778-8088 fax 630-778-8049
john@partnerswealth.com

Ernest T. George III, CFP, CLU
Investment Management Group, Inc.
102 South Jackson Street
P.O. Box 963
Starkville, MS 39760-0963
662-323-8045 fax 662-323-8030
eginvest@netdoor.com

Larry W. Gibbs, J.D.
Gibbs & Schwartzman
23859 Iron Horse
San Antonio, TX 78255
210-690-8858 fax 210-690-0024

Todd L. Goedeke, CFP
Raymond James Financial Services
1017 Fond Du Lac Avenue
Sheboygan Falls, WI 53085
920-467-1110 fax 920-467-0136
tgoedeke@rjfs.com

Douglas G. Goldberg, J.D., M.B.A.
Goldberg Law Center, P.C.
2500 North Circle Drive, Suite 100
Colorado Springs, CO 80909-1161
719-444-0300 fax 719-444-0342
dgoldberg@deathcheaters.com

Joseph M. Gordon, APM, CFP, ChFC, CLU
Invesmart Inc.
55238 Broughton
Chapel Hill, NC 27514
919-942-9818 fax 919-968-0203
joegordon@invesmart.com

Suzanne M. Graves, J.D.
Law Offices of Suzanne M. Graves
655A North Mountain Avenue
Upland, CA 91786
909-981-6177 fax 909-981-8859
graveplan@aol.com

Theron M Hall Jr., J.D.
Morris, Hall, Holdsworth & Kinghorn, PLLC
3300 N. Central Avenue, Suite 920
Phoenix, AZ 85012-2506
602-249-1328 fax 602-248-2887
tim@morristrust.com

Lewis B. Hampton, J.D.
Hagen, Dye, Hirschy & DiLorenzo, P.C.
888 S.W. Fifth Avenue, 10th Floor
Portland, OR 97204-2024
503-222-1812 fax 503-274-7979
lhampton@hagendye.com

Dean R. Hedeker, J.D., CPA, CFP
Dean R. Hedeker, Ltd
510 Lake Cook Road, Suite 105
Deerfield, IL 60015-5610
847-236-9900 fax 847-236-9901
dhedeker@taxdean.com

Rick O. Helbing, CFP, ChFC, CDP
Suncoast Advisory Group
1800 Second Street, Suite 756
Sarasota, FL 34236
941-955-9978 fax 941-957-0449
sagplan@gte.net

David P. Herrmann, CFP
Herrmann Financial Services, Inc.
370 Diablo Road, Suite 201
Danville, CA 94526-3438
925-831-0200 fax 925-831-8957
david@herrmannfinancial.com

Sandra Brink Heusinkveld, CLU
Financial Planning Perspectives, LLC
1333 Clubview Boulevard North
Columbus, OH 43235
614-785-0156 fax 614-785-0176
sandra@financialplanningperspectives
.com

Steven Andrew Jackson, J.D.
79 Woodfin Place, Suite 303
Asheville, NC 28801
828-252-7300 fax 828-254-6599
sajatty@aol.com

Reid S. Johnson, MSFS, CIMC, CFP, ChFC
The Planning Group of Scottsdale, LLC
8777 N. Gainey Center Drive, Ste. 265
Scottsdale, AZ 85258-2133
480-596-1580 fax 480-596-2165
reid@theplanninggroup.com

Thomas H. Keating, J.D.
T. H. Keating & Associates
18720 Mack Avenue, Suite 110
Grosse Pointe Farms, MI 48236
313-884-4200 fax 313-884-4298
mgoblue@mich.com

Ronald W. Kelemen, CFP
The H Group, Inc.
960 Liberty Street, SE, Suite 210
Salem, OR 97302
503-371-3333 fax 503-371-1410
www.kelemen.com

Thomas P. Kelly Jr., CLU, ChFC, CFP
Financial Options Incorporated/Phase II Planning
3000 Atrium Way, Suite 249
Mount Laurel, NJ 08054
856-778-8200 fax 856-778-1622
OPTIONSTK@aol.com

Bruce D. Ketron, J.D., LL.M.
Law Offices of Bruce Ketron &
  Associates
703 Second Street, 4th Floor
P.O. Box 64
Santa Rosa, CA 95402
707-542-1700 fax 707-542-1727
ketronlaw@metro.net

Charles P. KinCannon, J.D., LL.M.
KinCannon & Associates
1870 The Exchange, Suite 100
Atlanta, GA 30339
770-951-7033 fax 770-321-5495
chuck@us-law.net

**Steven M. Laiderman, J.D., LL.M.
  (Tax)**
The Laiderman Law Firm, P.C.
1067 North Mason Road, Suite 3
St. Louis, MO 63141-6341
314-514-9100 fax 314-514-9494
laido@aol.com

Jerry S. Lan, CPA, CFP, CMA, CLU
Lan, Liu & Co., LLP
12225 South Street, Suite 100
Artesia, CA 90701
562-924-9666 fax 562-809-4394
zendellson@yahoo.com

W. Vito Lanuti, J.D.
323 Main Street
Seal Beach, CA 90740
562-596-7550 fax 562-596-3661
habaeous@aol.com

Tim J. Larson, J.D.
Larson & Schainost, LLC
727 North Waco, Suite 255
Wichita, KS 67203
800-388-8529 fax 316-262-7408
tlarson@fn.net

William J. Maxam, J.D.
Law Offices of William J. Maxam, APC
404 Camino Del Rio South, Suite 605
San Diego, CA 92108
619-220-8666 fax 619-220-8788
maxamlaw@aol.com

Stephen D. Mayer, CPA, M.B.A.
Burr, Pilger & Mayer
600 California Street, Suite 1300
San Francisco, CA 94108
415-421-5757 fax 415-288-6288
smayer@bpmllp.com

Stephen A. Mendel, J.D.
Stephen A. Mendel, P.C.
1155 Dairy Ashford, Suite 104
Houston, TX 77079
281-759-3213 fax 281-759-3214
steve@mendelgammell.com

**Donna M. Miller, CPA, CFP, CVA,
  CPMA**
MillerMusmar
1861 Wiehle Avenue, Suite 125
Reston, VA 20190
703-437-8877 fax 703-437-8937
info@millermusmar.com

Lesa Oldham Miller, J.D., M.B.A.
Attorney and Counselor at Law
3802 East Third Street
Bloomington, IN 47401
812-320-3069 fax 812-332-3587
lomiller@homefinder.org

**Brandon W. Morgan, CFP, CSA, CIC,
  CPCU**
Bradshaw & Weil, Inc.
621 Broadway
Box 420
Paducah, KY 42001
270-444-7291 fax 270-443-9931
bwmorgan@bradshaw-weil.com

Dan R. Morris, J.D.
Morris, Hall, Holdsworth & Kinghorn,
  PLLC
3300 N. Central Avenue, Suite 920
Phoenix, AZ 85012-2506
602-249-1328 fax 602-248-2887
dan@morristrust.com

W. Aubrey Morrow, CFP
Financial Designs, Ltd.
5075 Shoreham Place, Suite 230
San Diego, CA 92122-5929
858-597-1980 fax 858-546-1106
aubrey@financialdesignsltd.com

Peter S. Myers, J.D.
The Myers Law Firm, LLP
260 California Street, Suite 801
San Francisco, CA 94111
415-951-8100 fax 415-951-9700
psmyers@themyerslawfirm.com

Michael R. Nall, CPA, CMA
Pencor, LLC
111 East Wacker Drive, Suite 990
Chicago, IL 60601
800-869-0491 fax 312-729-9800
www.advisor-alliance.com

David M. Nelson, CFP, CLU, ChFC, CFS
NelsonCorp Investment Services
880 13th Avenue North
Clinton, IA 52732
563-242-9042 fax 563-242-9062
david.nelson@lpl.com

Donald C. Nestor, CFP, CPA
445 Douglas Avenue, Suite 2005-22
Altamonte Springs, FL 32714
407-774-3032 fax 407-774-3014
dnestor@sigmarep.com

Michele Okin, J.D., LL.M (Tax)
Law Offices of Michele Okin
53 Burd Street
Nyack, NY 10960
845-358-2356 fax 845-534-3938
micheleokin@earthlink.net

Faith Hope Olsen, CFP
Dynasty Financial Strategies
102 Strathmore Village Drive
South Setauket, NY 11720
631-696-1554 fax 631-732-3533
faitholsen@portjeff.net

Debbie J. Papay, J.D.
Bayer, Papay & Steiner Co., LPA
4540 Heatherdowns Boulevard
Toledo, OH 43614-3157
419-381-8884 fax 419-381-7684
papay@plansthatwork.net

David C. Partheymuller, CFP, CEP
The Normandy Group
1675 Larimer Street, Suite 675
Denver, CO 80202
303-893-8700 fax 720-946-0226
david@rgsnormandy.com

L. Carl Peterson, CFP, CFS
Money Resources, Inc.
Baltej Pavilion, Suite 210
415 Chalan San Antonio
Tamuning, GU 96911
671-646-0000 fax 671-649-0014
invest@moneyresourcesinc.com

Henry B. Pilger, CPA, M.B.A.
Burr, Pilger & Mayer
600 California Street, Suite 1300
San Francisco, CA 94108
415-421-5757 fax 415-288-6288
hpilger@bpmllp.com

Gary F. Poling, CFP, RFC, CTFA, CFRC
Presidents Trust Company
125 Castle Heights North, Suite B
Lebanon, TN 37087
615-449-2904 fax 615-449-2906

Bruce D. M. Prescott, J.D.
Trump, Alioto, Trump & Prescott, LLP
2201 Walnut Avenue, Suite 200
Fremont, CA 94538
510-790-0900 fax 510-790-4856
bruceprescott@tatp.com

Chester M. Przybylo, J.D., M.B.A.
Przybylo and Kubiatowski, Attorneys
and Counselors at Law
5339 North Milwaukee Avenue
Chicago, IL 60630
773-631-2525 fax 773-631-7101
trustnow@ameritech.net

Donald Joseph Purser, J.D.
Donald Joseph Purser & Associates, P.C.
2735 East Parleys Way, Suite 303
Salt Lake City, UT 84106
801-532-3555 fax 801-537-1212
purserlaw@aol.com

Kevin D. Quinn, J.D., M.B.A.
Kevin D. Quinn, Attorney at Law
30 Hannum Brook Drive
Easthampton, MA 01027
413-527-0517 fax 413-529-8027
kdqplan@worldnet.att.net

W. Dennis Renter, CFP, RIAA, CEPA
Associated Securities, Corp.
20101 SW Birch, Suite 220
P.O. Box 10489
Newport Beach, CA 92660
949-756-1606 fax 949-757-0753
drenter@earthlink.net

Loren J. Richards, J.D.
Cook & Associates, P.C.
505 South Third Street, Suite 200
Laramie, WY 82070
307-745-7320 fax 307-745-6120
richardsl@cookandassociatespc.com

Michael J. Riley, J.D., MS
Law Office of Michael J. Riley
5854 Cinema Drive
Milford, OH 45150-1445
513-831-2227 fax 513-831-2228
michaelriley@fuse.net

Steven P. Riley, J.D.
Riley Law Firm, P.A.
4805 West Laurel Street, Suite 230
Tampa, FL 33607
813-286-1700 fax 813-286-3600
spr@rileylawfirm.com

Marvin J. Rudnitsky, J.D.
Rudnitsky & Hackman, LLP
9 Courtyard Offices, Suite 130
Selinsgrove, PA 17870
570-743-2333 fax 570-743-2347
mrudnit@ptd.net

Hugh Lucas Sawyer, CPA, CFP
Sawyer & Company Business and
   Financial Advisors
239 Business Center Drive
P.O. Box 129
Pawleys Island, SC 29585
843-237-0917 fax 843-237-0916
sawyer@sccoast.net

Robert G. Segura, OSJ
R.G.S. Investment Services, Inc.
1675 Larimer Street, Suite 675
Denver, CO 80202
303-893-8700 fax 720-946-0226
bob@rgsnormandy.com

Chris E. Steiner, J.D.
Bayer, Papay & Steiner Co., LPA
4540 Heatherdowns Boulevard
Toledo, OH 43614-3157
419-381-8884 fax 419-381-7684
steiner@plansthatwork.net

Joseph J. Strazzeri, J.D.
Law Firm of Strazzeri Mancini LLP
404 Camino Del Rio South, Suite 605
San Diego, CA 92108
619-220-8288 fax 619-220-8078
jjs@strazzerimancini.com

Daniel S. Swinton, J.D.
Daniel S. Swinton, Counselor at Law
95 Westfield Avenue
Clark, NJ 07066
732-381-3838 fax 732-381-3445
swinton1@aol.com

William G. Touret, J.D.
William G. Touret, P.C.
One Washington Mall, Fifth Floor
Boston, MA 02108-2695
800-345-0080
617-523-4880 fax 617-523-4876
wgtouret@bostonplanning.com

Daniel P. Trump, J.D., LL.M.
Trump, Alioto, Trump & Prescott, LLP
2280 Union Street
San Francisco, CA 94123
415-563-7200 fax 415-346-0679
dantrump@tatp.com

Christopher A. Vogel, J.D.
Brown & Vogel, Chartered
2035 East Iron Avenue, Suite 101
P.O. Box 2177
Salina, KS 67401
785-826-2525 fax 785-826-2588
chris@brownvogellaw.com

**Peter R. Wheeler, CLU, ChFC, CFP,
CIMC**
Wheeler/Frost Associates, Inc.
2665 Fourth Avenue
San Diego, CA 92103
619-491-0225 fax 619-491-0229
prw@wheelerfrost.com

Arnold F. Williams, J.D., M.B.A.
Arnold F. Williams, Counselor at Law
800 Wilshire Boulevard, Suite 1110
Los Angeles, CA 90017
213-316-6126 fax 213-316-6126
afwilliams@counsellor.com

appendix D

Geographic Listing
of Contributing Authors

Arizona
Theron M Hall Jr.
Reid S. Johnson
Dan R. Morris

California
Curtis A. Burr
Kyle S. Enright
Stephanie V. Enright
Jeffrey A. Forrest
Suzanne M. Graves
David P. Herrmann
Bruce D. Ketron
Jerry S. Lan
W. Vito Lanuti
William J. Maxam
Stephen D. Mayer
W. Aubrey Morrow
Peter S. Myers
Henry B. Pilger

California, *cont'd.*
Bruce D. M. Prescott
W. Dennis Renter
Joseph J. Strazzeri
Daniel P. Trump
Peter R. Wheeler
Arnold F. Williams

Colorado
Jack Anderson
Douglas G. Goldberg
David C. Partheymuller
Robert G. Segura

Florida
Kevan Boyles
David K. Cahoone
Neil R. Covert
John L. Csenge
David Etherington

Florida, *cont'd.*
Rick O. Helbing
Donald C. Nestor
Steven P. Riley

Georgia
Michael R. Bascom
Charles P. KinCannon

Illinois
John E. Freiburger
Dean R. Hedeker
Michael R. Nall
Chester M. Przybylo

Indiana
Brian A. Eagle
Lesa Oldham Miller

Iowa
David M. Nelson

Kansas
Steven W. Brown
Tim J. Larson
Christopher A. Vogel

Kentucky
Brandon W. Morgan

Massachusetts
Francis K. Brown II
Kevin D. Quinn
William G. Touret

Michigan
Robert H. Acker
Thomas H. Keating

Mississippi
Ernest T. George III

Missouri
Steven M. Laiderman

New Jersey
Thomas P. Kelly Jr.
Daniel S. Swinton

New York
Sidney Eagle
Michele Okin
Faith Hope Olsen

North Carolina
Joseph M. Gordon
Steven Andrew Jackson

Ohio
Gary J. Boecker
Jeffrey R. Dundon
Donna L. Freeman
Sandra Brink Heusinkveld
Debbie J. Papay
Michael J. Riley
Chris E. Steiner

Oregon
Lewis B. Hampton
Ronald W. Kelemen

Pennsylvania
Michael Cherewka
Richard F. DeFluri
Jeffrey J. Febbo
Marvin J. Rudnitsky

South Carolina
Hugh Lucas Sawyer

Tennessee
Philip J. Bryce
Paul T. Coleman
Gary F. Poling

Texas
Robert D. Bond
Larry W. Gibbs
Stephen A. Mendel

Utah
Stephen G. Chapman
Donald Joseph Purser

Virginia
Donna M. Miller

Washington
Margaret E. Brown
Stanley R. Byrd

Wisconsin
Bradley C. Baldridge
Todd L. Goedeke

Wyoming
Dennis C. Cook
Loren J. Richards

Guam
L. Carl Peterson

index